*The Great
Victorians*

Lascelles Abercrombie.
M. C. D'Arcy, S.J.
Martin Armstrong.
A. A. Baumann.
Edmund Blunden.
A. Y. Campbell.
Neville Cardus.
Lord David Cecil.
G. K. Chesterton.
John Collier.
St. John Ervine.
Katharine Garvin.
J. L. Hammond.
Laurence Housman.
H. J. Laski.
H. J. Massingham.
Hugh Massingham.
Charles Morgan.
J. H. Muirhead
J. Middleton Murry.
Harold Nicolson.
Sylva Norman.
H. C. O'Neill.
Lord Ponsonby.
Herbert Read
Sir Arthur Salter.
Clifford Sharp.
G. Elliot Smith, F.R.S.
J. W. N. Sullivan.
Frank Swinnerton.
Sir William Beach Thomas.
A. Wyatt Tilby.
H. M. Tomlinson.
W. J. Turner.
Hugh Walpole.
G. P. Wells.
Rebecca West.
Vita Sackville-West.
R. H. Wilenski
D. Willoughby.

EDITED BY
H. J.
MASSINGHAM
AND
HUGH
MASSINGHAM

THE GREAT
VICTORIANS

IVOR NICHOLSON & WATSON, LTD.

44 ESSEX STREET, STRAND, LONDON, W.C.

First Edition . . August 1932
Reprinted . . . September 1932
Reprinted . . . December 1932

D 818006963

Printed in Great Britain by
Hazell, Watson & Viney, Ltd., London and Aylesbury.

To
J. L. GARVIN

CONTENTS

CONTENTS

INTRODUCTION

THIS book has come out of a series of conversations that have lasted for over two years. For some time it has seemed to us that our generation had sufficiently thrown off the spell, evil and otherwise, of its fathers, and that having developed an individuality of its own, distinct from the literary and political generation that preceded it, it was in a position to see the Victorians clearly and dispassionately. Up to a few years ago we were too near the Victorians to get any nourishment from them. In a sense we were in the same mood as the early leaders of the Reformation, who could see nothing but faults in the system that had reared them. These growing pains are now subsiding. Even before the war England was being led out of the land of *laissez-faire* economics and into the land of scientific planning. Since then *laissez-faire* has been definitely abandoned. Spiritually we have left the old Churches long ago, and are busily building the new. Mr. Chesterton proposes a world that would safeguard the individual and make us all parts of one spiritual entity. Mr. Waldo Frank asks us to concentrate on the Whole with a very big W (we should be grateful to anybody who would explain to us exactly what Mr. Frank's philosophy means). A more serious American critic, Professor Irving Babitt, puts his faith in Humanism. The late D. H. Lawrence, one of the few men of genius of our generation, denounced the deadening influence of a conventional morality that has no conviction behind it. Mr. T. S. Eliot describes himself as " classicist in literature, royalist in politics, and Anglo-Catholic in religion." Mr. Middleton Murry thinks that the modern mind has to choose between Communism and the Chesterton-Eliot way, and has elected Communism.

It must be obvious that the modern generation has not

therefore reached finality in the sense that it is able to look at things in a homogeneous way: what is certain is that, numerous as our standards are, they are not the standards of the Victorians. Nor are they consciously anti-Victorian. In short, we have advanced far enough to see that the England of Queen Victoria is not something blindly either to praise or to curse; we realize that a clear understanding of it is necessary for our development. For to be aware of the present one must see it as part of the past, as a link in a definite, continuous chain of tradition and form which should consciously and unconsciously direct us. And the Victorian link is as vital as the others.

It was our original intention to write a joint book; but this idea fell through, partly because for the life of us we could not find out how these intricate mosaics were done. Dryden was part author of *The Rehearsal,* but although we studied this play long and anxiously, not to mention the works of Beaumont and Fletcher, the secret was not revealed to us. But the real reason why it fell through was that neither of us felt competent enough to undertake so majestic a task as the summing-up of the Great Victorians. For it is our deprecatory claim that this volume is a summing-up of one generation by another. We cannot claim that it is more than this, for other people will come after us with different ideas, different values, different convictions, and will find new virtues and faults both in us and in the Victorians which our own vision either misses altogether or sees as too obvious to need comment.

What, then, is the result of this study of some forty great Victorian figures, drawn from every branch of intellectual activity? First, they were great men and women, although they emerge after analysis shorn of many of their locks. Next, as to the age. There is a definition of epic which shows it as growing out of a great national struggle in which action leaves no time for speculation and introspection, and in which pride and fine consciousness of worth eclipse minor individual issues. Such a struggle was going on in the Victorian age. During the larger part of the century, England was in an heroic mood. On the one hand, she exulted in the apotheosis of English supremacy; on the other, her thinkers were left to construct a new order of society from the destructive thought that synchronized with, and followed on the French Revolution.

A popular conception of the Victorian age is that it was

a stagnant one, intrinsically derivative in thought and art. Actually it was an age when leading minds, as in the Renaissance, began to explore in every direction. Discovery was physical, scientific, historical, and religious. There can be no doubt that our own minds, suspicious, probing, experimental, meditative, owe a great deal to the courage and impetuosity with which the Victorians pioneered us into fields of scholarship and science, where they had not yet the right weapons to conquer.

The very novelty of their revolt against established canons of knowledge and philosophy caused them to assume and assert the infallibility of their discoveries. In most fields they really thought they had said the last word, with the exception of a few empirical and doubting spirits, who increased in numbers as the century progressed. The era consequently tended to become one of capital dogmas in capital letters. Although most of the figures in this book rebelled from this busy, officious, cocksure atmosphere of Victorianism, yet very few of the Victorians emerged clearly enough from the particular problems of the day to concern themselves with abstract verities and eternal values —whether in art, scholarship, science, or life itself. Unlike the great thinkers, they do not strike one as having their noses close to the ground, as pursuing a single quarry to the exclusion of everything else: the slightest red herring of emotion, of vanity, a passing scent of ephemeral interest, and the eager dogs suddenly disappear, wagging their tails and barking importantly, presently to return with a tremendous air of discovery. Indeed, there was obviously something impure in Victorian thought, and it is this which accounts for the tragic wastage of talent and genius. Comparisons are odious, but we should say that there was not more actual talent in the Elizabethan—the great period of English letters and music—than in the Victorian age; there was only greater achievement.

There are several reasons for this. The first is that the struggle that had been going on ever since the Reformation ended in the Victorian age with the triumph of the middle class. The middle class, panting but heroic, were thrown on to a secure shore by the wave of commerce and machinery. Professor Trevelyan has already pointed out that if the Squirearchy wanted to preserve its privileged position, it should not have opposed the Reform Bill: it should have beheaded Stephenson and Watt. For once men were congregated into towns, the old order was over for ever. The change that was coming over England can be traced by people more competent than ourselves, but a few obvious signs may be pointed out. The battle of Waterloo was the signal for an outburst of vulgar triumph hitherto unknown in English history. The Elizabethans did not perch themselves upon the housetops and begin crowing about the overthrow of the Armada—brilliant and officious cocks making a great deal of noise to a disgusted universe. Even Trafalgar was not celebrated as Waterloo was, for as soon as the wedding clothes were put on they had to be exchanged for mourning. Waterloo brought out quite a new spirit—the spirit which had such a profound effect upon Victorian manners, Victorian art, and Victorian literature.

It was the spirit of the middle class. Hitherto art and letters had played the tune for an aristocracy; and although aristocracies differ superficially, one does not differ fundamentally from another. Great social evils are connected with them; but their pressure upon the arts is fairly similar. Aristocracy has its definite creed, shaped and perfected by centuries of practice, and the arts in each successive age knew exactly how to respond. Social, spiritual, and artistic values were distinctly graduated. When Dryden wrote for the theatre he knew precisely what his audiences would stand and what they would not stand. The taboos—and they were mostly political—were sharply defined. It was understood that a minx was a minx, and probably no better than a harlot. Nor did Dryden think it absurd to put these words into the mouth of the " bold " Almanzor when he first saw the " fair " Almahide's face:

> " *I'm pleased and pained, since first her eyes I saw,*
> *As I were stung with some tarantula.*
> *Arms, and the dusty field, I less admire,*
> *And soften strangely in some new desire;*
> *Honour burns in me not so fiercely bright,*
> *But pale as fires when mastered by the light;*
> *Even while I speak and look, I change yet more,*
> *And now am nothing that I was before.*
> *I'm numbed, and fixed, and scarce my eye-balls move;*
> *I fear it is the lethargy of love!* "

Such extravagant language would be laughed out of any theatre to-day, but it seemed quite natural in the theatre

of the Restoration, and indeed was almost expected. But
the important point is, that the conventions of Dryden's
time were clearly understood by the dramatist, whereas in
the Victorian age no one was quite sure what the conventions were. It was this which enormously complicated the
task of the Victorian writers. When the Elizabethans or
the Restoration poets were confronted with a love scene,
they did not have to think whether it was quite nice to
leave two young things alone in a room : the Victorians had
to. In this way morality came to be mixed up with art,
and, *pace* the Ibsenites, a moral discourse is not a work
of art.

Had the Victorian writers inherited a definite tradition,
as the Augustans did from Dryden, the art of the Victorian
age might be a very different thing from what it is. Mr.
Roger Fry, in his essay on *Art and Life*, has pointed out
that the " revolutions in art " may not necessarily coincide
with the " revolutions in life " ; and when we think of the
tremendous change from paganism to Christianity, and
contrast this with the aloofness of the art that was being
done during the same period, there certainly seems some
evidence for his contention. But art and life do not always
remain apart, as Mr. Fry admits, and it seems to us that
the reason why the moral and political thought of the nineteenth century had such a profound influence upon art was
that art had no restraining tradition to fall back on.

Wordsworth in his youth broke away from the monotony
of the language and technique of Pope, and started a period
of experimentalism. The same thing had often occurred
before : Dryden, for instance, broke away from the free
verse of the Elizabethans. But this time the newly sown
seeds were to be prevented from growing to a fruitful
flowering by a series of accidents. Wordsworth grew old
and respectable : three new poets—Keats, Shelley, and
Byron—continued the journey he had begun. All three
died young. It was unquestionably a disaster. None of
them lived long enough to perfect a form to replace the old
one that had been rejected, and the result was there was
no anchor to steady the ship. Their successors were thus
made more aware of the middle class than they should have
been, and the influence of the middle class was not altogether happy, as anyone can see from a reading of these
studies. Literature was without form. In politics sense
and style went all to pieces—compare, for instance, the

prose of Clarendon and Bolingbroke with the prose of
Bright and Gladstone. The effect was not quite so bad on
science, although it was bad enough. Huxley and Spencer
made Darwin's scientific conclusions the basis for philosophical speculations that ministered to middle-class self-
satisfaction: only Clerk Maxwell pursued his lonely furrow.

In short, the middle class was triumphant in more senses
than one. No one, indeed, can understand Victorian literature, Victorian art, and even Victorian politics without
understanding Victorian domestic life. Who were the
people, then, who made up this middle class? Most of
them started in a small way, just as the Girards of America
started in a small way. They started with a one-man shop,
and built up by thought and industry and self-denial a big
concern. The end was material; but the virtues that got them
there were not wholly material. But there is, too, another
side to the account. Sin simply did not pay. Sin—and we
are using the word to denote conduct that diverged from respectable Victorian middle-class convention—costs money,
and money was needed for building up the business. This is
obviously quite different from the attitude, say, of the fourteenth century. In the Middle Ages, sin was referred to a
definite *moral* philosophy: in the Victorian age it was
referred to something that was part material and part moral.
In the end sin came to have such a restricted meaning that
when it appeared for the necessities of the plot, or later, as
a new discovery of the human soul, it was so unlifelike as
to give no conviction.

But the middle class demanded something more. No one
likes to be called a materialist. Just as the American
pioneer in the years of expansion between 1830 and 1850
liked to make the eighteenth-century idea of emancipation
the disguise of material aims, so the Victorian bourgeois
tried to give his earthly objective spiritual wings. This is
principally why the English Victorians did not produce a
Balzac. The French are realists, and if they steal your
money, they are not under the delusion that they are doing
you a service by saving you from drink. Balzac is the
bourgeois *par excellence*. He understands the excitement
of building up a business: he likes big things—big buildings, big orgies, finery, and immense lights. Arnold
Bennett was just such another. The authors remember a
certain occasion when, on ordering a car, he was asked
whether he wanted a taxi or a tram; and he very properly

replied that he wanted a motor-car, and (waving his arm to a terrified page-boy), "a big car, a huge car." Something tremendous and opulent. That is the attractive, boyish spirit of the best middle class; but it was not the spirit of the Victorian middle class. They wanted money and power; but at the same time they wanted to believe that it was manna dropped from heaven. And they wanted their writers to say so. It is to the great honour of the Victorian artists that they rebelled in one way or another, and that while they bowed the knee to Mammon they left their cards on the Deity on the way out.

While, therefore, these men in this volume were great, the marked decline in art showed that they had their limitations. Houses were not beautiful, but they were remarkably safe, secure, and solid. Furniture, for the most part, was hideous and cumbersome; the Bible reclined under the aspidistra, and the bluebottle buzzed suspiciously about the what-not. Painting, as Mr. Martin Armstrong shows, became decorative and illustrative and weakly charming. Music?—there was almost none. There was a lack of acuteness in the perceptions of the senses, which more than one poet tried to remedy. The result in many of the later poets was sensation in the place of emotion. Tennyson and Swinburne gave us music in words. Browning and Rossetti, trying desperately to cultivate in us the spirit of visual beauty, produced painting in words. It is pitiably evident that every artist excelled in his neighbour's field, but left his own unploughed.

Perhaps, if Victoria, so essentially unimportant a personality, had not been on the throne at the time she was, conditions might have been different. Elizabeth was a nasty old lady when she was old, and an extremely witty and attractive one when she was young, but she was unmistakably great both as a personality and as a queen. Like Lord Salisbury, she believed in doing nothing politically; but she did everything in other ways. She could both read and inspire beautiful and passionate poetry. She could lose her temper like a Billingsgate fishwife. She could dress magnificently and extravagantly. She could love extra-maritally and flirt royally. She could be jealous of a rival, and too jealous of her own greatness to tolerate a husband. Victoria could do none of these things. She was a good wife, mother, and a nice old lady that the sailors could fight for. But where Gloriana could temper her able grasp of politics with pageant and gallantry, Victoria, domestically minded, viewed politics personally, familiarly, and managed the nations as she would manage a kitchen. In short, Elizabeth was a coarse aristocrat, and Victoria was a sheltered product of the middle class, and its idol.

Since the sovereign was a woman, the women of the day took their tone from her; and though women do not create as splendidly as men, yet their inspiratory function is enormous. If they fail, men must be left in the lurch. The womanhood of an age not only does a great deal to set the tone of its culture, but also the pitch of its creative and intellectual life. The romantic inspiration of the beloved, of the companion, partner, and witty combatant to men gave place in the Victorian age to the subservient wife and mother. One remembers Millament's fear of wifehood. Partly whimsically and partly truthfully, one might find the explanation for so much frustrated idealism of the Victorian age in the real inequality between the sexes during the period.

The wonder is that, despite the comparative poverty of romance in normal domestic life, despite the restricting aims of the middle class, the Victorians could still be sincerely passionate, and that they could be something more than materialists. Greatness is a comparative term. If we compare any of the Victorians with Shakespeare, with Plato, with Napoleon or Cæsar, Charlemagne or Milton, they are not great. But they have the heroic greatness of the unreflecting stories and songs, an unconsidering devotion to a direct purpose or an uncomplicated ideal, like Ulysses, Beowulf, Æneas, Roland. They looked no farther than the immediate end. They were expressions of a national temper, as if they were agents of accomplishment. They failed of absolute greatness in comparison with the world's greatest because they were hampered.

Yet the number of momentous and significant figures that the age produced was nothing short of amazing. Even in art, while we must criticize its results, we must admit that its exponents stood big in their trade or profession. The doctrinaire confidence that is to most of us so unattractive and so mistaken itself made the century the prolific parent of eminent figures. The great men in the later Roman Empire were few. But there the domination of rich men was also a domination of men corrupt in manners; and the mob was not struggling for emancipation, but was parasitical. They failed to produce great men because there was no health in them, and because Romans had lost confidence in the Roman idea of life. The Victorians never for a moment doubted themselves. The middle class was rich and dominating, but not corrupt. It had a right to believe in its integrity; and similarly, even those who revolted most boldly from the Victorian idea of life, had the confidence in their own revolt that is an essential condition of monumental living and of great creative effort. That their quality is sometimes second-rate comes from the numerous conflicts of one ideal with another, from the fact that there was little united belief except the middle-class one.

II

It is our hope that the analysis of the great men and women in this volume will give an unprejudiced impression of the Victorian contribution to history. It is obvious that, by a careful selection of modern critics, we could have shown the period as a dark age or as a golden one. Neither would have been fair nor historical. We therefore decided to cast our net as wide as possible, and we have not allowed our personal opinions to interfere with our selection. Indeed, we have purposely chosen men who have entirely opposing views, such as Mr. Middleton Murry and Father D'Arcy. We have done this because, just as it is only convenient to talk loosely about a concrete mythical thing called the Victorian Age, so it is inaccurate to think of our own age as meaning a definite mode of thought and attitude to life. When we ask ourselves what exactly is this modernity we hear so much about, we find that it is impossible to define. Who, for instance, is modern? Mr. Aldous Huxley or Mr. Eliot?

Our own generation is, in fact, one of great variety, and in trying to get its view of the Victorians, it would have been obviously silly for us to have hunted high and low for forty contributors who would have taken exactly the same attitude to everything. We should incidentally have produced an exceedingly dull book, to say nothing of a very incomplete idea of what our age thinks of the Victorians.

Simple as the task of editing seemed to us in the first flush of enthusiasm, it did not take us very long before we realized that there were a thousand and one difficulties. We found ourselves confronted with a list of over a hundred and twenty Victorian figures, each with some particular virtue or vice—generally with both—that demanded analysis. Had we been asked to restrict our choice to literary figures, our task would have been comparatively simple; but unfortunately we had to show what was going on in every field of activity—in science, in politics, in religion, in economics, as well as in letters. For a moment the wild idea occurred to us of apportioning eight places to each category, but on second thoughts there seemed to us no sort of defence for including obviously minor economists, scientists, and politicians at the expense of greater men in other fields of activity. In the end, we boiled down our swollen, formidable list to a round fifty, and then set to work to reduce this still further. Many figures held, no doubt, in great affection by our readers, as well as by ourselves, have had to go in the process. Some of them—such as Brougham, Melbourne, and Grey—seemed to us clearly too early for the period; others—Oscar Wilde, Whistler, and Francis Thompson—are too late. These were therefore added to the numbers of the rejected which came to over eighty: Bulwer Lytton, Birket Foster, Watts, Lord Shaftesbury, Stafford Northcote, Lister, Bright, Bradlaugh, Gordon, Livingstone, Melbourne, Faraday, Manning, James Thomson, Fausset, Martin Tupper, Delane, William Barnes, Hartley Coleridge, Tom Hood, Tom Moore, Mrs. Browning, Bosanquet, Douglas Jerrold, Harrison Ainsworth, Kingsley, Maurice, Mrs. Gaskell, Prescott, Froude, Wilkie Collins, Charles Reade, Fenimore Cooper, Wakefield, Dr. Arnold, George Stephenson, Samuel Smiles, Pusey, Herschel, Dr. Whateley, Sir Charles Lyell, Hugh Miller, Professor Owen, Robert Owen, Harriet Martineau, Charles Waterton, Borrow, Henley, Keble, Edward Lear, Carroll, George MacDonald, Mrs. Oliphant, Christina Rossetti, Herbert Spencer, Bates, Jowett, Grote, Hallam, Sydney Smith, Freeman, Sir William Hamilton, de Quincey, William Crookes, Lord Brougham, Lord Durham, Anne Brontë, John Ramsay McCulloch, Irving, Gilbert, Sullivan, Parnell, Henry James, Whistler, Oscar Wilde, Francis Thompson, Clough, and Gerard Manley Hopkins. Nor is this catalogue complete.

The bald enumeration of this list may perhaps give the reader some notion of the problem that faced us in the early days of our editorship. We are well aware that our selection is open to many objections. There may seem to

xviii

be too many literary figures: there is only one philosopher, and only four scientists. All this we have pointed out to each other on the top of many London buses, in our lonely pacings up and down country lanes, and in those hundreds of conversations in London restaurants that were watched by dilapidated waiters in dilapidated evening dress. Mercifully some thirty great men walked automatically into this book—men like Gladstone and Disraeli and Darwin and Tennyson. We could have left it at that, and the volume would have given a very good picture of the Victorians in their amazing variety. But the picture did not seem to us complete, and we therefore decided to include other people who illustrated various important aspects of the Victorian scene. This is why we chose Patmore, for instance, who seems to us to be a more typical Victorian than James Thomson. After wrestling with Charles Reade, George Borrow, and Anthony Trollope, we decided that Trollope brings out the vitally important domestic life of the Victorians, and that nothing in the work of the other two novelists is as significant. De Quincey and Tom Hood were left out because they are Regency, but Peel, though early, was put in because he repealed the Corn Laws, and the Corn Laws started up the industrial engine. We have included Rhodes, although he is a little late, because he is the first picturesque personality who shows what was going on in the Empire meanwhile. Florence Nightingale goes in, because she was a pioneer in women's careers. Tylor, who may be unknown to some readers, is included because he was the father of Anthropology, and spiritually of Sir James Frazer, whose influence on modern thought has been so extensive. Incidentally, he indulged in " animistic " speculations that flatly contradicted his " diffusionist " principles, and this illustrates beautifully the conflict in the ideas of individual great Victorians. Fitzgerald might have been left out, but he is a powerful spreader of hedonism into respectable homes, and his influence on the popular mind was too great to be ignored.

A glance through the list of those whom we have included will show that we have taken the age from 1837 to 1890. Strictly speaking, there is not one Victorian age but two— the first lasts until about the sixties, when the tide that had been running since the French Revolution began to ebb. In Germany, Bismarck was consolidating his power. In America, the Southern cry of State rights goes down before

the Northern cry of union. In England the Whigs and
Radicals had had it all their own way up to Palmerston's
death: within the decade that followed the Tories were
returned with a majority. After this the quarrel between
the two parties is mostly on the Irish Question, and the
emphasis, as in the years immediately preceding the Civil
War in America, was on Union. The period definitely,
however, comes to an end in 1890. Henceforward the age
changes its line of development. In politics, the Labour
Party was born; in literature, moral earnestness gives way
to the gay nineties, and the dissatisfaction with conditions
which had previously brought about the dogmatic rebellion
of so many of the spirits in this book becomes unrest, doubt,
and disillusionment.

We might reasonably have decided that the age ran
between 1837, the first year of Victoria's reign, and 1865,
the year when Palmerston died, but unfortunately we found
it impossible to fit all the representative Victorian figures
into this category; we have therefore taken the period to
mean from 1837 to 1890. By doing this we hope we have
been able to give a picture of every aspect of the Victorian
age: its materialism, its spiritual tribulations, its artistic
individuality and its artistic lack of form, its scientific
keenness, its political and economic enthusiasm. The representation of this inner conflict is what we believe gives
coherence and unity to the book, and prevents it from
being merely a collection of essays about a given historical
period. The reader must be the judge. For ourselves, we
believe that these figures will emerge more distinctly
for the reading of this book than they did a few years ago,
and that they will give a true measure of their place in
history. Some reputations have gone in the process.
On the other hand, perhaps, we have succeeded in rescuing
a number of Victorians from a neglect that was sometimes
chargeable to popular prejudice or ignorance; and if so,
the book will have served a really valuable purpose.

MATTHEW ARNOLD

1822-1888

BY
EDMUND
BLUNDEN

B

MATTHEW ARNOLD

AFTER the display of English poetical genius in the
figures and the utterances of Wordsworth, Coleridge,
Scott, Byron, Shelley, Keats, and other men of the Regency, a period may be recognized during which the writing
of poetry became peculiarly hard to believe in, and the
reading of it was not widely attentive. A great many young
men—and women—of the necessary fineness of spirit
existed, and wrote; but over them seemed to hang the
shadow of their inefficacy. Greatness had flourished. For
them, the after-comers, the day of little though delightful
things; and if they attempted big things, they were inclined
to avoid main roads of style and subject and to grow
fantastical. Beyond the area of their literary indecision,
the new age offered them nothing of the challenge and the
excitement which had formerly, with drums and flags, with
surging ideas of "intolerable wrongs" and universal
rights, aroused young reformists and inspired political
poetry of the strongest conceptions. There had been a
world to set right; a vision to perpetuate; a religion of
philanthropy to establish. In England, after the eighteen-
thirties, the reformist had not such diet; the claims of
poverty were becoming the special study of those in power;
the National School, the *Penny Cyclopædia,* the elegant
cottage on the estate, the cheap edition of classical music,
the Mechanics' Institute, the county asylum, and other signs
are dated very noticeably from that time. Moreover, the
"Steam Intellect Society" was easier for such as Peacock
to ridicule than the march of the machine as an instrument
of a new society at large.

As yet, the labours of applied science appeared prin-

3

cipally in their kinder light, enriching all, diffusing ease
and advantage.   The railway certainly upset a wood or a
flower-bed here and there, and was capable of now and
then sending a man or two untimely to his grave, but the
obvious merits of cheap and rapid transport were undis-
turbed.   The mine, the mill were steadily multiplying their
useful arts.   What reasonable, simple expectations too were
felt over the power of the Press !   War itself was conceived
to be almost defeated, vanquished by that Power: by—

> " the little child, who, lighted by the single wick of a
> small lamp, sits at this moment perched above the
> great steam press of the ' Penny Magazine,' feeding it
> from morning till night, with blank paper, which at
> almost every pulsation of the engine, comes out
> stamped on both sides with engravings, and with
> pages of plain, useful, harmless knowledge, which, by
> making the lower orders acquainted with foreign lands,
> foreign productions, various states of society, etc., tend
> practically to inculcate ' Glory to God in the highest,
> and on earth peace—good will towards men.' "

Had Matthew Arnold come into the world a little earlier,
he would probably have suffered from the sense of indirec-
tion and of an unromantic but improved civilization which
compelled a generation of poets now little known to take to
the by-ways.   As it was, he was much inclined to bow his
head and accept the position of the unprofitable successor ;
there are many passages of his verse which only sigh out
that discouraged attitude:

> " *Goethe in Weimar sleeps, and Greece,*
> *Long since, saw Byron's struggle cease.*
> *But one such death remain'd to come.*
> *The last poetic verse is dumb.*
> *What shall be said o'er Wordsworth's tomb?*

> " *Ah! since dark days still bring to light*
> *Man's prudence and man's fiery might,*
> *Time may restore us in his course*
> *Goethe's sage mind and Byron's force;*
> *But where will Europe's latter hour*
> *Again find Wordsworth's healing power?* "

From the same source comes " Rugby Chapel," the elegy on the all-capable Preceptor:

> " *Yes! I believe that there lived*
> *Others like thee in the past,*
> *Not like the men of the crowd*
> *Who all round me to-day*
> *Bluster or cringe, and make life*
> *Hideous and arid and vile;*
> *But souls temper'd with fire,*
> *Fervent, heroic, and good,*
> *Helpers and friends of mankind.*"

And although, in that poem, Matthew Arnold introduces the note of the rally, requiring in at least some of his contemporaries a determined and influential activity, a loud unquavering Excelsior, still the very bleakness of his tune, the halting pauses of the metre betray the defeatist mood underlying all. At the present time, we may smile at this Wall of Weeping tendency; our world has had something to weep about; but our superior privilege of bitter contemplation is temporary. Man does not need world wars and economic chaos only to promote gloomy inner conflict:

> " *And sighs would sooner fail than cause to sigh.*"

Just missing the slack period of which I have spoken, and coming at his strength into the battle of life and letters round about the time of the Great Exhibition, Arnold was saved from the danger of being a delicate poet of asides. The silence that had seemed to brood (as the baffled great man Beddoes expressed it from his refuge in Germany) over England's oaky forest, had been dispelled; the era of a fresh, strenuous, various literature had opened; Dickens, Carlyle, Macaulay, Browning, Tennyson had made their places. It could not be feared any longer that nobody cared for the progress of genius because there had been a superflux of it to occupy day and night. Neither did the state of the race exhibit such serene improvement as to deprive the mind of its stimulus towards expression: discontent, and apprehension. Some temperaments might stick to their belief,

> " *Fine age is ours and marvellous,—setting free*
> *Hopes that were bending into gray despairs,*
> *Winnowing iron like chaff, outspeeding the airs,*

5

> *Conquering with smoky flag the winds at sea,*
> *Flinging from thunderous wheels immeasurably*
>   *Knowledge like daily light; so that man stares,*
> *Planet-struck with his work-day world, nor dares*
> *Repeat the old babble of what ' shall never be.' "*

Meanwhile, Thomas Hood had pointed out, in " Miss
Kilmansegg " and more famously in " The Song of the
Shirt," aspects of industrial domination which scarcely
fitted the age for the crystal floor; or you could hear Alton
Locke's song:

> *" Weep, weep, weep and weep,*
>   *For pauper, dolt, and slave!*
> *Hark! from wasted moor and fen,*
> *Feverous alley, stifled den,*
> *Swells the wail of Saxon men—*
>   *Work! or the grave! "*

Reference to the columns of Fonblanque's *Examiner* week
by week would readily fill in any dark colours of your
England, and mankind, that the poets of the people happened to have omitted. Under these circumstances, such
reflective beings as Arnold could not merely feel as though
they were without a constituency; vagueness had become
ample discontent; there was an enemy again in the field,
and frustration itself demanded expression. From such
conditions, I conjecture, it arose that the troubled thinker
under review succeeded, in spite of himself, in becoming
the only enduring poet [1] in England's lengthy list with the
Christian name " Matthew," one who is almost more likely
to be understood lately as intended by the use of that name
alone than the formerly popular author of a Gospel. And
although there are elements of poetical magic in which it is
arguable that Matthew Arnold was not rich in comparison
with some of his contemporaries—his " Works " savour
much of work—yet it has been my observation that the
poets of my time recall his name with a greater zeal and a
closer contact than they do those of any others represented
in the anthologies of the Victorians. I had scarcely written
the words when this observation on Arnold met my eye in
the newest critical volume of one of these poets, Mr. Charles
Williams: " Outside the three greatest, if one *had* to choose

---

[1] I would not except the eighteenth-century poet, Matthew Green,
from my own list of favourites; but he is not, I suppose, everybody's
reading.

6

a single poet for the rest of one's life, there are not many
who could rival him."

We read the other day of the sad case of Arnold's theological volumes of prose, sent with inscriptions of the
warmest admiration to—was it not Renan? The recipient,
although he acknowledged these with admiration not
less ardent, failed to cut open the pages. It is possible
that the simple story is the parable of Arnold's prose and
posterity. We all repeat with variations the sentences on
Shelley and the void, on Oxford and lost causes, on the
young lions of the *Daily Telegraph,* on Thomas Gray and
his never speaking out, with many more isolated *dicta,*
seldom allowed to pass unassailed. But we do not commonly meet those who have a conspicuous regard for the
following works: *Higher Schools and Universities in
Germany, A French Eton: or Middle-Class Education and
the State, Reports on Elementary Schools,* 1852–1882,
Isaiah of Jerusalem, A Bible Reading for Schools, or even
On Translating Homer. In these titles, and the others like
them, lurks the imp that urged Mr. Max Beerbohm to
record the person of Matthew Arnold at the moment when
his alleged niece asked him her stern question. " Perfectly
serious"! Nor will the *Study of Celtic Literature,* since
the development by specialists of the misty picture called
Celtic into something like clarity, hold a crowd again. The
prose writings of Arnold altogether are too technical to
have gained him a lasting existence in the library that will
soon collapse under the weight of expert treatises and
monographs. " Not here, O Apollo," did you descend to
bless your side-whiskered son. A dozen other Victorians
could hold their own in their bibliographies as critics and
polemical analysts of their age, in prose, with Arnold—
apart from the special signals of his personality.

The poet had not such rivals, and the infusion of pleasure
with the seriousness has enabled his verse, though not in
its attitude separated from his prose, to continue its life.
Indeed, we see in Matthew Arnold one of the most attractive
paradoxes in the history of our whole poetic inheritance,
which is so largely of a paradoxical kind. The prodigious
contrast of the ultimate reception of Fitzgerald's *Omar
Khayyám* with its first melancholy lucklessness is an instance; but near the popularity of that most cordial of
elegaic poems (for it is haunted with the darkness too) will
come the popularity of Arnold's " Scholar Gipsy." The

paradox of this idyll is not in its finding out so vast a number of delighted readers, nor in any temporary neglect and subsequent revival, but in the fact that it issued at all from the author's mind. The grimness of the intellectual habit was for the time transformed into a genuine " sweetness and light; " the search for a classical subject, or one involving the deliberate construction of a considerable framework, was for the time unnecessary. A simple fancy lured Arnold out of the common-room with its skilful argumentative variations on leading articles; such interests only recurred in order to make the poem at last, not a mere fancy, but a pathetic judgment on the other illusions of modern endeavour. The enjoyment of the "Scholar Gipsy" by many persons through many years was never in doubt. Tennyson thought it the best of Arnold's poems. A. H. Clough, at the close of 1853, wrote to C. E. Norton: "I send you M. Arnold's poems. I myself think that the ' Gipsy Scholar ' is the best. It is *so* true to the Oxford country." And that's true too; and conceivably a great many copies have been bought, read, and got by heart on that account; but the explanation of the very great hold the poem has even on our time does not begin and end in the Oxford country. Nor have there been wanting critics who did not think the Gipsy element in the poem at all explanatory of the said popularity, or who found the Scholar elusive in that regard particularly. The degree of escape from the practical world that the poem achieves has been measured, and has been stated to be insignificant.

Yet we escape with Arnold, on a long test, not into a picaresque or a Romany Rye world, but into a day-dream, and when that is disturbed and assailed by the traffic problem of our waking conceptions, still Arnold involves us in another benedictory dream. The Scholar Gipsy represents very closely the ghost of each one of us, the living ghost, made up of many recollections and some wishes and promises; the excellence of the study is in part due to the poet's refusal to tie his wanderer to an actual gipsy camp or any invention resembling a plot. We may be forced to say good-bye to that spirit, which Mr. A. E. Housman has also revealed to us, and in his poem Arnold himself utters such a farewell:

" *But fly our paths, our feverish contact fly!*
. . . Then fly our greetings, fly our speech and smiles! "

It is after that point, when it might seem that his beautiful fable was only to end in trouble and dejection, that he shows his poetry most strikingly; for, this tolerably logical figure of escape and bondage being worked out, he quietly brings on a new liberty, an even wider horizon, an apparent excursus, and in short the triumph of poetry itself over all " the pangs that pierce." He leaves the pastoral slopes and the divided aims behind, and we are away on fairy seas as in a picture, but not idle as a painted ship; the gale and the waves and sparkling sun are our liberators, and there seems no peril at all of this final transference being reasoned back into a cause of introspective regret. It is possible that some of Arnold's similes do fall under the heading of literary ornament, with a touch or two in them that contrive to obstruct the mere purpose of an emphatic comparison; but the one which concludes the " Scholar Gipsy," audaciously unsimilar as it is in element to what it pretends to parallel, is an original amplification, and changes the whole poem into an unanticipated glory of romance. While this subject of Arnold's instinct of poetry is being glanced at, some notice may be allowed of the relationship between the " Scholar Gipsy " and the " Ode to a Nightingale." The earlier poet has something of Arnold's theme, though he does not—in his youth, and in the world he knew—prepare it so fully. The Nightingale is the symbol of fulfilment and of freedom, in contrast with—

> " *The weariness, the fever and the fret*
> *Here, where men sit and hear each other groan,*"

as the Scholar is the lucky exception beyond our " sick fatigue." Many circumstances and turns of expression or tune in Arnold's piece are apparently harmonious with those in the Ode. Even the " perilous seas " of Keats seem to flow in to the other's " cloudy cliffs " and " sheets of foam." The dream of the Nightingale's ecstatic conquest over time and mutability fades into a " plaintive anthem " as the feigned Scholar Gipsy falls into dust:

> " *Long since, and in some quiet churchyard laid—*
> *Some country-nook, where o'er thy unknown grave*
> *Tall grasses and white flowering nettles wave*
> *Under a dark, red-fruited yew-tree's shade.*"

But, if there is a common measure of idea in the two poems,

B*

Arnold has naturally formed his work with no imitative submission; he has rather narrated than depicted, has enlarged the position from the personal to the Hamlet-like and universal, has humanized the allegorical media (for, though Nightingales are wonderful birds, we might spend our lives more gladly with Scholar Gipsies), and has left no doubt whether he was uttering a sweet and sad complaint or offering a criticism of life with progressive thought —and with a " last word " of singular faith.

In this place it may be agreeable to those who are aware that Time is a laughing philosopher as well as a sexton to look back at an example of the reviews of Arnold's poetry. The nearest to the hand of the present writer is contained in the *Edinburgh Review* for October 1856—the earliest number of that lordly periodical, I believe, to notice a poet named M. Arnold. When he did obtain notice in this quarter, he was not alone. The article (there were thirty pages of it, in those Macaulayese days) admitted: *Festus,* fifth edition, 1854, *The Angel World,* 1850, *The Mystic,* 1855—all by Philip James Bailey; *The Roman,* 1850, *Balder: Part the First,* second edition, 1854, and *England in Time of War,* all by Sydney Dobell, who collaborated with Alexander Smith, too, in *Sonnets on the War,* 1855; Smith's *Poems,* fourth edition, 1856; *The Music Master,* 1855, by William Allingham; *Poems,* 1851, by George Meredith; *Clytemnestra,* by Owen Meredith, 1855; *Poems,* 1856, by the Author of *Paul Ferroll*; *The Ballad of Babe Christabel,* fifth edition, 1855, by Gerald Massey; and *Poems,* by Matthew Arnold, second edition, 1854 and 1855. Among these authors, several fell under the heading of the " spasmodic school," which was being attacked; but Meredith and Arnold were not confused with those " feverish " aspirants. " Mr. Arnold's poems are very refreshing and instructive contrasts to the works of writers who engaged our attention in the first part of this article. Mr. Arnold seems to have been driven, by the consideration of the faults of those writers, into almost an affectation of indifference to minute verbal beauties." Then followed some praise; the versification of Mr. Arnold was excellent, the " coolness of head and warmth. of heart " which was typified in " The Buried Life " was good too. His critical perceptions were " very good, though not infallible." Yet the Edinburgh Reviewer, although he recognized in " Love in the Valley " a " little poem of singular sweetness, truth, and originality," did not spend a word on the "Scholar Gipsy"; and, as he shut up his last poetry book (with a hint to Gerald Massey "to tone down some of the amatory pieces" in the next edition), he began to feel the melancholy pangs of unsatisfied appetite. "Upon the whole, we cannot conclude this rapid survey of the latest poetical growth of English literature without arriving at a low estimate of its character and its tendencies. The harvest is great, but the labourers are weak, not few." Something might turn up. The critic pointed for a moment "from the regions of silence and obscurity into those of light and song." But only for a moment. "In spite of the fashion of the day, which may serve to raise this or that writer into a semblance of popularity"—in spite of Allingham, Meredith, Matthew Arnold on the critical table—"we must venture to record our opinion that the high places of English poetry are at this time unfilled, and that the man whose genius shall next enable him to embody in some living and original form the spirit and the feeling of our times has not yet revealed himself to us by his works."

What the entire spirit and feeling of mid-Victorian times were perhaps no single author could ever show; there may be no reason why a man of genius should be confined to the characteristics of his age; but Arnold certainly expressed, and is our man because he expressed, one aspect of his age. He was intensely concerned with responsibility, individual and national; and if he lacked the sense of humour, it was because of this concern, or scheme. The fabric entrusted to him and his contemporaries was prodigious; to maintain it demanded "laborious days," an attitude of greatness, a constant tirelessness. Now and then, particularly by moonlight, he retreated a little from the business of the vast priesthood into a personal affection simple and usual:

> "*Ah, love, let us be true*
> *To one another! for the world, which seems*
> *To lie before us like a land of dreams,*
> *So various, so beautiful, so new,*
> *Hath really neither joy, nor love, nor light,*
> *Nor certitude, nor peace, nor help for pain;*
> *And we are here as on a darkling plain*
> *Swept with confused alarm of struggle and fight,*
> *Where ignorant armies clash by night.*"

11

But he could not stay long away from the counsels of war.
He was in love with responsibility. As an inspector of
schools, of course, he had his weak moments, and a
" skilled assistant " was not disdained by him in some part
of his duties; but the larger, less tangible kind of inspection
—that of the country's civilization—was for him to perform
as though nobody else could help at all. If ever he wrote
a love poem (the Marguerite pieces being love elegies), it
was that excursus he makes from " Heine's Grave "—
odi et amo in a singular form, yet one known to many
Victorians whose wives saw little of them except in print.

> " *I chide with thee not, that thy sharp*
> *Upbraidings often assail'd*
> *England, my country—for we,*
> *Heavy and sad for her sons,*
> *Long since, deep in our hearts,*
> *Echo the blame of her foes.*
> *We, too, sigh that she flags;*
> *We, too, say that she now—*
> *Scarce comprehending the voice*
> *Of her greatest, golden-mouth'd sons*
> *Of a former age any more—*
> *Stupidly travels her round*
> *Of mechanic business, and lets*
> *Slow die out of her life*
> *Glory, and genius, and joy.*
> *So thou arraign'st her, her foe;*
> *So we arraign her, her sons.*
>
> " *Yes, we arraign her! but she,*
> *The weary Titan, with deaf*
> *Ears, and labour-dimmed eyes,*
> *Regarding neither to right*
> *Nor left, goes passively by,*
> *Staggering on to her goal;*
> *Bearing on shoulders immense,*
> *Atlantëan, the load,*
> *Well-nigh not to be borne,*
> *Of the too vast orb of her fate.*"

That wonderful portrait is inspired with sympathy, I suspect, from Arnold's own notion of himself undertaking
civil and moral and intellectual burdens beyond natural

12

strength; and one may read that, unhappy as the situation
might be, a grim happiness grew out of it. The heroic age,
after all, might not be beyond renewal. "Hear also what
Saint Paul saith." What would Arnold have done had he
lived now? or others of his time who so deliberately
assumed that their country should be the permanently
supreme power, and that only their own superhuman concentration of effort could attain that result? We have men
as energetic, as devoted, as patriotic; but the costly illusion
of "her fate" is hardly in them. They have witnessed the
indications of a new arrangement of burdens. But would
not Matthew Arnold have enriched the sessions of Geneva?

"Matthew Arnold, M.A., Foreign Assistant Commissioner to the Schools Enquiry Commission, one of Her
Majesty's Inspectors of Schools, formerly Foreign Assistant
Commissioner to the Commission for Enquiring into the
state of Popular Education in England, and Professor of
Poetry in the University of Oxford." Such was the author
of *Schools and Universities on the Continent,* 1868, a fine,
tall volume of three hundred pages, marking perhaps the
public retirement of Arnold from the poetical staff of the
State. The book is another version of his anxious love of
England and her problems as they appeared to him. It
reminds me of a vast manuscript work, analytical of human
progress and error, by a contemporary (one of the *Telegraph*
lions), which begins, "May we be of any use, however
humbly?" There is humility enough in Arnold's tone, but
he wishes to be of use in a mighty reconstruction. In
his statement, "I have seen Dutch, German, and Swiss
schools, I have seen their inspection; and I think both them
and their inspection, in general, better than our schools
and inspection at present: I think, as a matter of fact, they
are better; and I think, as a matter of likelihood, it seems
likely they should be better," there is austerity, pride of
place, but no vanity. He, like an umpire, knows the
system. Towards the end of the book he introduces the
theme of much of his verse, in plain, tranquil language,
but with Isaiah-like loftiness. He gazes over Europe. He
finds a phenomenon common to Austria, Rome, and
England: all these he detects "disregarding the inevitable
laws which govern the life of modern society," by their
failure to provide themselves with "a modern civil or-
ganisation." How his formidable question sounds from the
mountain: "Who will deny that England has life and

13

progress? But who will deny also that her course begins
to show signs of uncertainty and embarrassment?" There
is joy in him as he hints of the "immense task of transformation." His age was, or seemed, the age of "public
works." In his zest for those, not so much in his reasons
why, he is his age. Fortunate, in that he was not confined
to prose expression, for the mere tonnage of sociological
and ethical prose of his time has been its doom—

" And tottering empires crush by their own weight,"

the empires of those who, had they divined the beauty of
conciseness and reserve, would flash upon us still in the
welcome colours of genius separate and undying—Carlyle,
Ruskin, and even novelists like George Eliot and Charles
Reade.

And so this note on Arnold has returned to his verse, and
among his rivals there also, as it seems to me, he is fortunate
in the long run. It must be admitted at once that he wrote,
and was willing to preserve, some copies of verses quite as
unnecessary and as insipidly bad as any of his rivals from
Mrs. Browning to Sir Edwin Arnold ever did. His
"Modern Sappho" leans her head on the cold balustrade
in terms beyond the dreams of parodists and collectors of
Victorianism in bloomers. The lady, aware of competitors,
does her best to be a demon lover:

" So, to wait! But what notes down the wind, hark! are
*   driving?*
*   'Tis he! 'tis their flag, shooting round by the trees!—*
Let my turn, if it will come, be swift in arriving!
*   Ah! hope cannot long lighten torments like these.*

" Hast thou yet dealt him, O life, thy full measure?
*   World, have thy children yet bow'd at his knee?*
Hast thou with myrtle-leaf crown'd him, O pleasure?
*   —Crown, crown him quickly, and leave him for me."*

Even in the sonnet on the "Austerity of Poetry," which
yields in brief his opinion of the outward and inward nature
of this art, there is a strong suspicion of the Bathos. But
when these lapses have all been considered and assessed, it
becomes clear that Arnold reverenced poetry above all who
were then accepted as its guardians, and that he anticipated
more than those what modern judgment requires in poetry.

The temptation to produce verse, not out of a thorough conception and gestation of experience and tranquillity, but from the workshop of confident word-craft, did not subdue him, whether he followed the complete Greek spirit as he intended or not. He did not care to invent " beautiful lines " like marsh-mallows and liqueurs, while his laureated contemporary was brooding over such accomplishments as though " there all the honour lay." He could create such luxuries, but they did not occupy him; they were no more to his broader plan than the unadorned and bleak passages. " The instinctive mastery over metrical effects," accordingly, has been denied him, and a class of versification may be outlined to which he hardly contributes; and, if he tried once or twice, he was unsuccessful. In spite of that, he commanded a music of his own, and the only one appropriate, in its movement and its pause, to his train of thought, and the huge, rather dim, rather unsafe cosmos in which he imagined himself to move. You cannot be a skylark if the sky is falling. There is a peculiar tune for the deeper anxieties.

The second version of " Hyperion " is one man's record of that subtle, subterraneous concord. Arnold kept his own record, and certain master-images enabled him to think in metre not taught by main tradition. The waves on Dover Beach, the echoes of evening countryside, the courses of the great streams, were his prosodic tutors, and the sureties of his poetry in every sense. Sublime they must ever be, and by their sublimity he, calmly glad in the comprehension of their dignity and strength, is borne along. He tries no tricks on their majesty, either of universal " explanation " or of artful embellishments, such as should show the writer's acquaintance with the morning's scientific apocalypse or current painting or music. With such statements of what happens, though they may be devoid of conventions of hope and advantage, this generation has understood how to be happy; we " ask no kind returns," but watch with fascination the enigmatic flow of event. Arnold best expresses the power of his own poetry even while he describes that cool rapture:

> " *And the width of the waters, the hush*
> *Of the grey expanse where he floats,*
> *Freshening its current and spotted with foam*
> *As it draws to the Ocean, may strike*

Peace to the soul of the man on its breast—
As the pale waste widens around him,
As the banks fade dimmer away,
As the stars come out, and the night-wind
Brings up the stream
Murmurs and scents of the infinite sea."

GENERAL
BOOTH
1829-1912

BY
ST. JOHN
ERVINE

GENERAL BOOTH

I

WILLIAM BOOTH was born at 12 Nottintone Place, Sneinton, Nottingham, on April 10, 1829. His father, Samuel Booth, is said by Harold Begbie, the General's official biographer, to have been a man of means: a nail manufacturer and, later, an architect and builder. He sometimes described himself as " a gentleman " and sometimes as " a yeoman." [1] In these varied occupations, Begbie asserts, he earned " a fortune which enabled him to live in a fine house at Colston Bassett." All these statements are inaccurate, and the legend of his father's lost social grandeur, in which William Booth to the day of his death firmly believed, is a myth which his biographer might easily have exploded by a few inquiries. Samuel Booth was an ambitious but unsuccessful man, who bitterly attributed his misfortunes to the dishonesty and malignity of other persons when he might have attributed them to his own ignorance and vanity and business incapacity. He was never a nail manufacturer: he was a nailer, that is to say, a workman who makes nails. He was never an architect, for he was illiterate, being unable to read or write, nor was he ever a farmer, although for a brief and miserable period he held an allotment. He did not make a fortune; for a short time he earned enough money to live in what, for a workman, could be called style. The " fine house at Colston Bassett " existed in his romantic mind, which consoled him for his present miseries by glorifying his past. A man without occupation is sometimes described in legal documents as

---

[1] In his widow's death certificate he is described as a farmer.

" a gentleman," but to Samuel Booth the term, proudly claimed, denoted a man of family and fallen fortune. In the working-class district in which his son was born, Samuel Booth kept himself to himself, disdaining his neighbours, and constantly condoling with himself on the dreadful exigencies of life which obliged him, a man of former substance and style, to associate with such unimportant persons. His son, who had no respect for him, called him " a Grab, a Get," who only entered heaven by " the skin of his teeth."

William Booth's mother, Mary Moss, was Samuel Booth's second wife. Myths have been made about her. She is said to have been " the daughter of a well-to-do farmer." She was not. Her father was a hawker who, for a period, but most incompetently, tried to live on a small-holding. On his re-marriage, his daughter took a situation as a domestic servant in Ashby-de-la-Zouch, where she encountered Samuel Booth, a widower, newly bereaved of his only surviving child. Booth proposed marriage to her, but his proposal was declined. Its refusal mortified his pride, and so exasperated him that, after a precipitate flight from Ashby-de-la-Zouch, he returned a month or two later and pestered the girl, seventeen years his junior, until she accepted him. There is no proof, but a strong presumption which William Booth believed, that Mary Moss was a Jewess, or of mixed Jewish and Gentile blood. Her surname and her markedly Hebraic features, as well as the Rabbinical look of her famous son, which became more noticeable as he aged, and the strongly Jewish look of several of his children, especially his daughters, Catherine and Evangeline, support the presumption.

At the age of thirteen William Booth was taken from school, because of his father's financial misfortunes, and bound to a pawnbroker. The apprenticeship humiliated him, nor could he ever mention the occupation in his later life, although, through it, he had obtained a knowledge of poverty-stricken people which was invaluable to him. Five months later his father's widow, whose helpless condition was increased by her desperate efforts to be ladylike, removed to a poorer quarter of the town, and precariously maintained her young children by selling tape and toys. They lived on the verge of destitution, seldom having sufficient to eat. In 1844, before he was sixteen, the tall, gawky boy, with big, luminous, grey eyes, thick, black

hair, a high, Hebraic nose, and finely shaped hands, became "converted." He considered himself, prior to this
emotional experience, to have been a most wicked sinner,
but his offences were venial, and no more than any decent
lad might have committed. The worst of them would not
be noticed by the most exacting deity.

Booth was a predestined evangelist, pious almost from
his birth. The inescapable fact which confronts the student
of his career is that he was ordained to be devout from the
day he became intellectually conscious of life. So was the
woman he married. Four months before Booth's birth, on
January 17, 1829, there was born at Ashbourne, in Derby-
shire, a woman child, Catherine, the daughter of John and
Sarah Mumford. She, too, was one of a family of five.
Her father, a workman and local preacher, married a little
"above him." Miss Milward, as his wife was when he
met her, was in an acute condition of neurosis, which was
only cured or, at all events, assuaged by emotional piety,
such as the Methodists of her time provided. In one of
their meetings she met and fell in love with John Mumford,
a man of character and mind who, after a period spent in
the advocacy of total abstinence from intoxicating liquor,
became a drunkard, and involved his wife and his daughter
in poverty. Catherine Booth, the nervous child of a nervous
mother, was always pious, although, as is common with
persons pious from their childhood, she customarily thought
of her "unregenerate" period as one of appalling wickedness. She, like William Booth, was a destined evangelist.
Religion occupied her youth as closely as it occupied that
of Pascal. She was austere in her devotion from her infancy. At the age of twelve she had formed strong views
on intoxicating liquor and the Pope, and was firmly opposed
to the Catholic Emancipation Bill, of which her father
approved. In her fourteenth year her delicacy resulted in
spinal curvature, and she was compelled to cease from
school, and lie in a recumbent position for a prolonged
period. In this time she read and closely conned Butler's
Analogy and Newton on Prophecy and the gloomier works
of piety which were then thought to be particularly suitable
for invalids. Her father removed to London in 1844, where
her lungs became affected, and she seemed likely to die of
tuberculosis, but her piety prevailed over her physical distress, and she recovered, although her health for the whole
of her life was so poor that she could say, on her death-bed,

that she could not recollect a day when she had been free from pain.

In London, when he and she were twenty-one, William Booth and Catherine Mumford met for the first time. They were both members of a group of Methodists who had revolted against authority. Booth, who had been reared in the Anglican communion, joined the Methodists in Nottingham, because their worship was informal and warm. " I like my tea," he used to say to servants in houses where he was a guest, " as I like my religion—*hot!* " In his twentieth year, Booth, faring after fortune, went from Nottingham to Walworth, in South London, and there became a pawnbroker's assistant for a living, and an itinerant and unpaid preacher in his spare time, which was scanty. He would harangue the lost, after a long day in the receipt of pledges from the impoverished, and then run, panting, all the way to his employer's shop, lest he should be locked out; for the pawnbroker, although he affected to be pious, was not willing to leave his door off the latch after half-past ten, even for an assistant so religiously engaged as Booth.

Catherine Mumford, sadly disappointed with the tendency of religious persons to become comfortable, found no rest for her soul until one evening she heard the gaunt young man, Booth, preach from the text, " This is indeed the Christ, the Saviour of the World." She greatly esteemed him, and when, a few days later, she met him at a party where he enlivened the guests with the recitation of a long and lugubrious poem, called " The Grog-Seller's Dream," she and he discovered themselves to be in love. She encouraged him to become a minister, and on June 16, 1855, they were married in Stockwell New Chapel. Eight children were born to them in thirteen years, in which period both Booth and she preached their way through England, as a Methodist minister and his wife, attaining immense popularity and some envy as evangelists. They withdrew from the Methodist communion, because of the determination of their superiors that they should lead a pastoral rather than an evangelistic life, and started the East London Christian Mission, out of which the Salvation Army was evolved.

II

Booth's departure from the Methodist Church is more dramatically than exactly described in the official *Lives* of himself and his wife. He did not instantly resign in response to his wife's challenging cry uttered in the gallery of Bethesda Chapel, Liverpool. She shouted "No, never!" when the Conference proposed to restrict him to the pastorate of the Newcastle Circuit, and to prohibit him, except on rare and closely prescribed occasions, from evangelism. Nor is it true that when, six weeks later, Booth resigned from the Methodist New Connexion, he left Newcastle without a penny in his pocket. These are the romantic fictions which grow round the history of the founders of all religious societies. The resignation was tendered to the Conference Committee on July 18, 1861. Booth then left Newcastle for London, and, a few weeks later, began in Cornwall the peripatetic career of an evangelist which was to continue, more or less, for the remainder of his life.

It was not until the summer of 1865 that he started the mission which eventually became the Salvation Army. He was then thirty-six years of age, a man of moods and great energy and organizing ability, but made delicate by penury and years of ill-nourishment. His wife was more delicate than he, a woman of highly nervous temperament, but possessed of powers of endurance and recovery which such persons seem exceptionally to possess. They had six delicate and nervous children, one of whom was mentally afflicted, and another child, now Commander of the Forces in the United States, was on the way. They were poor and had few friends, and were without influence of any sort, and they had incurred the opposition, for enmity is too strong a word, of a considerable church. In that summer a firm of pious publishers, eager to promote both the Kingdom of Heaven and the circulation of their weekly paper, invited Booth to lead a Mission in a tent on the Quakers' Burial Ground in the East End of London. Mrs. Booth had already, and with immense success, led missions in Bermondsey and Rotherhithe. It was, indeed, her success which turned her husband's attention towards the Metropolis: he had previously thought of evangelizing the provinces. The invitation was accepted, and the Mission was successful enough to induce Booth to abandon his idea of a peripatetic preaching life and settle down to the making

of a permanent East End Mission. He became a pastor:
his wife remained an evangelist. While he worked in
Whitechapel, she invaded the West End, where her fervent
addresses evoked applause from pious peers, as well as
persons who were excited by the singular spectacle of a
woman preaching sermons.

III

Booth, throughout his life, found restraint irksome. He
disbelieved in democratic government and loathed committees, although he worked with them when he had to.
His temperament was despotic, but even if it had not been
despotic, he must, in the circumstances of that time, have
become a dictator; for the people with whom he had to
work had to be told what to do. They were not of the
sort that could usefully be consulted. The mission in the
tent ended with the collapse of the tent in a gale. It was
then transferred to a succession of halls of every sort, some
of them being so odoriferous, through contiguity to pigsties,
that Booth, whose nostrils were as sensitive as Shakespeare's, was overcome by the foul smell. After a succession of disappointing experiments, Booth suddenly made
the supreme decision of his life. He resolved to have done
with Churches, and to become master of his own Mission.
In 1865, therefore, he took his Bible and an umbrella, and
stood on Mile End Waste, a broad patch of derelict land
which lay at the side of the Mile End Road, Whitechapel,
where he preached, sometimes in front of The Vine public-
house, and sometimes in front of The Blind Beggar. He
could not foresee what he was doing when he banged his
Bible and waved his umbrella to attract attention, and
uttered his simple faith in a harsh, uneducated voice which
scattered aitches as wind scatters dust; but he then began
one of the greatest religious organizations in the world.

IV

But not without pain and loss. The Salvation Army is
now a universal society, everywhere respected and supported, and those who are acquainted with its members
and its work have difficulty in believing that Booth's first
followers were kicked and cuffed and persecuted and stoned
and imprisoned in almost every country in which they

worked. They were brutally beaten from one end of England to the other. They were assaulted in Great Britain and Ireland and France and Switzerland and Germany and the United States. Bands of hooligans, paid by brewers and publicans, formed a counter-force, called The Skeleton Army, which cruelly assailed the Salvationists, pledged not to retaliate for any injury they received, and blasphemously mocked their services. The police at first stood indifferently by, except when they arrested the Salvationists for provoking their assailants to commit assaults. As well might a man have been charged with tempting a thief by wearing a watch! Imprisonment became a common experience for a Salvationist. Assault was considered part of his regular routine. In one "barracks" plaster and ointment were kept for the soldiers who were certain to be wounded during any march! Booth's son, Ballington, was imprisoned in the North of England; his daughter, Catherine, was imprisoned in Switzerland and then deported. His son-in-law, Booth-Tucker, was several times imprisoned in India. Booth himself was accused of living on the pennies of the poor, and his followers were informed that they were credulous fools, who would presently discover that their precious leader had decamped with their cash, although he never drew a stipend from the Army's funds. Booth, in brief, experienced almost identically the persecutions which had been inflicted upon John Wesley and the first Methodists.

The Early Christians received the same treatment that was accorded to the Early Salvationists. Even the details of abuse were identical. Villains would let sparrows loose in the candle-lit rooms in which the Methodists prayed and preached and sang. The agitation which ensued generally resulted in the extinction of the light. The Methodists were then accused of practising abominable orgies in the dark! A similar charge was preferred against the Salvationists, who were accused of "groping for Jesus" or "crawling to Jesus" in the dark. Two bishops, their Lordships of Hereford and Oxford, charged Booth with promoting sexual promiscuity. The maternity wards of the workhouses, they implied, were full of pregnant unmarried girls who had been led astray through Booth's emotional meetings. Not one charge could be sustained, and the Bishop of Oxford subsequently apologized to two of Booth's officers for the pain he had inflicted upon him. All the bishops, however, were not antipathetic to Booth. If the Bishop

of Carlisle could denounce him from his cathedral pulpit,
the Archbishop of Canterbury (Dr. Tait) was temerariously
his friend, and incurred odium by contributing five pounds
to one of his funds. A suffragan bishop even preached at
a special service for Salvationists, and encouraged them to
do their work.

v

The Salvation Army was formally called by that name
on June 24, 1880, although it had informally borne the
title for several months before. Booth envisaged his Mission as a fighting force. He was at war with Sin. His
society was not a Church: it was an Army. He was not
a minister: he was a soldier. The methods which applied
to Church missions, therefore, were inapplicable to fighting
forces. Was a general to hold up his attack until he had
consulted every corporal on its advisability and conduct?
What would be said of a private or a company commander
who refused to go over the top until the details of the attack
had been expounded to him and a vote of the forces taken
on whether it should be made? The Devil was busy, said
Booth: God's soldiers must be busier. Satan was a wily
one: God's soldiers must be wilier. If the Devil seduced
men and women with jolly tunes, God's soldiers must take
his tunes and put God's words to them. . . . The important fact which was seized by Booth, as leader of the
Christian Mission and General of the Salvation Army, was
that the single relief which the deeply impoverished people
of the slums of England had from their misery was the
warm and well-lit public-house, in which there were congenial company and gaiety. The half-starved labourer
returned from arduous and ill-paid work to a dark and
dirty home in a dark and dirty slum, where his slatternly
wife and unkempt children completed his misery. The contrast between his home and the gin-palaces was too strong
for him to resist the allurements of the latter. The pub.
was the bright alternative to a dismal home. Had he looked
for comfort in any church, he would not have found it;
for the church doors, generally speaking, were closed from
one Sabbath to the next. Only the well-dressed were welcomed to worship! . . . As this fact, that the submerged
people had no alternative to their gloomy homes but the
brilliantly illuminated and warm and jolly public-houses,

26

seeped into Booth's brain, he realized that hot sin could be
successfully combated only by a hot religion. If there was
gaiety in the gin-palace, there should be gaiety in the
Salvation Army barracks. He would turn Hell's weapons
upon Hell. Like Whitfield, he disputed the Devil's right
to all the best tunes. He instructed his soldiers to sing
cheerful hymns; he gave them bright uniforms and bright
banners; he gave them drums and trumpets and tam-
bourines; he called them captains and commanders, and
told them that they must work for little or no wages. What
was left when expenses had been paid could be shared by
them. Garibaldi offered his Thousand wounds and death;
and got his Thousand. Booth offered half-educated or
illiterate workmen and servant-girls calumny and hunger
and pain and persecution and a strict and unquestionable
obedience to their General's commands; and he got an
Army that went across the world.

The devotion of his soldiers was such that in December
1878, while the Army was still the Christian Mission, he
had to issue a General Order against starvation, and forbid
his officers to go hungry for Christ's sake. The religion he
preached was a genial Fundamentalism, in which attention
was more often called to the gilt heaven than the red-hot
hell. His soldiers were not encouraged to dabble in
theology, nor were they permitted to use sacraments which,
Booth asserted, were active agents of discord and separation. They were told to believe that conversion was an
instantaneous process, and that a man could be immediately sanctified, but that he must be careful to keep himself
in that condition by starting to rescue those who were still
foundering soon after he had himself been rescued. The
half-drowned, on reaching shore, must turn and throw a
line to those still struggling in the sea. The soldiers were
encouraged to jump with joy. If the Spirit moved them to
leap in the middle of a hymn or a prayer, they were to
leap. They were to enjoy God.

VI

He was fortunate in his associates, as he was fortunate
in his wife and his children. When a young Scots mystic,
George Scott Railton, came to join his Mission, Booth
knew that God was with him, for this odd young man, who
was to invade the United States in company with six girls

and an elderly woman, and claim America for Christ, was
the first educated man to give up all he had to work with
him. Railton, at the age of nineteen, having learnt
Spanish, resolved to march to Morocco, carrying a little
banner, inscribed, "Repentance—Faith—Holiness," and
there begin the conversion of Africa. Ignatius Loyola
similarly started from Spain to take the Tomb from the
Turk! The British Consul, feeling certain that Railton
was demented, returned him to England, and soon afterwards the young Scot found his way to Whitechapel, where
he became a member of Booth's household, and eventually
was his first Commissioner. Booth was not afraid of a man
who was willing to be a fool for Christ's sake, and he
detected in Railton invaluable qualities when no one else
could see them, when, indeed, Railton seemed to be a
danger, because his odd ways and his contempt for committees, as great as Booth's, caused intense antipathy to
him. There was a time when members of the "station"
to which Railton had been appointed petitioned for his
removal. But Booth knew his Railton, and kept him, and
the Army learnt to appreciate and love him. Other invaluable helpers were Elijah Cadman, the converted chimney-
sweep, James Dowdle, the converted guard, and John
Lawley. Hundreds of simple, God-infested men and women
rushed to Booth's banner, and asked for no other reward
than to be striped for their Saviour. Girls of sixteen and
seventeen were made captains and lieutenants, and sent to
work in the worst slums in the country. When people
remonstrated with Booth for this action, he asked them
what sort of a general he would be if he hesitated to send
his troops into an attack because some of them might be
killed. Did they not know there was a war on? What did
it matter to a soldier if he were killed in the trenches, when
death meant instant promotion to Glory? The annals of
the Salvation Army are bright with the heroic deeds of
young working-men and women who endured hardship
and obloquy and obscene abuse for their God and their
General's sake.

VII

His wife was immeasurably helpful to him. Her beautiful and noble heart kept her in fighting-trim when her body
was trying to break her. There were times when, after a

meeting, she would lie panting for breath, or have to be
carried from the platform in a faint. She was a home-
loving woman, but her restless husband made her God's
gipsy, and sent her careering along the length of Britain,
as he himself careered, as he made his children career.
When he sent an expeditionary force to France, his delicate
daughter, Catherine, aged twenty-two, was appointed to
lead it, although pious people filled Mrs. Booth's mind
with forebodings of what would happen to the girl among
the ungodly and lascivious French. A Booth could not fail
to do what young servant-girls had gladly undertaken to
do in farther lands than France. All the Booths, so soon
as they could stand on a platform and preach, were sent
headlong into the war. The most brilliant of them was the
eldest, William Bramwell, who was showing talents at
sixteen that great *entrepreneurs* might have envied. He
became Chief of his father's Staff, and succeeded him as
General.

The formative years of the Army were the early eighties.
In those years, despite tremendous outbursts of abuse and
persecution, the strength of the Salvationists extraordinarily
increased. A young Indian judge, called Tucker, gave up
his post and a handsome salary to become an Army captain.
He led the first expeditionary force to India. America,
Australia, France, Switzerland, Sweden, South Africa, and
Germany were all invaded within two years. The first *War
Cry* was issued on December 27, 1879, at a halfpenny. It
speedily became a bi-weekly, and had a circulation of a
quarter of a million. *War Cries* were published from
America to China. Booth, like Wesley, had taken the
world for his parish. His troops were storming the Devil's
trenches everywhere. Their success was exciting the interest and sympathy, and sometimes the jealousy, of other
religious organizations. The Church of England made
tentative proposals for their inclusion in its communion,
but the proposals were not attractive, and seemed to offer
no inducement to Booth to subordinate himself to the Archbishop of Canterbury. He might, perhaps, be offered a
prebendal stall in St. Paul's Cathedral! . . . But Booth
was the commander-in-chief of his Army. He had made it
and intended to keep it. So he thanked the deferential
bishops, and allowed them to go. The Church Army was
formed thereafter. His success was singular. Queen
Victoria had frowned upon him, because of his military

pretensions, but King Edward approved of them, and received him at Buckingham Palace. Thereafter, emperors and kings were assiduous in their attentions to him. The organization rapidly grew, although harsh criticisms periodically were made of it, and every sort of social work was added to the spiritual crusade. The Army developed a commercial side, and it now transacts insurances, and has banks and printing works and emigration societies and several sorts of factories. It works in fifty-eight countries and colonies, and preaches in seventy-four languages. It has nearly twenty-six thousand officers, and issues a hundred and thirty different periodicals. It has children's homes, inebriates' homes, maternity homes, women's industrial homes, men's industrial institutions, labour bureaux, homes for the reception of ex-prisoners, farm colonies, hospitals, and social institutions of many kinds.

All these soldiers, so variously active, and all these institutions have grown out of the derided efforts of one God-infested, half-educated man, with a sick wife and a young sickly family, who stood, with a Bible and an umbrella, on the Mile End Waste and besought the ungodly to repent and sinners to seek salvation. A mouse had been in labour, and had produced a mountain.

VIII

There were heavy casualties on the way to this success. Two sons, Ballington and Herbert, and one dearly beloved daughter, Catherine, seceded from his Army. The Spartan father treated them as deserters, nor could they presume upon their blood. Booth had no father and no mother and no kindred. He was a soldier with a cause. Whoever was on his side was his father and his mother and his kinsman. Whoever flew from his side, though he or she were very Booth of very Booth, was no longer kindred of his. His daughter Emma, who had married Booth-Tucker, was killed in a railway accident in the United States. Some senior officers seceded, sometimes for trivial reasons. There were setbacks here and there, and indiscretions, and losses that, at the time, seemed trivial, but were subsequently proved to be serious. One of them occurred when a young man slipped into an Army meeting and found salvation, in which he did not long continue. His name was Alfred

Harmsworth, and he lapsed from grace and became a journalist and founded the *Daily Mail*.

Booth's heaviest loss befell him on October 4, 1890, when his wife, after enduring agony for two years from cancer, died. Her death was as heroic as her life. This great and good woman, who had triumphed over physical failures of the most distressing sort, lifted up her heart to the last minute of her life. Half-conscious, she called for her husband, and drew him down to her, so that her lips might be on his when she died; and in that dear embrace, a most noble spirit passed. Even in that time of trouble, there were some found callous enough to taunt the old man with the suggestion that it was his wife who made his Army, and not he. But Booth had no wish to defend himself from such taunts as those. Only God and he knew what was in his heart, and what was in his heart was in Catherine's too. Thereafter, the solitary old man, possessed now of one passion, to rescue the perishing, incessantly moved about the world, while his brilliantly executive son, Bramwell, managed his Army's affairs at home. His health, which had never been good, became poorer. He could eat little and with difficulty, for he was tormented by dyspepsia. He became blind. God used him as exhaustively and hardly as He had used Moses. Booth had brought his Army out of the wilderness, and had received more reward than Moses, but the end was difficult and dark. His enemies, in the first days, had cruelly accused him and his soldiers of groping in the dark for Jesus. Now, his friends could say that too, and not cruelly, but in loving pity. He fell over the chairs in his room, crying out in a religious rage because he could no longer lead his hosts. His strength failed, and quickly ran out. Speech became difficult. A short while before he died, he raised himself up, and said to his son, " Bramwell, the promises ! . . ." He could not continue for a few moments. He tried again, and again could not continue, but seemed to be confused. He made a third attempt to speak. " The promises ! " he muttered, and someone standing by helped him with the words, " of God." Booth rallied. Halting and hesitating, but with solemn emphasis, he said, " The promises . . . of God . . . are sure . . . are sure . . . if you will only believe." Later, he chaffed his son, for he had a grim humour. " I'm leaving you a bonnie handful," he said. That was the end.

On August 20, 1912, at his home in Hadley Wood, near

Barnet, he died. A great thunder-storm had beat about
the house when Catherine passed: a thunder-storm beat
about Hadley Wood when her husband followed her. The
Booths were *always* in storms. But they weathered them.
There was a suggestion that he should be buried in Westminster Abbey. The Dean declined it. But Booth would
not have cared for such a burial. His place was with his
fighting men who had died in the War and been buried in
Abney Park. A general should lie among his soldiers. His
body was carried through the streets of London, while
great crowds stood silent and uncovered to see it go by.
This was the same man who, forty-seven years earlier, had
stood alone on the Mile End Waste, uninfluential and derided, and had claimed the world for Christ. That claim
was now conceded, but even as he died he was not content.
When Bramwell whispered to the old man, dozing to his
death, " Is there anything you want, Father? " he stirred
and said, " Yes, I want to hear dear old Lawley say, ' Here
comes another one for God, General! ' " He was God's
soldier, His tireless recruiting-sergeant, who continually
called the careless civilians to enlist in the Holy War, and,
unlike the generality of such commanders, gave them
ribbons to wear in their hats and bright banners to bear in
their hands, and filled their hearts with the unquenchable
gaiety of God.

FRANCIS
HERBERT
BRADLEY

1846-1924

BY
J. H.
MUIRHEAD

c

J. H. MUIRHEAD

FRANCIS HERBERT BRADLEY

THE real history of an era is the history of the ideas which dominated it, and these ideas find their purest, if not always their clearest, expression in the works of its philosophers. The history of Victorian philosophy remains still to be written. When it finds its historian it will, I believe, be seen to consist in the gradual rediscovery, first by its chief poets, then by some of its more prophetic prose writers, finally by its professional philosophers, of certain great constructive ideas which had been the inspiration of the best periods of Continental thought, but had been largely obscured in England by the authority of some of her own great writers, chiefly that of Locke. When Victoria came to the throne, the current of thought, set in motion by Locke, was still running strong in the writings of Bentham and the Mills. A voice had indeed been raised in favour of a different type of philosophy by Coleridge. But his voice, if not of one crying in the wilderness, was of one who seemed to make a wilderness where he cried, and so to delay rather than accelerate the advent of the new order. To the prophetic writers of the succeeding period, led by Carlyle, technical philosophy under the name of Metaphysics seemed rather a disease than merely a particularly obstinate effort to discover the meaning of our experience. It was the sense that poetry and prophecy were not enough, and that the new generation had to be satisfied by other methods as to the rationality of its instinctive faiths, that gave its impulse to the important philosophical revival which took place in the 'sixties and 'seventies.

In this movement nothing can detract from the value of the pioneer work that was done by the men born before or

35

at the beginning of the Victorian age,[1] who were the first to set themselves the task of breaking ground and appropriating the results of post-Kantian thought on the Continent. Up to the middle of the 'sixties Hegel was little more than a name to English readers. In the course of the next ten years he had become a household word in the two Universities of Oxford and Glasgow. But the men who led the new movement had sufficient on their hands in the work of translation and exposition, added to that of University teaching in which most of them were engaged. It was to younger men released from these tasks and responsibilities that the work of carrying forward Hegelian ideas into fresh constructions in psychology and ethics, logic and metaphysics mainly fell. The names of two of these, F. H. Bradley, the elder by two years, and Bernard Bosanquet, will always be remembered as the exponents of a type of Idealism, which, whatever it owed to foreign sources, bore the stamp of originality, and gave a new distinction to British philosophy in the latter part of the reign of Victoria. In Bosanquet's case the release from teaching was a voluntary one, having for its motive the enlargement of his experience in the crowded and exciting life of London in the 'eighties. In Bradley's case it was the "curb of Theages" dooming a man, who otherwise might have been drawn by the same eager quest for experience and the "joy of eventful living" to the work of an explorer, to the life of a recluse, and exploration of quite a different kind.

In the result, Bosanquet's extraordinary vitality enabled him to combine with a life of devotion to philosophy a variety of interests somewhat remote from it. On the other hand, Bradley's almost monastic seclusion enabled him to devote himself with entire singleness of purpose to the work of "a writer on philosophy"—his own description of himself in the *Who's Who* of the time. It was this devotion, combined with elements not often found together since the time of Socrates—mysticism with critical power, unfailing ironical humour with a literary style comparable to that of Ruskin and Matthew Arnold [2]—that marked him out as the leader in the Argonauts' voyage, as it might be called, in which the later Victorian philosophy was engaged. What

[1] J. Hutchinson Stirling was born in 1820, Edward Caird in 1835, Thomas Hill Green in 1836, William Wallace in 1843.
[2] See T. S. Eliot's interesting essay on him in *For Lancelot Andrewes*.

were his credentials? What was the course he followed in the search for the Fleece? What may he be said in the end to have achieved?

I

F. H. Bradley was born in 1846, the eighth son of the Rev. Charles Bradley, the incumbent of St. James's, Clapham, the half-brother of G. G. Bradley, successively Head Master of Marlborough, Master of University College, Oxford, and Dean of Westminster, and the elder brother of Professor Andrew C. Bradley. After a school education at Cheltenham College and Marlborough, interrupted by an attack first of typhoid then of pneumonia, he entered University College, Oxford, as a Scholar in 1865. He took a first class in "Honour Mods." in 1867, a second in Greats in 1869. Rejected by his own College in the competition for a Fellowship, he was elected in 1870 to one at Merton College, which remained his home for the rest of his life. In the following year he was attacked by a violent internal inflammation, which left permanent effects, often involving long absences from Oxford, with consequent interruption to his work. In 1883 he received the degree of LL.D. from the University of Glasgow; in 1921 he was made a member of the Royal Danish Academy, in 1922 of the Accademia dei Lincei, in 1923 a Corresponding Fellow of the Reale Instituto Lombardo of Milan, and Honorary Fellow of the British Academy. In 1924 the King conferred on him the Order of Merit three months before his death in the same year.

In outward appearance he was tall and upright, singularly handsome, with well-formed forehead, grey-blue eyes under dark eyebrows and lashes, humorous and sensitive mouth, his finely modelled chin covered by a short pointed beard—the whole serving as an index of the mental alertness and the "strange mixture of daring and sensitive reserve" which his friends recognized both in his conversation and in his work as a thinker.

II

His three chief works were: *Ethical Studies,* published in 1876; *Principles of Logic,* in 1883; *Appearance and Reality,* in 1893. Each of them may be said to have been epoch-making in the history of philosophy in England and America. As the writer of the obituary notice in *The Times*[1] put it: " While never claiming finality, every work of his brought an argument to a definite close, and he was especially remarkable for the intense persistence with which problem after problem and consequence after consequence were elicited and confronted to the bitter end."

1. If there is one field of philosophy which British writers have made their own in a particular degree, and which has been coloured by the particular genius of the race, it is that of Moral Philosophy. In the 'sixties and 'seventies of last century interest in it had reached a crisis. The older Intuitionalism, resting on an appeal to common-sense judgments of right and wrong, combined with a belief in the infallibility of conscience as " the candle of the Lord," had ceased to satisfy philosophers, while proving itself useless to practical reformers, of whom the world at the time was full. On the other hand, the Utilitarianism which, since the time of Locke, had offered itself as the alternative, however useful it had been in politics, was showing itself, even in the " scientific " form made popular by Herbert Spencer, more and more inadequate to explain the deeper moral and religious experience of ordinary men. Carlyle's appeal to the duty of the moment as containing our ideal—the " America " of our desires—was magnificent, but it was not philosophy. Kant's " categorical imperative," as the pronouncement of our " reason," might commend itself to a Prussian disciplinarian, but was too abstract to provide a criterion of concrete right and wrong, good and bad. Where to turn for an ethic which would justify the essential distinction between duty and expediency, while remaining within the four corners of social experience, was the question of the moment.

Green was already working on this problem in the Oxford lectures, afterwards published in the *Prolegomena to Ethics*. Caird, in Adam Smith's old class-room in Glasgow, was expounding Hegelian ideas, as no one else could, to large classes of Scottish students. But Bradley's *Ethical Studies* was the first book in which these ideas were applied to the problem as it presented itself in the above form. Bosanquet tells us he had himself been meditating such a book, but the appearance of Bradley's volume blew his plans into thin air. Here was a book, as he put it, which, suffering

[1] September 20, 1924.

from an excess of thought and experience, was to most others on philosophy like a Dickens or Meredith to most novels: " A page of it would dilute into a hundred of any other." What it did was to restate and bring to a conclusion the long controversy with Hedonism, while offering a reinterpretation of Kant's Imperative of Duty which should give body to it.

In what is perhaps the most readable chapter of what is still the most readable book on the subject (that on " My Station and its Duties "), the conception of " law universal " to which Kant appealed was deepened into that of the call addressed to self-conscious beings by their place in a social organism whose ethos embodies, however imperfectly, the ideal of what human life should be. Waxing eloquent over the " objectivity " of this standard, the writer pours contempt upon all private interpretations " full of reflections and theories " as contrasted with the " honest will to do right." Those tell you—

> " to have no law but yourself, and to be better than the world. But this tells you that if you could be as good as your world, you would be better than you most likely are, and that to wish to be better than the world is to be already on the threshold of immorality. . . . We should learn to see the great moral fact of the world, and to reflect on the likelihood of our private ' ideal ' being anything more than an abstraction, which, because an abstraction, is all the better fitted for our heads, and all the worse fitted for actual existence," [1]

sentences that contain in a nutshell the difference between the sham Idealism of popular thought and practice and the real Idealism or ideal Realism from which Bradley took his departure.

Equally fatal to the popular idea of religious faith as belief in another world in which virtue and happiness meet and embrace each other was the view of the relation between morality and religion with which the book closed. Henry Sidgwick's book, on *The Methods of Ethics*, appeared while it was going through the press, and was the occasion of the essay on " Mr. Sidgwick's Hedonism " which Bradley added as a kind of appendix to the *Ethical*

---

[1] *Op. cit.,* pp. 180 and 181.

Studies. The passage in this rare pamphlet, in which the writer exposes the anachronism of the attempt to found morality on belief in another world, is an early example of the ironical humour that was to serve him in such good stead. For hedonistic ethics it was a matter of life and death to show that morality is the only true selfishness. But this cannot be shown from the internal nature of either. What resource, then, asks its critic, remains? We turn to the last few pages of Mr. Sidgwick's book:

> " Surely, surely it is our old friend the *Deus ex machina,* and anxiously we sit awaiting him: the crisis is at hand, the actors are at a deadlock, and we on the stretch. Vain expectation, for the days of Paley are gone by. The machine has grown old, and the God will not come to the front, and the stage is in confusion, and the curtain falls hurriedly in the middle of the fifth act."

With all this religious faith has nothing to do. It is not something that is added to morality to provide it with a motive that is the destruction of both. It grows up within the moral consciousness in a being whose nature commits him to belief in the essential reality of the ideal of a perfection that is beyond himself. In morality—in our station and its duties—the ideal is so far real, something " we feel or see and can not doubt. There is nothing to believe against appearances."

> " But in religion, despite of appearances, we have to believe that something is real. We must have an inward assurance that the reality is above the facts; and we must carry that out against facts in which we can not see the inward reality, and seem to see what is contrary thereto. It is by faith in our reconcilement with the invisible one reality that we are justified." [1]

In a later more critical mood Bradley was not wholly satisfied with this statement, and it was perhaps for this reason among others that he refused for forty years to allow a reprint of his book. In the end, in preparing it for a second edition, he was content to leave the passage practically as it was written.

2. With equal trenchancy and conclusiveness in his book

[1] *Op. cit.,* p. 302.

on *The Principles of Logic* Bradley carried out a long-called-for revolution in the accepted systems both of the formal logic of Kant and the empirical of Mill and Bain. The error of the former was, not that it was formal, but that it occupied itself too exclusively with the syllogistic form applicable to propositions, in which attributes are predicated of subjects but entirely inapplicable to those which express relations, spatial or other. Relational logic has been brilliantly developed since by Bertrand Russell and others, but Bradley stated the principle involved with a clearness that has not since been surpassed, and that contrasts with the obscurity into which it has sometimes sunk in its less philosophical advocates. Neither was it the error of the empirical logic that it was empirical and appealed to fact, but that by denying the existence of real sameness in the objects of experience and substituting for it " association by resemblance " it made valid deduction impossible. Extremes meet, and the empiricist lost his way in a mythology invented to fill the gaps his own defective analysis had left.

Bradley's exposure, in the central chapter of his book, of Bain's myth of " Primitive credulity," ranks with that above quoted on hedonistic religion. Bain's problem was to explain how, without assuming real identity, the mind could be led back from present to past experience. His example was the child's inference that sugar to-day would be sweet as it was yesterday :

> " Sudden at this crisis, and in pity at distress, there leaves the heaven with rapid wing a goddess Primitive Credulity. Breathing in the ear of the bewildered infant she whispers, The thing which has happened once will happen once more. Sugar was sweet, and sugar will be sweet. And Primitive Credulity is accepted forthwith as the mistress of our life. She leads our steps on the path of experience, until her fallacies, which cannot always be pleasant, at length become suspect. We wake up indignant at the kindly fraud by which the goddess so long has deceived us. So she shakes her wings and, flying to the stars where there are no philosophers, leaves us here to the guidance of—I cannot think what." [1]

---

[1] *Op. cit.*, 1st edn., p. 299.

The deeper defect of both systems was their failure to perceive that, behind the linear inference of the syllogism and the " methods " of inductive logic, as the real ground of their validity in any particular field, lies the whole system of accepted knowledge in it, with its claim to comprehensiveness and consistency. The real ground of all inference, whatever its form, as Bosanquet (developing Bradley's principle) afterwards put it, is: " This or nothing ": this conclusion, or the confusion of our reason and the destruction of our intellectual world. But there was another feature of Bradley's book that at the time struck Bosanquet and others who could read between its lines as of more ominous significance. As this was the growing point of his philosophy, to be afterwards developed in *Appearance and Reality,* a word or two must be said about it here.

There was none of Hegel's formulæ that had taken a firmer hold of his English and Scottish disciples than those of " the identity of thought and reality " and of " the real and the rational." But there was none that seemed more paradoxical. In what conceivable way could it be true that thoughts, concepts, bare universals give us the living touch and sense of reality? Must there not here be some mistake, either in the Master himself or, as was more likely, in his disciples' reading of him? The suspicion thus roused, Bradley expressed in a passage which, both on account of its metaphysical significance and its singular eloquence, has been more frequently quoted than any other in his writings:

> " Unless thought stands for something that falls beyond mere intelligence, if ' thinking ' is not used with some strange implication that never was part of the meaning of the word, a lingering scruple still forbids us to believe that reality can ever be purely rational. It may come from a failure in my metaphysics, or from a weakness of the flesh which continues to blind me, but the notion that existence could be the same as understanding strikes as cold and ghostlike as the dreariest materialism. That the glory of this world in the end is appearance leaves the world more glorious, if we feel it as a show of some fuller splendour; but the sensuous curtain is a deception and a cheat, if it hides some colourless movement of atoms,

some spectral woof of impalpable abstractions or un-earthly ballet of bloodless categories. Though dragged to such conclusions, we cannot embrace them. Our principles may be true, but they are not reality. They no more *make* that Whole which commands our devotion, than some shredded dissection of human tatters *is* the warm and breathing beauty of flesh which our hearts found delightful.'' [1]

No wonder his Hegelian friends were inclined to ask what this apparent break with the orthodox tradition portended. Was it a return to an effete dualism between thought and thing? Or was it the herald of an advance to a new form of monism? If Bradley himself at the time he wrote these words did not clearly know, he was not long in discovering.

3. *Appearance and Reality* owed its originality to the clearness with which he grasped the view—implicit, as he held, in all the greatest thinkers, including Hegel himself—that the Whole of Reality which philosophy knows as the Absolute is not, or at any rate not merely, a distant goal towards which the mind works by the process we know as thought, but is present to it from the beginning, wherever it has concrete experience of its world. When the mind does go forward, as under pressure of its own nature as intelligence it is bound to do, towards the conceptual systems of which Science and Philosophy consist, it does indeed possess its world at a new level and in a new form, but it is in the form of thought and theory in which it has parted with reality as an object of feeling and will. Before it can recover the real world of our common experience it must return, Antaeus-like, to the earth from which it draws its strength. It was the energy with which in *Appearance and Reality* he asserted the sole reality of the Whole in contrast to any one of its aspects when taken in abstraction from it, whether that of thought or feeling or will, *a fortiori* in contrast to any selected and isolated element within any of these fields, that gave many, even of his most instructed readers, the impression that his book was a revival of Spinozism. As in Spinoza, so here, all footprints seemed to lead to the cave of an Absolute that allowed of no return. It was probably this appearance of scepticism, especially as it was applied to the object of religious consciousness, that led to the strange fate of the book in its rejection by the Oxford Press of the period. It occurred to few at the

[1] *Op. cit.*, p. 533.

time that the stone which the builders rejected was to
become the head of the corner in the thought of the next
quarter of a century, both as heralding a new development
of idealistic philosophy, and as the starting-point of powerful and fertile movements of reaction. When, in the year
after his death, the second volume of *Contemporary British
Philosophy* was being prepared for the press, the contributors to it, representing all schools of thought, unanimously agreed to have it dedicated to Bradley as the writer
" to whom British Philosophy owed the impulse that gave
it new life in our time."

III

This impulse to the thought of others might perhaps be
regarded as achievement enough to justify the inclusion
of Bradley in this volume.   But the reader may fairly
ask, What were the positive conclusions which he sought
to establish on his own account? and What permanence
may be claimed for them?

1. In reply to the former of these questions, only the
most condensed statement in further exposition of what has
been already said is here possible. On its critical side the
doctrine of his chief book, so far from being sceptical, was
a sustained polemic against a cheap Agnosticism, and an
equally cheap Pantheism, the one teaching that " the Real
sits apart, that it keeps state by itself, and does not descend
into phenomena "; the other that " reality is immanent in
all appearances " in such a way that " everything is so
worthless on the one hand and divine on the other that
nothing can be viler or can be more sublime than anything
else."   As against both of these he maintained that " the
Reality comes into knowledge, and the more we know of
anything the more in one way is Reality present with us.
The Reality is our criterion of worse and better, of ugliness
and beauty, of true and false. It in brief decides between
and gives general meaning to higher and lower." If we
ask what this Reality more particularly is, a succinct answer
will be found in the concluding words of the book:

> " Reality is one experience, self-pervading and
> superior to mere relations. Its character is the opposite
> of that fabled extreme which is barely mechanical, and
> it is, in the end, the sole perfect realization of spirit.
> . . . Outside of spirit there is not, and there cannot

be, any reality, and the more that anything is spiritual so much the more is it veritably real."

If, finally, we ask what is meant by " spirit " and the " spiritual," we come to the crucial point in the whole system. Difficult though Bradley's conception is, it is perfectly clear cut, and he was prepared to give it condensed expression. " Spirit," he wrote, " is the unity of the manifold, in which the externality of the manifold has utterly ceased." In contrast to it we have Nature conceived of as a lifeless manifold of parts wholly external to one another. But he goes on to explain that neither of these extremes, neither Spirit, without one vestige of inner division, nor Nature, without one breath of inner unifying life, anywhere exists in fact. What exists always occupies a place between them, and stands higher or lower in the scale as it approximates to the ideal of Spirit—in his own language according as it partakes less of appearance and more of reality.

It was this contrast between existing things and a reality to which they may approximate but never succeed in attaining that drew the chief fire of Bradley's critics, seeming as it did to reduce everything to the level of illusion. What he really meant to assert was almost the direct opposite of this. So far from being an illusion, all things, even illusions, are a manifestation of reality in their own way and their own degree. We only go wrong and become the victims of illusion when we press a claim for them to be more than they are, *a fortiori*, when we take them to be the ultimate reality. This holds of existing things within the particular fields to which they belong: of objects of knowledge from the atom to the human soul; of feelings from bodily pleasure to the higher æsthetic and religious emotions, of actions from instinctive physical reactions up to the decisions on which the fate of empires or causes depends. But it also holds (and it was here that current intellectualism had failed) of these fields themselves. Neither in the world of thought, nor feeling, nor will alone can the supreme reality be found. Each even at its highest fails to give it, and leaves us either with a mere appearance or with something transcendent, of which our common experience gives us only the obscurest hint.

If this seemed to leave us in the end with a mystery, Bradley was content to have it so: " To love unsatisfied," he wrote in his note-book, "the world is a mystery, a mystery which love satisfied seems to comprehend. The latter is wrong only because it cannot be content without thinking itself right."

2. Our second question was, What may be said to be of permanent value in such a philosophy?

Fifty years have passed since the publication of *Appearance and Reality*. Fashions are apt to change in Philosophy as elsewhere. In a realistic age assertions of the coincidence of reality with "experience" and appeals to an Absolute Experience as the test and criterion of our own seem to mean less than they once did, if they can be said to mean anything at all. The one seems to carry us back to Berkeley, and to do scant justice to "the whole choir of heaven and furniture of earth" as we are coming to know them. The other seems to reduce the experiencing mind to a mode or adjective of the Absolute as the only true individual substance. Individuality may be difficult to define, but we know it when we see it as the direct opposite of the generality of adjectives. Of the use of Reality in this sense might we not retaliate *mutatis mutandis* on Bradley the words we have already quoted as used of the older Idealists' use of "thought."[1]

It is considerations of this kind that have led, in the intervening years, to the reaction in the direction of a more realistic philosophy asserting in one form or another the indefeasible rights of individual things and persons against the shadowy being of Bradley's Absolute. This is not the place to enter into any defence of his use of the conception, even though that were possible. Yet I believe that something has been lost sight of in the heat of the conflict, which Realism is beginning to rediscover for itself. Emphasize as we may the manifoldness of the world of existing things, their separation and apparent independence, it is only to the most superficial observation that they remain in isolation from one another. "A thing is only itself," writes Professor Whitehead,[2] "in drawing into its own limitations the larger whole in which it finds itself." "Nothing," writes another exponent of modern science,[3] "is isolated; everything makes reference to everything else. Every event by reason of its whole nature, requires the whole universe to be itself." Man, with whose life philosophy is

[1] See p. 42 above.   [2] *Science and the Modern World.*
[3] J. W. N. Sullivan, in *The Basis of Modern Science.*

mainly concerned, differs from all other beings, in that the whole to which natural things have reference comes to him as something to be realized, whether in social practice, in science, in art, or religion. In practice a man has " to be whole or join a whole," and to discover that in the end he can do neither effectively without doing both. In science he has to seek for the theory or way of looking at things that will hold all the facts and hold them together. In art he has to make something that, by its inherent unity, will reflect the unity and essential harmony underneath the apparent discords of the world. What finally is religion but the sense of unity of mind and will with the vital spirit and with what George Eliot calls the " high ambition of the world " ?

Interpreting what Bradley means by the Absolute in this sense as that which moves obscurely in everything, consciously in man as an ideal, we can perhaps see that, instead of the destruction of individuality and substantiality in things and persons, it is the very principle of their life. Anyone who asks for more of either than comes from self-identification with this principle asks for he knows not what. On the other hand, from the side of personality, as we know it in ourselves, we may thus come to see it as that by and in which the ideal is brought down into the world of fact, and thus becomes real also in the form of existence. To seek for anything higher for one's self than to become the bearer to a world of persons of values that come from beyond it is surely to pursue a shadow. Writing shortly before his death, Bradley expressed this in a couple of sentences:

> " Everything that is worth our having is (you may say) our own doing, and exists only in so far as produced by ourselves. But you must add that in the whole region of human value there is nothing that has not come down to us from another world—nothing which fails still to owe its proper being and reality to that which lives and works beyond the level of mere time and existence."

This I believe to be the essence of his teaching, and I venture to think that it is a truth which, if we are not content to accept it as an inheritance from Victorian Philosophy, we shall have to rediscover for ourselves with its aid or without it.

CHARLOTTE BRONTË
1816-1855

BY
REBECCA
WEST

CHARLOTTE BRONTË

THIS generation knows that Charlotte Brontë's own generation gave her too high a place in the artistic hierarchy when it exalted her above her sister Emily, but is itself tempted to place her too low because of the too easily recognizable *naïveté* of her material.

It is true that the subject-matter of all her work is, under one disguise or another, the Cinderella theme which is the stand-by of the sub-artist in fiction and the theatre, all the world over and in any age. She treats it in the form it takes in the hands of those who have moved just one degree away from complete *naïveté*: instead of it being supposed that Cinderella has the advantage of physical beauty over the Ugly Sisters, it is supposed (as an absolute and more magical compensation to the sense of inferiority which weaves and needs the story) that it is they who are beautiful, and she who is ugly, though possessed of an invisible talisman of spiritual quality which wholly annuls that disadvantage. This is the theme of *Jane Eyre* and *Villette*, and, with certain elaborations and feints, of *Shirley* also; and it cannot be denied that we have grave reason to associate it with work which is not artistic at all, which sets out not to explore reality, but to nourish the neurotic fantasies with which feebler brains defend themselves from reality.

Charlotte Brontë also uses material which many people denounce as naïve with, I think, less foundation. She records oppressions practised by the dowered on the dowerless, and by adults on children, and seems to many of her readers absurd and unpleasant when she does so; but that is perhaps not because such incidents never happen, but

51

because we dislike admitting that they happen. There is hardly a more curious example of the gap we leave between life and literature than the surprise and incredulity recorded by successive generations of Brontëan commentators at the passages in the sisters' works which suggest that the well-to-do are sometimes uncivil to their employees. In actual fact, all of us, even to-day, if we were connected with a young girl who was going out into the world as a governess, would feel an anxiety that she should be with "nice people," which would imply a lively fear of what nasty people are capable of doing to governesses; but these commentators write as if Charlotte and Anne must have been the victims of hysterical morbidity when they implied that governesses were sometimes treated rudely, although the idea then prevalent, that one was divinely appointed to one's social station, cannot have improved the manners of employers. It has been the opinion of all moral teachers from the days of the Psalmist that riches lead to haughtiness and froward bearing; yet when Miss Blanch Ingram tells the footman, "Cease that chatter, blockhead," the commentators shake their heads and smile, without reflecting that she was supposed to have made that remark in the year preceding Queen Victoria's accession to the throne, when much of the eighteenth-century coarseness of manners still lingered, and that even to-day women can be found who have the tiresome habit of being rude to waiters and menservants.

We may suspect, then, that the common objection to this material is not that it has no correspondence with reality, but that it is intensely embarrassing for us to contemplate. The feeling of inferiority, under which we all labour, may find a gratifying opportunity for self-pity in the accounts of the suffering which superiors can unjustly inflict on their inferiors, but only if they are not too vivid; for if they are, then we feel terror at the quality of the universe. And if that be so when the accounts refer to the relatively remote symbolism of social matters, which we all of us can discount by reference to some other system of values which we have devised to suit our special case, how much more will it be so when they refer to the actual and agonizing experiences of our childhood! In these days one is weaker than nearly all the world. However kindly one is treated, one is frustrated and humiliated, one's natural habits are corrected, and one's free speech censored; and if one is not kindly treated, one can take no revenge, one is without means of protecting one's dignity. There must be something shameful in such a phase to an organism as much in love with the idea of its own free will as the human being. Thus the descriptions of Jane Eyre's ill-treatment at the hands of the Reeds, and the sufferings of the pupils at Lowood, revive a whole series of associations in the readers' minds which the more imaginative and intellectually developed among them will hate to recall. They will turn from Charlotte Brontë's work with the accusation that it is infantile; but what they mean is that she exposes her own and their infantilism. She lifts a curtain, and reveals what the world usually keeps hidden. In her pictures of these oppressions she demonstrates the workings of our universal sense that we are worms; as in her use of the Cinderella theme she demonstrates our universal hope that, though we are but worms, a miracle will happen, and we shall be made kings of the world. It may be objected that any hack writer of penny dreadfuls does as much; but that is untrue. The hack writer spins the consoling fantasy, and so does Charlotte Brontë; but she also depicts the hunger that goads the spinner to the task. Her work, considered as a whole, is as powerful an analysis of the working of the sense of inferiority and its part in creating romanticism as the mind of man has ever made.

But colour is lent to the suspicion that Charlotte Brontë is not an artist but a sub-artist, that she does not analyse experience, but weaves fantasies to hang between man and his painful experience, by her frequent use of the sub-artist's chosen weapon, sentimental writing. This also is a feature of her work which is specially repugnant to the present generation's hyper-sensitiveness to the superficial decorum of literature; and it remains an indefensible defect. But it adds to Charlotte Brontë's power over our attentions, because in so far as she discloses it with her unequalled ardour and honesty, she gives us a picture of the eternal artist experiencing an eternally recurrent misadventure.

For Charlotte Brontë's tendency to sentimental writing was not due to an innate inaptitude for the artistic process, but to the pressure of external circumstance. In one important respect her life was unfavourable to the practise of art. This was not loneliness and privation: Emily Brontë, suffering the same portion of these ills, was the complete artist. It was not the misconduct of her brother Branwell, though that was a contributing factor to it. It was her specially acute need to make, by separate and violent acts of the will, the place in the world for herself and her two younger sisters which should have been made for them by their elders. Her realization of this need must have been panic-stricken and desperate, for the whole of her life was ravaged by a series of progressively bitter disappointments in the protection which children expect from adults and which women expect from men.

Mrs. Brontë died of cancer when Charlotte was five years old, and for some time before her death the progress of her malady and her regular confinements prevented her from giving her children much attention. Mr. Brontë was an eccentric recluse whose capacity for parenthood seems to have been purely physical. Even before he had taken to the bottle, he took no trouble to provide his children with either his own sympathy or proper companionship, or any but the barest preparation for adult life. Mrs. Brontë's sister, who came North from Cornwall to take charge of the orphaned children, disliked Yorkshire, retired to her bedroom, and cared for none of them except Branwell. From the terrible matter-of-factness with which Emily and Charlotte Brontë draw (in Nelly Deans and in Bessie) the servant whose unimaginative cruelty changes to a not very reliable kindness, one sees that there was no steady comfort for the children in the kitchen. It was in her sister Maria, the oldest of the family, that Charlotte found a substitute for her mother; we know that from the portrait of Helen Burns in *Jane Eyre*. But Maria died at the age of twelve, when Charlotte was eight; and her only other older sister, Elizabeth, died two months later.

About the time of Charlotte's ninth birthday, then, the negligence and death of her elders left her with her own way to make in the world. But that is an understatement, for it supposes her burdenless. It would be more accurate to say that she became the head of the family, with one brother and two sisters, all deeply loved, dependent on her for everything above the bare physical necessities of life. The records of the Brontës' childhood show her eagerly answering the call to leadership; but she was not then altogether to be pitied. She was still supported by her penultimate hope. Whatever the defections of Mr. Brontë, they would not be without a man to look after them as soon as their brother grew up. It is confessed honestly and

radiantly in Charlotte Brontë's books how she craved for
the support that the child-bearing faculty of woman logically entitles her to expect from man, and there was a special
factor in her environment to give intensity to that craving.
Victorian England was a man's country. She might well
have hoped that with Branwell Brontë's fine natural endow-
ment he would easily find a place in it, and that she would
see herself and her sisters decently maintained or helped to
decent employment. But she was still a girl when it became
apparent that Branwell, in spite of all his brilliant promise,
was growing up, not into a man, but into a pathetic
nuisance, who would not even decently maintain himself.
For the sixth time natural supports had failed her. She
knew the terrible fear felt by the young who begin to
suspect that they are going to be cheated out of the fullness
of life; and she was not fearful for herself alone, but also
for Anne and Emily, in whose gifts she had faith, and for
whose health she had every reason to fear. She had seen
her two elder sisters die, and she had probably forebodings
that she was to see the other two die also. It is known that
she had such forebodings about Anne.

During the years when it was becoming plain that Branwell was going to be of no help to them, but " a drain on
every resource," Charlotte became more and more desperate. By this time, it is interesting to note, she was half-
blind. But if no one would give her and her sisters their
fair share of life, she herself would see that they got what
she could snatch; and she snatched far more than one
would think possible. The astounding thing about the
Brontës' life is not its emptiness but—considering the bare-
ness of Haworth Parsonage—its fullness. There were
several friends; there was a good deal of employment,
including the Brussels expedition; there was the literary
adventure. And it was Charlotte who made the friends,
Charlotte who found the teaching posts, Charlotte who
wrote the letters to the publishers. Now, it is easy to sneer
at these achievements, on the ground that the greatest of
the three sisters, Emily, found them purely vexatious, since
she was shy of strangers, loathed leaving the moors of
Haworth, and would rather have kept her poems to herself.
Nevertheless, Charlotte's actions followed the natural direction of sanity. Like all living things, she strove for the
survival of herself and her belongings with the balance of
her impulses. It was hardly to be expected that reverence

55

for Emily's genius should oust the desire to keep her alive, and any change which removed her from the rigours of the Parsonage must have at first seemed favourable to that end. There is nothing to be said against Charlotte's frenzied efforts to counter the nihilism of her surroundings, unless one is among those who would find amusement in the sight of the starving fighting for food.

In the sphere of life they were unquestionably noble; but it unfortunately happened—and here lies the disconcerting value of Charlotte as a revelation of the artist-type—that in the sphere of art they had a disintegrating effect. They committed her to a habit of activism which was the very antithesis of the quietism demanded from the artist. In her desire to make a place in the world for herself and her family against time, she could let nothing establish itself by slow growth, she had to force the pace of every intimacy and every action, which means that she had constantly to work upon people with the aim of immediately provoking them to certain emotions. Sprightly or touching letters had to be written to the friends to keep them near in spite of distance; Miss Branwell had to be induced to finance the Brussels expedition, and Mrs. Wooller had to have her interest in the new school kept warm; Southey, Wordsworth, Tennyson, Lockhart, and de Quincey had to be addressed in the vain attempt to rouse their interest in Currer, Ellis, and Acton Bell. In fact, she was forced to a passionate participation in a business of working on people's feelings exclusive of the true business of art, and the root of the evil that we call sentimentality.

This, therefore, was Charlotte's special temptation: she was so used to manipulating people's feelings in life that she could not lose the habit in her art, and was apt to fall into sentimentality. All her novels are defaced to varying degrees by passages which have nothing to do with the organic growth of the story, and are inspired simply by guess-work as to the state of the reader's feelings. An extreme example of this is the scene where the Yorkes call on Miss Moore and find Caroline Helstone in her parlour, in the twenty-third chapter of *Shirley*. The same error is committed in an earlier scene of the book, but it is here more noteworthy and disastrous, because here there is promise of high poetic value. Caroline is sick with love for Robert Moore, and faint with despair. Mrs. Yorke looms over her like a personification of the

cruelty that must govern the world if it is true that she is
not to have her love ; the Yorke children have the fantastic,
unclassical quality that all objects not the beloved assume
under the lover's eye. When Caroline's veins are flushed
with quicksilver rage against that cruelty, the scene should
end, and she should be left still waiting for Robert at the
jessamined window. But Miss Brontë's habit of bustling
was too strong for her then. She could not trust her slow
magic to make the reader's interest slowly mount. She
felt she must put them under a swiftly growing debt to her
for entertainment. She remembered how Martha Taylor,
who was the original of little Jessy Yorke, had often enter-
tained her with her precocious tirades ; so she reproduced
one there and then. She also remembered what a poignant
effect had been made by this child's early death ; so she
inserted a description of her funeral. The continuity of the
scene is broken, the author's and the reader's contacts with
Caroline are lost, and whatever emotion is felt is diverted
from the real theme.

It would be easy to point to many other pages in Charlotte Brontë's novels where sentimental writing has been
allowed to destroy the structure of the work ; and there is
one case where sentimentality has been allowed to plan
such a structure faultily. The melodramatic plot of *Jane
Eyre* is not a symbol honestly conceived by extreme
naïveté, but was invented, in her own admission, to suit a
supposed popular demand for sensationalism. That was a
pity, for there are pages in the book, such as the scene
where the lovers walk in the orchard under the rising moon,
which deserve the best of settings. But great as is the
harm done to the valuable content of Charlotte Brontë's
work by her choice of certain episodes and series of episodes
simply for their immediate effect on her readers, still greater
is the harm done by the diffusion of sentimentality through
her style. It is crammed with direct appeals to the emotions,
which make it tediously repetitive, explosive, and irrelevant
to the deeper themes discussed.

That this defect was not inborn in Charlotte, but was the
product of her circumstances, can be proved by a reference
to a letter quoted by Mrs. Gaskell from *The Little Magazine*,
which the Brontës composed in their childhood. It begins :
" SIR,—It is well known that the Genii have declared that
unless they perform certain arduous duties every year, of
a mysterious nature, all the worlds in the firmament will be

burnt up and gathered together in one mighty globe," and
no style could be more decorous and more sincere. But she
wrote it at the age of thirteen, before she had become a
panic-stricken adept in the art of negotiation. She was
never to write such prose again until her passion for M.
Héger made her forget all her schemes and anxieties, and
changed her to the insanely honest instrument of one intention and one need.

The obviousness with which what was a virtue in Charlotte Brontë's life became a vice in her art, makes her one
of the most disconcerting among great writers to contemplate. She is suspended between the two spheres of art and
life, and not in a state of rest. She is torn between them.
But where this generation will probably err is in supposing
that her plight is unique, her helplessness before this temptation a personal defect. There is sentimentality in every
age, even in our own; and we swallow it whole if its subject-
matter is not of a sort that arouses suspicion. That was
where Charlotte Brontë erred. All of us not actually
illiterate or imbecile feel that something is wrong when a
writer attempts to compel his readers' feelings by the exploitation of early deaths, handsome sinners with lunatic
wives, and ecstatic dithyrambs. The march of culture has
forced such knowledge on the least of us.

But let us examine the current attitude to the great
Russians. A great many readers, and some of these drawn
from the professionally fastidious, place Tolstoy above
Turgeniev and Dostoievsky. Yet Turgeniev was, as Mr.
George Moore has said in that incomparable book of
criticism, *Avowals,* "a sort of Jesus of Nazareth in art,"
who gave himself to the artistic process with so little reser-
vation for his personal ends, that there is no conflict in his
work, only serenity; and though it is true, as Mr. Moore
says in the same book, that, before we can admire Dostoievsky's novels, "modern life must wring all the Greek
out of us," he also, albeit with constant cries of protest at
the pain it cost him, forced himself to the honest analysis
of experience. But Tolstoy is fully as sentimental a writer
as Charlotte Brontë. In *War and Peace, Anna Karenina,*
and *Resurrection,* he pushes his characters about with the
greatest conceivable brusqueness in order to prove his
thesis, and exhorts his readers to accept his interpretations
of their movements. He even admits in *What is Art?* that
he thinks this the proper way for the artist to behave.

Nevertheless, Tolstoy arouses no repugnance in this generation, although this use of art to prove what man already
knows is a shameful betrayal of the mission of art to tell
man more than he knows. This is only because the subject-
matter of his sentimentality is unfamiliar. He attempts to
influence his readers in favour of a thesis dependent on the
primitive sense of guilt, and the need for expiation by the
endurance and infliction of suffering, which had been forbidden expression above a certain cultural level in the
rationalist nineteenth century. We are not on our guard
against it as we are against Charlotte Brontë's Cinderella
theme; and we succumb to what must be an eternally
recurrent temptation.

Yet if Charlotte Brontë represents an eternally
recurrent defeat of the artist, she also represents his
eternally recurrent triumph. She told the truth even about
matters concerning which the whole civilization round her
had conspired to create a fiction; and her telling of it is not
an argument, but an affirmation, that comes and is, like
the light of the sun and the moon. It is not only true that,
as Swinburne said, again and again she shows the—

> " power to make us feel in every nerve, at every step
> forward which our imagination is compelled to take
> under the guidance of another's, that thus and not
> otherwise, but in all things altogether even as we are
> told and shown, it was, and must have been, with the
> human figures set before us in their action and their
> suffering; that thus, and not otherwise, they absolutely
> must and would have felt and thought and spoken
> under the proposed conditions."

It is not only true that she abounds in touches of that
kind of strange beauty which, dealing solely with the visible
world, nevertheless persuades us that the visible world is
going to swing open as if it were a gate and disclose a
further view: like the description of the stable-yard in
Thornfield at dawn, with the blinds still drawn in the
windows, and the birds twittering in the blossom-laden
orchard, when the mysterious stranger drives away with
the surgeon after his mysterious wounding. She does more
than that, she makes a deeper revelation of the soul.

In an age which set itself to multiply the material wants
of mankind (with what results we see to-day) and to whittle

down its spiritual wants to an ethical anxiety that was often
mean, Charlotte Brontë serenely lifted up her voice, and
testified to the existence of the desires which are the buds
of all human thoughts and actions. Her candid and clair-
voyant vision of such things is displayed again and again
throughout her works, but never more notably than in the
two instances which make *Villette* one of the most interesting of English novels. The first is the description of the
innocent but passionate love of the little girl Polly for the
schoolboy John. The second is the description of how
Lucy Snowe's love passed without a break from John
Bretton to Paul Emanuel ; never before has there been such
a frank admission of the subtle truth that the romantic
temperament writes a lover's part, and then casts an actor
to play it, and that nevertheless there is more there than
make-believe. To realize how rare a spirit it required to
make and record such observations at the time one must
turn to Miss Harriet Martineau's comments on the book as
given in Mrs. Gaskell's *Life* ; though one should remember
that Miss Martineau was herself to suffer from the age's
affectation of wantlessness. For when, as an elderly lady,
she received a present of money from her admirers, the
subscribers were greatly incensed when she proposed to
spend an undue proportion of it on a silver tea equipage ;
yet surely any earlier age would have understood this
belated desire for a little handsomeness.

But Charlotte Brontë did more than unconsciously correct
the error of her age ; she saw as deeply as poets do. There
are surely two scenes which have the dignity and significance of great poetry. One is the scene in *Villette,*
where the fevered girl wanders by night out of the silent
school, with the intention of seeking a certain stone basin
that she remembers to have seen, brimming with cool water,
in a glade of the park ; and finds the city ablaze with light,
thronged with a tide of happy people, which bears up to
the park that is now fantastic with coloured lights and
pasteboard palaces, a phantasmagoria in which she walks
and sees her friends, her foes, her beloved, but is not seen.
There has never before been found a more vivid symbolic
representation of the state of passion in which the whole
universe, lacking the condition of union with the beloved,
seems a highly coloured but insubstantial illusion, objective
counterpart to delirium. Yet even finer is the scene in
Shirley called " A Summer Night," when Shirley and Caro-

line creep across the moonlit fields to warn Moore of the
approach of rioters, and are too late. There, when the two
girls stand "alone with the friendly night, the mute stars,
and these whispering trees," listening to the shouts and
watching the fires of masculine dissension (which is their
opposite and what they live by), and while what is male in
woman speaks with the voice of Shirley, and what is female
speaks with the voice of Caroline, one perceives that a
statement is being found for that which the intellect has not
yet stated in direct terms.

Charlotte Brontë was a supreme artist; and yet she was
very nearly not an artist at all. That will make her an
unsympathetic figure to many in these days, when a school
of criticism, determined to exert authority but without the
intellectual power to evolve an authoritative doctrine, has
imported into this country its own puerile version of the
debate between romanticism and classicism which has
cut up the French world of letters into sterile sec-
tionalism, and trots about frivolously inventing categories on insufficient bases, rejecting works of art that
do not fit into them, and attaching certificates to those
that do. But she will inspire and console those who realize
that art is a spiritual process committed to imperfection by
the flesh, which is its medium; that though there are artists
who seem to transcend the limitations of that medium, like
Bach and Mozart and Emily Brontë, they are rare as the
saints, and, like them, sublime but not final in their achievements; and that the complete knowledge and mastery of
experience which would be attained in a perfect world of
art is like the *summum bonum* of the theologians, the vision
of God which is to reward the pure in heart, and cannot be
realized until time is changed to eternity.

EMILY BRONTË

1818-1848

BY
CHARLES
MORGAN

EMILY BRONTË

"IT is Friday evening near 9 o'clock—wild rainy weather. I am seated in the dining room, having just concluded tidying our desk boxes, writing this document. Papa is in the parlour—Aunt upstairs in her room. She has been reading Blackwood's Magazine to Papa. Victoria and Adelaide are ensconced in the peat-house. Keeper is in the kitchen—Hero in his cage. We are all stout and hearty. . . ."[1]

This is the opening, written on her twenty-third birthday, of one of the few pieces of directly biographical material that have come to us from Emily Brontë. There are two stiffly formal letters from her to Charlotte's friend, Ellen Nussey; there is the "document" from which I have quoted, written on July 30, 1841, as part of a scheme, arranged with Anne, whereby each should set down her summary of four years past and her forecast of four years to come; there is this document's successor, dated 1845. That time will reveal other letters of hers is scarcely to be doubted. If they were written to Branwell, they might well make necessary a new biography of the Brontës. If they were written to Charlotte, it is unlikely that they will reveal anything; if to Anne, though Emily seems to have loved her, they will be as discreet as though they were addressed to a child.

It is an instance of Shorter's obtuseness in all things relating to Emily Brontë that he should have written: "It is certain that her own letters to her sisters, and particularly to Anne, must have been peculiarly tender, and in no way

[1] *The Brontës and their Circle,* by Clement K. Shorter.

D

lacking in abundant self-revelation." If by "abundant
self-revelation" Shorter meant no more than chatter about
dogs and birds or domestic details that he might have
hastened to publish in a domestic journal, he may have
been justified. Emily had two lives. It was the essence
of her genius that they were distinct. One, the superficial
life, the life of the daughter at the parsonage, which she
is commonly praised for having led with dutiful heroism,
was not in her eyes heroic. It was the activity in the midst
of which she had learned how to feed upon the spirit within
her. Those biographers who insist that she sickened and
came near to death when separated from her moors have,
I think, missed the root of her desire for Haworth. That
the bleak countryside was friendly to her is true, but can
scarcely have been all the truth of a hunger so imperative.
She clung to her duties at the parsonage as visionary and
contemplative men cling always to the discipline that they
have cultivated as an enablement of their vision. The
vision was her secret, but of the unconcealed life that was
its condition she could write with a pleasing candour.
Never did feminine genius whine less against household
drudgery, for the good reason that her acceptance of it was
complete and her spirit too powerful to admit it as an impediment.

> "I am quite contented for myself: not as idle as
> formerly, altogether as hearty, and having learnt to
> make the most of the present and long for the future
> with the fidgetiness that I cannot do all I wish; seldom
> or ever troubled with nothing to do, and merely desir-
> ing that everybody could be as comfortable as myself
> and as undesponding, and then we should have a very
> tolerable world of it. . . . Anne and I should have
> picked black-currants if it had been fine and sunshiny.
> I must hurry off now to my turning and ironing." [1]

For one who remembers of what other writing she was
capable, there is reason enough here for loving her. Thus
she may have written to her sisters, and her letters would
enable us to see her at work in the kitchen at Haworth,
and to love her as much for her reticences as for what she
told. But such letters would not abundantly reveal her self,
for Emily's self was set apart from all these things and was
profoundly secret. She communicated it in her art because,

[1] *The Brontës and their Circle.*

being an artist who drew from the distillations of her spirit, and not, as Charlotte did, from external and observed sources, she could not do otherwise, but she was reluctant that her art should confess her to the world. She was angry when Charlotte dragged out her poems. She played for years the Gondal game with Anne, because to write poems and histories about an imaginary people gave her, even at her own fireside, a saving anonymity of form. "Emily," says Anne, "is writing the Emperor Julius's life. She has read some of it, and I want very much to hear the rest. She is writing some poetry, too. I wonder what it is about?" It was probably about one of three things—the complete mystical experience that Emily appears to have enjoyed at some time in her early youth; her abiding desire, which made all other desires relatively unimportant to her, for repetition of it; or a partial re-experience—one of many, as I interpret her—from which, in an agony of spiritual disappointment, she had been dragged back.

When her critics have wearied of calling her "pagan," which she was not, some have spoken of her as a mystical poet without fully appreciating how much truth is contained in their own words. Miss May Sinclair [1]—though an underestimate of Branwell has led her to dangerous conclusions and a strangely irrelevant twinge of feminism has darkened her counsel now and then—is fully aware that Emily is of the company of Blake, not indeed in manner nor in faith, but in her capacity for spiritual absolutism. Miss Sinclair speaks of her as having been "in love with the Absolute," and we need seek no phrase more apt. She adds that Emily "was a mystic, not by religious vocation, but by temperament and by ultimate vision," and that none can comprehend her genius who does not himself, with "passion and sincerity," embrace the idea of "the illusory nature of time and of material happenings." This could not have been better said. But neither Miss Sinclair nor Madame Duclaux, whose early biography [2] has proudly endured long critical tests, seems to have realized how concrete, how definite, how specialized Emily Brontë's spiritual adventure may have been.

Here we are on dangerous ground—dangerous because no theory about Emily Brontë's inner life is capable of

[1] *The Three Brontës,* by May Sinclair, 1912.
[2] *Emily Brontë,* by Mary F. Robinson (Madame Duclaux), 1883.

final proof, doubly dangerous because, in many minds, the Brontës are an obsession which, while it lasts, attaches to them the privileges and penalties of Cæsar's wife. We know that they were passionate writers, and that Emily was the most passionate. We know, or should know if we have remarked elsewhere the fruits of imaginative genius, that to infer from this alone that Charlotte was in love with Héger or that Emily experienced the satisfactions or even the desires of the flesh is unwarrantable. But Miss Sinclair, writing in 1911, went too far. She was violently scornful of those who then accepted the possibility of Charlotte's having been in love with Héger ; she regarded the suspicion as an attempt to belittle the genius of a woman novelist ; she said that Charlotte, being " pure, utterly pure from all the illusions and subtleties and corruptions of the sentimentalist," was incapable of " feeling in herself the possibility of passion " ; and, following Mrs. Gaskell, the only source then available, she quoted a fragment of one of Charlotte's letters to Héger in support of the conception of her heroine as a " fiery-hearted Vestal." Two years later this letter and three others were published in full in *The Times* (July 29, 1913). It was seen that Mrs. Gaskell, who may have been shown the originals by Héger, as Mr. Benson [1] supposes, but who more probably worked from a copy or copies retained by Charlotte, had been discreetly selective. That Charlotte loved Héger was established. The indignant rhetoric of Miss Sinclair was seen to have been thrown away, for the artist's repute was not touched ; and all but those who had believed that a virginal soul was a necessary support to an impassioned imagination wondered what all the fuss had been about.

The incident would not be worth its place here if it were not that rhetoric of the same colour has been, and is still being, used in defence of Emily's absolute chastity of act and wish, and that the publication of new material might at any moment cause this rhetoric to perish. Someone may dare to say that Emily too was in love. " But we shall at least know that he has made it up," says Miss Sinclair. " And even so, it will have been better for that man if he had never been born. He will have done his best to destroy or to deface the loveliness of a figure unique in literature." What an obsession is this ! Who would feel that anything essential in the woman was defaced if it were

[1] *Charlotte Brontë*, by E. F. Benson, 1932.

proved that she had loved a man, or whose adoration of her genius be lessened? It is true that fiery genius is extremely rare in women who lack sexual impulse, and there may exist, in some minds, a wish to preserve so great a rarity, but this is not a good reason for saying, with Miss Sinclair, that " when Emily wrote of passion, she wrote of a thing that, as far as she personally was concerned, not only was not and had not been, but could never be." There is none but speculative evidence for this sweeping statement. There is at present none but speculative evidence against it. In each reader's knowledge of women and in his biographical interpretation of the works, the subject may be allowed to rest until new evidence is forthcoming.

Let us, then, examine the works without seeking to prove in them either that Emily was in love with her brother or with any other man, or that she was incapable of bodily desire. It is unnecessary to proceed to either of these extremes, for the poems do not require them, and, though the closeness of Emily's later association with Branwell is deeply relevant to the authorship of *Wuthering Heights*, there is no just cause for assuming or suspecting that her love for him, if she loved him, was abnormal, except in the sense in which all emotional states were, by intensification and a disease of secrecy, made abnormal within the walls of Haworth. It is true that Charlotte's behaviour to Branwell, her envenomed exclusion of him from her life during the period in which *Wuthering Heights* was being written, is not fully accounted for either by his pleasures of the inn or by the suggestion that, having been herself denied in her passion, she was made morally indignant and resentful by her brother's disgrace at Thorp Green. Charlotte had many faults, but she was not a petty, spiteful spinster : there must have been better reasons than these for the long continuance of her hatred. It is true, also, that she displayed an extraordinary eagerness to obliterate all traces of her sister's private life, and that there is a hint of baffled terror in her reticences when she writes of Emily. On these and other indications it might be possible to build up a theory that the relationship of Branwell and Emily was one that displeased Charlotte, and that she wished to conceal the nature of it. But the evidence is all conjectural, and reacts against itself. We shall be wise to put this theory out of mind, and to proceed, for lack of available proof, on the assumption that it is altogether unfounded.

It remains as fact that Emily wrote poems of love, that many lines in those poems have the quality of supreme genius, and that supreme genius does not appear in love-poems written by those who are without experience of love. This argument has been a stumbling-block to those who are determined to disallow in Emily the love of man, but it need not have been so. They have gone to fantastic lengths in an endeavour to avoid a logic which seemed to them to be destructive of their theory. They have divided the poetry into Gondal verses and personal verses, being careful always to classify the love poems as Gondals—that is, as poems expressing the passion, not of Emily herself, but of one fictitious character in the Gondal cycle for another.

To this argument there are two replies: the first, that many of the Gondal ascriptions are extremely doubtful; the second, that even where a poem is Gondal beyond dispute, it is often personal also beyond reasonable dispute, the Gondal form being no more than a cloak, perhaps even a liberation, of personal feeling. Clear proofs that Emily so used the Gondal form are to be found in two familiar poems, "The Prisoner" and "Remembrance." The opening of "The Prisoner," telling how narrator and jailer visit a dungeon and speak with a female prisoner confined there, is evidently fictitious, probably Gondal, and, like all Emily's work, when written deliberately and not dictated by the spirit within her, second-rate.

> *" About her lips there played a smile of almost scorn:*
> *' My friend,' she gently said, ' you have not heard me*
>   *mourn;*
> *When you my kindred's lives, my lost life, can restore,*
> *Then may I weep and sue,—and never, friend, before!"* [1]

No genius was needed for the composition of that; but suddenly, with so violent a flash that I am inclined to wonder whether the connexion between the earlier and the later sections of the poem is not an editorial error, Emily Brontë speaks.

> *" ' Still, let my tyrants know . . .'"* [1]

The superb stanzas, the clearest, the most persuasive de-

---

[1] *The Complete Poems of Emily Jane Brontë.* Edited by Clement Shorter. Arranged and Collated, etc., by C. W. Hatfield (1923), p. 15.

scription of mystical experience in our language, are so
familiar that they need not be quoted here. They are
enough to undermine the theory that the poems, having
a fictitious form, are necessarily impersonal. An examination of " Remembrance " completes the destruction of that
theory. Whose death is lamented in these verses we do not
know—not Branwell's, for it was written not later than
March 1845.

> " *Cold in the earth—and the deep snow piled above thee,*
> *Far, far removed, cold in the dreary grave!*
> *Have I forgot, my only Love, to love thee,*
> *Severed at last by Time's all-severing wave.*" [1]

If words have meaning—above all, if the music of poetry
has a significance distinct from that of its words—this is a
lament written by one experiencing a personal emotion. We
must not be over-precise in our interpretations. The poem
is unquestionably Gondal in form, one of the two MSS. in
which it exists being headed, " R. Alcons to J. Brenzaida."
The external circumstances may well have been dictated by
the necessities of the Gondal fiction, and we should be rash
to assume that the creature lamented in Emily's own heart
had been dead while " fifteen wild Decembers, From those
brown hills, [had] melted into spring." Nor is it necessarily to be believed that when she cried:

> " *Sweet Love of youth, forgive, if I forget thee,*"

she was providing commentators with evidence of an early
amour. It is by no means impossible that the personal
thought within the Gondal form was directed to her dead
sister. But speculation on this identity is unfruitful. It is
enough that the poem, together with " The Prisoner," be
accepted as disproof of the theory that verses with a Gondal
form are to be regarded as impersonal.

Thus the whole body of poems is released to equal
criticism, and we may range them, side by side with
Wuthering Heights, as the basis of our interpretation of
the author. I would add here, in parenthesis, that I accept
Emily as substantially the author of *Wuthering Heights*
without believing for a moment that Branwell was physically incapable of collaborating with her, or that he lacked
qualities of imagination and experience that would have

---

[1] Shorter and Hatfield, p. 7.

given value to his collaboration. The evidences that he had some share in the work are numerous and independent; Mr. E. F. Benson has so ably and so recently martialled them in his life of Charlotte that they need not be reviewed. Miss Alice Law [1] takes in Branwell's defence an extremer position, into which it is hard to follow her, but her research has done much to make it certain that the brother contributed to the sister's work. What was the extent of that contribution we cannot know. Mr. Benson would " assign the first two chapters, pompous and monstrous in style, with their Lockwood *motif* which once announced is heard no more," to Branwell, and, though the admitted structural flaw in the opening does not persuade me, in a book of such confused architecture, that two hands have been at work, it does seem to be true that the two opening chapters are burdened with a facetiousness from which the rest of the book is exempt.

What gives to Emily her unique place among English novelists is that her imagination, when in full cry, was unembarrassed by the curse of " humour," which, when found in a tragic writer, is often equivalent to destructive self-consciousness. *Wuthering Heights,* said a contemporary reviewer [2] in one of the cuttings preserved by Emily in her desk,

> " is a strange, inartistic story. . . . *Jane Eyre* is a book which affects the reader to tears; it touches the most hidden sources of emotion. *Wuthering Heights* casts a gloom over the mind not easily to be dispelled. . . . The book sadly wants relief. A few glimpses of sunshine would have increased the reality of the picture and given strength rather than weakness to the whole. There is not in the entire *dramatis personæ* a single character which is not utterly hateful or thoroughly contemptible."

This, as Charlotte indicated in her preface, is untrue; the reviewer who wrote it was a fool. But when he pleaded for " a few glimpses of sunshine " he was representative of a school of criticism that persists to our own day. *Wuthering Heights* is great, not for its story, which is rash

---

[1] *Patrick Branwell Brontë*, and *Emily Jane Brontë and the Authorship of " Wuthering Heights,"* both by Alice Law.
[2] Quoted in *Emily Brontë*, by Charles Simpson, 1929, pp. 174–5.

and confused; not for its drawing of recognizable or virtuous character, though, as Charlotte said with Charlotte's irrelevance, Nelly Dean has " true benevolence and homely fidelity " and Edgar Linton is " an example of constancy and tenderness " ; but for its power to communicate a vision and, in communicating it, to concede nothing to those who clamoured then—and clamour still when they cannot endure the ecstatic fire, the " horror of great darkness "— for " relief," for " glimpses of sunshine," for " increased reality." And it is not to be denied that the hand which wrote the first two chapters was capable of these concessions. It was not cheerful, but it had a funereal, polysyllabic facetiousness strikingly contrasted with the lightning of Emily at her best.

> " ' The Lord help us ! ' he soliloquized in an undertone of peevish displeasure, while relieving me of my horse ; looking, meantime, in my face so sourly that I charitably conjectured he must have need of divine aid to digest his dinner, and his pious ejaculation had no reference to my expected advent."

This could scarcely be worse: Branwell may have written it. But if we harshly attribute it to him, we are in danger of repeating the error common in Shakespearian scholars who will not permit their Homer to nod. Emily may well have been guilty, if she was writing self-consciously before the genius within her had possessed her pen.

That Branwell had a hand—or, if not a hand, a contributory mind—in the book is sufficiently established by evidence external to the text. That Emily was the substantial author is, nevertheless, beyond doubt. Charlotte, we know, could lie in a good cause, particularly when the secrets of authorship were at stake ; but all her letters about Ellis Bell go to prove that she believed *Wuthering Heights* to have been written by Emily. This—the contacts of Haworth being what they were—is itself strong evidence for Emily's authorship. Nor is there any reasonable motive to account for prolonged deception by Emily, or for Branwell's having permitted her, if the book was not hers, to rob him of his author's vanity. It has been said by one theorist [1] that Charlotte wrote it—a suggestion manifestly

---

[1] *The Key to the Brontë Works. The Key to Charlotte Brontë's " Wuthering Heights," etc.*, by John Malham Dembleby, 1911.

ridiculous; as well attempt to prove that Sir Walter Scott wrote *Kubla Khan*.

Emily's genius is plainly dominant in *Wuthering Heights*, unless we are to assume that the manuscripts of the poems are fraudulent; for whoever wrote the poems wrote *Wuthering Heights*, the same unreality of this world, the same greater reality of another, being in them both, and in nothing else that the human mind has produced. The poems and the novels are twins of a unique imagination. They have the same prosaic lapses, the same poetic transcendence; they have the same obsession with the idea of imprisonment and of supernatural visitants; the same swift alternation between two seemingly contradictory ideas of death.

One instance of this from the novel must suffice. In Chapter XV Heathcliff visits Catherine, who is dying and big with child.

"Heathcliff had knelt on one knee to embrace her; he attempted to rise, but she seized his hair, and kept him down. . . . 'Don't torture me till I am as mad as yourself,' cried he, wrenching his head free, and grinding his teeth. The two, to a cool spectator, made a strange and fearful picture. Well might Catherine deem that heaven would be a land of exile to her, unless with her mortal body she cast away her mortal character also."

But later Catherine says:

"Oh, you see, Nelly, he would not relent a moment to keep me out of the grave. *That* is how I'm loved! Well, never mind. That is not *my* Heathcliff. I shall love mine yet; and take him with me: he's in my soul. And,' she added, musingly, 'the thing that irks me most is this shattered prison, after all. I'm tired of being enclosed here. I'm wearying to escape into that glorious world, and to be always there: not seeing it dimly through tears, and yearning for it through the walls of an aching heart; but really with it, and in it. . . . I shall be incomparably beyond and above you all. I *wonder* he won't be near me!' She went on to herself. 'I thought he wished it. Heathcliff, dear!

74

you should not be sullen now. Do come to me, Heathcliff.' "

The contrast between these two passages is not to be mistaken. It is the contrast between the two planes on which Emily Brontë conducted her life—the plane on which Ellen Nussey and Charlotte observed her and the plane that was the basis of her mystical poetry. On the first, she deemed " that heaven would be a land of exile to her." When death approached, she struggled against it. " I have seen nothing like it," wrote Charlotte, " but, indeed, I have never seen her parallel in anything. Stronger than a man, simpler than a child, her nature stood alone." She was not, as her own diary proves, discontented ; she was reconciled with life, and could, in her own solitary way, be happy ; to which Ellen Nussey bore testimony, confirming Charlotte. " On the top of the moor or in a deep glen, Emily was a child in spirit for glee and enjoyment ; or when thrown entirely on her own resources, she could be vivacious in conversation and enjoy giving pleasure." And Miss Nussey supplies the link between the two aspects of this girl whose " extreme reserve was impenetrable." Few people, she said, " have the gift of looking and smiling as she could look and smile. One of her rare expressive looks was something to remember through life." These looks were all that Emily revealed of that other plane, experience of which made her feel that on earth she was a prisoner. She was tired of being enclosed. She was weary to escape to " that glorious world " of which, I believe, she had once enjoyed immediate apprehension. All her life, all her poems, all those parts of *Wuthering Heights* that bear the stamp of vision were dedicated to her desire that this direct experience might be repeated, that she might be again " really with it and in it—not seeing it dimly through tears and yearning for it through the walls of an aching heart."

There are in the poems indications enough that this experience, this achievement of the Absolute with which she was ever afterwards " in love," was identified in her mind with an individuality, known to be ghostly in its relation to the earthly plane, but having for her an unforgettable reality and probably an anthropomorphic form. If this be true, there is no need for the curious to ask with which of her father's curates Emily was in love, nor for the too eager advocates of a virginal and sexless soul to explain away her passion as Gondal. Nor, in recognizing this truth, need we give to it the harsh outline of Romer Wilson's Demon Lover.[1] Emily Brontë may, or may not, have loved in the flesh; certainly no love poems have ever been more free than hers of erotic imagery; but, however this may be, the key to her art, with which alone we are deeply concerned, lies, not in a bodily passion, but in a spiritual ecstasy having, for her, the form of possession at once blissful and terrible. This idea is continually expressed in her poems:

> " *What I love shall come like visitant of air,*
> *Safe in secret power from lurking human snare;*
> *Who loves me, no word of mine shall e'er betray,*
> *Though for faith unstained my life must forfeit pay.*" [2]

From the possession of night when—

> " *Thought followed thought, star followed star*
> *Through boundless regions on;*
> *While one sweet influence, near and far,*
> *Thrilled through, and proved us one!* " [3]—

she awoke to the agony of daybreak and consciousness of the earthly plane. The sun rose; she hid herself in her pillow.

> " *It would not do—the pillow glowed,*
> *And glowed both roof and floor;*
> *And birds sang loudly in the wood,*
> *And fresh winds shook the door.*" [4]

In October 1845, having described the spirit that " sent his dazzling gaze down through that ocean's gloomy night," she told how she had sought continually and in vain for him:

> " *I've watched and sought my lifetime long;*
> *Sought him in heaven, hell, earth, and air,*
> *An endless search, and always wrong.*" [5]

And often, I think, when she seems to be lamenting the death of a human being, and thrusting from her mind the too powerful memory of the " sweet love " of her youth,

[1] *All Alone,* by Romer Wilson.
[2] Shorter and Hatfield, p. 53. [3] *Ibid.*, p. 3. [4] *Ibid.*, p. 4.
[5] *Ibid.*, p. 6.

the power of this spirit to elude her is the force behind her words:

> " Then did I check the tears of useless passion—
>   Weaned my young soul from yearning after thine;
> Sternly denied its burning wish to hasten
>   Down to that tomb already more than mine.
>
> " And, even yet, I dare not let it languish,
>   Dare not indulge in memory's rapturous pain;
> Once drinking deep of that divinest anguish,
>   How could I seek the empty world again? " [1]

Seven years earlier (November 3, 1838), she was already telling of the same loss:

> " O Dream! where art thou now?
>   Long years have passed away,
> Since last from off thy angel-brow
>   I saw the light decay." [2]

On May 25 of the same year her statement, within the Gondal form of *Gleneden's Dream,* is direct and unmistakable:

> " Watcher, in this lonely prison,
>   Shut from joy and kindly air,
> Heaven, descending in a vision,
>   Taught my soul to do and bear. " [3]

But she cannot deny herself her ecstatic voyages, though their incompleteness is torment to her.

> " Oh! dreadful is the check—intense the agony—
> When the ear begins to hear, and the eye begins to see;
> When the pulse begins to throb, the brain to think again;
> The soul to feel the flesh, and the flesh to feel the chain.
> " Yet I would lose no sting, would wish no torture less. . . ." [4]

Sometimes the vision approached her by day:]

> " Methought, the very breath I breathed
>   Was full of sparks divine,
> And all my heather-couch was wreathed
>   By that celestial shine! " [5]

[1] Shorter and Hatfield, p. 8.
[2] *Ibid.,* p. 97.   [3] *Ibid.,* p. 85.
[4] *Ibid.,* p. 16.   [5] *Ibid.,* p. 19.

Sometimes by night she longed for it:

> " Yes, Fancy, come, my Fairy Love!
>   These throbbing temples softly kiss;
> And bend my lonely couch above,
>   And bring me rest, and bring me bliss." [1]

Page after page of her poems proclaims the same hunger
for an experience, having the force of absolute possession,
once known, still tasted, but now, in its finality, denied
to her.

> " Burn then, little lamp; glimmer straight and clear—
> Hush! a rustling wing stirs, methinks, the air:
> He for whom I wait thus ever comes to me;
> Strange Power! I trust thy might; trust thou my con-
>   stancy." [2]

To one who had known this reality, all other failure was
less than her failure to recapture it, and over such a one
the world had no power. Death appeared to her, in one
aspect, as an end of the blissful torture she would not
have lessened; in another aspect, as a possible reversal
of her failures—an opportunity to be " really with and
in " the supreme familiar spirit. She did not know
whether to dread death as a cessation or to desire it as
an opportunity. She did not know whence her familiar
spirit came, from Heaven or from Hell; she did not know
whether, in the Christian view, her blisses were evil or
good; she was not certain that, in going from this world,
she might take her ecstasy with her. " I shall love (my
Heathcliff) yet; and take him with me: he is in my soul,"
said Catherine, and though it would be foolish to suggest
that Heathcliff was no more than an embodiment of Emily's
vision, seen in its aspect of evil, it is unquestionably true
that he often, while she wrote the novel, so appeared to her,
and that Catherine's passion for a man was, in this sense,
an expression of Emily's passion for her absolute visitant.
" ' Heathcliff, dear! you should not be sullen now. Do
come to me, Heathcliff.' "
    Novel and poems are one. Both, in the intervals
when genius slackened and talent was needed to fill the

---

[1] Shorter and Hatfield, p. 21.   [2] Ibid., p. 53.

gap, weakened, for Emily had not a tutored talent, consistently at her service. She could write verses as trivial as Anne's; she could compose a strange " inartistic story." But she had an extraordinary power, when the secret virtue commanded her stresses and her open vowels, to change a commonplace metre into a winged charge of the squadrons of the spirit, and, because she was delivered from humour and could permit a woman, vehement with a lover, to retain " in her closed fingers a portion of the locks she had been grasping "; because she wrote, when she wrote well, on the plane of her own vision, without embarrassment, without fear, she has left behind her a novel that cannot perish. That cannot perish, not because it is faultless, but because it has already transcended its faults. Its appeal is not to reason, but to perception; it is not an argument, but a spell. Like the poems, it is not a criticism of this life, but the evocation of another, and, like its author, it is not to be compared. " The worst of it is," wrote Charlotte to Mr. Williams, having tried laboriously to explain Heathcliff by his unfortunate upbringing; " the worst of it is, some of his spirit seems breathed through the whole narrative in which he figures : it haunts every moor and glen, and beckons in every fir-tree of the Heights." This is the book's miraculous unity. It is possessed by Heathcliff, who was " in " Emily's soul.

ROBERT BROWNING

1812-1889

BY
LASCELLES
ABERCROMBIE

ROBERT BROWNING

I

ANYONE who had some knowledge of literary history might have expected that the great reputation which Robert Browning won in the latter part of his lifetime would be followed by a reaction. The process is familiar and understandable; but is no more rational than the decision of the Athenian voter, who was tired of hearing Aristides called " the Just." It is, however, a process which usually endeavours, somehow or other, to rationalize itself. The heaviest count against Browning, in the reaction of common opinion from his Victorian reputation, seems to have been the charge of " optimism." It will be a question of considerable interest in social history why this accusation should have proved so damaging. The answer will hardly be the simple one which the War at once suggests; for the charge had weight before the War. But the discussion of Browning's poetry need not concern itself with the seriousness of the charge until it is sure of its justice. Common opinion is not always accurate in its indictments. When reaction against an author's reputation has well set in, it is natural that those who are affected by it should not read him; for why read what you are certain you will not like? But something is known about him; and out of this something is engendered a rumour of what he was and what he wrote; and the rumour turns out, of course, to be of a kind which seems to justify the reaction against him.

It was known that Browning had a robust and hearty disposition; it was known that he had specially pleased many of his admirers by poetically vociferating the courage with which he faced the problems of mortality—" Greet the unseen with a cheer ! " for instance. All this was not exactly " optimism " itself, but it made that injurious accusation plausible ; and the accusation became inevitable when, by one of those accidents to which all great poets are liable, a phrase of Browning's took such hold of the popular mind that, like " one touch of nature makes the whole world kin," it could completely detach itself from its context and, throwing off the peculiar significance which its author intended by it, enter into the miscellaneous use of everyday speech. It was common, all too common, knowledge that Browning was the poet who wrote:

> " God's in his heaven,
>   All's right with the world " ;

and was not this the very quintessence of an " optimism " which would justify the strongest reaction against its author? So this unfortunate quotation became the motto of anti-Browning criticism ; this celebrated remark formed the nucleus round which grew the rumour of Browning's fallacious cheerfulness and his paralysing satisfaction with things.

Thus Browning became the " optimistic " type of that Victorian hypocrisy which so revolted the Edwardians and the Georgians. The reaction against him seemed to have succeeded in rationalizing itself. However, the justice of the rumour on which it relied may be fairly measured by the worth of the one distinct piece of evidence it brought against him:

> " God's in his heaven—
>   All's right with the world ! "

For if we take that as it was written, and keep our minds within the wholly unmistakable intention it has in its context, what do we find? Two very obvious things. First, this is a quotation from a lyric, from the expression of a momentary mood. Now, it cannot be argued that whenever a poet is expressing the mood of a moment, he is declaring his philosophy. There are many moods so familiar to ordinary human nature that their expression commits no one to any particular view of life whatever; and surely one of them is, that simple, unreflecting sense of well-being on going out of doors on a glorious morning with nothing to do the whole day long but please oneself. And just that is what Browning expresses here. If we did not know what pranks reaction can play on criticism, should we not say that anyone who had to bring in " optimism " to account for such a lyric as this must be either a very whimsical sort of critic or strangely deficient as a human being ?

But this is not all. The second thing we notice if, instead of taking these lines as a detached quotation, we read the poem· in which they occur, is that Browning himself professes nothing in them at all, not even the primitive sense of well-being they express. The lyric is a dramatic lyric. It is the utterance of a character he has imagined, and it helps to delineate that character. The poet is telling a story ; and at a certain point it was necessary for his story that this character—Pippa—should intervene in an entirely characteristic manner. She does so by singing a song, which is not merely the right sort of song for such a person as she is to sing, but the right sort of song for that moment of the story. Out of this double artistic necessity, how could anyone extract evidence of Browning's personal " optimism " ? Only by taking as true the rumour by which an essentially irrational reaction sought to rationalize itself.

The quotation from *Pippa Passes* was so immensely famous, and seemed so pat to the point, that the reaction scarcely troubled to look for any further evidence of Browning's " optimism." Pippa's exclamation turns out to be no evidence at all ; and, in fact, there is no further evidence to be found. In the sense which the accusation intends, no poet was ever less guilty of " optimism " than Robert Browning ; for no poet was ever more clearly aware of the evil of life, or expressed his sense of evil more unmistakably. We do not need, to assure us of this, the remarkable confession he uttered towards the end of his career :

> " *I must say—or choke in silence—' Howsoever came*
>   *my fate,*
> *Sorrow did and joy did nowise,—life well weighed,—*
>   *preponderate.' "*

This was only to be expected from the poet who wrote (to take two very different instances of evil prevailing in life)

The Heretic's Tragedy and *Mr. Sludge the Medium*. For
Browning could enter into, and make himself the very
mind and nerves and speech of evil, while yet at the same
time perfectly loathing it. Look, for an example even
more striking than those just mentioned, and of a kind
entirely peculiar to himself, at the brilliantly horrible
soliloquies of the advocates in *The Ring and the Book*.
The wickedness which tortured and destroyed innocent
Pompilia is bad enough ; but there is something even worse,
and Browning dreadfully understands it—the profession-
alism to which wickedness and innocence alike are simply
articles in a trade. But the whole body of Browning's
poetry testifies past mistake to his interest in life as the
manifestation of evil as well as of good. It might be said,
nevertheless, that the good on the whole, in Browning's
view of life, outweighed the evil. If that could be said, it
would be a very different thing from the " optimism " of
which he has been accused. But it is doubtful if it can
truthfully be said, quite apart from his definite assertion
that in his own personal experience " sorrow " outweighed
" joy "—an assertion which would not in itself be incompatible, for a man may well experience more sorrow than
joy, and yet believe that in life as a whole good is stronger
than evil.

But that seems to have been just what Browning did not
believe. It might be nearer the truth to call him, as far at
least as this present life is concerned, a " pessimist " rather
than an " optimist," were it not that all such terms are
equally futile for a mind so rich and complex as his.
Browning's attitude to life and estimate of it were religious
rather than philosophical. Throughout the very considerable changes which his religious opinions underwent—he
began in the Broad Church creed and ended in a position
which can hardly be called Christianity—he maintained in-
alterably his belief in two things : he believed in a personal
God, and he believed in immortality. The first involved
him in metaphysical difficulties (*Fears and Scruples,* for
example) with which he never managed satisfactorily to
cope. It was the second that gave him security ; and
the chief thing against which he required security was the
apparent overplus of evil in mortal affairs. During the
whole of his life, the doctrine of immortality seems to have
presented itself to him as the one possible escape from the
conviction that evil had, on the whole, the mastery in

existence. If he could not believe in immortality, there would be for him—

> *" no reconciling wisdom with a world distraught,*
> *Goodness with triumphant evil, power with failure*
> *　　in the aim."*

This, he says, summing up his whole career, is what he has " learnt and taught " ; and so far as we can read his career in his poetry, it is the truth. It was in the security given him by his belief in immortality that he could profess (somewhat noisily) the courage with which he faced man's incomprehensible destiny, and maintain in perfect sanity that vivid energy of mind and feeling with which he was so splendidly endowed. But when we admire (as we must) his magnificent enjoyment of life, we ought to remember that, so far from ignoring or being blind to evil in the world, he saw so much of it that only in a future life could he believe that the good would prevail. It certainly will not do to call him a cheerful pessimist, though that is by no means an impossible creature ; but, just as certainly, between Browning's magnificent enjoyment of life and anything which can be called " optimism," the distance is as far as the East is from the West.

II

There was, however, an even deeper misunderstanding of Browning than this, in the attempt the reaction against him made to rationalize itself. For it is not for any sort of valuation of life, not for any ethical or intellectual contribution to man's sense of himself and of his place in the world, not for any philosophy, however vaguely and loosely the word may be used, that his poetry is important ; and it must be added, not characteristically for any religious thought or feeling or intuition, though there are a few passages (one of them scarcely to be equalled elsewhere) which notably express some aspect of religious experience. The reaction, however, can scarcely be blamed for this misunderstanding, which it merely took over, and caricatured, from the reputation Browning's poetry had in his lifetime. Indeed, in the long run, the reaction has no doubt done good service to the true appreciation of Browning. It accused him of a false valuation of life. When we test this accusation, we find not merely that his poetry does not give us a false valuation of life, but that its importance does not consist in giving us any valuation of life at all. All the more should our attention now fix on that in which the importance of his poetry does consist.

The reaction against him was, as has been suggested, a quite blind and irrational process. One cannot but be amused at those critics who, in expressing it, did so as though they were the messengers of a daring and original innovation; whereas they were but embodying one of the most ordinary phenomena of literary history. It would be as futile to protest against the reaction as its efforts to rationalize itself have been. It must just run its course; and probably by now it has done so. But it must be with Browning as it has been with Tennyson: the figure that emerges from detraction is a Browning somewhat altered from what he was; some traits have disappeared from serious discussion, others require a more decisive emphasis. Against Browning's reputation, reaction came somewhat later than against Tennyson's. This was no doubt due to the contrast which contemporary criticism liked to make out between them, though it would be hard to find two poets who can be less profitably contrasted than Tennyson and Browning. The formula was, that Tennyson had the art, Browning the matter. The formula will only work as regards their failures. Where Tennyson fails (as in *The Lord of Burleigh* or *The Children's Hospital*) there is nothing wrong with the art: it is the matter that is so dreadful. Where Browning fails (as in *Red-cotton Night-cap Country* or *The Inn Album*) there is nothing wrong with the matter; but the art has ceased to exist. Elsewhere, all that can be said is that, both in their matter and their art, Tennyson and Browning differ as widely, perhaps, as two poets can differ; but that, both in their matter and their art, each is in his kind as good as the other.

There is a theory that art and matter are, at bottom, the same thing. This is true only in the sense that all things are, at bottom, the same thing. Art and matter in poetry are perfectly distinguishable; but the truth is obvious, that neither is of any value without the other. Nevertheless, the notion is often proclaimed, that matter is the thing that really counts in poetry; perhaps because it can be more easily discussed. Members of the Browning Society were fond of proclaiming this: it followed naturally on their doctrine that Browning was the poet of his time who most conspicuously had matter in him. This view of Browning's superiority took the popular fancy; and that, no doubt, is why reaction against him was delayed a good while after it had overtaken Tennyson, who, it was supposed, had only art in his favour. That, too, is why the reaction, when it did come, seemed chiefly concerned to caricature Browning's matter, though his art, as Calverley had long since wickedly shown, is much more vulnerable. Admittedly, when Browning did fail, he failed in art; but it is the law of reaction in literature that it is set in motion by success, not by failure. And Browning's success was taken to be in his matter.

The result of all this is, that Browning's real and permanent merits have not yet emerged from the reaction against him as clearly as Tennyson's have. The real and permanent merit of his matter was not, of course, obscured in his lifetime; there is no question of qualities unsuspected by his contemporary admirers being at last revealed, now that the reaction against him is passing away. But it was not this, or not chiefly this, which gave him his reputation as a poet pre-eminent for great matter. That was because his poetry was regarded as being extraordinarily rich in what may roughly and compendiously be called *thought*, which was assumed to be specially valuable for its philosophical concern, discursive or intuitive, with the nature of things and the destiny of man: the sort of matter we get in Lucretius or in Wordsworth, or, indeed, in Tennyson (as, for example, in *The Ancient Sage*).

Now, if we take Browning at his best—say, in that superb collection, *Men and Women*—we certainly do find that thought takes an unusually large part in his poetry; and not so much the *result* of thinking, in wise reflection and considerate judgment, as the very activity of thinking, the actual movement of ratiocination, and even casuistry. But this thought does not belong to the poet's matter: it belongs to his art. Browning is not thinking on his own account: he is attributing thought to certain characters he has imagined, and making them delineate themselves by the manner of their thinking. It is the peculiar and highly developed method of his art of expressing matter which is also peculiarly his own, by reason of his unerring instinct for it; and this matter is human character, the vivid and intense imagination of all sorts of personalities—or perhaps we should put it more generally, and say, of all sorts of

E

habits and energies of living. When this is Browning's matter, and when that peculiar art of his, which we may describe as *characteristic thinking,* succeeds, as it often so finely and powerfully does, in expressing this matter, then we perceive the real and permanent merits of his poetry ; then we find—and this is the test of a great poet— that the more closely we attend both to its matter and its art, the more its importance is felt.

But elsewhere, though much less frequently, it certainly is *thought* that is the matter of his poetry. This is when he is thinking on his own account, and thinking, as his contemporary admirers awefully noticed, about the great problems of existence. And when this happens, the matter of his poetry is of scarcely any importance at all. The two most conspicuous instances are *La Saisiaz* and *Christmas Eve and Easter Day*. Fortunately, in both *thought* is not the whole of the matter. *La Saisiaz* is a very noble elegy ; but its thought is somewhat inconclusive, as no doubt thought on such topics—the mystery of evil and the case for immortality—must always be. But it is jejune and unexciting thought ; and thought in poetry, however inconclusive, should always be at least exciting. *Christmas Eve and Easter Day* (as perhaps befits a much earlier poem) is even more ambitious : it is the nature of God that is the topic here. For the first time in his poetic career—it may be because Elizabeth Barrett, now his wife, had urged him to it—Browning spoke in his own person. The result was less a transformation of thought into poetry than a kind of emulsion of the two, as of oil and water. The poetry is in the admirably managed contrast of vividly grotesque and humorous realism with a most individual kind of apocalyptic vision ; but the thought is a doggerel rendering of abysmally dull sectarian theology, futile, small, and profitless, which can never, one would think, have had much importance, and now has none whatever. Is this, we ask in our astonishment, this insignificant stuff, what a great poet calls *thinking*? And thinking about the grand problems of existence ! Such a failure as this is often thought to be characteristic of Victorian England. But we need not go to foreign literature to see what poetic thinking of this kind ought to be : we have only to compare *Christmas Eve and Easter Day* with Matthew Arnold's *Obermann Once More*.

It is much the same with the other poems of Browning's

which passed in his day for something philosophical. The truth is, that Browning's intellectual life was spent in a backwater. The great current of European thought in his day scarcely moved his mind. This would not have mattered if he had had any notable thought of his own. But he had not: he believed he was taking his part in the great intellectual campaign of his age. But for all his courageous expressions, he was not one of the fighters. His was rather the fighting spirit of the non-combatant. He was like a war-correspondent at the base, occasionally seeing, but never smelling, the smoke of powder, and cheerfully sending home encouraging messages, not very well-informed, and of a most transitory importance.

All this detracts nothing from his real greatness. We can see now that Browning was not a poet whose mission could ever have been the interpreting or even the valuing of life. The poems in which he attempted such a business are the mere aberrations of his genius. There are not very many of them: in the whole mass of his work their bulk is comparatively small; and they should not be allowed to distract our attention from his success, much less trouble our admiration for it. Inclination and talent alike took him in a direction quite different from philosophizing about life: they took him in the direction Chaucer and Shakespeare went. It was not for him to judge life, but simply to portray it. Human nature in all its infinite possibility of variation—that was his subject. He needed no other, and he could seize on any kind or aspect of this with incomparable relish and exquisite understanding. It is true, as has been said, that he had a very strong sense of the evil in life, and the hearty detestation of it which such a sane mind as his must have; but when he is portraying evil (as he very often is) his hatred of it is combined with his delight in human nature as such—his joy in understanding one more specimen of its inexhaustible variety. Such perfect co-existence of opposite feelings is nothing to be surprised at in a man like Browning, though perhaps in a less capacious mind it would be. It is true, too—and this perhaps is more remarkable—that in the process of portraying a character he sometimes wrote poetry of great speculative power, as though, kindled by the energy of creation, his mind could do for a person he had imagined what it could not or would not do for himself. But, indeed, this merely shows that it was not his business to interpret life

on his own account and for its own sake; it only became
his business when it was *in the character* he was drawing.
Instances are *Johannes Agricola, Kharshish, A Death in
the Desert;* but by far the most splendid is the conclusion
of *Saul,* when David becomes physically aware of the
infinite spiritual life of the universe: one of the greatest
passages in modern poetry of speculative intuition, whether
we call it religious or metaphysical.

III

Browning's pictures of human nature are not always,
strictly speaking, studies of character, like Blougram,
Sludge, and Cleon; they are often rather aspects of life and
studies of situation, like *Love among the Ruins, The
Heretic's Tragedy, A Grammarian's Funeral,* or *The Flight
of the Duchess.* But from first to last his characteristic
method is substantially the same: it is to make life argu-
mentatively expound itself and, above all, justify itself to
its own satisfaction. This extraordinary talent of his, which
would not be suppressed, was the very thing that made it
impossible for him to write plays which would act, though
in dramatic poems it worked admirably: witness *Para-
celsus* and *Pippa Passes.* He was a dramatist for whom
plays were the wrong medium. To present human nature,
not as it looks to the poet or to us, but as it looks to itself—
that is what it is to be a truly dramatic poet; and that was
Browning's work. The soliloquy was the right medium
for him. Life active in endless variety of conscious self-
assertion, and always for the purpose of justifying itself to
itself—he could make the whole gamut of life, from Caliban
to Rabbi ben Ezra, soliloquize in that style.

What is the meaning of this ceaseless passion for self-
justification which Browning so notably attributes to
human nature? That man, whether he be good or bad,
cannot live without protesting, however speciously, at least
his *effort* to obey some monitor within him, to conform
at any rate to his own standard? That perhaps is as near
as we can get to a philosophy of life from Browning. All
his methods and powers reach their climax in *The Ring and
the Book,* possibly the most originally conceived of all long
poems. After that great achievement, the decline is sudden
and woeful. The falling off in the latter half of Browning's
work is worse than in Wordsworth's: though, as with

Wordsworth, there are very striking exceptions (*Ned Bratts,* for example). He no longer designs his poems; his methods have become a mere mechanical habit, out of which he tirelessly but most wearisomely improvises. But what matter for that? We can, with one or two exceptions, let all his later work go, and be nobly satisfied with what is left. *Dramatic Lyrics, Dramatic Romances, Men and Women, Dramatis Personæ*—what a range he has, in the poetry which shows his real and permanent merits! If we fix our attention on those merits, we shall find it difficult to praise him too highly.

EDWARD
BURNE–JONES

1833-1898

BY
MARTIN
ARMSTRONG

E*

EDWARD
BURNE-JONES

THE critic, like the joiner, the plumber, and the doctor, is a person who goes about the world with a bag of tools. If you wish to size up a painter, a poet, a composer, or any other artist, and are unable to do so yourself, you call in the critic. He arrives with his bag, unpacks his set of standards, applies them more or less skilfully, and gives you his diagnosis. If his standards are not your standards, he has told you nothing you want to know about the artist, though incidentally he will have told you much about himself. He is a very limited creature: he can use only his own tools, the tools which are the product of his age and his experience. If you were to hand Ruskin's bag to Mr. Roger Fry or Mr. Clive Bell and ask either to do a critical job for you, he would probably tell you that the tools you had provided him with were of little or no use for his purpose. Unhappily, the trade of critic is much more difficult than those of the joiner, the plumber, and the doctor, for his application of his standards is hampered, unless his intellect and his sensibilities are impeccable, by all sorts of prejudices, some private and personal, others belonging to his period. It would be dishonest to disguise the fact that we are nowadays in violent reaction against most of what constitutes the art of Burne-Jones.

Let me state my own difficulty clearly. I came across the work of Burne-Jones in my young days before I knew anything of art beyond the English cathedrals, the English water-colourists, and William Morris and modern English arts and crafts. I admired him prodigiously, and no wonder, for his paintings, whatever they may be as pictures, are the perfection of handicraft. To-day I have

97

reacted from them so violently that I find it extremely difficult to judge them impartially. But not all of my antipathy is personal and prejudiced, for the standards I am forced to apply to him are not the standards by which he painted: few of the appliances by which we estimate him are to be found in Ruskin's tool-bag.

What I hold to be of prime importance in a picture are design and colour. A picture, however complicated, however full of shapes and colours, must be a balanced unity. Every shape, every colour, must be a necessary and indispensable part of that unity. Yet if I were pressed to explain what I mean by good design, balanced unity, I could not do so: I could only assert that a good design stimulated in me pleasant physical sensations, and that a bad one made me feel physically uncomfortable; that a good design drew me into the picture and held me there contented, while a bad one led me a wild-goose chase after a destination which I never discovered. " Then you offer us," I might be asked, " no other touchstone for a fine picture than these physical sensations of yours? "

To that I should reply that there was, as a matter of fact, a large number of people who shared my sensations. If my questioner asserted that he did not share them, I should have no more to say. And it would be the same with colour. I could only say that good colour was colour that pleased my eye and produced pleasant sensations in me, that seemed to me to add power and significance to the design.

Fine design and fine colour are in themselves a revelation, but a picture must be a revelation in another way. It must, as a poem must, tell us something new about its subject, whether its subject be a landscape, a naked figure, an abstraction, or anything else. But what it tells us it must tell directly and not obliquely. The revelation must be visual, plain for the eye to see: it must draw us into the picture and dismiss us from it satisfied. It must not send us to dictionaries and story-books to discover its meaning: it must draw no red-herring across our quest for instant revelation by means of coloured design. Anyone who has spent an over-conscientious morning in the Arena Chapel at Padua, which Giotto has covered with frescoes that tell the stories of the lives of Christ and His mother, will not need to be told of the wearisomeness of story-telling in pictures. Fortunately, Giotto was so great

98

an artist that each picture is a joy in itself, and we need
not exhaust ourselves in unravelling the story, which, as
regards painting, is irrelevant. It is not only irrelevant,
it is also impossible to tell, for the best that a picture can
do is to show very incompletely one moment in a story.
For completion of even that moment it must rely on the
knowledge which the spectator brings to it from other
sources. To a man who knew nothing of the Christian
story, those frescoes would mean nothing—nothing, and
yet everything that a picture should mean, for they would
remain a series of wonderful paintings, complete in themselves.

But it is pertinent to our subject, the art of Burne-Jones,
to look farther into those frescoes of Giotto's at Padua.
I have treated them as pictures, but the object with which
they were painted was not purely pictorial: it was also
illustrative. As the pictures in a book of fairy-tales show
the child in visible form scenes of which he has already
learned the meaning from the tale they illustrate, so these
frescoes offered to the pious and illiterate Christian illustrations to the holy stories familiar to him. The frescoes,
then, are illustrations, and it is obvious from them that
Giotto was a great illustrator. It is a fortunate chance that
he was also a great painter.

Obviously, then, illustration is irrelevant in a picture,
and if the picture-painter fixes his aim on illustration and
not on coloured design, he runs a risk of painting a bad
picture. The logical and horrible conclusion of the picture
which is primarily an illustration is the problem-picture—
the picture which does not even refer to a well-known story,
but tries to set you guessing at the conundrum it poses.
The picture called " Too Late," by W. L. Windus, in the
Tate Gallery, is an example. One can never discover why
the female invalid rising from her chair is so startled, nor
why the gentleman on the right is so conscience-stricken
or so shocked. But the artist insists that we shall go on
guessing, and it is not till we have given up the problem
that it occurs to us that we are in the presence of a picture,
and had better look at it as such. When we do so, in the
present case, we are grateful to the artist for the red-
herring, for the picture is not a picture ; and as there is
no text, so far as we know, to the illustration, it is not an
illustration. It is merely a conundrum without an answer.
But it might have turned out to be a picture, and in that

99

case we should have blamed the artist for disguising the fact by introducing inescapable irrelevancies.

I have stated the first essentials which I demand, and believe it right to demand, in a picture, and I have pointed the difference between pure painting and illustration. I must now make clear another matter—truth to Nature. The original Pre-Raphaelites and the later Pre-Raphaelism to which Burne-Jones belonged insisted on a copying of Nature as close and accurate as possible. This did not mean, of course, that their pictures must be copies of actually existing scenes, but that every object in their pictures—trees, flowers, human beings—must be faithful, one might even say photographic, copies of these things as seen in the outside world. They would, for instance, utterly have condemned the painting of a face by Matisse or Modigliani, and a landscape by Cézanne or Van Gogh. Also, if they were consistent, they would certainly have condemned the faces painted by those Pre-Raphaelite painters Cimabue and Giotto, and the landscapes of most of the early Italians. But the artists and critics of to-day recognise no obligation to copy Nature. There is no objection to it and no necessity for it. If an artist wishes, he may differ as widely as possible from the photographic aspect of things. Accurate representation of Nature, then, is no longer a criterion of artistic excellence. The realm of visual imagination is free, and recognises no laws but its own.

Having described, as well as I am able, the critical standpoint from which the artist is to be viewed, let me turn to the artist. The first thing that strikes one in a picture by Rubens or Cézanne is the artist's preoccupation with paint and design; the first thing that strikes one in the majority of Burne-Jones's pictures is his preoccupation with the subject—the subject not as form but as story. It is evident, not only from the pictures themselves, but from a mere list of their titles : " King Cophetua and the Beggar Maid," " Clerk Saunders," "Love Among the Ruins," " Love Disguised as Reason," " The Blessed Damosel." " The Merciful Knight." And if that is not enough, we have only to turn to the man himself, his letters and talk, to discover at once his constant preoccupation with romantic literature : the story of the Holy Grail, Malory's *Morte d'Arthur,* the Sagas, Chaucer, Dante, and so on. In a youthful essay he writes : " When shall we learn to read a picture as we do a poem, to find some story from it, some little atom of human interest that may feed our hearts withal, lest the outer influences of the day crush them from good thoughts?" It would be unfair to quote a man's youthful pronouncements as evidence of a permanent attitude, were it not that his later pictures and statements reveal so clearly this cloistered and literary attitude of mind.

Twenty-eight years later he writes in a letter: "All this has eaten up much time; also, to put on the beggar maid a sufficiently beggarly coat, that will not look unappetizing to King Cophetua—that, I hope, has been achieved, so that she shall look as if she deserved to have it made of cloth of gold and set with pearls. I hope the king kept the old one and looked at it now and then." There, too, the preoccupations are purely literary, and let us note, not irrelevantly, in passing, that the beggar maid as she finally appears in the picture might, with the addition merely of shoes and stockings, pass at an evening party to-day as an extremely well-dressed young woman. "Lord!" he wrote in 1898 at the age of sixty-five, "how that San Graal story is ever in my mind and thoughts continually. Was ever anything in the world beautiful as that is beautiful? If I might clear away all the work that I have begun, if I might live and clear it all away, and dedicate the last days to that tale—if only I might." Is it not obvious that at heart Burne-Jones is an illustrator? That, let us remember, recalling Giotto, does not prevent his being a painter; but it does mean that, in considering him as a painter (when I say painter I mean a painter of pictures), we shall often have literary red-herrings drawn across our path.

Take the picture of "King Cophetua and the Beggar Maid." The fact, as I have pointed out, that the Beggar Maid is a beggar maid is a literary fact. It is not in the least apparent in the picture, but it is so in the title and, if we wish to be quite certain about it, we can turn up the story to which the title refers. A less literary artist would have called the picture "Knight and Maiden," and a pure painter would have called it, for the sake merely of identification, "Interior with Figures." That last title would have left us free, unattracted or unrepelled by red-herrings, to regard the picture at once as a picture, namely, as a coloured design.

Before we look at " King Cophetua " as a picture, I must say something of what Burne-Jones calls " finish " in painting. I think that by " finish " he means, in the last analysis, *that quantity of photographic detail without which a picture is not a picture.* Here are some of the things that he said of Whistler's pictures at the Whistler-Ruskin trial: " I think that nothing but perfect finish ought to be allowed by artists, that they should not be content with anything that falls short of what the age acknowledges as essential to perfect work. I have seen the pictures by Mr. Whistler which were produced yesterday in court, and I think the Nocturne in Blue and Silver is a work of art, but a very incomplete one; an admirable beginning, but that it in no sense whatever shows the finish of a complete work of art." Of " Battersea Bridge " he said: " The colour is even better than the other, but it is more formless, and as to the composition and detail, it has neither." " The danger is this," he said on the same occasion, " that if unfinished pictures become common we shall arrive at a stage of mere manufacture, and the art of the country will be degraded." Lady Burne-Jones, in her Memorials of her husband, refers to Impressionism in perfect good faith as " the doctrine of the excellence of unfinished work."

But what is finished, and what is unfinished work? Why is " Battersea Bridge " unfinished and " King Cophetua " finished? This is what Burne-Jones says: " When is a picture finished? Never, I think—and is a symbol of life itself in that way: so when I say it is finished I mean it is cut off and must go away." He used to say, Lady Burne-Jones records, " that it was only the van coming to take it away that finished a picture for him." Apparently, then, one can go on applying " finish " for ever. Yet what can such finish mean but the applying of more and more meticulous detail? And does it not imply that the artist is much more preoccupied with this than with the design as a whole? Certainly one feels this when one confronts the " King Cophetua " itself; for though there is no difficulty here in disregarding its story, we cannot disregard its mass of exquisitely finished detail. The significance of the design is drowned in it. One feels that if the van had come many years earlier, the picture which it rescued from its painter would have been a very much finer one. It seems as if he believed that the quantity of patience and labour expended bore a direct relation to artistic excellence. Was not his friend Ruskin preaching the dignity of labour?

The artist's own feelings when the picture was at last finished are, I believe, a true reaction to it, and not merely the result of a natural physical weariness. " I am very tired of it—I can see nothing any more in it, I have stared it out of all countenance and it has no word for me." Just so. For a picture on which a prodigious amount of labour has been expended by a highly skilled craftsman, it produces, I feel, surprisingly small effect. But if it is not very effective as a picture, it is a marvellous decoration, a marvellous piece of handicraft.

In the same room in the Tate Gallery there is another " King Cophetua " by Burne-Jones, a small one of a totally different design, which some happy chance rescued from completion. Of all his pictures that I have seen it is the most beautiful. Though even an Impressionist would call it unfinished, it reveals Burne-Jones's qualities as an artist—his feeling for design, his sense of rhythm, his beauty of line—much more effectually than any of his finished pictures. There is no distracting detail to smother the design and break up the telling effect of the colour. And what a lovely design it is ! no mere flat pattern, but a strong, beautifully balanced, three-dimensional design with a surprising sense of space. I think it is true to say that " finish," in the sense in which he understood it, is the bane of Burne-Jones's work. If he could have believed that it is no slur on a picture to have been painted in two and a half hours, he would have produced much finer work than he did. But there is a sense in which patience and labour are of infinite value to the artist, and that is, as a means to the technical mastery of his craft. No artist or critic would disagree with him in that. He himself certainly acted up to his belief. His diligence was stupendous, not only in painting his pictures, but in the constant drawing and sketching by which he sought patiently and humbly to perfect his powers. His pencil drawings are miracles of delicate accuracy : I have heard that he never erased, and from the sureness of his touch I can well believe this to be true.

Yet of his pictures I think it would prove to be true that the less time he spent on the painting of them the better they were. Prolonged labour not only overloaded them, it also took the life out of them. In the little water-colour,

" Clara von Borck," in the Tate Gallery, the detail is not over-laboured, and it is strictly subordinated to the design. The result is alive and instinct with movement. Who Clara von Borck was I have no idea, but the reference does not matter. The little picture is a picture, not an illustration. Take another in the same gallery, " The Nine Muses on Mount Helicon." The spacing of the simple, unadorned figures in a bare landscape skilfully produces a delightful three-dimensional design. It is not the Muses on Helicon, it is figures in a landscape ; and, in any case, the Muses on Mount Helicon is not a story, it is a fact ; therefore the artist was not distracted from his task by the irrelevant interest of literature. That interest, like his craze for " finish," is a dangerous and often fatal influence. We deprecate it wherever it occurs in his work, but we cannot ignore it in our judgment of him ; and, as we consider it, it gives us the key to the surprisingly unstimulating effect of Burne-Jones's paintings. For the stories he loved and illustrated were wistful tales of the remote past. Not only this, but he expressed them, not in the various spirits of their various authors, but in the one, uniform, sad, other-worldly spirit which was his own invariable mood as an artist. His people are gently tearful or, at best, palely calm. Everybody is young, joyless, and feminine. The skies and seasons are calm, the weather neither hot nor cold, and, except in a very few pictures, everybody, everything is absolutely static. The wind that whirled those draperies into spirals ceased to blow before the picture was painted, and the draperies have ceased to whirl, and hang suspended, frozen into immobility. The girls in " The Golden Stairs " will never get downstairs. His pictures are one sweet, melancholy puppet-show, and when he achieves something like tragic intensity, as in his " Death of Orpheus," he surprises us by his unlikeness to himself. Though he went back to the painters of the Italian Renaissance, his mood is utterly alien from their sunny humanity : it was only their forms that influenced him. When he designs stained-glass windows (windows beautiful in design and colour) for Gothic churches, their gentle beauty is as remote as it could be from the grim force of the Gothic spirit. In his pictures and the people that inhabit them vitality is reduced to the lowest pressure.

It is worth noting that all that I have just said of the spirit of his pictures has to-day an inevitable note of disparagement, although I have tried merely to state facts. The reason is that we of to-day have reacted violently from that spirit. We are interested in contemporary life: we do not—though goodness knows we would have good excuse for doing so—seek refuge in dim Edens of the past. Yet most, if not all, of what I have said would have implied no disparagement at all to the majority of Burne-Jones's contemporaries. For them I should have been describing a singularly beautiful and poetic spirit. But it is undeniable that his mood, beautiful or repellent, is extremely narrow, so narrow that it is astonishing that he should have lived in it throughout a long life and expressed it in such profusion. For those that love the mood, the profusion is, perhaps, welcome: for those alien to it, it becomes excessively cloying. From either point of view it must be apparent that he allowed his prolific fancy to beguile him into expression far too easily. Far too large a proportion of his work consists of visions and fancies too tenuous to be worth expressing: his immense fluency of invention results in a serious lack of tensity. We hear of the young artist and his friend William Morris carrying with them to Oxford " the banner of Art and Revolt," and it is hardly credible to us to-day that this quiet, gentle art could be a revolt against anything. But it was a revolt, none the less, and a valuable and successful one, against the ugliness of industrialism and the apathy of the Victorians to the hideousness of their homes and their furnishing and decorating of public buildings and churches. It was, no doubt, the absence of beauty in the life about him that drove Burne-Jones into his dim other-world, and forced him to over-beautify his pictures.

It would be possible, I believe, to collect in one room twenty or thirty of his best pictures, which would show him to be a much more considerable painter than we at present hold him to be; but even so, we cannot for a moment, as the Victorians did, rank him as a great painter. He is a great decorator, a great handicraftsman and, within the narrow limits of his mood, a great illustrator. As Meier-Graefe says in his *Modern Art*: "Burne-Jones always contrives to make a picture of some kind. His song, though slight, is true. There is an unfailing rhythmical beauty in his figures." Yet when we disentangle our heads from the veils of his myth and legend and look out on the world in which he lived, we discover to our amazement that Cézanne, Manet, Monet, and Renoir were his strict contemporaries. To visit the Pre-Raphaelite rooms in the Tate Gallery immediately after the Modern French section is to receive, with deadly effect, the most direct criticism of Burne-Jones and his fellows as pure artists. Their revolt seems to us now little more than a regrettable act of insubordination in a convent. A few of the votaries, it seems, broke out; but they immediately built themselves another convent, in which they found permanent protection from the grosser world of painting that rioted about them.

SAMUEL
BUTLER

1835-1902

BY
H. C.
O'NEILL

H. C. O'NEILL

SAMUEL BUTLER

TOWARDS the close of his life in 1902 Samuel Butler wrote a list of his " finds." It is a strange document; but it has this value: it presents a fairly complete picture of the Victorian period in its tenets and in its temperament. It is not, of course, a direct picture. It is the obverse of the medal that appears in Butler. Of the instinctive reactions of the two classes into which the thinking minority of mankind can be divided, his was the critical rather than the appreciative. To every complacency of the Victorian period his mind reacted sharply. He not only riddled each, severally: he exploded the whole temperament. He grew up into a world which was supremely content with its outlook, social, theological, scientific, musical, artistic, and literary. " Logic is like the sword," he wrote. " Those who appeal to it shall perish by it." And he wrote to Charles Darwin that one of his most ingenious and provocative ideas was developed " for mere fun, and because it amused me." He wished, he said, to imply: " See how easy it is to be plausible, and what absurd propositions can be defended by a little ingenuity and distortion and departure from strictly scientific methods."

This was, of course, the unforgivable sin. But a certain impish perversity drove him on. He might have been forgiven differing from accepted opinion on some points. No absolution was possible for one who differed upon so many. Still less was it tolerable that he should deny the validity of the mental processes by means of which such opinions were sustained. He wrote quite sanely but equally strongly of the insufficiency of reason; and the Victorian Age prided itself upon nothing so much as the dependableness of the

foundation of its system. To the dogmatic statements upon
one subject or another he opposed equally dogmatic
counter-statements; but whereas the majority of those he
attacked were content with their conviction, his views were
tentative, suspensory, subject to revision.

There is a complete opposition between these types of
mind; and Butler was at least desperately serious about
that. If he established one thing in the career he regarded as
something of a failure, it was the supreme and vital necessity for *life* in thought. He first fell foul, very early in the
career which his decision shaped, of the accepted theological position. It was not a very mature criticism.
Indeed, it is the fact that his serious attacks upon the
current religious views have much less ground for consideration than the refined irony in *Erewhon* and *Erewhon
Revisited*. But having rejected the Established Church in
its then impressive position, he was determined by all the
gods not to allow the establishment of another orthodoxy
in the place of the old. It was much less this or that tenet
he objected to than the mere infirmity of the vast majority
of all minds to economize thought by a series of arrests.
Hence he drifted quite naturally from some mild satiric
comment upon the superficial aspects of "Darwinism"
into a long, subtle, sustained onslaught upon the very
stronghold of the biology of his day.

In his account of his finds, six are scientific, one-third of
the total; and in the most important of them, the "exposure
and discomfiture of Charles Darwin and Wallace and their
followers," he was more right than wrong. Of the painful
personal encounter he had with Darwin it is necessary to
say little. Butler had grave cause for complaint. But he
made far too much of it; and it was felt that he fought too
bitterly. The disclosed complaint, serious as it was, was
not the real ground. He thought himself contemptuously
elbowed out of the company of those whose scientific
opinions had to be seriously considered. He was quite
right. Even in those days, when the experimental side of
science was in its infancy, the systematic scientist had no
respect for the *amateur*. But to Butler this attitude was
gall; and he had much of it to drink before he died. It is
perhaps true that he attacked a crude Darwinism; but it is
at least as true that the biologists of the day saw only a
crude Lamarckism.

Butler derived from *The Origin of Species* the impression

that evolution and natural selection were practically the same thing. Such a reading owed almost everything to the jubilant reception of Darwin's work, since the author was at pains to point out that natural selection was the " main but not the exclusive " means of modification. But this misconception had a profound effect upon Butler. In four books, dealing with one aspect of evolution or another, he restored to general circulation such honourable names as Buffon, Lamarck, and Erasmus Darwin, and showed that the idea of evolution, and much speculation as to its mechanism, were antecedent to Charles Darwin. The idea of evolution is, of course, as old as Aristotle. But Butler's misconception as to the claim of *The Origin of Species* produced, in *Evolution Old and New,* the best account extant of the views of Buffon, Erasmus Darwin, and Lamarck. This, however, was not his most important contribution to the subject. He saw quite clearly that Darwin held the main means of the modification of species to be extrinsic and undesigned. Upon both grounds he " exposed " Darwin. He insisted that the modification of species must depend upon intrinsic reasons, and that design must be restored to the world.

The four books in which he set forth his own views of evolution, *Life and Habit* (1877), *Evolution Old and New* (1879), *Unconscious Memory* (1880), and *Luck or Cunning* (1887), suggest in their titles the main points of the theory by which his actual scientific contribution must be measured. Names and terms are of little value in assessing it. The initiate may contend that he was a Lamarckian. It may be admitted, without advancing the discussion appreciably. As against Darwin, what he held was that by an inherent cunning the cell controls its destiny, and that useful habits, stored in unconscious memory, are transmitted.

There can be no doubt that time has avenged the neglect of Butler by his contemporaries. Even before his death, the idea of unconscious memory, independently put forward by Hering, was fathered by some of the most orthodox biologists ; and Francis Darwin made some amends upon this point later on. There cannot be two serious opinions as to whether the origin of specific modification is intrinsic or extrinsic. Any difference there may be is reducible to a question of terms. As to the choice between design and chance, the scientist logically cannot hesitate, and whether the shaping agent be called cunning or will matters nothing. The main battle over his opinions has always revolved about the question of the " inheritance of acquired characters." For two generations it has been impossible for the student to maintain this obvious proposition without suffering a scientific ostracism. At the present moment, however, the battle has apparently been won. Lamarck is now being read more carefully. It is realized that " habit " must be substituted for the term " character "; and, as MacBride says, " There is abundant experimental evidence for the effect of acquired habits on the next generation."

It says much for Butler that, in this long and difficult discussion, he saw in what direction the truth lay. He never did justice to the theory which Darwin advanced, and it is quite possible that the next generation will similarly depreciate the principle of Natural Selection. But he most generously admitted the services of Darwin. " To the end of time," he wrote, " if the question be asked, ' Who taught people to believe in evolution ? ' the answer must be that it was Mr. Darwin. This is true, and it is hard to see what palm of higher praise can be awarded to any philosopher."

The point which must be realized is that Butler was not, in the general acceptance of the term, a man of science. It is useless to rail at this use of the term or at the inevitable result of it. Only those who have not had a scientific training minimize its immense advantage. And those who rail loudest at the refusal of the scientists of his day to accept Butler at his own valuation make their own economies in mental effort. One does not seriously discuss the theory of idealism with the yokel, however developed his natural logical ability. But this ready reckoner, by which everyone calculates, takes no account of the entirely exceptional, and it is for this reason that Butler is only gradually coming into his own.

When he began to write about Darwin he was a sheep farmer ; and in his first recognition of Darwin's work, he was accepted as a friend, and even stayed at Down. In point of fact, Butler had some family connection with Darwin. His father had been at school with Erasmus Darwin, and Charles must have known of Butler's early history. It was far from what then and now would be accepted as the training of a scientist. Samuel Butler, born in 1835, came of clerical stock. His father was the Rev. Thomas Butler and his grandfather Dr. Samuel

Butler, Headmaster of Shrewsbury School and later Bishop of Lichfield. He was himself destined for the Church, had the training of a clergyman, and worked under one of the curates of St. James's, Piccadilly, in preparation for Ordination. It was owing to his doubts that he declined to be ordained, and returned to Cambridge hoping, ultimately, for a Fellowship. And it was when that hope seemed to fail that, after some trouble with his father, he at length went out to New Zealand and set up a sheep farm.

There is nothing in this that suggests the man of science. On the contrary, he was a first-rate Classical Scholar, and was twelfth in the first class of the Tripos. Not classics, nor theology, nor sheep farming suggests either the temperament or training of the man of science. But it is significant that in 1862, he contributed, unsigned, to the Press "Darwin on the Origin of Species. A Dialogue." He was, at this time, only twenty-seven years of age. He had had the conventional training of a gentleman, and was at the moment engaged in the pursuit, unconventional for a gentleman, of sheep farming; and yet he is found taking to writing—scientific writing—as though to the manner born. That one thing stamped him as exceptional. And there came from his pen, in the following year, a characteristic letter, "Darwin among the Machines." The next year he sold his sheep run, returned to England, and entered upon a mode of life which persisted to the end. He began seriously to study painting; and, as seriously, resumed that series of letters, pamphlets, and books, in which one side of his life found expression.

It is remarkable that, at this early stage of his career, he had begun to trifle with the thought, which he notes among his finds, of "emphasizing the analogies between the development of the organs of our bodies and of those which are not incorporate with our bodies and which we call tools or machines." And a few years later there appeared the book, which is still his best-known work, *Erewhon, or over the Range*. His friend and biographer calls his memoir, *Samuel Butler, Author of Erewhon,* and there is much more justice in the apposition than at first appears, for in *Erewhon* almost all that was characteristic of Butler appears either in germ or fully developed. The impulse that drove him to find expression in art is suggested in a few pages of admirable description. The main body of his social criticism is to be found there. His early comment upon the

F

Darwinian theory of evolution has its place. His criticism of religion finds a voice. There is even a suggestion of his love of music in the Handel motif of the guardian images. And above all there is a satire, already a finely sharpened weapon, which he used to the end of his life for the suggestion of his views.

Erewhon is, of course, the least coherent of his works, and yet, in many ways, it remains the most readable, stimulating, and suggestive. Up to three years before his death, it had sold more than all his other books put together. It is not difficult to find a reason for this preference. In the account of his sales, Butler does not include *Erewhon Revisited,* which appeared the year before his death; and, apart from this, only one of his books had so good a chance of acceptance. It is a little difficult to understand why *Alps and Sanctuaries,* which appeared only eight years after *Erewhon,* should have achieved only one-twelfth of its sale. When Butler cast up his accounts, only 332 copies of this book had been sold, and it represented a loss of £110 in his balance-sheet. And yet it has a lightness and charm that are absent from all his other books. Butler was at his best in Italy. At home he was always in reaction to an environment that he felt oppressive, even though he gave it a wide berth. In Italy he was a tolerant, tolerable, courteous gentleman, and his fun tended to be real fun and not the vitriolic wit he vented upon his own race.

Erewhon is a satire on the life and thought of his time. Mr. Birrell mentioned *Gulliver's Travels* in connection with it; but Swift's was a compact, coherent work. *Erewhon* was the result of a number of pieces of criticism thrown together in book form. Three chapters of it, " The Book of the Machines," were based upon his earliest extant writing. A considerable amount of it deals with the current system of education. Some of it, the " emphasizing the analogies between crime and disease," apparently the most fanciful, has long since passed into current thought. But it was written with so much ingenuity and daring that it still seems irresistibly amusing. The trial of a consumptive for " labouring under pulmonary consumption " will never be forgotten. The prisoner pleaded not guilty, and his counsel urged that the man was " simulating consumption in order to defraud an insurance company, from which he was about to buy an annuity, and that he hoped thus to obtain it on more advantageous terms. If this could have been shown to be the case, he would have escaped a criminal prosecution, and been sent to a hospital as for a moral ailment.'' The case, however, was only too clear, '' for the prisoner was almost at the point of death, and it was astonishing that he had not been tried and convicted long previously. His coughing was incessant during the whole trial, and it was all that the two jailers in charge of him could do to keep him on his legs until it was over.'' He was found guilty, and the Judge, in the preamble to sentence, said he could only conclude that the man's distressing condition was due to a ' radically vicious ' constitution. He had already been convicted of ' aggravated bronchitis.' He was sentenced to imprisonment, with hard labour, for the rest of his ' miserable existence.'

The '' fun and naughtiness '' which he admitted in much of *Erewhon* had in this and other passages a deeply serious purpose. '' The Musical Banks '' were a satire upon religion, as were '' The Colleges of Unreason '' upon the educational system. But it is strange that the book, launched on the book-buying public under the mistaken notion that it was by Lord Lytton, should have found as many readers as it did. Butler announced his responsibility for the book, and the demand fell 90 per cent. From Lytton the public could tolerate the unintelligible it would not stand from a nobody.

There is one line which Butler opened up in *Erewhon* that deserves more attention. Religion was a ruling interest in his life. He seemed, indeed, to be hag-ridden by it to the end of his days. Whatever he might say of it, he could not exorcise its influence from his life. His writing is steeped in the language of the Bible and the Book of Common Prayer. Up to the very last he was still engaged in attempting to kill the hateful, obsessing thing. *Erewhon Revisited,* which appeared in the year before his death, is, perhaps, the most biting satire upon Christianity that has appeared since the mediæval *Passiones*. The thought is suggestive. Still more pertinent it is that only one out of his eighteen '' finds '' is theological. This is how he states it himself: '' The clearing up the history of the events in connection with the death, or rather crucifixion, of Jesus Christ, and a reasonable explanation, first, of the belief of the founders of Christianity that their Master had risen from the dead and, secondly, of what might follow from belief in a single supposed miracle.'' He notes three refer-

ences, *The Evidence for the Resurrection of Jesus Christ,
The Fair Haven*, and *Erewhon Revisited*; but the last,
being a finished piece of satire, and not a direct attack, is
far the most damaging. *The Fair Haven*, an ironical work,
is built upon an earlier MS.; and the theme recurs in *A
Clergyman's Doubts* and *God the Known and the Unknown*. In the event, the force of his criticism falls more
upon the practice than the theory of Christianity, and it is
notable that he showed real appreciation for simple religious
people.

Butler left a novel, *The Way of all Flesh*, which was
published after his death. It is a full canvas, but painted
with the brushwork of a miniaturist. It has had the wildest
praise lavished upon it, and there can be little doubt that
it is a great piece of literature. But the real foundation of
it is, admittedly, too near autobiography to be judged as
pure fiction; and taken as some picture of the truth, it is
deeply cruel. It is a satire upon English life in the mid-
Victorian period; and, as it was on the stocks for at least
twelve years, each stroke is well weighed. But it is gross
caricature, and the picture of his home life under his
parents ("Theobald" and "Christina") is pitiless.

It has nevertheless been taken as illustrating, by its truth,
the philosophy of the relations of parent and child. This
is sheer moonshine. Butler could no more depict the normal
than he could be interested in it; and anyone who imagines
that the son was an entirely trustworthy witness on his
parents had better study his life. He was, in fact, a prickly
person, always prone to the most immature reactions to the
company which he recognized ranked high in other people's
estimation. He writes completely contradictory statements
on the sort of tuition he received from his father: nothing
but that forceful method could have made him learn such
a Latin grammar, he could learn nothing at all under force.
He made the most arrogant demands from life. He must
be maintained in a certain minimum comfort to do just
what he pleased, although, in fact, it was costly rather than
lucrative. It was a congenial source of merriment between
him and his friends to caricature the behaviour of his
parents and relations. To take his account of his parents'
behaviour towards him, or even the behaviour itself, as
typical, is to take the exception for the rule; and the
majority of readers will find *The Way of all Flesh* to be
rather heavy going for this reason if for no other. But it is

116

full of good things if one will but take them with at least
a modicum of that rational care the necessity of which
Butler urged continually.

There are some other sides of Butler's activity which
must be considered if one is to appraise him justly. He
made an ingenious case for a feminine authorship of the
Odyssey, which he tried to prove was written at Trapani.
The attempt fell flat. Moreover, he translated the *Iliad*
and the *Odyssey* into " Tottenham Court Road English."
Alas! even Tottenham Court Road proved insufficient
gilding for such a pill. He also " elucidated " Shakespeare's sonnets—ingenious, penetrating, and—like *The
Authoress of the Odyssey*—small beer. Moreover, he wrote
some verse, sonnets in the irregular mode, and the joyous
" O God! O Montreal! " which is still his sole passport
to the hospitality of many.

However one may regard him, he was an extraordinary
man. He had the scholar's aptitude and technique for
co-opting new faculties. At forty-three he began to learn
German, and in six months had a real working knowledge
of it. Three years later he learned book-keeping by double
entry. Each was useful; and he characteristically added
them without any fuss. Upon his return from New
Zealand he set himself to the serious study of Art. He had
about a dozen pictures shown in the Academy, and one,
" Mr. Heatherley's Holiday," was hung upon the line,
and is now in the Tate Gallery. Art, in fact, represented
a necessary outlet. Five of his " finds " are purely artistic :
the discovery of portraits of the Bellinis, the identification
of Holbein drawings, the finding of a statue of Leonardo
by Ferrari, and so on.

With the same competent ability he set about the study
of music later on, and in " Narcissus," a cantata in the
Handelian form, and " Ulysses," he claimed, with his
friend and biographer H. F. Jones, to " return to the
principles of Handel and take them up where he left off."
Music, also, was a necessity of his well-being.

He looks, at this point, something of a dilettante. In
truth he was. But he was the rarest of all dilettantists, the
dilettante equipped with the finest weapons, extraordinary
ability sharpened by hard training and uncommon powers
of concentration. From his return to England he lived in
Clifford's Inn, and in time gathered about him a little circle
of congenial friends. One of these, Eliza Mary Ann Savage,

was, from his first acquaintance with her, his most faithful friend and literary adviser. It was an odd relationship. The Temple, looking down, saw an intercourse after its own heart—cold, egotistical, inconclusive, and entirely profitable upon one side. Even Butler felt some compunction in looking back upon that episode, and noted that he could not read some of her letters unmoved. Only a heart of stone could have been unmoved at the spontaneous, ingenuous, unguarded words to which Butler felt himself unable to reply in the sense desired. He owed an immense debt to her criticisms of his work, and he used her services fully and freely.

In person Butler gave the lie direct to his real quality. He looked commonplace, undistinguished; and dressed the part. He might have been a small grocer, with a little house-property. (He *had* house-property! Does it revenge itself on its possessor?) With his brick-dust complexion he suggested, perhaps a little more, a sailor, a master-mariner of, say, a coasting steamer. His *vera effigies* is in the portrait gallery, so that one can verify this impression. He looked, in fine, everything he was not. In congenial company he was apt to be voluble, and the brilliant stream of his conversation shot forth continuous stimuli, like those electrical gadgets which the experimental physiologist uses to produce tetany. He was kindly, courteous, ingenuous in his generosity, and liable, as in one amazing instance, to be thoroughly humbugged. He was a good Tory, and had the happy and sound conviction that "few Radicals have good digestions." He was most lavish in his dislikes. He disliked Leonardo, Pater, Renan, Lamb, Carlyle, the Brontës, George Eliot, Blake, Dante, Virgil, Tennyson, and so many more that a list becomes wearisome.

It is well to remember these human foibles in a man of genius. He was certainly that. He has to his credit some real and important achievements in science; and, in sociology, so much of his thought has passed into the background that it is extremely difficult to disentangle his contribution. In his *Notebooks*, surely a unique legacy, he left something more. Not a page, scarcely a paragraph, hardly a line that is not full of stimulus. Much of it is, as he would say, naughty. "An honest God's the noblest work of man." "Jesus, with all Thy faults, I love Thee still." "We want a Society for the suppression of Erudite

Research." " *De minimis non curat veritas.*" " If a man
is not a good, sound, honest, capable liar, there is no truth
in him." These are but the froth of his work. And there
is a certain lees. Many of this generation have drunk of
this heady mixture to their own hurt. But in between
there is a golden fluid which is food and drink and the
light of the mind.

THOMAS
CARLYLE
1795-1881

BY
A. WYATT
TILBY

F*

THOMAS CARLYLE

"CARLYLE," said Froude in the final words of the great biography of his master, "made an eternal memorial for himself in the hearts of all to whom truth is the dearest of possessions." Allowing for the exaggeration of farewell, this means that everybody who matters ought to read Carlyle, as everybody who matters has read Isaiah and St. Paul and the Four Gospels—not because of their literary style, but because, in the opinion of competent judges, these works contain truths which the world cannot do without, and which it cannot find elsewhere.

It is a high claim to be one of the major prophets, and the fifty years since Carlyle's death have dealt rather hardly with it and with him. His *French Revolution,* of course, is definitely a popular work; no series of cheap reprints is complete without it. But in spite of the post-war interest in dictators, *Cromwell* is certainly less read than it was. As for *Frederick,* I happen to have read it myself—the whole thirteen volumes, during a winter in Germany. But I have never met anybody else, whether in Germany or England, who has read it from cover to cover; nor am I likely ever to tackle it a second time. Immortal masterpiece or not, the book is definitely far too long.

The minor works, though less of a tax on leisure, seem to be going the same way. *Past and Present* remains an admirable interpretation of the Middle Ages; but the Victorian Radicalism of this piece and the *Latter-day Pamphlets* is now strangely archaic. The problems are still with us, but that particular treatment of them is old-fashioned. *Heroes and Hero-worship* survived the New

History; I doubt if it will permanently survive the New Psychology. As for *Sartor Resartus,* its unhappy fate is now to be set as a holiday-task by schoolmasters to adolescent youth; and it is safe to say that no ordinary schoolboy can make head or tail of it.

If Carlyle, then, is one of the immortals, he seems to be gradually approaching the numerous and respectable company of those who are much praised and little read, rather than joining the small and select band of stars in the literary heaven who are not appreciably dimmed by time and distance. Milton and Wordsworth and, I imagine, Browning belong to the former category; Sophocles and Shakespeare and, I suppose, Dante to the latter.

This distinction between survival as shadow and survival as substance is not, of course, entirely a question of merit. Few students of the nineteenth century would deny that Carlyle was at bottom a greater man than Macaulay. Yet the famous Edinburgh Reviewer is still read by everybody who reads anything at all of serious literature, while it is no longer a disgrace to confess ignorance of the protests and prophesyings of Ecclefechan.

For this neglect there is more than one reason.

In the first place, of course, the style of Carlyle is obscure. It is not merely that the frequent inversions of substantive and predicate are as awkward in English as a left shoe on a right foot; it is the general helter-skelter and rumble-tumble, the invocations and objurgations and repetitions that bother even the appreciative reader. Much of this, no doubt, is due to the over-emphasis which was habitual in Carlyle's conversation as well as in his writing (he once confessed that he was not actually dying every time he cried " Murder ! "). But over-emphasis and exaggeration are themselves a sure sign that one is uncertain of one's position—it is an attempt to silence doubt by shouting, as the damnatory clauses of a creed are an attempt to silence doubt by threat.

Language is, after all, simply a method of conveying thought, and when the language is obscure, it is almost always a tacit admission that the thought behind the language is uncertain of itself. Macaulay never wrote a sentence whose meaning is doubtful, because that clear and superficial mind was cocksure about everything. Carlyle often wrote whole paragraphs, and occasionally whole pages, which are at once over-emphasized in content and obscure in conclusion. As a piece of literature it is, therefore, unsatisfactory, even though the actual treatment of the subject shows that a greater mind is here at work, which is at any rate more aware of the problem as a whole, and not merely as the cross-section that Macaulay had envisaged.

But this brings us to the second reason why Carlyle is less read to-day than in his lifetime. The fact is that, tricks of speech and style apart, there is a definite contradiction in his outlook and attitude towards life and the external world which has gradually reduced his influence.

It does not, of course, really matter that the Carlyle who was always appealing to the Eternal Silences was one of the most loquacious talkers and prolific writers of a loquacious and prolific age. It is not really important that the man whose trade was words affected to despise oratory and rhetoric, and exalted men of action—and more especially men of violent action, like Danton and Cromwell and Frederick—above men of contemplation and research. These inconsistencies may happen to anybody who writes or talks for a living, and they are as venial a sin as the parson's, who prays for humility and dreams of an archbishopric.

What does really matter is a deeper and in fact fundamental cleavage in the Carlyle philosophy. He was, for example, a Radical in politics, but he always believed in authority. He was an iconoclast in religion, but he distrusted the clergy who would have followed him in modernizing the doctrines of Christianity. (" There goes Dean Stanley, boring holes in the bottom of the Church of England.") He believed in moral, not material, progress, with the result that he derided, denied, and distrusted science ; but at the same time he failed to think out his own moral principles to a final conclusion, with the result that thousands of his readers thought he exalted Might above Right, until he was driven to protest that in his opinion it was Right itself that made Might. The protest was, of course, sincere, but it is significant of a muddled presentation that it had to be made.

It is probably no more than coincidence that throughout his married life Carlyle either neglected or fratched with his wife when they were together, and regularly fell in love with her again as soon as they were separated for a few days. But this in itself suggests a difficult and contentious personality, ill-adjusted to its environment whether natural or self-acquired; and it must be remembered that the fifty eventful years from 1820 to 1870 which covered the active life of Carlyle presented quite exceptional strains and stresses to a character of this type.

The idea is abroad to-day that the Victorian Age was a prolonged period of static peace. Never was a greater delusion. The first three-fourths of the nineteenth century were years of industrial revolution, of economic and therefore social change, political readjustment, scientific discovery, and religious disputation. It was only in the last quarter of the century that these various movements diminished for a time, and thus gave rise to the superstition of a quiescent epoch in which men lived and worked, but did not think.

We must visualize Carlyle against this background of intense activity and continued secular and spiritual change, or we shall not visualize him at all.

Carlyle, like all men of large vision, sought the eternal verities. Unluckily these are not as a rule readily discoverable in current temporal values, and this is more particularly the case when temporal values are themselves in process of rapid change. Whether we like it or not, we are all influenced by environment, and changed conditions mean changed social and individual values.

The transition from a rural to an urban basis of life, which was the outstanding feature of nineteenth-century civilization, was bound to affect the structure of society from top to bottom. As a minor economic point, it manifestly reduced the part played by production and increased the part played by distribution in the world of commerce; as a major political point, the mere compulsion of physical contiguity in town and city necessarily modified the older social environment of countryside and village. The crowd does, after all, limit the bodily freedom of the individual, and it does not necessarily enlarge his mental freedom; a relevant fact which the estimable John Stuart Mill—whom Carlyle, as pitiless to friend as foe, once compared to sawdust—naturally failed to observe when he wrote his celebrated treatise on Liberty.

To Carlyle himself, a country-bred man whose profession demanded residence in a great city, the limitation of space and the consequent limitation of opportunities for physical exercise were a harmful influence. Hence, no doubt, some of the dyspeptic thunders of Chelsea; we shall not, I think, go far astray if we regard these outbursts simply as nostalgia for the beloved Ecclefechan.

Further, the transition from a rural to an urban basis of life was bound to change manners; and manners, after all, are simply morals *in petto*. Kant's Categorical Imperative and Carlyle's Everlasting Yea might be true as a whole, but analysis and observation showed more than sufficient local and temporary exceptions to embarrass the universal affirmative. In ethics, then, as in economics the eternal verities were somewhat to seek in an age of social and political transition; and it was Carlyle's peculiar misfortune as a prophet that he could find neither comfort nor enlightenment in art, religion, or science.

He was too nearly a poet to have been ever a philistine, but his attitude to painting and music was simply that of the impercipient; there is no indication that he was aware of the age in which he lived as one of the great creative periods of art—outside England. Yet the name of Chopin surely stands for as much as that of Carlyle; while Wagner's rendering of the love of Tristan and the renunciation of Parsifal has moved the world more deeply than Carlyle's splendid battle-pieces of the victories of Frederick the Great.

Towards all the rival and competitive forms of Christianity Carlyle was frankly critical and often contemptuous. He had rejected in youth the formal logic of his native Presbyterianism, but he retained till death its intense preoccupation with original sin and the problem of evil. Common sense compelled him to refuse the later religious extravagances and enthusiasms of his unfortunate friend Edward Irving, whose gift of tongues first edified and then amused the metropolis. And the Oxford Movement, with its longing, backward look at the Middle Ages, which stamped itself upon the Church of England and even to some extent influenced the mind of England during the thirty years of Carlyle's maturity, meant nothing whatever to him. Keble was merely "a little ape," and Newman had "the intellect of a rabbit." Even allowing for the habitual exaggeration of Carlyle's table-talk (which poured forth in cataracts oddly at variance with his adoration in print of the strong, silent man), these misjudgments were merely grotesque.

It seems at first sight strange that Carlyle should have

had much the same contemptuous attitude towards the new science as towards the old religion; for science was in fact transforming the industrial and social life of the nation, and was soon to change its mental approach towards almost every problem and principle of the past. It is not necessary to dispute Carlyle's view, that moral progress is everything and material progress is nothing; but it is at least a relevant comment that the mere bald statement as it stands is so incomplete as to be misleading. Material changes do in fact affect and modify moral attitudes; and even on Carlyle's own doctrine, that the truth is the only thing that counts, the exclusion of any form of truth must be a sin against the light.

Yet here his position was clearly defined among the obscurantists, in a curious and even comical chronological declension of honour that is almost a caricature of conservatism. He honoured Kepler, he thought considerably less of Newton, he derided Faraday, and he sneered at Lyell and Darwin. The older the brew the better the vintage is no doubt an excellent rule in most things, but in this connection it is simply untrue.

" Science, as the understanding of things worth knowing, was once a far different matter from this melancholy maundering and idle looking into the unknowable, and apparently the not worth knowing." This misjudgment of contemporary geology and biology is as grotesque and as foolish as was his misjudgment of the contemporary Oxford Movement: it simply shows that prejudice had limited and consequently distorted his values. But it is even more significant than his dissent from the new Anglicanism of the Tractarians; for the sneer in fact conceals a fear that the theory of Evolution might turn out to be right. But in that case a great deal of Carlyle's philosophy would turn out to be wrong.

Carlyle, then, could find the ultimate verities he sought neither in old tradition nor new discovery. And the reason is simple. In the last analysis, religion and science both place their ultimate standards outside and far above humanity: " What is man, that thou art mindful of him ? " is common ground to David and Darwin. But Carlyle, for all his protests and prophesyings of the Eternal, was a pure humanist. Man was the measure of his universe, and absolute truth for him must therefore be expressed in moral values and none other.

This exclusively moral standpoint helps to explain the apparent contradiction, so curious to a later generation, in Carlyle's political philosophy, which made him both a Radical and an advocate of authority. It is easy to show that in his case the two opposites were simply different sides of the same face.

In the famous Edinburgh address, which was virtually his last public act, Carlyle affirmed that the age (which to most men of that day seemed a constructive and even a creative period) was one of anarchy and disintegration; and since he could not share the easy optimism of those who believed that a time of spreading bricks and mortar, of increasing wealth and segregated poverty would automatically solve its own problems by some unexplained process of enlightened self-interest, he regarded the outlook as definitely evil.[1]

It is an open question, too large for argument here, whether self-interest, as the guiding rule of life, is antisocial or not; at any rate it has not so far produced the perfect political equation in any State. That being so, there was clearly something to be said for Carlyle's doctrine that reform was necessary, or evil was bound to increase automatically as population grew. But since the majority of men, according to him, were foolish and incapable of reforming themselves, far less of reforming the State which tolerated the abuses and inequities of human society, what was done must be done for them. In a word, they must be led—or driven—to take the right path; and it is clear that men can only be led or driven by some recognized authority or leader who can persuade—or force —them to obey.

From this it is but a step to the Great Man theory of history, which the Radical Carlyle maintained against the Liberals, who believed in liberty, and equally against the Conservatives, who disliked the Great Man's mission to reform society; and it is manifestly only two, or at the most three, steps from the Superman theory with which Nietzsche impressed the Germans a little later.

[1] Perhaps the clearest statement of the optimist standpoint, with which Carlyle emphatically disagreed, was made by his friend Emerson: " Give no bounties. Make equal laws. Secure life and property, and you need not give alms. Open the doors of opportunity to talent and virtue, and they will do themselves justice; and property will be in good hands."

The heroic or Great Man theory of history has one considerable advantage over the rival and opposite theories of democracy and mass-action: at its best, it ensures unity against division of purpose, and therefore it can point to definite results, and frequently to spectacular results, whereas democracy often means a mere conflict of wills that precludes effective mass-action. But in practice, and particularly in the long run, this dictator business is subject to such grave deductions that as a permanent solution of the intractable problems of human government it can hardly be considered much more successful.

Neither Carlyle nor Nietzsche, in fact, for all their argument and rhetoric, went to the roots of the matter. The truth is not in the least that men will not follow leaders: all gregarious animals in fact do so, and since man (like other animals) usually follows the line of least resistance, the majority of men are always ready to follow those who are better equipped, or more forceful and successful than themselves. The actual trouble is more complicated and difficult.

In the first place, the Great Man is not great enough for the job. Alexander was hardly more than a world-show-man and died prematurely, Cæsar failed to carry his friends or control his enemies in Rome and was assassinated, Napoleon towered and fell.

In the second place, the Great Man cannot provide for the succession. Richard Cromwell loses what Oliver has gained. The indecision of Louis XVI dissipates the policy of Louis XIV. Bethmann-Hollweg muddles away what Bismarck has achieved.

And in the third place, men often fail to recognize their leaders when they see them. The man who founds a State is visible to all, because he works in concrete symbols of power that cannot be ignored. The man who founds a Church may be despised and rejected by the majority, because he works in ideas and not in force; but the time may come when his Church, which is the creation of an idea, destroys the Empire, which is the result of a fact. And finally, the man who makes a new discovery in applied or abstract science may not even be despised but simply ignored; yet in time this leader, who is not even recognized as a leader at all, may undermine both Church and State, because he deals in the high explosive which men call truth, and which is greater than the physical forces which men control, and greater even than the mental ideas which men conceive.

Progress may come from one source or any source, but the mid-nineteenth century, as it happens, could not be expected either to believe in Carlyle's radical-authoritarian theories or to analyse their weakness. It believed, indeed, in progress as a law of nature—which it is not—but since 1848 it had lost faith in revolution, by 1870 it was beginning to lose faith in Radicalism, and before the century was out it had lost some of its faith in reform.

Optimism, the natural result of easy conditions and an expanding material civilization, was in the air of the eighteen-sixties and seventies. The prosperous Victorian really believed Browning's *non sequitur* of " God's in His Heaven—all's right with the world "; and Tennyson's noble falsehood, that " We needs must love the highest when we see it," was acclaimed as a splendid but a simple truth. Such an age, in such a mood, could easily accept the theory that if only you let things alone, all things (including even evil) would work together for good in the long run; and to such an age, in such a mood, Carlyle's insistent proclamation of the reality of evil and the necessity of reform could be no more than an astringent but beneficial tonic.

Southey, the simple Tory, and Cobbett, the shrewd Radical, had agreed in advance with Carlyle that the tendency of the times was bad, and said so—upon which Macaulay, the optimistic Whig, had castigated Southey for his doubts in a famous essay, and proved to his own satisfaction that things were good and getting better. Actually the industrial-social revolution, as Kingsley and Disraeli both realized from very different points of view, was more complex in its causes and consequences, and was bound to produce both good and evil; while Carlyle, always more conscious of the evil than the good in the process, reluctantly conceded that good might in the end come out of the evil that he saw around him, if and when the wise minority ruled the foolish majority, and the leader of the Right came by his own.

It is a vision, almost a melodrama, of the past, which is worked out in the histories and biographies with an exquisite skill and cunning that almost carries conviction. Almost but not quite; for the truth is that the problem of existence is over-simplified by Carlyle's purely moral treatment, and that life is not quite like that.

The multitude, no doubt, are foolish and inconstant and short-sighted, because they live too close to the ground to see far ahead. But they are not quite so foolish as Carlyle contemptuously suggests, and they are certainly not incapable of heroism and self-sacrifice in following a leader whom they can trust.

It is the choice and quality of the leadership which Carlyle approves, and the means and ends which it attempts, that give one pause. His whole philosophy is one of action, and of action for the right and for righteousness against a sombre and sinister mass of sin and suffering and evil. Prominent in the foreground is the Hero, the God-given leader of the inert and foolish multitude; and the dramatized chronicle of history is invoked to show this sublime He-Man scaling the heights of achievement in search of the good, the true, and the (morally) beautiful. But can we honestly affirm that Frederick the Great really fills the bill? Right, as Carlyle formally maintained, ultimately makes Might. But when all is said and done, and the last entry made in the account, Frederick's biographer comes near the counter-proposition that Might makes Right.

The reason for the contradiction, so curious in one who was above all a moralist, is simple. Might almost inevitably means Action, and the visible and even violent and spectacular expenditure of energy; whereas Right is often passive, and works as a corrective and a retrospective idea rather than as a crusade. Carlyle seems never to have seen this: his philosophy was so completely one of action that the whole world was for him a stage set for action, and God Himself became a God of Action—a kind of super He-Man using lesser human heroes as His chosen instruments in that endless and therefore ineffective warfare against sin and suffering and evil which an ethical God of Action must be presumed to maintain. This, too, is a point of view, though ultimately an untenable one; for the facts are against it, as they are against all such methods of explaining the problem of evil.

" God is all-powerful and all-loving—and the world is what it is! How are you going to explain that? " said the great Lord Salisbury once, to the confusion of complacent orthodoxy. Carlyle had never been orthodox, but there survives a curious confession that, towards the end, his own God of Action had been weighed in the balance and found wanting. " God does nothing," he said with a cry of pain shortly before his death.

It looks as if he saw, too late, that the moral foundations on which he had built his philosophy were insufficient to support the facts of life.

RICHARD COBDEN

1804-1865

BY
J. L.
HAMMOND

RICHARD COBDEN

SOME thirty years ago two young men were travelling on one of the old horse trams through the melancholy streets of Camden Town. "How just," said one of them, "was the instinct that prompted Cobden's friends to put up his statue on the doorstep of this district. Here, if anywhere, is Cobden's England: this drab, colourless, dingy squalor, with nothing to take a man's mind from the dreary business of making money." "It is odd," said the other, "that you should say this at this moment, for it was only yesterday that Morley remarked that there were three English statesmen who stood out in the nineteenth century as men of original and commanding views: two of them were Disraeli and Gladstone, the third was Cobden."

The great interest of Cobden's career is that, though the second of these views would be accepted to-day by all serious critics, all discriminating admirers would admit that the first is not wholly false. For while those who deplore Cobden's influence in English politics would have to admit that the state of Europe when he died shows that he was a man of remarkable power, those who admire his spirit and achievements will allow that it is not altogether a co-incidence that at a time when the Manchester School was drawing upon itself the eyes of the world, the streets of Manchester were so mean and miserable that a magistrate of the Roman Empire in the days of the Antonines would have been ashamed to call it his native city.

The most dramatic and the most familiar way of looking at the domestic history of the first half of the nineteenth century is to regard it as an epic struggle between the land-lords and the manufacturers, between the spirit of feudalism

137

and the spirit of commerce. Cobden, as a protagonist in that struggle, is regarded as a man of business. In this there lurks a danger. If we think of commerce to-day we think of offices and banks, of business men dictating to typists, of clerks making up ledgers, of a brisk but sedentary life spent in Manchester or London or some other great city. Of course, all this life can be clothed with romance, if you picture these men and women moving in fancy from one continent to another, watching the rise and fall of prices at the ends of the world, thinking at one moment of coffee in Brazil, at another of rubber in the Malay Archipelago.

But commerce in history has a more exciting aspect than this. The merchant in the Middle Ages did not merely visit the ends of the earth in imagination, he visited them in his caravan. He was the man of action, the man of adventure. At home he had all the prestige and popularity of the traveller who can tell his neighbours what life is like somewhere else: how people keep themselves, what are their habits, their manners, their religion. Such a man was more like Herodotus than Mr. Marshall or Mr. Snelgrove. He was more like Strabo than Mr. Swan or Mr. Edgar. He was the travelled man, the experienced man, the man of wide interests and outlook, for, like Odysseus, he had seen many men and many cities. And at a time when newspapers and newspaper readers were much less common, the traveller occupied a very important place in society. Man is always curious about man. To-day there is a new interest in archæology just because we seem to have ransacked and to have standardized the whole world, and it is only by unburying the past that we can learn about peoples that differ from those with which we are familiar. That is why new light on Troy and Mycenæ, which could take Gladstone's mind from his most pressing public cares in the first days of Schliemann's discoveries, stirs curiosity and excitement to-day in the man in the street. But a century ago that kind of curiosity was satisfied by travellers from Turkey or China or—

> " *Golden cities, ten months' journeys deep*
> *Amid Tartarean hills.*"

To speak of Cobden as a business man, putting himself at the head of a business party, is misleading, unless we remember that he belonged to commerce in this special and romantic tradition. He was the most travelled man in the House of Commons. Nobody among his contemporaries had seen so much of the world, or talked to so many of its rulers and its merchants, its politicians and its peasants. He knew Europe in its diplomatic politics as Stanhope knew it at the beginning of the eighteenth and Castlereagh at the beginning of the nineteenth centuries, but he knew Europe also in its underlying passions and submerged desires, an aspect of which Stanhope and Castlereagh knew relatively little. To understand his power and his ideas, we must remember that he became a great leader, not because he was a business man, as we understand the term, but because, travelling in muslins, he could collect the wisdom that comes with experience to alert and observant minds. By nature an adventurous man, a man, that is, eager for a wide and various experience, he was always on the look-out for the significance of the world which, at any given moment, he found himself observing.

If he had not possessed this quality, he would never have overcome his early disadvantages. He was one of eleven children, born under the shadow of family disaster. He was educated by an uncle at a school in Yorkshire, where he remained for five years, " a grim and desolate time," " ill-fed, ill-taught, ill-used." His chance came when his uncle, who was in business, sent him to Ireland and Scotland as a commercial traveller. He made so good an impression that, although his uncle's firm came to grief in the financial storm of 1826, he was offered a partnership in a merchant's house. Seeing that the repeal of the heavy excise duties on calicoes would stimulate that industry, he turned calico printer. But though his business prospered for a time, it came to misfortune later. This was not surprising. The ordinary business man spends his time making himself into a better business man : Cobden spent his time making himself into a politician. He worked hard at his own education. As a clerk in his uncle's warehouse he learned French ; as a partner in a merchant's business in Manchester he studied Latin and mathematics. Like all reformers of his type, he read widely and eagerly. He became an admirable writer, and though the play he offered to the manager of Covent Garden as a young man did not deserve, Lord Morley tells us, more than the slight and slighting consideration that it received, his letters on his travels are agreeable reading, reflecting the play of a mind that soon finds itself at home in a new atmosphere, and settles down to look about and understand new and unfamiliar surroundings.

Thus Cobden was a calico printer in the sense that Grote was a banker. His fundamental interest was not in muslins and cottons, but in the men and women of the world. He resembled Marco Polo or Jonas Hanway more than he resembled the Manchester merchants who helped him to repeal the Corn Laws. This came out clearly enough when his friends, rightly thinking it a scandal that a man who had given to public causes the most persuasive tongue in England should suffer personal shipwreck from neglect of his affairs, came to his rescue as Fox's friends had come to the rescue of that noble spendthrift half a century earlier. Cobden, with a map of Illinois before him and a fortune in his pocket, was about as good a business man as Fox when he sat down to the faro table at Brooks's, fingering all that was left of his father's plunder. Cobden threw his fortune into the Mississippi with the generosity of a man whose imagination moves faster than the facts.

Cobden's optimism, his habit of letting his imagination outrun the facts, blinded him to the truth that if he lacked the business man's prudence, the business men whom he summoned to his banner lacked his large outlook. There was a wide and ultimately fatal difference between leader and led. This was plain from the outset of his career. The first thing Cobden did when he became a calico printer was to agitate for a village school; the first cause he took up was the cause of education. When he went into public life he meant to devote to this cause the incomparable gifts of persuasion which were ultimately given to the cause of Free Trade. But he was indifferently supported. Many of the business men in the North of England had the kind of self-satisfaction which is produced by success that has been gained in the face of great difficulties. Some of them were large-minded enough to prize the education which they had missed, but most of them were doubtful whether the education which they had not found necessary for their own development was worth much public money or much public effort. Another difficulty was the extreme sectarian spirit of the times. Most Churchmen and most Nonconformists preferred that the towns should be left in ignorance if the alternative was a form of education of which they disapproved. In this intolerant world the few men such as Cobden and Hook, the great Vicar of Leeds, who put education first, believing, as Cobden said, that Cicero and Seneca had done greater service to humanity than the average gladiator or peasant of their time, although neither Churchman nor Nonconformist would have approved of their education, made little impression.

Another great obstacle to the civilization of the new towns, as Dickens saw, was the Sunday imposed on the working classes, a Sunday in which the church or chapel and the public-house offered them their only escape from their dwellings in the slums. Every visitor from the Continent was astonished to find that beauty, fresh air, music, and reasonable recreation were kept out of the reach of the working classes on the only day on which they had leisure. We know what Cobden thought of this bleak and barbarous institution from the letter he wrote in Germany. " If you think this is an improper picture of a Protestant Sunday," he wrote to his sister, " on the other hand, the sober and orderly German thinks that drunkenness, the filthy public-houses, the miserable and moping mechanic that pines in his dark alley in our English cities on the Sabbath day, are infinitely worse features of a Protestant community than his Tivoli Gardens." Here again there was a wide difference between leader and led.

Cobden was blind to this difference. His outlook was coloured and dominated by his buoyant nature. He was an optimist, and his optimism resembled that of Macaulay both in its range and in its source. A century ago Macaulay, criticizing Southey's pessimism, made a guess about the state of England in 1930. " If we were to prophesy," he said, " that in the year 1930 a population of fifty millions, better fed, clad, and lodged than the English of our time, will cover these islands, that Sussex and Huntingdonshire will be wealthier than the richest parts of the West Riding of Yorkshire now are, that cultivation, rich as that of a flower garden, will be carried up to the very tops of Ben Nevis and Helvellyn, that machines constructed on principles undiscovered will be in every house, that there will be no highways but railroads, no travelling but by steam, that our debt, vast as it seems to us, will appear to our great-grandchildren a trifling encumbrance which might easily be paid off in a year or two, many people would think us insane."

Macaulay went on to say that he would not prophesy,

but he asked his readers to imagine how a person who had predicted the England of 1830 would have appeared to the Parliament which met in perplexity and terror after the South Sea Bubble crash of 1720. What would that Parliament have thought of a picture of England in which men would be in the habit of sailing without wind and beginning to ride without horses, and in which the annual revenue would equal the principal of the debt which that Parliament considered an intolerable burden?

Cobden, as he moved about, felt towards all the new energy in the world as Macaulay felt. He was not one of those men who have no eyes for the life of the past. When he stood before the Parthenon he declared that his own age could not match such beauty of design or perfection of workmanship. Disraeli, speaking in the House of Commons after his death, said that reverence for the past was one of his distinguishing characteristics. But he found the vitality of his own age expressed and symbolized in this new power. He believed that the Industrial Revolution had done what the French Revolution had done, that it had shaken " the dead from living man." Looking at this world, he made in politics the same mistake that he made in business. He gambled on the virtues of a class. He thought that if you could put on one side all that belonged to the dead world, and throw power to the class that had come to life in this new world, England would be guided and governed by the energy of a new and generous public spirit. Cobden, in fact, was ready to stake everything on his belief that the British mill-owners and the British bankers and the British tradesmen would create a new city life recalling the city life of Italy or Flanders in the great days of Michelangelo or Rembrandt.

Unfortunately, large numbers of the new class resembled Charlotte Brontë's neighbours, as described by Mrs. Gaskell—" Men with hundreds of thousands of pounds who bring up their sons with only just enough learning to qualify them for overseers during their father's lifetime and greedy, grasping money-hunters after his death." These gentlemen, it will be remembered, defeated the efforts of Charlotte Brontë's father to obtain a water-supply for Haworth, and Cobden was expecting them to emulate the munificence of Cosmo de' Medici. Those who formed larger views for their families did not always form larger views for their towns. Cobden lived to deplore the haste with which business men who made fortunes turned themselves into country gentlemen, neglecting the claims of their city life. He was let down by the merchant princes as Disraeli was let down by the landlords. Disraeli, looking for a Herodes Atticus among the landlords, who grew fabulously richer with every new smudge on the face of Lancashire, found his followers voting steadily against Bills for Public Health, abandoned his mission in despair for twenty years, and gave his brains to the tactics of his party.

Cobden's mistake about the middle class was as disastrous as his mistake about the Mississippi, for he had staked everything on this illusion. Trusting that this new class would rise to a great occasion, he taught the fatal doctrine of public parsimony. He gave Peel no support when Peel was bold and wise enough to re-impose the income-tax. Yet the new England could only have been civilized by large public expenditure, for the new towns lacked for the most part water, light, streets, drains, not to speak of decent schools, libraries, parks, theatres, and the amenities that other ages had counted among the necessities of city life. When Cobden was telling Place to bless himself that he was living in this age of railways and steamboats, Palmerston was telling the House of Commons that the report of the Board of Health on the state of Newcastle was enough to make any civilized man shudder. England was adding slum to slum as fast as she added railway to railway or ship to ship.

About Cobden's place in English history there must always be differences of opinion. No one doubts that the Repeal of the Corn Laws was one of the main causes of the immense development of our commerce and industry between the forties and the eighties. All classes shared in some degree in the benefits of that development. Factory conditions improved. Civilization began to lift its head again out of the smoke of the industrial towns. Parks, libraries, theatres, the necessities of ancient civilization, gradually came back into social life as the luxuries of this age. If you study the history of the English towns you see that a new page is turned, with however timid a finger, after the middle of this century. On the other hand, many would argue that the spectacle of dazzling commercial success blinded the age to the dangers of a headlong industrialism, and that the belief which grew up of an endless and automatic progress was an obstacle to reform as serious as the old vested interests that Cobden attacked. And even those who give the Repeal of the Corn Laws its full share of credit for the improvement in the material conditions of the time, might hold that Repeal, passed in 1846, was a less important influence in civilizing this new world than the passing of the Ten Hours' Act in 1847. By that time the factory agitation, which had started as a crusade for the protection of children, had become a campaign for the recognition of the workman's right to a larger life. Cobden was not so bitter an opponent of the Bill as Bright, but like Peel he was nervous about the risks to which industry would be exposed by this experiment. As we watch the new English town struggling out of the grim prison in which it was born, we may be pardoned for doubting whether the cause of civilization owed as much to the reforms carried by Cobden as it owed to those carried by Shaftesbury. For unless the nation had taken the risk of limiting the hours of labour, the new amusements and culture which began to develop after the fifties, reviving the long-lost habit of common enjoyment, would only have intensified the difference between those who could share in the pleasures of life and those whose lot it was to bear its burdens.

When we look from England to the world, Cobden's place in history becomes clearer. That strong sense for the unity of civilization for which we look in the world of science and culture, struggles against special obstacles in the world of politics, for politicians have to manage the mixed passions of class and nation, of religion and race. Those obstacles grew more difficult in the nineteenth century as popular feeling and national sentiment became stronger forces. Of the British statesmen of that century two were distinguished by the possession of that sense, and one of them was Cobden. He has suffered in some degree from the custom of linking his name with that of Bright. The custom is natural enough. Their friendship, generous, sincere, and lasting, made a strong impression in a world so much embittered by fierce competition as the world of politics. It is true, also, as was said of them, that the power of these two men was greater than the power of each added to the power of the other, for their remarkable gifts were complementary. If some of the arts of advocacy were practised by Cobden with dazzling success, there were others of which Bright was a master without rival. But the association of their names leads to a misconception. There was as much difference between Cobden and Bright as between Gladstone and Palmerston. In comparison with Gladstone, Palmerston was an insular Englishman with the high spirit of a schoolboy; in comparison with Cobden, Bright was an insular Englishman with the stern conscience of a Quaker. To understand Cobden's place in history it is necessary to see what he had in common, not with Bright, but with Gladstone.

Gladstone, brooding over the pages of Dante, saw the moral relations of peoples with an imagination more vivid and powerful than any man who took part in the government of Europe in the nineteenth century, unless we count the few hours when Mazzini ruled in Rome. His letters on the Naples prisons, his magnanimity after Majuba, his hesitation between two dangers in the Soudan, his crusade for Ireland, are all explained by his regard for public law, at a time when a man who cared about public law had to act as if something that existed only in his imagination could be made a force in the life of the world by the power of a noble example. On the one great issue on which he differed from Cobden, the Crimean War, he differed widely from most of those who were on his side. They thought of Russia as a danger to England: he thought of Russia as a danger to public law. He held that Russia had taken into her own hands a problem that ought to be decided by Europe.

What Dante was to Gladstone, Adam Smith was to Cobden. The sense for the unity of the world which had inspired the mystical poetry of the thirteenth century dominated the cold prose of the eighteenth century, revealing itself in *The Decline and Fall of the Roman Empire* and *The Wealth of Nations*. Cobden had learnt from Adam Smith to look upon commerce in this relation. He saw, as he surveyed its history, that the discoveries of Columbus and the other great mariners had been followed by two centuries of struggle, and that the passionate desire for the new wealth of the world had turned the Atlantic into as lawless a sea as the Mediterranean in the savage days of Mithridates. To the ordinary business man this was idle history. He was for British commerce. If commerce flourished by peace, he was for peace; if by war, he was for war. To Cobden that past was a haunting shadow. For the things to which many of those who followed him

G

were indifferent were just the things that mattered to him above everything else. Just as in education and religious tolerance, so in commerce he moved in a world beyond their understanding. This difference came out in two great controversies. When Palmerston gave the British merchants the war for which they asked in China, Cobden denounced the use of violence to open doors for trade, and the men who had put him into Parliament, when his principles seemed to them to agree with their interests, threw him out on finding his principles and their interests in conflict. When the Russian and Austrian Governments floated loans in London because they needed money for their struggle with their revolutionaries, the business man said that it was no concern of his what was done with his money, if the interest was paid on it. Cobden denounced this doctrine, and asked whether the man who lent his money to those Governments for such purposes would be equally ready to lend his money to finance a brothel. No statesman was less willing to accept the formula that business is business than this leader of business men. For he was not a business man who had taken to politics, but a politician taught, warned, and, let us add, sometimes misled by experience of business. He saw the economic disorder of the world in the same vivid light in which Gladstone saw its political confusion, and he pursued his remedy with the same single-minded devotion.

For the discovery that guided and governed Cobden's mind was a truth too important for anybody who had grasped it to give it half-hearted service. The British people, as the pioneers of the Industrial Revolution, had created an economy which made the whole world one. In such a world strife must be more disastrous than in a world where nations still lived on their own resources. It must also be more frequent, for just as the penalties of defeat would be more severe, so would the prizes of victory seem more tempting. While many of his followers were merely thinking of free trade as a means of adding to Britain's commerce and riches, Cobden's mind was brooding on this prospect. He called on the British people to help the world out of this danger by renouncing monopoly; by throwing open its markets; by declaring that the British Empire welcomed anybody who wanted to trade with it. In this way he hoped to save the world from repeating the crimes of the seventeenth and eighteenth centuries; from opening up the undeveloped parts of the world by violence and wrong; from nursing a sense of property that would be too strong, in case of conflict, for the sense of justice. In this sense he was well described in Carlyle's famous phrase, "an inspired bagman with a calico millennium." For these words might be taken to mean that he was a traveller who had seen men and cities, with a mind lighted by genius, teaching a faith and doctrine that could deliver calico itself from the crimes that had stained the pirate seas.

Some who agree with Cobden's aim would argue that his plan for bringing the world to Free Trade was not the best plan; that Europe, which under the force of his teaching moved so fast towards Free Trade in the sixties, would have learnt his lessons better if England, instead of making a bold and generous gesture, looking to the world to follow, had pursued the more gradual method of commercial negotiation; the method of which his own treaty with France was so successful an example. Some, again, would hold that it was dangerous to expect other peoples to draw from Britain's success under Free Trade the conclusions drawn by Cobden's converts among the British manufacturers and cotton spinners. List had produced the rival view, that Free Trade suited the powerful, and that the nation making its uphill way needed Protection. The argument from example was in some respects a dangerous argument. When the United States and Germany, after the Civil War and the Franco-German War, and partly in consequence of those wars, turned to Protection and grew into prosperous industrial States, that argument went over to the enemy.

Free Trade again occupied in Cobden's analysis an importance that most people to-day would think excessive. Too much was expected from it. Few people would hold that universal Free Trade gives the answer to all the economic problems of a world that has become a single economic unit. If every tariff was thrown down at this moment, the statesmen, the bankers, the manufacturers, the workers of the world would still have some hard problems to settle by conference and regulation. And there is no doubt that the solution that would be found of those problems would strain the principles that Cobden held. For the principles that he formed, looking at a world in which Governments were chiefly occupied in holding down the populations submerged beneath the treaties of Vienna, would lead in a world living by our elaborate system to a chaos not unlike that which afflicted the politics of Europe in his day.

All these considerations could be urged in criticism of Cobden's statesmanship and foresight. But they do not touch his position as an intellectual and moral power in Europe in the nineteenth century. He stands out as a man acting consistently on a large view of politics. He brought his own nation to accept his conclusions, and he almost brought the world to accept them. These conclusions, though most persons would consider them a less complete answer than he supposed to the international problem set by the Industrial Revolution, were based on a fundamental truth. The world was moving towards a new unity, with opportunities and dangers greater than it had ever known in its history. For the Industrial Revolution had created an elaborate world order, based on a system of exchange which was gradually drawing all peoples into a single plan of life. Cobden saw that every civilized people had a new duty to its neighbours under this system, and that this duty was specially binding on the people now enjoying the kind of ascendancy that had belonged at one time to Venice and Genoa, at another to the Portuguese and the Dutch. He asked of his nation that it should look beyond its own immediate desires and use this power in a spirit of generosity and forbearance. We need not turn back to distant centuries or search the civilizations of the past, recalling Isocrates and Cicero, Epaminondas and Scipio Africanus, to determine whether a man who brings this wider wisdom into the violent atmosphere of politics deserves to live in history. All observers are agreed in tracing the confusion of the world to-day to the want of this guiding sense, in the hour when victory had put the fortunes of Europe in the hands of a dozen politicians, trembling before popular passions, so lately their servants and now their masters. If mankind could summon the dead to its rescue, the two Englishmen to whom it would first turn in its distress are the men who, learning from different prophets, tried to teach their age this larger sympathy.

CHARLES ROBERT DARWIN

1809–1882

BY
G. P.
WELLS

G. P. WELLS

CHARLES
ROBERT DARWIN

"SOME are born great, some achieve greatness, and some have greatness thrust upon them." It is hard to tell to which of these categories Charles Darwin should be assigned. He was certainly not born into the limelight. He came into it with dramatic abruptness, but belatedly. For the first fifty years of his life he was a little-known man, except to a small circle of his professional colleagues, and throughout that period he produced nothing to merit a wider recognition. He was sent to Edinburgh at the age of sixteen to study medicine; soon, being obviously unfitted for that profession, he was removed to Cambridge to become a clergyman. At the latter university he divided his energy between hunting, shooting, and the industrious collection of beetles, and his clerical ambitions (or rather his father's), to quote his own words, "died a natural death." Immediately after graduating, he joined the staff of a research ship, the *Beagle*, in which he sailed about the world for five years. Returning with his collections from this adventure, he went at first to London, where for a while he was Secretary of the Geological Society, and where he married; at thirty-three, already broken down in health, he retired for the rest of his life to a country house at Down, in Kent.

"During the first part of our residence," he wrote of this phase, "we went a little into society, and received a few friends here; but my health almost always suffered from the excitement, violent shivering and vomiting attacks being thus brought on. I have therefore been compelled for many years to give up all dinner-parties. . . ."

Happily, being the son of a prosperous and affectionate country doctor, he had no need to work for a living. From thirty-seven to forty-five he devoted himself to the preparation of an exhaustive monograph on recent and fossil barnacles.

Suddenly, at fifty, this invalid naturalist became famous. In *The Origin of Species by means of Natural Selection*, he put forward an idea which he had been unobtrusively incubating for twenty years. The success of this book was immediate and astounding. His publishers were quite unprepared for the reception it received: a small first edition of 1,250 copies was exhausted on the day of publication, and the second did not appear until two months afterwards. In a very few years, the *Origin of Species* had brought about a revolution in the whole framework of contemporary philosophy. It had been translated into almost every European tongue, and even into Japanese. An essay in Hebrew had appeared, which proved that its theory was contained in the Old Testament.

To understand this eager reception, we must consider for a moment the state of mind of the world into which the book was published.

Before the latter half of the nineteenth century it was generally believed that the species of animals and plants were fixed and immutable. God created them in 4004 B.C. His handiwork had persisted unaltered since that date, having been saved by Noah from untimely destruction, and it would continue to persist until He saw fit to revise it in the very thorough manner described in the Book of Revelation.

But the crust of the earth was teeming with eloquent witnesses against this belief. Scattered through the rocks were the fossilized remains of animals and plants. The significance of their testimony was long obscured by the interpretations they received. Aristotle declared that they had germinated spontaneously where they were found, and when, in the seventeenth century, the unquestioning faith with which his writings had been accepted waned, and this view was discarded, it was replaced by another false explanation. Most of these fossils were of marine creatures, preserved by the fine sediments that slowly collect on the sea-floor, so their occurrence in the rocks of large landmasses, far from any sea, was attributed to the Deluge. In this way, the fossils became proofs of the literal truth of

Genesis. But as the collection and study of fossils progressed, this theory in turn became untenable.

In addition to the fossils, a host of other puzzling facts
awaited the evolutionary interpretation. There were manifest imperfections in the structure of many creatures—such
as the useless little vestigial leg-bones embedded in the
belly of a whale—which suggested that creation, if it had
occurred, had been, to say the least, uneconomical; and
there were odd resemblances between animals of different
kinds, and points about the geographical distribution of
animal and plant species, that were hard to reconcile with
the generally accepted story of the origin of the world.

As these facts accumulated, a number of naturalists came
to question the immutability of species; and here and there,
more or less explicitly, the idea that a species may slowly
change into something quite different began to appear in
scientific writings.

When Darwin began his studies, at Edinburgh and at
Cambridge, the immutability of species was still the generally held doctrine, even among biologists, although the rival
view had already been put forward.

> " It has sometimes been said," he wrote in a later
> retrospect, " that the success of the *Origin of Species*
> proved that ' the subject was in the air,' or ' that men's
> minds were prepared for it.' I do not think that this
> is strictly true, for I occasionally sounded not a few
> naturalists, and never happened to come across a single
> one who seemed to doubt about the permanence of
> species."

And when, after long thought, Darwin first confessed his
evolutionary suspicions in a letter to Sir John Hooker, he
expressed himself as follows: " I am almost convinced that
species are not (it is like confessing a murder) immutable."
Nevertheless, although the majority of biologists were still
creationists when the *Origin of Species* was published, the
evolutionary idea had been vigorously expounded by the
Comte de Buffon, by Darwin's own grandfather Erasmus,
by Lamarck, by Saint-Hilaire, by Treviranus, and less
conspicuously by a number of other authors.

One of these pre-Darwinian evolutionists is of peculiar
interest. In 1813, a Dr. W. C. Wells read before the Royal
Society, and subsequently published, " An Account of a
White Female, part of whose skin resembles that of a

G*   153

Negro." This essay contains a clear description, not only
of the gradual modification of a race, but of Darwin's own
hypothesis of Natural Selection. Dr. Wells discusses the
fact that negroes and mulattoes are better adapted than
white men to live in hot climates. To explain their fitness,
he points out that all animals tend to vary slightly from
each other, and that breeders steadily improve the races of
domesticated animals by picking out the most suitable
variations to breed from. What the breeder does

> " by art, seems to be done with equal efficacy, though
> more slowly, by Nature, in the formation of varieties
> of mankind, fitted for the country in which they in-
> habit. Of the accidental varieties of man, which would
> occur among the first few and scattered inhabitants of
> the middle regions of Africa, some one would be better
> fitted than the others to bear the diseases of the
> country. This race would consequently multiply, while
> the others would decrease ; not only from their inability
> to sustain attacks of disease, but from their incapacity
> of contending with their more vigorous neighbours.
> The colour of this vigorous race I take for granted,
> from what has already been said, would be dark. But
> the same disposition to form varieties still existing, a
> darker and darker race would in course of time occur ;
> and as the darkest would be the best fitted for the
> climate, this would at length become the most preva-
> lent, if not the only race."

The white woman, part of whose skin resembled that of
a negro, was of course an example of the kind of variation
upon which the selective process could act. This very remarkable essay was published when Darwin was nine years
old, but it attracted little attention, and did not come to
Darwin's notice until after the appearance of the *Origin of
Species*.

The biologists, then, had before them a mass of evidence
for evolution, and a number of expositions of the theory,
but, with rare exceptions, they still believed in the fixity
of species. It is curious to note how they were made to
change their belief.

Darwin's own conversion was characteristically slow.
He was by nature a cautious man. He collected and sorted
relevant facts for over twenty years before he published
the *Origin of Species*. Herein lies one reason for the

enthusiasm with which his work was received. It is a thoroughly documented book. In this it differs from the writings of his predecessors. Buffon was an attractive writer, and a brilliant sweeping thinker, but not a painstaking collector of evidence. Lamarck wrote heavily and with difficulty, and lapsed often into unprofitable speculation. Huxley lamented with good reason that the theory of evolution had been " sadly damaged by some of its supporters."

But much more important than this in determining its success is the fact that the *Origin of Species* contains two entirely different ideas. It presents evidence for believing that evolution has occurred, and it also presents a mechanism by which evolution can be explained—the hypothesis of Natural Selection.

We have already traced the main features of that hypothesis in an extract from a paper by Dr. Wells. Darwin applied it, not only to the adaptation of human races to the regions in which they live, but to the whole spectacle of organic evolution. In all organisms without exception, the number of young produced is far greater than can possibly grow to maturity and reproduce their kind. There is, therefore, in every generation a massacre of the young, an intensive competition to survive to maturity. Assuming that organisms vary, and that the variations are inherited —inheritable variations are known now in a great variety of different species—there will be a tendency for the better-adapted animals or plants to out-live and out-reproduce their brethren, and for the race to be steadily modified, generation by generation, in this way.

This hypothesis of Natural Selection is clearly quite distinct from the hypothesis of Evolution. Natural Selection is no more than a suggested explanation of the evolutionary process. There may be other and better explanations. Nevertheless, in the *Origin of Species,* these two ideas are not kept apart; they are inextricably confused with each other. Darwin does not first establish the truth of evolution, and then produce Natural Selection as a possible mechanism: for him, the two ideas stand or fall together.

Now this is precisely what we are looking for—the reason why the *Origin of Species* created such a violent revolution in contemporary thought. It contained, not only evidence that evolution had occurred, but a plausible explanation of the occurrence. This, above all, was what the major treatises on evolution had hitherto failed to produce. The world was waiting for the explanation. Until it had the explanation, it would not trouble to accept the fact. Why should it? In the *Origin of Species,* Darwin achieved a tremendous feat of rationalization. He substituted rational evolution for miraculous creation. But if the evolution had not been rational, there would have been no great advantage in the change.

In Darwin's own mind, one can see how the final recognition of the fact awaited the explanation. He suspected the truth of transformism while he was travelling round the world on the *Beagle,* and he opened his first note-book on the transmutation of species a few months after his return. But not until he had conceived and elaborated his hypothesis of Natural Selection did he dream of working up his material for publication. He wrote of—

> " the innumerable cases in which organisms of every kind are beautifully adapted to their habits of life— for instance, a woodpecker or a tree-frog to climb trees, or a seed for dispersal by hooks or plumes. I had always been much struck by such adaptations, and until these could be explained it seemed to me useless to prove by indirect evidence that species have been modified."

Thus, mounted on the back of Natural Selection, Evolution attacked and conquered the nineteenth-century world. It is interesting to trace the subsequent fate of the rider and the steed.

There followed upon the publication of the *Origin of Species* a tremendous outburst of critical scientific research into the truth of evolution. Animals and plants were dissected and compared with each other in the light of the new teaching; classifications were overhauled and revised; the study of embryonic structure received a freshening inspiration; the fossil record was scrutinized with the most minute and painstaking care. The verdict of an army of investigators has been unanimous. The result of seventy-odd years of intensive inquiry has been to place Evolution on an unshakable foundation of fact. It has become the central generalization of biology. Looking back, one is amazed at the relative slenderness of the evidence that supported the earliest evolutionists, and at their temerity in basing upon it so revolutionary a doctrine.

But what of Natural Selection? What has happened to the hypothesis that made evolution acceptable to mankind? The answer is—practically nothing. While our knowledge of the steps through which organisms have evolved has been progressively consolidated, the hypothesis of Natural Selection rests pretty nearly where it did at the time of its formulation.

If one were to take a census of the biologists of to-day, one would find them—except in Tennessee, where the law forbids it—unanimously evolutionists. But one would probably find only a small proportion of active believers in Natural Selection—except in Russia, where it is part of the official creed. This does not mean that the majority of biologists believe the hypothesis of Natural Selection to be wrong; it means that they are neutral. They leave it alone. There is of course a big difference between believing that a proposition is false and abstaining from the belief that it is true.

Oddly enough, the very qualities that enabled Natural Selection to serve as sugar for the evolutionary pill make it unsatisfactory as an instrument of modern scientific thought.

We have already seen that Natural Selection affords an intelligible explanation of adaptive features, such as the feet of woodpeckers and tree-frogs, or the hooks and plumes of seeds. But it is evident that the selective process will only operate in favour of characters that confer some advantage on their possessors. One of the most dangerous objections that have been raised against Darwinism is that many characters are apparently not advantageous. Most of the differences which enable the systematist to distinguish one species from another serve no apparent purpose; and there are several well-established fossil pedigrees in which useless structures have been evolved—such as the strange bifid horns that slowly grew on the noses of the Titanotheres, an extinct group of rhinoceros-like mammals, or the fantastic ornamentation with which many of the Ammonites decorated their shells.

The selectionist has a ready reply to this criticism. Often a single inheritable variation affects more than one character of the organism. The various anatomically distinct strains of wheat differ also in their susceptibility to the disease called rust; the white and coloured populations of America die from different illnesses; and there is evidence that immunity to measles is correlated with hair and eye colour. One may therefore account for the evolution of useless characters by supposing them to be accompanied by unknown advantages. Even a disadvantageous character might prevail if it was linked to a sufficiently profitable adaptation.

It will at once be seen that the hypothesis of Natural Selection is a very formidable explainer of data. Indeed, it is not easy to imagine any facts (short of downright, repeated discontinuity in the fossil record) that, properly manipulated, it would fail to explain. Let us illustrate this point, which is of great importance, by considering for a moment one of the best-known chapters of the record of the rocks—the evolution of the horse. The story is now known in considerable detail, and is based on tens of thousands of specimens. It begins about forty million years ago, with an animal about as big as a medium-sized terrier, having five toes on each foot, comparatively short limbs, and simple teeth. Gradually this creature evolved into the modern horse. Its bulk increased; its legs became longer so that it could run more swiftly, and at the same time one of the toes on each foot grew into a stout lever, its nail becoming a hoof, while its neighbours dwindled and disappeared; the molar teeth became larger and more complicated, so that they could thoroughly grind up vegetable food. Manifestly, these facts lend themselves to a Darwinian explanation. The modern horse is much better fitted to its mode of life than its five-toed ancestor, and the whole history can easily be attributed to selection of favourable variations.

We may observe in passing that there is not a shred of positive evidence for this view. It has yet to be shown that at any period the less advanced horses died younger than their brethren; indeed, there is not a single case known to science where a gradual evolutionary change can be shown to coincide with selective mortality. The interpretation is nevertheless a possible one.

Now suppose the fossil record turned upside down. Suppose that we suddenly discovered that we had been mistaken, and that the race had really evolved in the opposite direction, from the horse to the little unspecialized ancestor. Would this afford a confutation of Natural Selection, or would the hypothesis adapt itself to the reversal?

There is no doubt at all that in the hands of a skilful

exponent—and it has had many—Natural Selection could account for the new facts with the utmost ease. The foot of a one-toed horse, he would argue, is possibly very serviceable in running, but it is not plastic; it is limited in the things it will do, and by evolving five less specialized toes the race has acquired a more adaptable limb. The horse has raised itself to a new level of biological efficiency. Similarly, the reduction of the teeth was desirable, because they had previously occupied a disproportionately large part of the skull. (These supposed arguments are only mild caricatures of the ones with which an anatomist consoles himself for lacking the powerful arms and jaws of a gorilla. There are plenty of examples in the literature of reasoning as specious as this.) In the last resort, our selectionist could of course call linked characters to his aid, and suggest that the more toes a horse had, the more immune it was against diseases.

It was this very ability to explain any and every fact that gave Natural Selection its initial importance. The world was weary of unquestioning faith in Genesis, and was hungry for explanations. But the scientist of to-day has different needs. His hypotheses must not only explain, they must discriminate. There must be possible facts that they would fail to explain. Just as a warrior is not really a warrior until he has fought and killed an enemy, so a theory, until it has run the risk of disproof, is not satisfyingly true.

As an illustrative contrast to the Darwinian hypothesis, we may take the brilliant generalizations known as Mendel's laws of heredity. By means of these laws one can make definite prophecies about the outcome of particular crosses. One can first anticipate, not only the different kinds of progeny that will emerge, but the relative numbers in which they will appear, and then test the inference experimentally, and see whether its theoretical basis is correct. Thus, if one hybridizes pure-bred yellow and green peas, and inbreeds the hybrids, the second generation should consist of yellows and greens in the ratio of three to one. Seven different investigators have made the experiment; their results, added together, come to 152,824 yellows and 50,676 greens —a ratio of 3·01 to 1. The departure from expectation is trivial. If the ratios had been four to one or two to one, there would have been something wrong with the laws.

These laws of heredity were obscurely published by the

Abbé Mendel in 1865, but the world was not ready for them, and they attracted little attention until they were rediscovered by a group of botanists in 1900. Their resuscitation gave a world-wide impetus to the study of genetics. They were tested again and again and found to be good; with their aid a magnificent structure of accurate knowledge about heredity has been built up in thirty years. This is one of the major triumphs of twentieth-century biology.

On the other hand, although the *Origin of Species* was published three-quarters of a century ago, the hypothesis of Evolution by Natural Selection has yet to undergo a really critical test. Because of the very facility of the theory, such a test would be difficult to devise, and probably even harder to execute. But one may safely prophesy that until it is brought within the range of possible disproof, Natural Selection will play no further part in the development of biological knowledge.

Happily, there are indications that the hypothesis will not remain permanently inaccessible to critical investigation. J. B. S. Haldane and R. A. Fisher in England, and S. Wright in America, have performed the extraordinarily complicated feat of describing mathematically the action of Natural Selection on populations of different types, so that the various possibilities can be stated and discussed with more precision than hitherto. H. J. Muller, of the University of Texas, has shown that the rate with which inheritable variations appear in a fly can be increased about 150 times by irradiation with X-rays. It may soon be possible, by choosing a rapidly breeding species, so that the experiments can cover a large number of generations, to make an animal adapt itself to a variety of different environments. Then we shall be able to assess more accurately what part selection plays in the process.

There we have a problem that may be tackled at some future time. For the present, Natural Selection is in ill favour because it explains too much and too readily. It is too unassailable. Hypotheses must live dangerously nowadays if they are to live at all. Until the position of Natural Selection is made more dangerous the theory will remain what it is and what is has been ever since its formulation— a perfectly credible explanation of the evolutionary process, but not necessarily the true one.

CHARLES DICKENS

1812-1870

BY
G. K.
CHESTERTON

CHARLES DICKENS

IN considering Dickens as a Victorian, perhaps the first necessity is considering him as a pre-Victorian. It is not so much a matter of dates as of derivations; it must be remembered, to begin with, that he is much less completely inside the period, much less covered at both ends by the conventions of the period, than many great men whom some would call more original, like Ruskin or Meredith or Browning. On this side, indeed, Dickens is outside the Victorian enclosure, not so much because he was original as because he was traditional. Though labelled Radical, where others were labelled Tory, he carries on a rank, rowdy, jolly tradition, of men falling off coaches, before the sons of Science and the Great Exhibition began to travel primly on rails—or grooves. He carries on the old English legend of the coarse and comic novels of Smollett and Fielding; and none the less because, under the gradual pressure of Victorianism, his work is still comic but no longer coarse. The sort of comicality that commonly went with coarseness is apparent enough, especially at the beginning; while many of the other Victorians seem to have grown up, not merely Victorian—but something that should rather be called Albertian. This is the first and perhaps the frankest phase of Dickens; and but for refinements that really started later than this phase, it might easily have been even more frank. It may or may not be right to call him a caricaturist. But certainly, considered as a caricaturist, he starts straight away out of the world of Gilray and Rowlandson; a world widely different from that of Du Maurier or even Keene. We hardly feel any such direct heritage of the old comic writers even at the beginning of the other Victorian novelists; because they are more completely Victorian. And before we come to the application of this fact to his fiction, it has some application even to his life. For circumstances started him almost unconsciously with a certain very ancient tradition, which for special reasons had become a very English tradition. It makes an immortal appearance in his first great masterpiece of *Pickwick*; but it is connected also with something in his personal position as well as in his literary lineage. It is perhaps the simplest figure in which we can summarize his primary position both in life and letters. I will call it for convenience the great tradition of The Comic Servant. And though in special ways it had been softened by being Christian and emphasized by being English, it is a very venerable tradition, which works back to the position in antiquity of The Comic Slave.

To explain this, we may briefly allude to his life, though there is no space for his biography. He was born in Portsea, a part of Portsmouth, in 1812, but was soon removed to Chatham, around which neighbourhood his early life largely revolved. His father was an impecunious old party, whose occupation was often shadowy and what the hasty will describe as shady. But he was the model of Micawber, and therefore must have had in him something great and good. He and his son later went to London, where they both became parliamentary reporters; but the son soon turned from reporting politics to reporting life. As a journalist he wrote under the name of "Boz," and certain sketches of his attracted attention; a friend and patron named Hogarth had a family of daughters, among whom he found first a wife and afterwards a friend; but his first great opportunity came with the offer to write a story round Seymour's sketches of the pranks of the Nimrod Club, which he managed to turn into the more famous Pickwick Club. The book was hugely popular, and ever afterwards he was busy, successful, laborious, inventive, excited, and exhausted until he died. *Oliver Twist,* which stands somewhat alone, was followed by a serial scheme of stories within a story called *Master Humphrey's Clock,* in which *Barnaby Rudge* and *The Old Curiosity Shop* both appeared. Later, at regular intervals, came *Nicholas Nickleby, Martin Chuzzlewit,* and *Dombey and Son*; and with the latter we reach and recognize a change in his mood and method; the frank farce begins to fade away, and the more subtle, sober, and realistic Dickens of later years develops. He reaches his most sincere moment in the semi-autobiographical *David Copperfield*; his most earnest social philosophy in *Hard Times*, with something of the same graver reforming spirit in *Bleak House*; and his most restrained and delicate artistic success in *Great Expectations*. *Little Dorrit* was something of an interlude; and then he gathered up into his last complete book, *Our Mutual Friend*, all his growing knowledge of the realities of society, of the growth of plutocracy, and the peril now threatening the national tradition. His furious industry, combined with yet more devastating tours in America, to say nothing of the private tragedy that separated him from his wife, gave something gloomy and feverish to his end; and he died in 1870, leaving unsolved other mysteries besides *The Mystery of Edwin Drood*.

It is rather symbolic that he died in that year of Prussian victory, which was the eclipse of Liberty throughout the world. For he had grown up with the growing Liberalism of England, and is perhaps the one great Englishman who consciously devoted himself to democracy as a feeling as well as a theory. He stands for all the hearty humanitarianism of that age at its best; and yet there is a deeper and older element in him, which I have put first because it came first. I mean, what I have already called the tradition of The Comic Servant.

I mean, that if we call Dickens democratic, we must qualify it by saying that he is the derisive democrat rather than the dignified democrat. If he looks down on worldly rank, it is not from the severe status of the citizen of antiquity; it is not even from the solid status of the peasant in any peasantry. It is rather with that inverted and comic contempt which looks down when it looks up. It derives, not so much from any levelling dogma that Jack is as good as his master, in the sense that he should have no master; it derives rather from the old joke, found in many an old legend, that Jack is better than his master; that in the last scene the last are first and the first last. We could hardly summon the solemnity to say that Samuel Pickwick and Samuel Weller are two equal citizens; if only because in some ways the servant is the superior. But the superiority is the superiority of a comic servant, not of a master or even a peasant proprietor; superiority in wit and satire and cunning, but not superiority in status or seriousness or dignity. Now, despite the growth of more grave and ideal democratic views, this did long remain the real attitude of the real Dickens. He was, first of all, the poorer man making fun of the richer; but instinctively using fun as his weapon, and not minding if in the process he seems merely the funny man. This was complicated afterwards, as will be noted later, by many less natural ambitions touching rhetoric and sentiment. But when Dickens is most like himself, he is most like Sam Weller, and least like Wat Tyler or William Tell. He is more really concerned to show that the tyrant is undignified than that the slave is dignified.

The point is that the comic Dickens existed before the tragic or melodramatic; the comic was older than the tragic; the comic was deeper than the tragic. It was partly because there was already a tradition of popular joviality rather than popular justice; of riot rather than revolt. It was partly because Dickens as an individual had lived for a long time amid this laughter of the populace, before he began to think more seriously of that social ideal; which is not merely the populace, but rather the people. Just as Sam Weller had run wild as a sort of guttersnipe, before he became a gentleman's servant and something of a philosopher, so Dickens had been one of the old English crowd, from which a nameless voice cries, " Three cheers for the Mayor; and may he never desert the nail and sarspan business as 'e made 'is money by," long before he had ever dreamed of seeing the tragic vision of a French crowd, as in *The Tale of Two Cities,* through the visionary eyes of Carlyle. That is the real comparison between Dickens the humorist and Dickens the sentimentalist, the sociologist, the realist, the reformer, and all the many aspects that have been unfavourably or favourably compared with it. Not that his social criticism was bad, not even that his sentimentalism was always necessarily bad; but that his humour was the elder brother, more hardy, more mature, more expert and experienced, more genuine and more national and historic. For the English populace has lived on laughter—its substitute for religion, for property, and sometimes even for food.

We may say that in this matter there is a curious contrast to Scott. We may also say that in this matter Scott was really Scottish, and therefore the reverse of English. For the Scots, having a real religion of the people, have had a real dignity in the democracy. Nothing is more notable than this curious contradiction: that while Dickens called himself a Radical and really was a Democrat, and Scott called himself a Tory and really rejoiced in some qualities of the older aristocrat, Scott had a far nobler sense than Dickens of the natural human dignity of the poor. Small farmers or fishermen in Scott do not have to become comic servants in order to score off their masters; do not have to become Court fools in order to criticize the Court. They can be eloquent in plain words: they can be eloquent in poor man's speech; they can be eloquent in broad Scots. Nobody doubts the sincerity of Dickens or the justification of Peggotty; but they could not speak over the ruined hearth with the tongue of Meg Merrilees over the gipsy fires; a speech that almost rises into song. Nationality is not a matter of praise or blame, for by its very nature a nation gives a colour to things both good and evil; but it is important to realize that Dickens could no more have imagined Meg Merrilees than Scott could have invented Mrs. Wilfer.

Oddly enough, Dickens could only write good rhetoric when he meant it for bad rhetoric. When he himself seriously meant it for good rhetoric, it was generally bad. So completely was the comic spirit his spirit, almost in the sense of his soul, that anything he wrote with expansion and exaggeration was for him a liberation of the soul, and took on swelling contours of the comic, which really have their own beauty and even their own harmony. But when he was only making his serious characters dramatic, he often only made them melodramatic. When he was only stuffing the gaps of the mere story with serious matter, he was not enjoying himself so much; and the stuffing was often poor stuff. His fools could talk poetry, while his knaves could only talk sentiment. Therefore, strange as it may seem, the one or two occasions on which Dickens may actually be said to be an English stylist, are those in which he is a satirist of what he considers a pompous and preposterous style. About as good a piece of English as he ever wrote in his life is Mr. Serjeant Buzfuz's speech, which is really an uncommonly good speech. We can see the difference at once, when we compare it with the really pompous and preposterous speeches he was putting, almost at the same time, into the mouths of his serious villains. For instance, *Nicholas Nickleby* is an early work; but

Pickwick is even earlier. But the raving of Ralph Nickleby is not even good as raving; while the ranting of Serjeant Buzfuz is very good as ranting; nay, is classical and almost rational as ranting. Few, I imagine, who have had business interviews with a money-lender, or even a stingy uncle, have ever heard him conclude the conversation with the words, " My curse, my bitter curse upon you, boy ! "; or formed a high opinion of his literary style if he did. But then Dickens was not enjoying himself in writing about Ralph; and he was enjoying himself in writing about Buzfuz. Therefore, as I say, he so heartily enters into the real spirit of the old forensic eloquence, and so fills it with his own ecstasy of emphasis, that he really writes a piece of good style worthy of a great stylist. After describing darkly how " a being, erect upon two legs and bearing all the outward semblance of a man and not of a monster," entered Mrs. Bardell's lodging-house, he has the art and restraint to close the passage with simplicity and severity. " This man was Pickwick; Pickwick the defendant." Then, by a true stylistic inspiration, he starts afresh, as with a new paragraph: " Of this man Pickwick I will say little. The subject presents but few attractions; and I, gentlemen, am not the man, nor are you, gentlemen, the men, to delight in the contemplation of revolting heartlessness and systematic villainy." Which is, quite seriously, a rattling good piece of English rhetoric; a thousand times better than anything Dickens could have written when he wanted to be serious.

It would be an exaggeration to say that this is because Dickens was not serious about being serious. But it is true to say that his whole soul was seldom in anything about which he was wholly serious. He was a man with much of the actor in him; he was, in fact, an admirable amateur actor; the real, sound, old-fashioned sort of actor, who was proud of versatility and the taking of varied parts. When he took the part of a rhetorician or a sentimentalist or a social idealist, he was sincere as an actor is sincere; that is, as any other artist is sincere. He had something to say and he said it; not always perfectly, but often very well. But when he was describing something funny, he was himself. He was not acting but enjoying; he was almost the audience rather than the artist. There was something gigantic, as of the joy of a whole crowd, in his enjoyment. He was essentially the man who laughs at his

168

own jokes, and his own jokes inspired him like wine to wilder and wilder creation; but always to the creation of beauty in his own department of the far-fetched and the fantastic. What is more to the purpose here, they could inspire him even in the department of the forensic or the classic. When he was giving us Buzfuz at his funniest, he could not help giving us Buzfuz at his best. Dickens does not record the speech of Mr. Serjeant Snubbin, the Counsel of Mr. Pickwick, who was equally eminent and doubtless equally eloquent. But then Snubbin had the misfortune to be on the right side, and especially the reasonable side, and reasonableness would never have inspired such rhetoric. In Dickens it is the man who is entirely in the wrong who invariably says the right thing.

All the genius is in that saying of the right thing; that is, of the exquisitely and ecstatically wrong thing. His fun is a form of poetry; and quite as personal and indefinable as poetry. Like poetry, it is for the moment on one note, and making the most of one notion; like poetry, it leaves us amazed at what can be made out of one notion. That is what the critics mean who say it is not like life; because it is more living than life. It is a magic accelerating growth; so that one seed out of a thousand seeds of fact visibly springs and sprouts into a tree, as in a fairy-tale. Certainly this is not dealing with all the facts; but it is releasing all the potential life in one of them. Dickens saw something, whether in a man's notions or in his nose, which could be developed more than dull life dares to develop it. The Dickens comic character is in that sense real and in that sense unreal. We may call it a caricature; though indeed it is a caricature of Dickens to call him a caricaturist. The very criticism itself has exactly the over-simplification of a caricature. But if anybody thinks that anybody can do it, that it is a vulgar trick of exaggerating anything, that it is not a work of art, that it is not a work of genius—then that critic may be curtly recommended to become a great comic novelist, and create a score of Dickens characters out of the next twenty people he meets. He will soon find that he can no more do it than he can become a great poet merely by admiring the sunset. In this sense we may say that Dickens was really too subtle and distinguished; and that is why it was easy to call him obvious and vulgar.

We may here recur to the fact first stated: that Dickens,

who was in a family sense almost as new and nameless as
a foundling, or at least almost as lonely as an orphan, had
in a literary sense something like a pedigree. He called
one of his sons Henry Fielding Dickens, and we instantly
feel that he had a sort of natural right to make a godfather
out of Henry Fielding; more than he had, in that sense,
to make one out of a pure Victorian like Alfred Tennyson.
But the comic literature was not all great literature, nor
its exponents all men like Fielding; and there were two
sides to the very broad farce prevailing before the time
when the Tennysonian refinement finally prevailed. In some
ways this crude comic tradition did him harm even then;
and in one particular way it does him even greater harm
now. It is notable that he took over certain stock stage
figures, of the farcical sort, and many modern readers are
still repelled by a general impression that the story is stale,
before they go on to discover that the story-telling is almost
startlingly fresh. For instance, they feel that it is not very
funny that Mr. Tupman was a fat man who dressed up as
a dandy and a lady-killer. It is not very funny; and for
that reason Dickens really tells us very little more about
Mr. Tupman. It marks the inspired inconsequence of his
method, that the story of Pickwick is not chiefly the story
of the Pickwickians. Dickens started with the stock characters, but he crowded the stage with superb supers who
have nothing to do with the play, and who are the making
of it. By the end, the story is full of entirely new and
original characters, and none more new than Mr. Samuel
Pickwick; who has somehow changed from a goggle-eyed
old buffoon to a most mellow and well-mannered old
English merchant. Nobody does justice to Dickens the
creative artist who has a general prejudiced impression of
Dickens the caricaturist. He actually began with a commission to write what were little more than captions for
caricatures. The point is that while the caricatures remained stiff or vulgar, the new captions grew more and
more inventive and imaginative. The test is not in the
situations, but in the treatment of the situations. There
must have been many tipsy clerks, in many comic novels,
who roystered in their cups in the manner of robbers
carousing. But only one of them, whose name was Richard
Swiveller, when crying, "Some wine here, ho!" ever
carried dramatic versatility so far as to hand the flagon
to himself with profound humility and then receive it

haughtily.   There must have been many jokes about
Valentine's Day as vulgar as the valentines; but only in
the Weller family was there that remarkable debate on
diction, which decided whether " circumscribed " or " cir-
cumvented " is a more tender word.   Many allusions
less than delicate were made to Mrs. Gamp's profession,
but only one gave us a flashing glimpse of that distracted
husband, and the invalid who was told " to ease 'er mind,
'is 'owls was organs."

Nevertheless, Dickens did gain something essential to
his greatness from that old tradition of England, and even
from that relatively old tradition of revolution.   I know
not what it should be called; if I had to invent a name for
it I should call it The Great Gusto; something whole-hearted
and precipitate about the mirth and the anger of that age,
when there were mobs and no ballot-boxes.   When all is
allowed for, the many noble names that are native to the
Victorian time as such, and their several forms of sincerity
or self-direction, it is true that the great force, or even the
great violence of Dickens flows through them all, like an
ancestral river coming from older places and more historic
hills.   He is all the more traditional because he is ignorant.
He has that vast, silent, incessant traditionalism that we call
the ignorance of the populace.   And it is right to say that
when more sophisticated Victorians set up fads like fences,
and established new forms of narrowness, that flood of
popular feeling, that was a single man, burst through them
and swept on.   He was a Radical, but he would not be a
Manchester Radical, to please Mr. Gradgrind.   He was a
humanitarian, but he would not be a platform pacifist, to
please Mr. Honeythunder.   He was vaguely averse to
ritual religion; but he would not abolish Christmas, to
please Mr. Scrooge.   He was ignorant of religious history,
and yet his religion was historic.   For he was the People,
that is heard so rarely in England; and, if it had been
heard more often, would not have suffered its feasts to be
destroyed.

BENJAMIN DISRAELI

1804–1881

BY
ARTHUR A.
BAUMANN

ARTHUR A. BAUMANN

BENJAMIN DISRAELI

I HAPPENED to have a seat under the gallery in the House of Commons last April, when Mr. Neville Chamberlain moved the introduction of the Finance Act 1932. The whole House rose, cheering and waving the order papers over their heads, one or two, I fear, clapping their hands. Dear me, I said to myself, whatever is this for? The House has grown very emotional in these days. For I have seen Gladstone and Harcourt and Randolph Churchill rise to make a big speech without exciting any of this shouting, or getting up, or waving of order papers. The speech was a good House of Commons speech, nothing out of the way, and frequently inaudible—how they do mumble in these times, the Speaker worst of all! The peroration was well conceived, making the point that one son of Joseph Chamberlain was listening to another who was proposing a Protectionist Budget! This I read next morning in *The Times*, for the Chancellor's emotion showed itself in complete inaudibility at the Bar of the House.

There was an omission of a name which struck me as I left my seat—there was no mention of Disraeli. And yet seventy-six years ago Disraeli, a young and not much respected member, had the courage to stand up and tell Peel, at the peak of his parliamentary power, backed by three-fourths of the Tory Party, all the Whigs, the Radicals, with the Anti-Corn Law League thundering out of doors, that they were all wrong, and that they were ruining the agricultural interest and the territorial system, which had made England great and alone could keep her so. The present generation is apparently devoid of the historic sense. To mention the country's return to Protection with-

175

out naming Disraeli is like talking of slave-emancipation without remembering Wilberforce.

I quote the following passage, published in 1912, from the second volume (Monypenny's) of the great *Life of Disraeli*:

> "The repeal of the Corn Laws was the first decisive step in that policy of sacrificing the rural life of England to a one-sided and exaggerated industrial development, which has done so much to change the English character and the English outlook, and which it may not impossibly be the business of subsequent generations to endeavour to retrace."

The repeal was followed, as everyone knows, by the fifty years of expanding prosperity, which coincided with Queen Victoria's reign, and had very little to do with free imports. The reaction has come, as Disraeli warned us that it would, and this generation is endeavouring clumsily and half-heartedly to retrace its steps. But because Repeal was followed by prosperity, and because Disraeli said, in his epigrammatic way, "Protection is not only dead but damned," his enemies accused him of insincerity. What he did was to accept the *res judicata*. His views on trade were liberal from the first to the last; he never became, like Peel, the slave of a formula. A tariff, he often explained, was not a principle, but an expedient, and he dwelt steadily on the value of reciprocity. He was the one statesman of the age who kept his mind clear on the subject of tariffs, and refused to be blinded by the commercial success, due to quite other causes, of the Victorian era; and he regarded with scorn the muddle-minded enthusiasm of the academic experts, who wrote the system of free imports up to the level of a religion. He lived long enough to see the beginning of the Fair Trade movement, which was started in Lancashire in the late seventies, just when three wet summers washed him out of office in 1880.

For one of the greatest party leaders that ever lived, Disraeli's consistency is wonderful. He formed his opinions on political fundamentals before he entered Parliament, and he never changed them. His period of gestation was between 1830 and 1837, when he was fighting unsuccessful contests at Wycombe and Taunton. These early convictions are mostly to be found in his pre-parliamentary writings, such as *The Spirit of Whiggism*, his *Runnymede*

Letters, and the *Vindication of the English Constitution,*
which are well worth reading, or would be, if anyone cared
a straw to-day about anything but keeping his seat. Disraeli was quite determined to prevent parliamentary reform
from being made a monopoly of the Whigs, who regarded
this young man as a poacher on their preserves when he
put forward any plan for the extension of the franchise.
But the difference of Disraelian reform from that advocated
by Gladstone and Bright and the Manchester school, was
that the Radicals proclaimed a vote to be an abstract right,
a claim belonging to every Briton, while Disraeli maintained that a vote was a privilege, a prize, as it were, for
proved civic capacity. Thus he distinguished between
popular principles and democratic rights.

The distribution of political power was to him a matter
of political convenience to be decided by the Government.
No man had any right to participate, in however small a
degree, in the government of his country unless he had
given some evidence of stability of character or willingness
to support the most obvious duties of a citizen. Residence
for a year or two as a householder and the payment of
rates, the payment of a small amount of imperial taxation,
a university degree, the position of a foreman of works,
were some of the qualifications which he proposed in his
first Reform Bill in 1857, which, it is needless to say, were
laughed out of court as " fancy franchises " by the provincial Bright, the doctrinaire Russell, and " the flesh and
blood " demagogue Gladstone.

In his 1867 Reform Act, which he carried through a
House with a Liberal majority, he brushed aside as childish
the making a particular figure of rental, £10, or £7, or £5,
the basis of the franchise, which he anchored to a two-
years' residence and the personal payment of rates. It
was not his fault if the Liberal Government that displaced
him in 1868 abolished his qualification, though it is interesting to note that the system of compounding for rates introduced by the building workmen's blocks of flats has been
modified by returning to Disraeli's qualification, by stating,
in the demand for rent, the proportion that stands for rates.
The local authorities have discovered how right Disraeli
was in fixing on the payment of rates as a test of civic duty.
Disraeli received undue praise and undeserved abuse for
this Reform Act. It was the Queen and Lord Derby who
pressed him to settle this Reform question once for all as

H

is clearly shown in the correspondence between the three, published in Buckle's *Life*. Having defeated Gladstone's Bill, Disraeli would have gladly allowed the question to ripen in the public mind for, at any rate, a few years.

When the working classes of the towns realized in 1874 what Disraeli had done for them, they showed their gratitude by giving him what was then thought the handsome majority of 50. But by that time Disraeli had lost his wife and his health, and the energies that gout, asthma, and bronchitis had left him were absorbed in saving Turkey from Russia, a stroke of policy which, so far from " putting our money on the wrong horse " (Lord Salisbury's sneer), must be recognized with gratitude by the present generation. All that Disraeli could do in domestic politics was to choose the right Ministers, and carry their Bills for them. He chose Cross as Home Secretary. I believe even the extreme wing of the Labour Party now freely admits that Disraeli gave them the charter of Trades Unionism. The Act which Cross passed, amending the law of conspiracy, made trades unions legal combinations, and the Workmen's Dwellings Act was the beginning of the policy of *sanitas sanitatum omnia sanitas,* which a shallow lawyer like Henry James could describe as " a policy of sewage," but which subsequent Governments have found so popular that they have sometimes carried it to excess.

All this sanitary and trades union legislation is merely another proof of Disraeli's consistency, for you can find it all in *Sybil,* which was written thirty years earlier. Superficial students, who never get beneath formulas and slogans, misquote Disraeli to prove that he was at heart a Democrat or a Socialist, and he certainly did say, " the Monarchy of the Tories is more democratic than the Republic of the Whigs." The danger to which every epigrammatist is exposed is misquotation by phrases being wrenched from their context.

His two pet objects of political dislike were middle-class Nonconformity, with its Puritanical horror of enjoyment, and the arrogance of the Whigs, who regarded themselves as a caste born to rule the mob, political Brahmins, to whom Dizzy himself was an "untouchable." He was determined to break down what he looked on as the hypocritical professions of charitable sympathy with the lower classes, whose suffering the Whigs exploited for political purposes. Disraeli supported the Chartists when they presented their monster petition to Parliament in 1840, though he pointed out to them that they were " barking up the wrong tree " in thinking that their wrongs were political. With a few other Young Englanders, he supported Lord Ashley's Ten Hours' Bill, which Bright, Cobden, and the Manchester Radicals denounced as an interference with freedom of contract, Cobden declaring that a nice warm factory was a better place for young children than cold, wet fields ! (see Hammond's *Lord Shaftesbury*).

That Disraeli was a Socialist in his belief that society was capable of improvement by a " judicious combination of private and public effort " is true, as I imagine it to be true of every sane Conservative.   But that he was a Democrat or a Socialist in the sense that he believed that State ownership, however gradual or modified, was better than private property, is so untrue that he did not even believe in the possibility of such a policy.   A policy built on confiscation he refused to consider, except as the fantastic scheme of some presumptuous pedant.   It was his only bad blunder.   In *The Spirit of Whiggism* (1836) he ventured on the astounding prophecy that " there is no probability of ever establishing a more democratic than the present English Constitution."   His syllogism is flawless, granting the major premise: " Whatever form a government may assume, its spirit must be determined by the laws which regulate the property of the country."   That is quite true.   " You may have a Senate and Consuls, you may have no hereditary titles, and you may dub each householder or inhabitant a citizen ; but if the spirit of your laws preserves masses of property in a particular class, the government of the country will follow the disposition of property."

Quite so ; but how if the property should be transferred from the upper to the lower classes?   The question is then put: Is there any probability of a different disposition of property in England ?   Disraeli decided that there was not, because " the nation that esteems wealth as the great object of existence, will submit to no laws that do not secure the enjoyment of wealth.   Now we deprive wealth of its greatest source of enjoyment, as well as its best security, if we deprive it of power.   The English nation, therefore, insists that property shall be the qualification of power."   This was written the year before Disraeli was elected to Parliament.

In his own Reform Act, twenty-six years later, he still clung to the payment of rates as a qualification. But these absurd arguments show how little the farthest-seeing amongst us can penetrate the future. That Conservative and Socialist Governments should seize from 40 to 60 per cent. of a man's income, and at his death appropriate a like proportion of his accumulation or inheritance, was not dreamed of in Disraeli's philosophy, any more than that universal suffrage for both sexes should be carried into law by Conservative Party leaders. Mr. Lloyd George was not more beyond his ken than Lord Ullswater and Mr. Baldwin. How Disraeli would have financed the War and social services, it is idle to speculate. But to one who has studied his writings and speeches, it does not seem too bold a conjecture to suppose that he would have recurred to tariffs at the outset.

Against his " howler " about the distribution of property must be set off his prediction that the decline of the House of Commons, which had filched power from the Crown and the House of Lords, would be as rapid as its rise. " The depositary of power," observes Sidonia, " is always unpopular " ; " an educated nation recoils from the imperfect vicariate of what is called representative government," and will prefer the Press, as " a more direct and less costly method of representing public opinion."

His prophecy that the influence of the Crown would revive is, of course, taken from Bolingbroke. But it is remarkable that Lord Balfour, writing an Introduction to Bagehot's *English Constitution,* republished in 1927 by the Oxford University Press, should have concluded with these words:

> " The Empire in its modern shape is a bold experiment, and a very novel one. On its success hangs the assurance of peace, happiness, and prosperity, over no small portion of the world ; and when we reflect that without the Crown the experiment could never even have been tried, we cannot doubt that among the transformations which by insensible degrees have converted our most ancient and most venerable institutions to the most modern uses, not the least fortunate and successful has been the transformation of the British Monarchy."

Nor can we doubt that the practical romance which Lord

Beaconsfield wove about his " Faëry Queene " had a hand
in that transformation.

Dating parliamentary government from the Whig Revolution, there have been three statesmen who have applied
thought consistently to politics, and written about them like
men of letters—Bolingbroke, Burke, and Disraeli. Matthew
Arnold has told us that the first is one of our classics, of
whom we ought to know more. I have read most of
Bolingbroke's writings, from the *Letter to Sir William
Wyndham* to the *Patriot King,* and *pace* my friend Mr.
Walter Sichel, am inclined to agree with Burke, that he
was " a presumptuous and a superficial writer," though
there was more than a touch of Whig malice in the query,
" Who now reads Bolingbroke ? " Bagehot, indeed, has
paid him the compliment of a humorous homily on his
moral delinquencies ; but in truth he has faded away into
something of a myth. Burke had the inestimable advantage of being his own reporter, in days before the reporters'
gallery existed, for all his speeches were written before or
after delivery, and most of his output was in the form of
the essay or pamphlet. For the weak digestion of the
modern student Burke is too strong meat. Lord Newton,
to whom I sent a copy of Eyre and Spottiswoode's
republication of *A Letter to a Noble Lord,* with an Introduction by myself, wrote that he preferred my preface to
the pompous and stilted phraseology of Burke !

That in his free-lance days Disraeli should have written
sentimental novels, pamphlets, and letters to the newspapers (for which he refused payment), is what we might
expect. It is more remarkable that, after he had been
in Parliament seven years, had made many successful
speeches, and was a serious candidate for office, he should
deliberately have chosen the novel as the medium for the
advancement of his political ideas. The celebrated trilogy
of *Sybil* (as he misspelt it), *Coningsby* and *Tancred* was
Disraeli's *cri de cœur,* a trumpet-sermon to a stagnant and
decaying Tory Party. *Lothair,* in which the vulgar saw
nothing but a description of lords and ladies, and which
even his friends thought beneath the dignity of an ex-Prime
Minister, dealt the Church of Rome a blow from which she
still reels, and as a political move was twenty times as
effective as Lord John Russell's anti-Popery manifesto.

Disraeli knew what he was about in writing political
novels : he knew that " Where truth in closest words shall

fail, when truth embodied in a tale shall enter in at lowly doors." For one who has read his Corn-law speeches or his *Life of Lord George Bentinck*—though his attacks on Peel and his account of the two years' struggle in Parliament are packed tight with wit and historical truths—there are millions who have read *Sybil* and *Coningsby* and *Lothair*.

Political novels written by a Prime Minister must necessarily be unique. I have heard people compare Trollope's political novels with Disraeli's. The politics in Trollope are merely the setting for his admirable and immortal characters. His description of the debates between Mr. Gresham (Gladstone) and Mr. Danbeny (Disraeli) have always seemed to me very poor stuff, whereas Planty Pal, Lady Glencora, the Greshams, De Courcys, etc., live to-day. Thackeray and Dickens made fun of elections. But anyone who reads the Disraelian novels will learn as much political history as the readers of Shakespeare learn about pre-Stuart history; and honest people will tell you that all they know about Richard II is got from the play.

I hear it often said that Disraeli was a feminist, meaning that he would have given the vote to women. Disraeli was fond of saying that he owed everything in life to women; which was partly true. For without the jointure and devotion of Mary Ann at a point of his life when he had been in Parliament two years and owed about £20,000, it is difficult to conjecture what his fate might have been. He would probably have accepted the Vice-Royalty of India, like Canning, who was only stopped from sailing by the death of Castlereagh and the offer of the leadership of the House of Commons.

He also owed much, socially, to Frances, Lady Londonderry, in the early days. His father left him £10,000: Mr. Brydges Williams left him £40,000; and the Bentincks (Titchfield, Henry, and George) advanced him about £30,000 on a mortgage of Hughenden, subsequently taken over at 2 per cent. by Andrew Montagu. Curiously, it was almost exactly the sum lent by Lord Rockingham to Edmund Burke to buy the Gregorics at Beaconsfield. I think there is little doubt that Queen Victoria was very nearly in love with him, and that he was desperately in love at seventy-four with Lady Bradford the ruthless publication of his letters by Lord Zetland proves beyond a doubt. Indeed, the theme of his last novel, *Endymion,* is

that a nincompoop lad in the post office may become Prime
Minister by the influence of women. Nevertheless, in spite
of all this, I do not believe Disraeli would have committed
the folly of throwing the balance of political power into
the hands of women. The incorrigible romantic had a
substratum of realism. Beneath the flowers of his Oriental
imagination there lay a bottom of sound common sense.
" Where is the merriment? " angrily asked Dr. Johnson
of a group of giggling women. " I say the person was
fundamentally sensible," as was Disraeli.

To place Disraeli rightly in the bede-roll of English
statesmen you have only to see for yourself what has
become of the Tory Party since his death in 1881. Headless
and nameless, it lies upon the strand.

" Avolsumque humeris jacet et sine nomine corpus."

Afraid to call itself Tory, apparently thinking the name
Conservative not modern enough, it resorts to the name
Unionist, meaningless except to remind us of one of the
least creditable chapters of recent history.

It is true that for twelve years, from 1881 to 1903, the
late Lord Salisbury kept us out of war abroad, and preserved a semblance of unity between the two wings of the
Unionist alliance. Lord Salisbury possessed in an eminent
degree the virtue which the Greeks valued so highly—
balance, sanity, sobriety of mind. But he was not inspiring,
and when he died the quarrel between Chamberlain and
Balfour rent the party in twain. From 1916 to the present
hour the Conservatives have been content to fulfil what they
appear to regard as their natural function of supplying
votes to be used by the Socialist and Liberal chiefs for purposes and aims other than those of Toryism. These were
succinctly defined by Disraeli in 1872 to be, " the maintenance of our institutions, the preservation of our Empire,
and the improvement of the condition of the people."
Fifty years of Balfour, Bonar Law, and Baldwin, co-operat-
ing with Socialists, have left us with a disabled House of
Lords; a lost Ireland; a vanishing India; and a class war
fomented by the robbery of the minority in order to buy
the votes of the majority.

GEORGE ELIOT

1819-1880

BY
VITA
SACKVILLE-WEST

GEORGE ELIOT

1819-1880

BY

VITA

SACKVILLE-WEST

GEORGE ELIOT

IN the National Portrait Gallery, among other records of the memorable dead, hangs the portrait of George Eliot. Near it hangs the portrait of three Brontës—Charlotte, Emily, and Anne—that unskilled and yet revealing canvas, creased and blistered, which provides so startling a contrast between the three delicate, visionary, almost mediæval faces, and that other face which looks out at us from the canvas of Sir Frederick Burton, reassuring as the face of an old-fashioned Nannie, solid, sensible, and eminently Victorian—the face of George Eliot.

Not unsuitably, we reflect, was she christened Mary Ann. Not unsuitably did Mr. Lewes, in intimacy, call her " Polly." We are not surprised, looking at that face, to read that she could weep " bucketfuls [*sic*] of tears." We are not surprised to learn that she was born only six months later than Queen Victoria, or to find every biographer, male or female (with one notable exception), insisting on her femininity. We are not surprised to hear it suggested that one of her hands, her shapely hands, was larger than the other, because of her work, butter-making, in the dairy.

" The only ardent hope I have for my future life," she wrote, " is to have given to me some woman's duty, some possibility of devoting myself where I may see a daily result of pure blessedness in the life of another."

George Eliot is one of those authors of whom it is almost impossible to think without instantly recalling their physical appearance. It is just possible to read even *Mazeppa* without giving a thought to Byron's curly mouth; just possible to read even *Atalanta* without reference to Swinburne's fiery hair; but it is difficult to consider *Scenes of Clerical Life* without an involuntary evocation of that large, serious, and benevolent countenance.

The verbal descriptions of George Eliot are almost more vivid than the sketch in the National Portrait Gallery. "Bishop-like," Lord Morley called her. "A large, thick-set sybil, dreamy and immobile," wrote Sir Edmund Gosse, "whose massive features, somewhat grim when seen in profile, were incongruously bordered by a hat, always in the height of the Paris fashion, which in these days commonly included an immense ostrich feather; this was George Eliot. The contrast between the solemnity of the face and the frivolity of the head-gear had something pathetic and provincial about it."

Yet this was not all. It might be wittily said, it might be accurately said; but neither wit nor accuracy contains the whole truth of the matter. They seldom do. It should not be forgotten that a new acquaintance, having once enjoyed an hour's conversation with George Eliot, came away under the impression that she was beautiful; though, seeing her later in repose, she could hardly believe her to be the same person.

For there proves, indeed, to be something misleading about both this thick-set sibylline and this old-fashioned, comfortable Nannie conception of George Eliot, when we come to examine her a little more closely. Without going so far as to suggest that anything resembling a dual personality existed in George Eliot, it is certain that her inner life and her consequent actions were by no means entirely in accordance with the large placidity of those familiar features. As we contemplate those features, it is hard to believe that she could ever be described as "wayward and hysterical." Yet such is the fact. Outwardly serene, she was inwardly tormented by ill-health, religious doubt, nervous troubles, acute headaches, and night-terrors. She appears herself to have been aware of some discrepancy in her make-up, for she hated herself "for caring about carpets, easy-chairs, and coal-fires—one's soul is under a curse, and can preach no truth while one is in bondage to the flesh in this way. . . . We are reprobates, and shall never enter into the kingdom of heaven."

Outwardly, she cared about the carpets and the easy-chairs. She liked to have her house ordered as a woman likes to have her house ordered. Above all, she thought she would like to devote her life to a man—but,

though in theory she did so, in practice it worked out that
the man devoted as much of his life to her as she of hers
to him. He watched over her as tenderly as any Victorian
wife was supposed to watch over her husband. He kept
any offensively critical article away from her; he sheltered
her fame from any breeze from an outspoken world. He
cupped her life in his hands, lest any hostile breath should
blow out its candle.

She had given up a great deal for his sake. Her elopement with him, however—a married man—was not the first
gesture that she had made in the cause of personal independence. Her father had already had good reason for
sorrow and for a quarrel with her over her break-away
from orthodox religious views. She grieved over the
breach, but she persisted. Docile though she might appear
—and does still appear to us in her portraits—Mary Ann
Evans had a mind of her own.

The curious thing is, that she should have acted rebellion
rather than preached it. She preached many things—
rather too many, which damaged her as an artist—but
among the things she preached were not the things she had
practised in her own life. In her own life she had broken
away from her Church and had transgressed the laws of
wedlock and morality—Victorian morality. It is baffling
to think that the owner of that face, and the author of *Amos
Barton,* could be the same person as the woman who ran
away with George Henry Lewes; though far less baffling to
think that that woman was also the creator of Maggie
Tulliver.

It was a bold act, in those days, for a daughter to defy
a parent. It was a bolder act for a woman to run away
with a man she could not marry. It must have required,
indeed, a degree of moral courage almost inconceivable to
our minds. And Mary Ann Evans, one must remember,
was not only a woman, but in some ways a very womanly
woman, and a Victorian woman into the bargain. She
was no flaming rebel, with a desire to scandalize and startle
her generation. No dreams that her example might speed
up the emancipation of her sex ever entered her head.
Rather, she disapproved avowedly of the " unsexing " of
women, which was beginning to be talked about as she
grew older—though she did approve of equal education for
women, and actually bestowed £100 on Girton College,
" from the author of *Adam Bede.*"

No, she was no rebel by temperament, although she took the step of committing herself to this surprisingly irregular union. Irregular though it might be, she entered into it with as much earnestness as was ever accorded to a projected marriage. She was doing something highly unconventional, but she would do it in the most decorous way possible; and she would regard her voluntary bonds with as much respect as any bonds knotted in a church. She spoke truly when she said, " If there is one action or relation of my life which is and always has been profoundly serious, it is my relation to Mr. Lewes. . . . Light and easily broken ties are what I neither desire theoretically nor could live for practically."

She became, then, " Mother " to Mr. Lewes's sons; she became, nominally though never legally, Mrs. Lewes, and Mary Ann Evans ceased to exist. The change of name was significant, occurring as it did half-way through her life. Miss Evans had ceased to exist; Marian became Polly; Mrs. Lewes took Miss Evans's place. Still, a third personality, hitherto unsuspected, remained to be born; and out of the womb of years emerged George Eliot.

The name was fixed on because George was Mr. Lewes's Christian name, and because Eliot was " a good mouth-filling, easily pronounced word."

It seems strange that so great a novelist should have lived till the age of thirty-seven in ignorance of her own peculiar talent. In a memorandum she notes " a vague dream of mine that some time or other I might write a novel," but this vague dream had never got beyond the writing of an introductory chapter. Mr. Lewes was encouraging but cautious. He warned her that the projected story might be a failure; it might be that she was unable to write fiction. On the other hand, it might be just good enough to warrant her trying again. On the whole, it was worth while for her to try the experiment.

She tried it, and wrote *Amos Barton*.

The story was not a failure; both the Lewes's cried over it; Mr. Lewes sent it as the work of an unnamed friend to John Blackwood, and John Blackwood immediately accepted it for publication in his magazine. He wrote presently that he was glad to learn that Mr. Lewes's anonymous friend was, as he had supposed, a clergyman. Such a subject, he said, was best in clerical hands. Mr. Lewes, however, with characteristic honesty dispelled this misunderstanding, putting Mr. Blackwood into direct touch with the still anonymous author, whose first letter to Blackwood records " his " sensitiveness to the merits of cheques for fifty guineas, but still more his sensitiveness to the appreciation displayed by Mr. Blackwood, a guarantee that the work was worth doing for its own sake. The anonymity of this correspondence becoming inconvenient, the author of *Amos Barton* is shortly to be found writing to Mr. Blackwood: " Perhaps it will be well to give you my prospective name, as a tub to throw to the whale in case of curious enquiries ; and accordingly I subscribe myself, best and most sympathizing of Editors, yours very truly, GEORGE ELIOT."

One wonders what her feelings were, when for the first time she signed that name at the foot of a letter ? Did it look very strange, and did its masculinity slightly discompose her ? Did she and Lewes laugh together over it as a good joke, or was she too much filled by a sense of the sacredness of her new calling ? One suspects the latter, for there is no doubt that being a novelist was, to George Eliot, a very solemn mission indeed. One could speak to men's hearts, one could touch their souls ; it was not a power to be lightly or frivolously used. " A blessed hope," she called it, " to be rejoiced in with trembling." " Every hand," she wrote later, " is wanted in the world that can do a little genuine, sincere work."

The deception as to the name and sex of the author proved almost entirely successful. Dickens and Mrs. Carlyle, it is true, had some suspicions, Dickens giving it as his opinion that if the new author was not a woman, then no man ever before had had the art of making himself mentally so like a woman since the world began. (In point of fact, I believe Dickens's suspicions to have been next door to certainty, and his respect for the innocent mystification merely an ironical and courteous compliance.) Jane Carlyle suggested a two-deep explanation : the author, she thought, might be a middle-aged man, brother or first-cousin to a clergyman, and might have a wife who provided him with those " beautiful feminine touches." Others, however, were satisfactorily deceived. Froude began his letter " Dear Sir," and was doubtful whether he addressed an old man or a young. Thackeray accepted George Eliot without question as a man, saying definitely that the *Scenes* were *not written by a woman*. (Italics not mine.) Mrs.

Blackwood was *sure* they were not written by a woman;
so was Mrs. Oliphant. Blackwood himself was completely
taken in, for, having given up the idea that his contributor
was a clergyman, he wrote that " it will be curious if you
should be a member of a club, and be hearing your own
praises."

There must have been a charming little scene when
Blackwood called on Lewes, more than a year later, and
having talked for some time about *Clerical Scenes,* finally
asked, " Well, am I to see George Eliot this time? " Lewes
said, " Do you wish to see him? " " As he likes," said
Blackwood—had he by then any idea at the back of his
mind?—" I wish it to be quite spontaneous." George
Eliot then left the room, followed after a moment by Lewes,
and gave him the necessary permission. One can imagine
the whispered confabulation that took place outside the
door. Blackwood, we learn, " was kind "; missed his
train, and came back for further talk.

A schoolfellow of Marian Evans, who had known her as
a girl of thirteen, once told Mathilde Blind that it was impossible to imagine Marian as a baby; that it seemed as
if she must have come into the world fully developed like a
second Minerva. The same remark might have been
applied, twenty-four years later, to George Eliot the
novelist. She was born fully equipped from the first. No
trace of a fumbling amateurishness marks even her earliest
compositions; *Scenes of Clerical Life,* in fact, must be
reckoned among the best work that she ever did; and the
reasons for this immediate exercise of her skill and powers
are probably various. In the first place, she was a mature
woman when she turned to fiction, a woman of thirty-seven,
thoughtful and earnest by nature, ripened by her unusual
experience of life. " I feel," she wrote to Mrs. Bray, " that
all the terrible pains I have gone through in past years . . .
has [*sic*] probably been a preparation for some special
work that I may do before I die." In the second place,
she was firm from the outset in her own mind. " I cannot
stir a step aside from what I *feel* to be *true* in character,"
she wrote to Blackwood, who had ventured on some suggestion or criticism. In the third place, she had the good
sense to apply her talents to scenes and characters which
she intimately knew. As in her actions she had had no
desire to *épater le bourgeois,* but only to fulfil her in-

congruously unconventional destiny as conventionally and
decently as possible, so in her writings she seems to have
recognized from the first (with a few subsequent lapses)
that her principal gift was for the reproduction of her own
familiar rural England and the personalities that might be
met with, leaning over a stile or gossiping in the village
street. Her fiction, in short, was less fiction than truth:
she had but to place the paper beside her own memory,
and transcribe what she found therein; and her readers fell
upon it with delight because, apart from its other qualities,
it provided them with the flattering pleasure of recognition.
Her talent was a steady and sober talent, far, far removed
from the flash of genius; and, characteristically, she
accepted this rather mortifying fact, and squeezed the best
out of it; a very good best, too.

The pity is, that she did not permanently restrict herself
to that humble but respect-worthy ambition. Unfortunately, there was another side to George Eliot the realist,
George Eliot the interpreter of Mrs. Poyser, Mrs. Holt,
Caleb Garth, Rufus Lyon, and the Tullivers. Even Gwendolen Harleth and Dinah Morris may take their honourable
place in that company, as representing another facet of
George Eliot's mind, though on a different plane. But
what are we to say of the incredible Deronda, his mouth
" beset with abundant soft waves of beard "; his eyes " of
a dark yet mild intensity "; his " dark-blue shirt and skull-
cap "?—or of that attractive cad, Tito Melema?[1] George
Eliot the realist had her romantic side; few realists are
without it; in George Eliot it took the form of creating
impossibly romantic scamps or prigs of men, and of writing
Romola.

Romola, I think, is psychologically interesting as the
cuckoo in the nest of George Eliot's novels. Not that it is
interesting as regards the characters portrayed—Romola
herself is a dry though beautiful stick, Savonarola a mega-
phone, Tessa a charming ninny, Lillo the most decorative
but the least convincing of George Eliot's children; Monna
Brigida alone is really alive and immortal, sharing the

---

[1] A curious error appears in Sir Leslie Stephen's article on George
Eliot in the *Dictionary of National Biography*. He describes Tito
Melema as " one of her finest feminine characters." But possibly he
intended this statement deliberately and ironically, for in his *Men of
Letters* biography, he refers to Tito as, " thoroughly and to his fingers'
ends a woman."

quality of Mrs. Poyser and of Juliet's nurse—that Shakespearean quality of rich and rooted life which George Eliot
so frequently recaptured. Monna Brigida and a few sub-
sidiary characters excepted, *Romola* is superficially nothing
more than a painstaking costume novel, over whose details
the author expended enormous and conscientious trouble.
The interesting thing about *Romola* is that it represents
George Eliot's one attempt to escape from her own particular province of rural English life, of English politics as
she saw them (*e.g.* in *Felix Holt*), and of English character
as she knew and appreciated it in country people. She
went to Italy in her customary serious mood, but the sense
of romance was strong in her: " We had left our everyday
conventional world quite behind us," she wrote, " and were
on a visit to Nature in her private home." Nature in her
private home, as she believed, meant " the anticipation of
the new elements it would bring to my culture rather than
the hope of immediate pleasure." Travel, she thought,
could hardly be without a current of disappointment, if the
main object were not enlargement of one's general life, so
as to make even weariness and annoyance enter into the
sum of benefit. A truly Victorian point of view. What
actually happened was that Italy and especially Florence
released a flood of romanticism in George Eliot at the age
of forty-one, such as it has released at a perhaps more
appropriate age in many an English school-girl. Elopement, apparently, had not been enough for her. But, then,
elopement had been a solemn undertaking, rather than a
romantic excursion.

Being George Eliot, she managed to combine even in
Romola the romantic with the factual, the picturesque with
the improving. She let herself go, and go badly, over Tito ;
she let herself go, less badly, over Tessa, who at any rate
may claim relationship with Hetty Sorrel in *Adam Bede*.
(George Eliot had a persistent weakness for kittenish
women.) Then the whole background of fifteenth-century
Florence provided her with an orgy of romantic indulgence :
young men in scarlet tights, *barrette, zazzere,* and *scarselle*
—cod-pieces, too, though she averted her pen from those, if
not her eyes. Only when she came to Savonarola did she
return with energy to the young Marian Evans who had
been tormented by ideas of right and wrong. She was said
to resemble Savonarola in feature ; I cannot see that her
heavy face bears any greater resemblance to his burnt-out

and emaciated profile, than *Romola* bears to the rich,
pagan, masculine life of Renaissance Florence. Both were
Victorian falsifications; and the net result of *Romola,* however interesting it may be as an indication of George Eliot's
several repressions, is of a Victorian line-engraving, remin-
iscent of *Hernani* or *Ruy Blas.*

But it is not by *Romola* that one must judge George Eliot.
Romola should not be read by anyone over the age of
seventeen. *Romola* was a freak in an otherwise orderly
intellectual existence. We should not measure Tessa against
Tess; but the great solid block of George Eliot may without
shame be measured against the block of Thomas Hardy.

EDWARD FITZGERALD

1809-1883

BY
A. Y.
CAMPBELL

EDWARD
FITZGERALD

FITZGERALD was the Gray of the nineteenth century;
a sensitive and scholarly recluse, a fine critic and letter-
writer, a dilettante, a sad man; warm and yet wistful in
his friendships; author of the only other comparable elegy.
His poem is as Oriental in colouring as the elder is English;
yet the stuff of its sentiment is, in a sense, more durable; our
native rusticity is extinct; but the hedonist, the philosopher,
the lover—these in their widely different reactions will remain
throughout all ages confronted with the fact of mortality.
The quatrains (the " heroic " and the Persian) wind their
lovely sustained rhythms through either composition with
equal mastery and range. There is nothing in the *Rubáiyát*,
certainly, to rival the grave, deep harmonies, and richly
sensuous evocation, of those five great opening stanzas
which immortalize an English evening. But there is
mystery, which the other has not. And if the poignant and
searching wit of parts of FitzGerald's monody must have
been alien to all the majesty of Gray's, there is yet also a
plangency unattainable by any eighteenth-century poem,
there is a sympathetic sincerity and vibrant individual tone,
sensible in every modulation and indeed in every characteristic line of this exquisitely melodious testament of a
Victorian pagan. Its author, in one of his own several
tributes to the earlier masterpiece, refers to the *Elegy* very
simply as " a something which we all love to keep ever
about us." But the truth is, we need no more trouble to
keep than to love. Those are both poems which have this
above all others as their surest title to immortality, that
different as is their music, it is equally and supremely a
music which, once heard, no one can forget. And it is

in youth that one stumbles upon the *Rubáiyát*, and
then—

> " *Dreaming when Dawn's Left Hand was in the Sky,*
>   *I heard a Voice within the Tavern cry,*
>   ' *Awake, my Little ones, and fill the Cup*
>   *Before Life's Liquor in its Cup be dry.*' "

Gray's poem begins with twilight, FitzGerald's with the
dawn ; " Awake ! for Morning in the Bowl of Night "—in
that opening stanza the almost breezy call of his incense-
breathing ashes excites youth to a sensitivity that, in
measure as it saddens, enhances and itself enriches this
our brief and only life.

Such is in fact FitzGerald's achievement ; the contemporary of Tennyson and Browning, he left to posterity one
of the most beautiful long poems of the Victorian age ; a
poem highly original, for all it was a translation, because
so new and so peculiar ; a poem, whatever its limitations,
purely, and one may even say flawlessly, poetical. And for
everyone but the specialist, he did virtually nothing else.
From the standard biographies, indeed, those who care to
may elicit his simple annals. He was born, he died ; he
even, in a manner, married, anxiously but not for long.
He formed lasting and deep friendships with Tennyson,
Thackeray, Carlyle, and Spedding—to name no others ;
he corresponded with Fanny Kemble ; he contracted an
enthusiastic affection for a handsome young mariner,
Joseph Fletcher, nicknamed Posh, a gentleman after
Nature who united simplicity of soul to hair " strictly
auburn," and who cultivated one taste in common with
the old Persian poet.

> " *Indeed, indeed, Repentance oft before*
>   *I swore—but was I sober when I swore?*
>   *And then and then came Spring, and Rose-in-hand*
>   *My threadbare Penitence apieces tore.*"

Tennyson, Thackeray, and Mr. Joseph Fletcher—in all
three FitzGerald recognized great men ; but the greatest of
these was Posh. In his later years the lonely old gentleman
in the grey shawl and green eye-shade had become well
known locally as an eccentric. When his sight deteriorated
he employed a boy to read to him, while he would sit in a

low chair with his feet on the fender, wearing a top-hat.
For many reasons his memory should remain worth consideration, at least, by the connoisseur in personality.

And he became, of course, a man of letters. His first
book, *Euphranor,* a short dialogue on the Platonic model,
published when he was forty-two, is, truth to tell, but a
trivial and inconsequent preciosity; though its over-
praised conclusion is certainly a most graphic description
in virtually flawless rhythm. All his characteristic works
were free translations with excisions, amounting sometimes to paraphrase and sometimes (particularly in his
Agamemnon) to independent and indeed indefensible
embroidery, of works of Spanish, Persian, or Greek poets,
into English verse of rare accomplishment and even distinction. The blank verse into which exotic poetry has
often been rendered generally possesses no merit except
that it scans; FitzGerald's verse (blank or otherwise)
purely as verse is fine, it has music and it has vigour. Yet
after the single great exception, there is (as will appear
presently) only one of all these versions that the modern
reader might be advised to try; unless, indeed, I ought to
add the swashbuckling comedy *Beware of Smooth Water,*
to my taste much the most effective of the eight plays translated from the Spanish of Calderon, and a work which
goes with unflagging spirit on the stage, if I may testify
from an amateur performance. Critics have raised, but
never perhaps satisfactorily answered or even conscien-
tiously faced (you can see the very sentences in which they
shirk it), the question why these other works are after all
so immaterial. The fact is, it was not always for the same
reason; FitzGerald was so exquisitely qualified for his self-
chosen task of transfiguration by translation, that upon the
one occasion when there was no impediment, he simply
succeeded to perfection.

Of the *Six Dramas of Calderon,* published in 1853, one is
the comedy which I have in fact partially exempted just
above, four are clearly and admittedly not good enough in
themselves; and even of *The Mayor of Zalamea* one can
only say, as of *The Mighty Magician* and *Such Stuff as
Dreams are Made of* which he rendered twelve years later,
that if plays on themes no subtler than the plots of these
are really among the best of Calderon, then Calderon is not
a great dramatic poet, and therefore cannot be made into
one. With the three Greek tragedies, on the other hand,

the *Agamemnon* of Æschylus (1865 ; 2nd ed. 1876) and the two *Œdipus* plays of Sophocles (1880–1), the mistake was to attempt any transfiguration of masterpieces. The centos from Sophocles are indolent as well as capricious ; but the *Agamemnon,* had it been a version (and correct) instead of a fantasia, would have been in fact the best of such ; it is free from the academic tritenesses which deaden its plodding rivals, and in its dignity, clarity, and beauty remains the one readable poem among our author's minor adaptations. Even he did not sufficiently disencumber the *Salámán and Absál of Jámi,* nor the *Bird-Parliament* of Attár, pretty though these translations are in parts.

The letters to friends are another story ; not merely as agreeable reading, but because here one may come upon really sagacious comment upon life, whether as criticism, humanity, whimsicality, or wit. Of Carlyle's *French Revolution*—" An Englishman "—but false, a Scotsman— " writes of French Revolutions in a German style." Why Spedding, who had an unforgettably lofty brow, was bald : " No wonder that no hair can grow at such an altitude." Upon social evolution : " Humanity grows clear by flowing, very little profited by any single sage or hero "—the latter part surely untrue, but the former profound. Of *In Memoriam* : " It is monotonous, and has the air of being evolved by a Poetical Machine of the highest order." Of Lucretius : " He makes some music even from his hardest atoms." Apropos of reading Tacitus on Nero in a sunny garden—" But . . . the weather is not always clear, nor nightingales singing, nor Tacitus full of pleasant atrocity." On himself : " I am a man of taste, of whom there are hundreds born every year " (not now that taste has become no longer fashionable) ; and elsewhere : " I am credited with the Aphorism, ' Taste is the feminine of Genius ' " (it is the geniuses that are now born in hundreds per annum).

But his really cleverest *mot* comes by accident from an unpublished (because too merely technical) series of letters : it is quoted in that finely sympathetic monograph by A. C. Benson—but surely without having been properly under-stood. " I am not always quite certain," writes the puzzled student of Omar to his Orientalist professor on the subject of his translational labours, " of getting the right sow by the ear." What a persuasively homely picture does this evoke of tumbling around among comparatively raucous, promiscuous, gross originals, and of high-handed selection and haling, before the magical transmutations could be effected, and the silken Tassel of each Purse be tied.

Among other nice paradoxes: " I have been all my life," he wrote, " apprenticed to this heavy business of idleness, and am not yet master of my craft "; and when his easy circumstances got on his conscience, he began to feel that " one really ought to dip for a little misery "; I like " dip." He concludes a description of the gruelling monotony of life in Woodbridge with—" I see, however, by a Handbill in the Grocer's Shop, that a Man is going to lecture on the Gorilla in a few weeks; so there is something to look forward to." Now " Grocer's Shop," excellent as it is, must have been true; but it was FitzGerald, it was not that Handbill, who said that what was going to lecture in a few weeks on the Gorilla was " a Man." A real live exhibit, that.

The letters contain much about music, in which his tastes were simple but his relish was acute. He is for ever insisting on the necessity of melody, which to him meant " that which asserts itself independently of harmony." It is dumbfounding, however, to read of his having " heard an Opera (*Carmen*) on the Wagner model: very beautiful accompaniment to no Melody." What he writes, here and elsewhere, about the art of translation, is reasoned and uncompromising. " A Translation must be Paraphrase to be readable." At all cost, the thing must *live*: " Better a live Sparrow than a stuffed Eagle." On the other hand, the atmosphere of the original must be preserved: " Rub off as little Oriental colour as possible," he writes to Cowell about Hafiz.

The finest piece of prose in FitzGerald is surely not that favourite of Tennyson, the conclusion of *Euphranor*; a description of a boat-race has some limitations that are inevitable. It was Benson who drew attention to the passage, in a letter to Cowell, from which the following is an extract:

" Lyell, in his book about America, says that the falls of Niagara, if (as seems certain) they have worked their way back southwards for seven miles, must have taken 35,000 years to do so, at the rate of something over a foot a year! Sometimes they fall on a stratum that crumbles away from behind them more easily;

but then again they have to roll over rock that yields to them scarcely more perceptibly than the anvil to the serpent. And those very soft strata which the Cataract now erodes contain evidences of a race of animals, and of the action of seas washing over them, long before Niagara came to have a distinct current; and the rocks were compounded ages and ages before those strata! So that, as Lyell says, the Geologist looking at Niagara forgets even the roar of its waters in the contemplation of the awful processes of time that it suggests. It is not only that this vision of Time must wither the Poet's hope of immortality; but it is in itself more wonderful than all the conceptions of Dante and Milton."

No mere " vision of Time," naturally, can be in truth more wonderful than the vital conceptions of the poets; there is more force in Patmore's rhetoric about the idle and tedious vastness of our universe, the expression, he suggested, of its Creator's intention " to make dirt cheap "; but here is impressively presented a step in the development of the Victorian (and therefore of the human) mind. θνῄσκει δὲ πίστις, βλαστάνει δ' ἀπιστία. " Faith dies, and Unfaith waxes in her turn." So wrote Sophocles when aged about ninety, survivor from a period of achievement and confidence into a period of defeat and despair. Everybody knows that there were two strands in the thought and literature of the Victorian era—optimism and pessimism, to name them after their attitudes to the ultimate destiny of man. It was the pessimism that, waxing throughout the second half of the nineteenth century in spite of progress and prosperity, inspired the truer poetry. In the best of Arnold and the Rossettis and Swinburne there is a depth of feeling, a poignancy enriching the very tone of the verse, which is not to be found among the brilliances of Tennyson, and which among the volubilities of the semi-articulate Browning one would not, naturally, so much as seek. The vein leads on to Housman. Of this melancholy FitzGerald's *Rubáiyát* is the crowning expression:

> " *Ah, Love! could thou and I with Fate conspire*
> *To grasp this sorry Scheme of Things entire,*
>   *Would not we shatter it to bits—and then*
> *Re-mould it nearer to the Heart's Desire!* "

If poetry must be picturesque, or if it must be nationally

representative, then Tennyson is still the greatest poet of
the Victorians. But if poetry must be intellectual, then
neither Tennyson nor any of them is to be matched with
Arnold; and if poetry is to be intellectual it must be sad,
because it is true of men that "when they think, they
fasten their hands upon their hearts." For myself, I must
say, such works as *Mycerinus, A Picture at Newstead, Saint
Brandan,* the third *Rachel* sonnet, numbers two and three
of *The Church of Brou,* the last 113 lines of *Tristram and
Iseult,* and many another passage from the same hand and
heart, represent a far richer spiritual development, are
things that I care incomparably more to keep about me,
seem far more original, than any other body of poetry (our
present theme excluded) between the Romantics and *A
Shropshire Lad*.

FitzGerald was the one Victorian to continue that still sad
music of humanity which is to be heard (for instance) in the
Ode to a Nightingale. It is the nightingale's own music,
"high-piping Pehlevi."

It was pointed out by Edmund Gosse as long ago as
1889 (*Fortnightly Review* for July) that, alike in date and
in mood, the *Rubáiyát* links itself with the poetry of the
Rossettis, Morris, and Swinburne; despite its author's indifference to the work of these fellow-craftsmen—two of
whom were, as is notorious, far from indifferent to the
Rubáiyát. In it Gosse finds "the same reassertion of the
sensuous elements of literature, the same obedience to the
call for a richer music and a more exotic and impassioned
aspect of manners, the same determination to face the
melancholy problems of life and find a solace for them in
art." These tendencies represent, of course, the reaction
against that general complacency—material, social, spiritual
—which is so apt to be labelled "Victorian" by those who
would ignore the fact that the reaction was Victorian
also.

But one need hardly refer to a certain roughness of texture in the work of Morris, nor to a slight stiffness in that
of the Rossettis, in order to emphasize by contrast that the
Rubáiyát has the true lyrical *cry*. Swinburne, indeed, is
another matter; the lyrical cry he has, and conspicuously,
in all his best work; but his music is not "still," and his
sadness is much less "human" than that of the *Rubáiyát*.

Half the secret of FitzGerald's music is in the stanza-
form which he took over from the Persian. Of the rhyme-

series *a a x a* he himself acutely and happily remarked that
" the penultimate line seems to lift and suspend the Wave
that falls over in the last." " Somewhat as in the Greek
Alcaic," he adds, and this is curious. What is like the
Greek Alcaic is not his own quatrain, but that in which,
with a shorter line and some metrical variety, Tennyson
had anticipated his discovery of the *a a x a*; this was in
1853–4, with those charming and very clever experiments
The Daisy and *To the Rev. F. D. Maurice.* FitzGerald's
use has, however, naturally the monopoly of that elegiac
gravity which it gets from its length of line. Thrice in the
first edition he employs to very subtle effect the variation
a a a a, itself also Persian.

> " *Oh, come with old Khayyám, and leave the Wise*
> *To talk; one thing is certain, that Life flies;*
> *One thing is certain, and the Rest is* Lies;
> *The Flower that once has blown for ever dies.*"

Here the unexpected rhyme lends to the word above roman-
ized an emphasis amounting to cogency, and turns " dies "
by consequence into a distant echo.

> " *'Tis all a Chequer-board of Nights and Days*
> *Where Destiny with Men for Pieces plays:*
> *Hither and thither moves, and mates, and slays,*
> *And one by one back in the Closet lays.*"

Here the suggestion is one of ruthlessness. The *nuance* in
stanza 32 may be left to the reader to analyse; stanza 10
had its third line remedied in succeeding editions.

Every man should arrange his own *Rubáiyát.* Mine is
simply the original version, plus nine of the later stanzas
(33, 62, 64–7, 74, 78–9 of the fourth edition), and with here
and there a bare word or two from the later revisions.
Almost invariably, the revision was (I feel) unfortunate;
in general he was evidently solicitous to intensify the expression of the *thought,* to add point or antithesis; often
this resulted in over-refining or over-loading, almost everywhere in loss of tone. Just occasionally he is equally
anxious to dissolve some feared obscurity. Observe him
in the opening stanza progressively remove the poetry
throughout his four editions. If some of us do not know
that to drop a stone into a bowl was the desert signal for

striking camp, how very little that matters in comparison with the ideal propriety of this novel figure in its application to a sunrise. Similarly with the first line of the stanza following. Again, in 64 he not only loses that admirable Doomsday apparition of the sooty Tapster, but disconcerts us with the ceramic and eschatological monstrosity of tossing Pots to Hell. This is not to regret that he continued his adaptations; of the new quatrains, 64–67 alone would be sufficient justification, particularly the latter two.

After the characteristic measure, the next essential of this unique creation must surely be the Oriental *milieu*. So completely do I disagree with Platt's offhand assertion that "the Persian allusions" are "a nuisance." What is imparted to the whole poem by this Persian colouring is mystery—the necessary mystery. A certain indefiniteness, imaginatively very suggestive, is one of the assets of our *Rubáiyát*.

> "*One Moment in Annihilation's Waste,*
> *One Moment, of the Well of Life to taste—*
>   *The Stars are setting and the Caravan*
> *Starts for the Dawn of Nothing—oh, make haste!*"

I cannot imagine what other choice of thirty words would so effectively convey the unaccountable urgency and anxiety which hourly attend our tantalizing and sandy pilgrimage to extinction, this life where—

> "*. . . each day brings its petty dust*
>   *Our soon-choked souls to fill,*
> *And we forget because we must,*
>   *And not because we will.*"

Some Nemesis of the benigner kind must have overheard FitzGerald's misgiving upon being told that Tennyson was composing *In Memoriam*: "Don't you think the world wants other notes than elegiac now?" The age needed (amid much else) the elegiac note, and it was Fitz-Gerald who supplied it. His *Rubáiyát* is an elegy upon human life. Its original was an epicurean poem, satirizing religion, denying the soul's immortality, and exhorting us to appreciate the pleasures of this world. Omar is certainly not without his own tenderness and pathos; but what he glorifies in Wine is wine. FitzGerald,

I*

who supplied good wines for his guests, but himself lived
upon " milk and meal and grass," with the occasional
indulgence of a turnip, was not the man to sing the praises
of alcoholic elation.   The Wine of his poem is obviously
emblematic ; it indicates mortal joy.   Life is a Tavern :

> *" You know how little while we have to stay,*
> *And, once departed, may return no more."*

Or by an alternative and more ingenious image, we ourselves, wrought of clay as we are, vessels by some inscrut-
able magic made temporarily loquacious, fancy in our
simple credulity that we must have some individual importance for the Potter; but various as are our teleologies,
we have all one and the same craving (stanzas 59–67). That
craving is not, except in some few individuals, and then
per accidens, for any so thin stuff as champagne.   It is not
the dull material temptations, the bait of gulls ; it is the
finest, keenest, steadiest intoxications of the mind and
spirit, such as the ecstasies of intellectual pursuit and discovery, or the sustaining flood of seemingly inexhaustible
inspiration welling up from this or that delight in beauty
or in personality—it is these far more insidious and dominating idolatries that give to this life its real danger, as well
as its truest zest and pathos.

That such memories as those will one day perish with us,
that life itself is but a stimulant whose reaction inevitably
leaves us as the " senseless Nothing " out of which we were
originally " provoked "—that realization, even when fully
apprehended, is one which it must ever require some forti-
tude to accept.   The knowledge that even our good deeds
cannot save us, that the highest activities are as evanescent
as the commonest, obvious though it be, is apt at some time
to descend on us in its full force suddenly, like the sentence
of the Egyptian oracle that staggered the just and clement
Mycerinus.   After that one can but cheat the gods as he
did ; vice or virtue, midnight oil or revelry, it is a matter
of individual preference.   The oracle that revealed his
destiny to the poet was from the inner sanctuary that tells
truth twice as plain.

> *" I sent my Soul through the Invisible,*
> *Some letter of that After-life to spell:*
> *And by and by my Soul return'd to me,*
> *And answer'd, ' I Myself am Heaven and Hell:*

" *Heav'n but the Vision of fulfilled Desire,*
   And Hell the Shadow from a Soul on fire,
      Cast on the Darkness into which Ourselves,
  *So late emerged from, shall so soon expire.' *"

The doctrine is orthodox Epicureanism; *Quæcumque Acherunte profundo prodita sunt esse, in vita sunt omnia nobis.* And similarly for Swinburne, God is " the shadow of the soul of man." As for Heaven, enough is as good as a feast, and there are things by virtue of which even our Wilderness can become a Paradise enow.

What FitzGerald makes of this philosophy is sweeter music than anyone else. His poem is unique, not merely in the Victorian period, but in literature. The quality of its grief is nowhere flawed with bitterness, not even in the stanzas in which Man forgives his iniquitous taskmaster. The poetry of hedonism has been sometimes mutinous and sometimes mundane, according as the soul had been beaten or drugged. The *Rubáiyát* by contrast is always sensuous and always melancholy. It never lets us forget the sadness of life, it never disturbs our sense of the enjoyment of the moment. In it one seems to find the most perfect fusion of artistic rapture with the spiritual pang. If the rest that can be told of its author may seem to our strenuous epoch merely a pathetic waste, we must remember, not only that every fine friendship or affection is itself an achievement, and one which posterity can seldom or never appraise, but that to produce some kinds of poetry it is probably necessary to submit to no other intellectual harness.

WILLIAM
EWART
GLADSTONE
1809-1898

BY
LORD
PONSONBY

WILLIAM EWART GLADSTONE

TO write about Gladstone is like writing about Mont Blanc or Niagara. Not only has it been done before from every angle, at length in volumes and briefly in numberless sketches, but in Gladstone's case it has been done critically as well as enthusiastically, with a cold lack of sympathy as well as with enthusiastic admiration. No branch of his activities has escaped the searchlight of those who knew him as well as of those who have since found more material about him. What else, then, can be done with so notable a personality? Like Mont Blanc and Niagara, there is something rather obvious about this great figure. The psychologist will look in vain for intriguing subtleties, and the mere description of big lines is always in danger of being commonplace.

A fresh perspective, however, can be given by the passage of time. As we travel away from the great citadel of the nineteenth century we can see all the notable figures grouped together, and we can view the relative size and merits of the more prominent edifices with perhaps a better capacity to estimate their dimensions than could be possessed by those who lived in their midst. Some who seemed to tower have shrunk in stature, while the wider judgment of posterity sometimes brings into prominence others whose proportions seemed of no particular consequence in their day.

There is a tendency in this country to over-estimate the importance of politicians, to give an exaggerated amount of publicity to the mere handling of public affairs, and to enlist a large chorus either to idolize or to denounce the men of the hour as heroes or miscreants. Considering the far-reaching implication of policies, this is natural; and considering the need for public discussion and political education in matters which now reach into the recesses of the homes of the people, this is necessary. Moreover, we are rightly anxious that politics should be the occupation of public-spirited, disinterested, and if possible notable men, and not be spurned by them and left to the care of second-rate minds, as sometimes happens elsewhere. Nevertheless, when a judgment is formed of a politician, it rests less on definite achievement than in the case of the creative artist or even the man of action; and imponderable elements, such as reputation and contemporary but passing judgments, have to be taken into account, strongly biased as they sometimes may be by political predilections.

Like actors, politicians appear taller when they are before the footlights than when they are off the stage, and contemporary estimates are to a large extent based on the stage performances. Many a civil servant has done every bit as much as a politician to frame policies and to direct administration, but he remains behind the scenes out of the reach of the limelight, and whatever credit may be due falls to the politician. Yet the great constructive speech propounding the new policy and the great destructive speech denouncing the policy have an effect which, though immediate, moving, and exciting, quickly dwindles even in memory and certainly in history. Of all forms of literature political speeches are least re-read. At most they may be skimmed by the modern politician in search of a quotation. Oratory, of all the arts, is the least enduring. On oratory in all its conceivable branches was Gladstone's reputation made. Had he not been an orator we should not be still discussing him to-day. That he was not only an orator is of course true. But in his very remarkable equipment his power of speech stands out as something abnormal, and is therefore a very useful index, not only to his power, but to his weakness.

The influence of the spoken word is misleading. Its immediate effect is so striking as to appear far more significant than it is in actual fact. Assemblies, when they disperse and are freed from the spell of the orator's personality, are very apt to find the persuasion exercised on them vanish, and seldom do they re-read and ponder over what they have heard. The influence of the sermon is notoriously ephemeral. The power of the rhetoric of

Demosthenes, judging by contemporary opinion and also
by what remains to us of his orations, gives him an almost
legendary position as the greatest orator of all time. Yet
the Greek dramatists, not to speak of the sculptors, have
left the world a greater legacy than his. Savonarola moved
his congregations to hysterical passion and frenzy like
many revivalists since his time, yet the same capricious
multitude saw him burn at the stake without protest.
Burke's magnificent eloquence gives him a position in
British political history which few can rival, yet his achievements are hardly remembered. The great preachers of
the past are all forgotten, their sermons are never read,
yet in their day they stood very high in the estimate of
their fellows. Demosthenes was more intellectual than
Gladstone, Savonarola more emotional, and Burke more
literary. But Gladstone had perhaps greater ease and
aptitude for a spontaneous flow of eloquence than any other
orator that could be named. His prepared speeches were
effective, but his sudden interventions in debate were more
striking still. It was not only the set oration, but the cut
and thrust of combat in which he delighted and in which
he excelled. He was not dependent on form or phrase, he
did not study style and composition, nor did he polish
memorable epigrams. But, assisted by a very noble
presence, a flashing eye, broad gestures, and a wonderful
voice the range and modulation of which he managed to
perfection, he was able with ease, possibly too much ease,
to arrest the breathless attention of the most listless of his
hearers, and subdue a crowd into rapt attention. With
this amazing power it was impossible for him to enter the
political arena without making his mark. Bagehot, writing
as early at 1860, says, "England is a country governed
by labour and speech. Mr. Gladstone will work and speak,
and the result is what we see." He speaks of "the singular
vivacity of his oratorical impulse," but adds a note of warning as to the excitement of oratory being inimical to calm
reflection.

Gladstone loved conflict, and was always ready to step
into the fray. Opposition stimulated him, and his contributions were seldom negligible. He was too fond of
abstractions, and was apt on occasions to confuse the issue
by a mere torrent of words. He was also inclined to use
this ever-ready and effective weapon when there was no
need for so much sound and fury. But he elevated debate,

he enhanced the calling of a politician, and he raised the level of House of Commons controversy. He was never long on his feet before the course seemed clear to him, and a driving sincerity of conviction carried him through, regardless even of the feelings of his bewildered colleagues.

There have been many great men who have been largely made by circumstances. Gladstone, on the contrary, moulded circumstances and created his own opportunities. As Huxley said of him: " Put him in the middle of a moor with nothing in the world but his shirt, and you could not prevent him from being anything he liked." In one circumstance, however, he was fortunate. His flint required steel, his foil required a counter-foil. No antagonist could have been found better than Disraeli to draw his fire, to rouse his indignation, to be a target for his invective; and in this way Gladstone was of as great service to Disraeli as Disraeli was to Gladstone. Not only did the two men represent different and opposing schools of political thought, but no two men could have been more different in outlook, disposition, method, and even appearance. Their very rare courtesies to one another were only perfunctory concessions to convention. Hostility, bred of mutual incompatibility and incomprehension, may be jarring, but it is real. They were bitter antagonists, not play actors or advocates who can have a friendly laugh together behind the scenes in the intervals, but men who regarded one another as public dangers, while each had to keep his wits about him and exert himself to the full in order to meet the attack and denounce the nefarious policies and the pernicious influence of his rival. This is politics at its best. Controversy carried out on these lines is not only genuine, but has an educative value of immense importance to an electorate, with whom rests the final decision. Disraeli never suffered from the same unpopularity as Gladstone, but at the same time he never inspired quite the same rapturous devotion. Where Gladstone was impetuous Disraeli was calm, where Gladstone trusted to a rush of eloquence Disraeli was content with an epigram, where Gladstone was moved to passion Disraeli countered with a cynical retort. Both were leaders unquestioned, unrivalled, and pre-eminent. Gladstone swept impetuously forward, Disraeli chose his steps carefully. He realized better than Gladstone the importance of studying the personality of those with whom he had to deal. It was by this means that he gained his unique position in the favour of his sovereign. Apart from their political views, it might seem more probable that Queen Victoria would prefer the robust simplicity of the great Liberal to the subtle and almost Oriental advances of the great Tory. But Dizzy studied his method, and found that the most extravagant and indeed absurd exaggerations of flattery were acceptable, while the G.O.M., always deferential but ponderous in his social approaches, was kept till the very end at arm's length, and became the victim of the most biased prejudice which the Queen ever displayed to any of her ten Prime Ministers.

The depth of Gladstone's convictions was the fuel which gave the driving-power to all his utterances on matters great as well as small. It was combined with a certain religious fervour which often found expression in outbursts of righteous indignation and was apt to exasperate not only opponents, but minds more inclined to dispassionate analysis of the subject in question. He always thought that he was not only politically but morally right. Each question presented itself to him as a moral issue, while his opponent never debated it beyond a matter of expediency. Lord Palmerston accused Gladstone of fanaticism and hypocrisy, and the same charge was made against him often enough in after years. Indeed, through his oratory he sometimes gave the impression of a self-righteousness which he, personally the humblest of men, never actually felt, and further, a charge of self-delusion if not insincerity was sometimes invited. It was the inebriation of his eloquence which was responsible for this. Two such different people as Queen Victoria and Huxley (who never met) agreed on this point. The Queen said, "He can persuade himself that *everything* he takes up is right, even though it be calling black white and wrong right." Huxley said, "If working men were to-day to vote by a majority that two and two made five, Gladstone would believe it, and find them reasons for it which they had never dreamed of." Benjamin Jowett, another outside observer, said, "It was the first time that anyone of such great simplicity had been in so exalted a position." But he regarded the sequel as "full of peril," because the great statesman was "so powerful and so unsound." George Meredith thought him "too much of an actor."

These opinions, and many other contemporary judgments which could be quoted other than those of his political

colleagues and opponents, were largely founded on his
public utterances. Whether in the House of Commons, in
Midlothian, at Blackheath, or wherever it might be, his
words rang out and roused a turmoil of enthusiasm and
indignation. In great causes his course was clear, his argument sound, his convictions justified. But when the same
drive of invective and flow of words were used on question-
able issues, there was some reason for a suspicion of mistrust and some justification for the criticism of his " tenacity
in supporting dubious opinions." It was his defective
judgment which Sidney Herbert in quite early days complained of.

Gladstone described his method of speech-making to
Morley: " Collect facts and figures as accurately and con-
clusively as you can, and drive them home as if all the
world must irresistibly take your own eager interest in
them." He succeeded to a degree which can hardly ever
have been reached by any political leader. His stoutest
opponents were spell-bound, mesmerized by the brilliant
eye, hypnotized by the wonderful voice, whatever they
might think when, after leaving his presence, they had
recovered their senses. But Gladstone the orator was not
quite the same as Gladstone the man. When oratory
reaches this pitch it ceases accurately to illustrate personality. Meredith was not wrong. People formed their
judgment of the actor not of the man. They were fascinated
by the genius, they enjoyed the mannerisms, they rejoiced
in the brilliance of the weapon. In the present century
oratory has fallen almost into disrepute. It is character
in a politician which counts more than speech and gesture.
Gladstone had character outstanding and clear-cut, but concealed rather than exposed by his soaring flights of rhetoric.

When Jowett rightly used the word " simplicity," it was
from personal intercourse with Gladstone, not from listening to his speeches. He was indeed simple, not to say
unsophisticated. As Morley observes in his *Recollections*:
" He is too healthy, too objective, too simple for all the
complexities of morbid analysis, and knows not the very
rudiment of *Weltschmerz*." In a way this ingenuousness
was his strength, but it prevented him from having any
fine sense of quality, and, combined with his lack of any
sense of proportion, led him to enthusiasms for things that
did not much signify, even second-rate novels. His great
vitality and zest were not reserved only for public life.

They were felt in his family circle; they were exercised on the humblest of his acquaintances. Mrs. Gladstone notes that she engaged a cook " after a long conversation on religious matters chiefly between her and William."

Gladstone's pen was notably inferior to his tongue. Although he found relaxation in absorbing studies, his conclusions on Homer and Dante lacked real profundity. Nothing that he wrote will survive. Disraeli the successful novelist was always sarcastic on this point. He condemned Gladstone's style as " involved," and "so wanting both in melody and harmony that it always gives me a headache " ; and went so far as to say, " He has not produced a page which you can put on your library shelves." However, he revised his first condemnation of the style of the pamphlet on Bulgarian atrocities, and said that Gladstone must have dictated it. It had in it something of the flow of the spoken word. As a writer Gladstone would never have been famous; as a preacher he probably would have made a name, although his range would have been considerably narrowed and his opportunities too much restricted.

Oxford gave him his ecclesiastical bias, Lancashire gave him his grit, and his Scottish ancestry gave him his astonishing capacity for argument. The barest record of his career makes the most casual student of history ask for an explanation. Sixty-three years a Member of Parliament (1833-1895); twenty-eight years the leader of a party (1866-1894), and four times Prime Minister (covering some fourteen years), he was a man about whom more violence and bitterness of language was used than any in our parliamentary annals. Often throughout the country his admirers were unable to have any social intercourse with his detractors. The issues which have occupied Parliament in recent times would seem to be more vital, more disturbing, and more fundamentally affecting the lives of the people and the very constitution of society itself, yet no such intensity of feeling has been displayed about any modern statesman. Gladstone was at times intentionally provocative. To him the duty of a leader was not to seek tepid compromise, but to drive with all the force at his command towards what he conceived to be the logical conclusion of the principles he upheld. Even now an attempt to estimate his achievements leads at once to an atmosphere of keen controversy, as must be the case when the record of any party leader is examined.

There is undoubted difficulty in singling out particular measures or special results from the long career of a statesman and crediting him because of the passage of a Bill or the pursuance of a certain line of policy with a definite and lasting accomplishment. Gladstone's prolonged and arduous term of service is no exception. That he had a wonderful grasp of the most intricate financial question is not disputed by anyone. His five-hour speech on the introduction of the Budget in 1853 stands out as one of the most memorable Budget statements ever made, although there may still be differences of opinion about the soundness of his financial principles throughout the period he held office as Chancellor of the Exchequer. Economists may differ, they generally do. But there is a consensus of opinion as to the high position he held as Controller of the country's finances. On domestic questions there must be more differences of view. On Irish Home Rule subsequent events have mitigated, if not dispelled, the conflict of opinion, and it was this question, to which he devoted practically the last twenty years of his life, which will chiefly be associated with his name. He was converted to it, not as an abstract principle, but as a matter of expediency, because he conceived it wise to acquiesce in a demand supported by so large a proportion of the Irish people. It was a splendid instance of his tenacity. In the vicissitudes of the long-drawn-out struggle of which he never witnessed the finish, he encountered the bitterest opposition and the most staggering rebuffs that any statesman could meet in the advancement of a cause. The Tory Party, with the assistance of the House of Lords, twice defeated his Bills; he was confronted by the undisguised disapproval of his sovereign, and, worst of all, he lost an influential section of his own followers. A weaker man would have yielded to the force of circumstances, and made an excuse of one check or another to drop his great project. But it was only old age and the compulsion of his retirement from politics which prevented him, after the defeat of the Bill of 1894, from continuing the fight. He had prepared the way and laid the foundations; and the justification of his policy, the vindication of his foresight, and the consummation of his ideal came some twenty-five years later, not through the instrumentality of any other great statesman, but through the inexorable pressure of unforeseen circumstances.

In foreign and imperial questions the policy pursued by his Governments is most of all open to criticism. The Liberal reluctance to engage in war and hesitancy to continue hostilities once begun, combined with a conscientious desire to carry out imperial obligations and uphold British interests, led to dilemmas and even disasters which reflected little credit on some of the administrations. But apart from this, there were occasions when the leader, taking up some great moral issue, was able to make an appeal of such force that it rang out and echoed far beyond the shores of England. This was the case in his denunciation of the misgovernment of Naples, his condemnation of the Turk, and his crusades over the Bulgarian, and later the Armenian atrocities. Such occasions filled him with inspired fire, and the persecution of oppressed peoples gave him just the theme most suitable for his unsurpassed eloquence. To take only one instance: in 1877, after a debate in the House which continued till the dinner-hour, he sprang to his feet, and in a speech which lasted two and a half hours he denounced with great vehemence the government of Turkey. " As a mere feat of physical endurance," wrote Arthur Balfour, a keen critic, and an opponent who was an eye-witness of the scene, " it was almost unsurpassed; as a feat of parliamentary courage, parliamentary skill, parliamentary endurance, and parliamentary eloquence, I believe it will always be unequalled." J. R. Green, the historian, understood the political significance of these incursions on behalf of the victims of misgovernment in whatever part of the world it might be. " I begin to see," he wrote, " that there may be truer wisdom in the ' humanitarianism ' of Gladstone than in the purely political views of Disraeli. The sympathy of peoples with peoples, the aspirations of nationalities after freedom and independence *are* real political forces, and it is just because Gladstone owns them as forces and Disraeli disowns them that the one has been on the right side and the other on the wrong."

On the whole we find, however, in perusing the history of the last half of the nineteenth century that it is not the triumph of an accomplished purpose nor special measures of social progress nor the great sagacity of some definite line of international policy which we can pick out and associate with the name of Gladstone. It is rather the astonishing dominance of a great personality, the powerful authority of leadership, the indefatigable toil of a parliamentary giant, and the ceaseless moral endeavour of a noble character which pervaded the political atmosphere while Gladstone lived. He had his definite limitations, and in these perhaps lay his strength. He was rigidly orthodox, intolerant of any approach to frivolity, unaware of the humour in any situation, oblivious of the subtleties of human intercourse, impatient at the hesitancy of the philosophic outlook, and contemptuous of the opposite view. Had he been heterodox, easily genial, and acquiescent, with a lively sense of humour and a broad tolerance for other courses and for weaker natures, he could never have achieved the position he held. Had, in fact, the banks of the stream been more broadly set, the gush of the torrent would never have had the same tremendous force.

The younger generation of to-day may pass over Gladstone merely as a name, and even discard him as the personification of Victorian virtues which they heartily despise and condemn as hypocrisy. Moreover, a new political party has arisen since his day, breaking with past traditions, and deriving few of its principles from nineteenth-century Liberalism. To them, however, his powers of leadership stand out as a notable episode in our history. But the student of politics of the older generation, looking back over the past, does not see him as one who has lost in stature; on the contrary, although the voice on which so much depended is for ever silent, he still seems to tower, the more perhaps because hardly one of his nine successors has reached anything like a comparable height. He and his great rival still have their bands of admirers ready to worship at the shrine of these supermen of the past. The one still presides as an almost legendary figure over the destinies of a great and powerful political party, as the idol of a particular creed, and the emblem of a particular policy; and one looks up at his statue to see if he is smiling. The other stands aloft with no compact or powerful party to do him homage, no longer as a politician, but as a man above the turmoil of controversy. He stands as the embodiment of the spirit of disinterested combat for great causes, and as one for whose reputation and honour numbers of his fellow-countrymen for generations to come will always be proud. You look up at his statue, and his eye still flashes.

WILLIAM
GILBERT GRACE

BY
NEVILLE
CARDUS

1848-1915

WILLIAM GILBERT GRACE

A MONGST the eminent Victorians was W. G. Grace; he enjoyed the proper authority. The nation called him the G.O.M., and, like another monument called the same, he looked the part. There is a lot in " appearance " if the crowd is to give full respect and worship. W. G. Grace possessed physical size—and he was bewhiskered. I have seen faded photographs taken of Grace when he was under twenty years of age; the beard is already profuse and impressive. To catch the popular sense of dramatic fitness, Grace simply *had* to be big, for he stood for so much in the history of cricket at a time when hardly any other game challenged it as the national out-of-door sport and spectacle. Also there is another point which was to Grace's advantage in his character of a G.O.M.: he lived in a period which not only believed in great men but actually insisted on them and went about looking for them. And because there was no idea then of the trick of exploitation called nowadays publicity, a politician, actor, jockey, or a cricketer could remain at a romantic distance from the eyesight of the multitude: he did not get too familiar. Grace was a household possession, true, but only by reason of the performances he achieved day by day. Advertisement did not give him a spurious reputation and wear out belief in him by damnable iteration. Off the cricket field he was concealed in suggestive anonymity, and if people saw him in the streets, they turned round and gazed and gaped, and were pleased if they could feel that no mistake had been made.

Astonishing that by means of a game of bat and ball, a man should have been able to stamp his shape and spirit on

K

the imagination of thousands. As I say, no rhetorical Press pointed out his prowess incessantly. Not long ago I had cause to look through the files of an old newspaper in search of some bygone fact of cricket. I found a match at Lord's in which W. G. scored 152 not out; the game was reported in very small type with no headlines but this—in tiny print:

ANOTHER GOOD SCORE BY DR. GRACE

Grace got his renown during the years that did not know the literary persuasions of cricket writers who describe an innings by Hobbs in the rhetoric of a Macaulay; alone he conquered—with his bat and (this is certain) by his beard.

When I was a boy I lived in a family that did not interest itself in games. Yet often at breakfast W. G. Grace's name was mentioned. Everybody understood exactly who he was and what he signified in the diet of the day's news. From time to time, *Punch* used him as the subject for a cartoon; the Royal Family occasionally inquired after his health. When he was reported not out at Lord's at lunch, the London clubs emptied, and the road to St. John's Wood all afternoon was tinkling with the old happy noise of the hansom cab. Sometimes he would play, at the height of his fame, in a country cricket match in some village in the West of England. And from far and wide the folk would come, on foot, in carriages, and homely gigs. On one of these occasions Grace had made a score of twenty or so when he played out at a ball and missed it. The local wicket-keeper snapped up the ball in his gloves triumphantly, and swept off the bails and—seeing visions of immortality—he screamed to the umpire: " H'zat! "

The umpire said: " Not out; and look 'ee 'ere, young fellow, the crowd has come to see Doctor Grace and not any of your monkey-tricks."

I have always been amused that W. G. Grace became famous while the Victorians were endowing cricket with moral unction, changing the lusty game that Squire Osbaldeston knew into the most priggish of the lot, and stealing rigour, temper, and character from it. Cricket was approved at the private schools for the sons of gentlemen; the detestable phrase, " It isn't cricket," was heard in the land. The game acquired a cant of its own, and you might well have asked why two umpires were necessary at all, and why the bowler ever appealed for leg-before-wicket. W. G. could not have contained his large humanity in any genteel pursuit; he was of more than ordinary human bulk, and therefore he had more than ordinary frailty. He exercised his wits, went about the job of winning matches with gusto.

"Did the old man ever cheat?" I once asked an honest Gloucestershire cricketer, who worshipped Grace.

"Bless you, sir, never on your life," was the quite indignant answer. "Cheat? No, sir, don't you ever believe it—he were too clever for that."

When Grace and Gloucestershire met Hornby and Lancashire, there was sport indeed. Grace had a habit of moving a fieldsman surreptitiously from the slips to fine leg, while the batsman was concentrating his vision on the next ball. Once on a time at Old Trafford, A. N. Hornby decided to hoist Grace with his own petard. So, even as Grace was standing with his left toe up from the ground, getting ready for a stroke while the bowler was running to the wicket—at that very moment A. N. Hornby quietly signalled to first slip, who on tiptoe moved towards the leg side behind Grace's back. But he was not half-way there before W. G.'s high-pitched voice cried out: "I can see what you're doin'; I can see what you're at!"

If a man is going to give his whole life to a game, let him play it like a *full* man, with no half-measures and no repressions. Cricket was a battle of wits with Grace, first and last. His enormous technique was saved from mechanical chilliness because he never practised it without some artful end in view; he larded the green earth wherever he played; he dropped juicy flavours of sport; he loved an advantage, and hated to be beaten.

In his long career, which lasted from 1863 to 1908, he scored more than 54,000 runs and took 2,664 wickets. I write down these statistics here to give some slight idea of his mastery over the two main technical departments of cricket. But one of the purposes of my essay has really no use for records, which mean nothing to folk who are not cricketers. I am trying to get Grace into the Victorian scene, to see him as a Representative Man, and also to see him in relation to the crowd that invented his legend. "Was he a fraud?" a young man at Oxford asked me not long ago. "I fancy there is a bit of the fraud in all the Victorians."

The question was, on the face of it, senseless: no charlatan can be a master and forge a lasting technique. There would have been no Hobbs if Grace had not extended the

machinery of batsmanship and achieved a revolution in
bowling, by his great synthesis of offensive and defensive
stroke-play.

The hint of the triumphant charlatan which comes to us
when we read of Grace (just as the same hint comes to us
when we read of Gladstone and Irving) arises from a habit
of mind supposed to be peculiar to the Victorians. They
rather lacked flippancy, and for that reason they appear
to this flippant generation to have blown out fulsomely all
the objects of their admiration; they seized on the day's
heroes, and invested them with the significance of a whole
tradition. In an epoch of prosperity, when the idea of
material expansion was worshipped for its own sake, even
the vast runs made on a cricket field by W. G. Grace
seemed symbolical; his perpetual increase of authority and
performance suited a current love and respect for size and
prosperity. W. G. became an Institution in a day of
Institutions, all of which, like the Albert Memorial, had to
be impressive by sheer bulk. W. G. himself, of course,
did not know what he stood for in the national consciousness: he was content to be a cricketer. He shared none
of the contemporary modern habit of self-exposition.

To-day, even though we pretend to possess a humorous
sense of proportion, all sorts of small persons regard themselves much too seriously, and are ready to submit to an
" interpretation," psychological or scientific. I expect any
moment a treatise by Bradman on " The Theory and
Economy of Batsmanship." And I would not be surprised
to hear, any Sunday evening, an address broadcast from
St. Martin's by Jack Hobbs on " The Cricketer as an
Ethical Influence," with some moving metaphors about
" The Great Umpire " and " Playing the Game." W. G.
Grace never lapsed into solemnity about himself. Once he
was asked to explain the best way to stop an off-break.
He did not let loose a cartload of theory, or drag in the
blessed word " psychology." He simply said: " You must
put your bat to the ball." Frequently I wonder whether
the " Victorian age " has not been a consequence of the
modern tendency to write " studies " of everything; and to
turn irony against itself by too close a search for significant
overtones. Grace, I am sure, would be the last person in
the world to regard himself a theme for such a " study "
as I am attempting now; I can see his great ghost stroking
the immortal beard, and saying: " Get on with the game."

228

It will be as well for me to do so ; let me keep myself hence-
forth to the man's cricket; there's a deal to be said on
behalf of it.

To be first in the field in any activity is a good thing :
there's so much room in the beginning ; the earth is virgin,
and admiration is eager and sensitive. If a Grace were
born to-day, what would there be in cricket left for him to
do ?—and a man cannot express an original nature by
moving along worn tracks, emulating and not creating.
When Grace began to stamp his personality on English
sport, cricket was scarcely established, save as a rough-and-
ready pastime on the village green. The technical elements
of the game had yet to be gathered together ; the counties
had to be organized. A spectacular interest was wanting
to attract the crowds; and the money was required to
make a national game. W. G. came forward, at the ripe
moment ; the technique of cricket stood ready for expansion
and masterly summary ; the period was also ready for a
game which everybody could watch, the gentry as well as
the increasing population of town workers. Grace's skill
as a batsman may be said to have orchestrated the simple
folk-song of the game ; his personality placed it on the
country's stage.

He came from out of the West Country, and though in
time his empire stretched from Lord's to Melbourne, never
did he forget the open air of Gloucestershire, and the
flavours of his birthplace. In an orchard at the dawning
of June days, he learned his cricket; yet in his prime, at
the age of forty-seven, he was still waking every summer
morning fresh as a lad, eager for a match. If he knew
that the other side were about to give a trial to a new bowler
of awe-inspiring reputation, Grace would get up all the
earlier, make haste to the field, and take a glance at the
latest demon.

Once it happened that the Australians brought to England a bowler of unknown witchery; Grace straightway
went to their captain, W. L. Murdoch, and he said : " And
so you've found a good bowler, eh ? What does he do with
the ball ? Is he a fast 'un, or slow ? "

" Ah," was the sinister reply, " he mixes 'em."

" Very well, then," answered W. G., " I'll have a look
at him this afternoon; I'll have a look at him." And that
afternoon he went in first with some old professional, whom
we'll call Harry.

W. G. played a few overs from the new bowler most warily; the devil might have been in every ball, so carefully did Grace keep his bat down, and so suspiciously did his eyes sharpen. After a short time he hit the new bowler for two fours and a three off successive balls. And while the two batsmen were passing one another up and down the pitch, Grace's voice cried out, in immense glee: "Run up, Harry, run up! We'll mix 'em for him; we'll mix 'em!" Is it any wonder that the man's vital character made cricket seem part of the English way of life in summer-time, lusty and manly, yet artful and humorous? A great company of "originals" grew around the Old Man: Tom Emmett, A. N. Hornby, Crossland, Barlow, Johnny Briggs—scores of them, all men of ripe comedy, home-spun and fresh, each of them as vivid as characters on a page of Dickens or Surtees.

Cricket is not the best game *as* a game. There is more excitement in Rugby football; as much style and skill in tennis at Wimbledon; a swifter and more certain decision in a cup-tie. But cricket is without a rival amongst open-air pastimes for the exhibition of native characteristics in Englishmen. It is a leisurely game on the whole, and its slow movement enables the cricketers to display themselves. A lot of nonsense is talked about the "team spirit" in cricket; but as a fact the greatest batsmen and bowlers and fieldsmen have been those who have stood out from the ruck and have taken charge of a situation in ways entirely their own. You could not merge into a drilled efficient mass the Johnsonian bulk of Grace, or the Figaro alacrity of a Macartney. In no other game than cricket does the result mean so little to true lovers of it. As the years pass by and cricketers become old and sit by the fireside talking of the past, they do not remember matches won or lost, or the scores piled up, or the technical excellences seen on a hundred fields of play. No; the memory is a sunlit scene, and all the heroes are deathless, because they somehow told the old tale of every man in his own humour, in this our land. W. G. Grace put his heart into the game, and perhaps it is that which keeps cricket alive to this day, despite many changes and vicissitudes.

At the present time, nearly all the performances of W. G. Grace have been surpassed by cricketers here and there— some of whom will not be remembered a year after they have ceased playing the game. Hendren of Middlesex has scored more hundreds than W. G. Grace scored in his long career. Yet the fact of Grace's posterity remains to this moment: he is still the most widely known of all cricketers amongst folk who have seldom, if ever, seen a match. After all, he really did transcend the game; I have tried in this article not to treat him with less proportion than he would have treated himself. But I cannot, and nobody possibly could, contain the stature of the man within the scope of bat and ball. Nobody thinks of Grace in terms of the statistics recorded of his skill; like Dr. Johnson, he endures not by reason of his works but by reason of his circumferential humanity. I always think of him as the great enjoyer of life who, after he had batted and bowled and fielded throughout the whole three days of a match between Gloucestershire and Yorkshire, was at the end of the third afternoon seen running uphill from the ground, carrying his bag, in haste for the train to London—running with a crowd of cheering little boys after him, and his whiskers blowing out sideways in the breeze.

THOMAS HARDY

1840-1928

BY SYLVA NORMAN

K*

THOMAS HARDY[1]

I

THE author of *The Dynasts* is an awkward figure to place accurately. Set him on the ground amongst mortals, and it is at once apparent that his head and shoulders are in the stars. Raise him to the skies, and his feet remain entangled in earthly undergrowth. His range is immense, and paradox pervades it; for he appears often as a novelist in his poems and a poet in his novels, and in work fired with a brave conception, he will mercilessly cheat probability by successive twists. It is an axiom that no writer can be insensitive to the particular tenor of the age he works in, whether he defy or surrender to it. Hardy, doing both to a remarkable degree during his first twenty years of authorship, contrived to please by the tricks we now condemn, and to offend by the candour we have so heartily adopted as to forget its Wessex origin.

A genial minor novelist of the late 'nineties presents us with a commentary that may be taken as expressing the intelligent, if hardly profound, opinion of the day. David Christie Murray, writing on " My Contemporaries in Fiction " with a bold show of finality (it is always the bright and hasty critic who achieves this), expressed astonishment and grief that the author, whose earlier manner could delight his readers, then followed Zola by dealing in the poisonous and obscene. Murray echoed the reviews of *Jude,* where Hardy, sturdiest of idealists, was condemned as a decadent for dwelling on foul details. " There are passages," says

[1] Part II of this essay contains personal and hitherto unpublished recollections of visits to Thomas Hardy by Mr. Edmund Blunden.

235

the *National Review,* "which will offend men in direct proportion to their manliness, and which all women, save the utterly abandoned, will hurry over with shuddering disgust." Here, too, we are to believe him "caught by the fashion of the period," which enjoyed a problem novel. Meanwhile, these inferior critics were themselves bound in by fashion, and made no more of Hardy's development as a novelist than a change from a manner they approved to one they censured.

They appeared to forget, too, that this "decadence" was creeping, from the outset, over the writer for respectable magazines. Leslie Stephen, editing the *Cornhill,* noted in 1874 an "unexpected Grundian cloud," condensing into the protests of three ladies against an improper passage in *Far from the Madding Crowd.* We are inclined now to consider the outrage lies, not in the wounding of these ladies, but in the necessity for a literary artist to pour his work into the serial mould. It was not only that gentility had to be catered for—Hardy never did so, though a provisional dismembering of *Tess* was the alternative. Sentimentality had to be respected in *The Return of the Native* by ringing incongruous wedding-bells in the gloom of Egdon. Above all, the crude beast Curiosity had to be goaded by continual sensations, so that, to take one instance, long passages in *The Mayor of Casterbridge* show Hardy desperately inventing out of a tired and temporarily bored mind. "After all," he noted at the time of writing it, "it is not improbabilities of incident but improbabilities of character that matter."

And "after all," the serial exigency only added a twist to Hardy's natural bent. "The real, if unavowed, purpose of fiction," he records, "is to give pleasure by gratifying the love of the uncommon in human experience, mental or corporeal. . . . And the writer's art lies in shaping that uncommonness while disguising its unlikelihood, if it be unlikely." For art, he might have written "craft." The definition is that of a professional novelist, and less trimmed for public exhibition than Wilkie Collins's remarks on the interplay of circumstance and character. Disguising unlikelihood is a part of plot-machinery. That Hardy often failed is manifest in *The Woodlanders,* where the story bumps and creaks by the continued dependence upon accidents with horses, storms, and man-traps. And how the novels bristle with those undelivered letters, untold

236

secrets, missed occasions, without which, as honest authors used to write, " there would have been no story ! "

Essentially, then, Hardy cannot claim as his licence dissatisfaction with the existing rules for serial structure. Within their limits the professional novelist in him finds room to create characters not too often made improbable by incident; to mellow the sharp outlines of his story by the humour and dialect of a Shakespearean breed of rustics, and to wrap all in a physical environment that becomes a presence. It is not by heresies of form that he " disturbs the order " (his contemporaries would say it is by moral impropriety), but—

> " *Let him to whose ears the low-voiced Best seems stilled*
>   *by the clash of the First,*
> *Who holds that if way to the Better there be, it exacts*
>   *a full look at the Worst,*
> *Who feels that delight is a delicate growth cramped by*
>   *crookedness, custom, and fear,*
> *Get him up and be gone as one shaped awry; he dis-*
>   *turbs the order here.*"

When these lines were written, not only Clym Yeobright, but Tess and Jude had lived and suffered. The obligation of a novelist to his readers is an external question of tact and craftsmanship; but Hardy's tragic sense of an unheeding, pitiless First Cause brings bitter and close shackles that ought, by their nature, to be unescapable. Whatever reading we adopt of the *Prometheus Bound,* the central agony of his bondage must remain. For the characters of Æschylean drama are symbolic. Each one has a degree of power and dominance according to a recognized convention (which explains why, on impassioned speakers, masks did not offend). Here is the simplicity, not only of ultimates, but also, let it be admitted, of an age and order that bear fewer responsibilities. That the Greek conception entered deeply into Hardy's thought would be apparent through the rhythm and burden of his writings, even without specific references. (" Things are as they are," quotes Jude, " and will be brought to their destined issue.") Yet there could be no retreating into simplification. The novelist in Hardy had to create individuals, even while the fatalist decreed their end. And it is *Tess of the D'Urbervilles* and *Jude the Obscure* which, more than any of the former novels, stretch to the uttermost these two traits of passionate independence and helpless bondage. The key to Hardy's vast growth and expansion of vision is in them; for, together with *The Dynasts,* they mark the shifting of his primary interest from the personal to the general pattern. It seems more than mere coincidence that this same shift is apparent in modern thought and science. Is Hardy following the fashion again? He has not been so accused, since he is slightly in advance of it. But no outside reference is required to light his progress; only a retrospective view of his own work.

Lionel Johnson, surveying the novels when *Tess* was newly published, lamented the insistent protests against moral and social laws. And it is true that Tess, viewed as a solitary jewel, needs none of them. There is not another heroine in Hardy's works so individual, so humanly unconscious of the part her master has decreed for her. Bathsheba Everdene and Grace Melbury move stiffly through a field of obstacles; Eustacia Vye is partly shadowed and romanticized by the dark giant Egdon; but Tess, whose lower lip " had a way of thrusting the middle of her top one upward," is so closely, truthfully, and honestly presented, that again and again the clear notes of an eternal phrase of music can be heard. It is not that concerted music of a losing battle which is echoed in so many of the poems. Nor does it depend on a philosophy. To-day, when Tess's outrage is no longer made the theme for drama, when Clare seems something between a useful pivot, a disciple of Grundyism, and one of those mortal fingers of the Will which crowd *The Dynasts,* the inherent personal tragedy moves with an ultimate and unrelated power.

> " Nobody could love 'ee more than Tess did! . . .
> She would have laid down her life for 'ee. I could
> do no more."

Such a sentence is supreme in its simplicity; just as the final " I am ready " is supreme. Under its spell one wishes Hardy need have felt no urge to lose this individual grandeur in a cosmic scheme. It may be merely personal opinion that, as a lyric poet, moving between the moods and scenes, the persons and philosophy of his novels, without notable development, he achieves no keener utterance.

If the " dramatic monologues " sing more clearly than the novels, by their freedom from machinery, they lose the dearer kind of detail which brings an experience of closely felt and individual truth. Bald melodrama could, in fact, lead Hardy into some deplorable misfirings. Take, for example, " The Brother " in *Winter Words,* who, having killed his sister's seducer, finds the two had " churched it," and goes in haste to join him in death. It might be a parody by Max Beerbohm of Hardy's worst contrivances for dolour. Only human characters in the place of skittles could save it. Though swift, strange intimacies do haunt the poems (of a woman: " I thought of the first with her *eating eyes* "), yet the sighing of young pines newly planted is keener in the prose than in the rhymed version, and the dark-green islands, where the cows had lain on the grey moisture of the grass, are seen on the same morning that " minute diamonds of moisture from the mist hung, too, upon Tess's eyelashes, and drops upon her hair, like seed pearls." And when Tess sees numbers of to-morrows, " very fierce and cruel, and as if they said, ' I'm coming ! Beware of me ! Beware of me ! ' " it is still the outbreak of Tess the individual, while Hardy's reflection on it as " the ache of modernism " is put into Clare's mind.

Tess never speaks a word that is not hers. In spite of the net that has been woven round her, she exists, from the artistic standpoint, as the last free tragic individual in Hardy's work. (In 1892 the *Spectator,* zealous guardian of the vicarage and the country home, was concerned only with her morals, and repeated a denial of her purity some eight times. One may note that Hardy's later years saw no abatement of his grievance against this paper.)

What should a character need for fuller personal awareness except the power to analyse and understand ? Sue Bridehead, human as Tess in trivial actions, has it. But she is given an intellect for Hardy's own convenience, that he may speak through it of the First Cause working as a somnambulist. Both she and Jude, exquisitely conscious of their own predicament, are so, not with their own, but with their author's consciousness, and in character, word, and action must submit to him, at times so jarringly that we hear the bump. Consider that scene where Sue, as Mrs. Phillotson, meets Jude at night through the chance crying of a snared rabbit. It is a moment of deep personal intensity ; and in answer to Jude's cry, " I wish you were happy, whatever I may be!" Sue answers (with passion, we must believe):

> "I can't be. . . . It is none of the natural tragedies of love that's love's usual tragedy in civilized life, but a tragedy artificially manufactured for people who in a natural state would find relief in parting!"

An exclamation mark is not enough to transform this clumsy expression of Hardy's thought into emotional utterance. He has gone behind her character in the urgent necessity to pursue his aim. And as the bitter incidents pile up—with Sue stretched into constraint to re-marry Phillotson, Jude drunkenly re-marrying Arabella, and so providing those rectangular lines that Hardy insisted came by chance—a sense of strain passing into a new "unlikelihood" emerges, caused by individualism and symbolism at war. The influence of Greek drama surely is responsible for that aged child, whose bloody deed is the old stroke of vengeance, heaping ill on ill. But the scene is almost crazy; unbearable if the child is truly human, incongruous if he is a symbol. The effort to create completely dominant mortals, who are yet dominated utterly by a celestial cause, tears *Jude* in pieces. Or very nearly tears it. The rival forces appear locked in struggle. Neither classic drama nor Victorian fiction can be called on to decide the combat; both are inadequate, for something comparable to Melville's White Whale fills the picture. It is too large to give first place to the story of four human beings in Wessex, and the four humans are too intimately drawn to yield to it.

Hardy's notebook gives a hint of the solution ten years before the appearance of *Jude*. "Novel-writing as an art cannot go backward. Having reached the analytic stage it must transcend it by going still further in the same direction. Why not by rendering as visible essences, spectres, etc., the abstract thoughts of the analytic school?" And again: "The Realities to be the realities of life, hitherto called abstractions. The old material realities to be placed behind the former, as shadowy accessories."

Like many a philosopher before or since, Hardy is snared by the vague word "reality." But "the old material realities" conveys enough for us to understand that Sue and Jude were bound to fail; that the battle—not against society or the universe, but against Hardy's insistence on

the cosmic scheme—was lost at Christminster, and had
never to be fought by Napoleon, Pitt, or Wellington in
The Dynasts.

In the relieving of so taut a strain, a certain loss is un-
avoidable. Report goes that Hardy, begged in latter days
by admirers to write more fiction, would merely comment on
the stretch of years that lay between him and his last novel.
One sees a good enough reason why he wrote no more.
Responsibility to individual characters was the ballast he
threw out of the balloon. The tragic intensity of Tess
Durbeyfield could never recur, but neither could the tricky
juxtaposition of uncommon events and normal characters.
Hardy had gone so far from the old craftsmanship that
now, instead of watching stars from hilltops with expansive
gratitude, like Gabriel Oak, or with a horror of immensity,
like that too romantic young astronomer Swithin, he
looked down from " high amongst the clouds, which, opening and shutting fitfully to the wind, reveal the earth as a
confused expanse merely." On it may be seen—

> " *An object like a dun-piled caterpillar,*
>   *Shuffling its length in painful heaves along,*
> *Hitherward. . . . Yea, what is this Thing we see*
> *Which, moving as a single monster might,*
>   *Is yet not one but many?* "

It is Napoleon's Grand Army on the march from Moscow.
It might, when an attempt was made to stage *The Dynasts,*
have been any army in that later war. Hardy appeared
prophetic:

> " *So the season's intent, ere its fruit unfold,*
>   *Is frustrate, and mangled, and made succumb,*
> *Like a youth of promise struck stark and cold!* "

Granting that prophecy is not the foretelling of future
events, but the ability to discern the universal, Hardy has
attained it. There is no obstructive system of philosophy
in *The Dynasts*. Hardy's own utterance, clumsily tacked
on to the narrative in *Tess*, stilted and cramped in *Jude* by
its intrusion, is not only freed, but dances off to various
tunes: and in the Sinister, Ironic, and Pitiful Spirits there
can be found the whole expression of numerous post-war
writers, each limited to his one aspect. European and

THOMAS HARDY [*The Great*

American dramatists, experimenting technically with mega-
phonic voices, crude symbolical figures, jumbled scenes that
plunge from heaven to a brothel or inside a human brain,
are only throwing out restless and imperfect fragments of
the logical scheme whereby Recording Angels chronicle
decisions, Spirits of Rumour report distant action, and the
point of vision, roaming from the upper air to the interior
of a cellar, everywhere reveals continuity and clarity. The
argument is not " Hardy as a modernist " (though *Late
Lyrics* can provide some verses on a railway cutting, harsh-
lined and angled as a cubist picture, and named slyly
" After a Romantic Day "); it is rather that he has so
transcended fashions in *The Dynasts* that adventurous
writers, whether consciously or unconsciously, approach
him at some one point and fall short of him. German
expressionists, moved by the Revolution or the active antagonism of mass machinery, still broke their plays by the
post-Hardian effort to convert an individual into a symbol.
In America, Eugene O'Neill, writing a present-day trilogy
around the old Greek curse, sets out again, and less successfully than Hardy, to achieve " the modern expression of a
modern outlook " on a basis of the classical simplicity. If
there is an English dramatist who, dropping the individual
for the general theme, appears to follow Hardy, it is C. K.
Munro, in his dramas of the genesis and conduct of a war.

This is a proud estimate; and still it leaves the poetic
element untouched. In the spirit utterances, thought and
diction seem at times to rise together into a music beyond
the confines of humanity and its attendant Pities:

" He of the Years beheld, and we,
Creation's prentice artistry,
Express in forms that now unbe

" Tentative dreams from day to day;
Mangle its types, re-knead the clay
In some more palpitating way;

" Beheld the rarest wrecked amain,
Whole nigh-perfected species slain
By those that scarce could boast a brain;

". . . Heard laughters at the ruthless dooms
Which tortured to the eternal glooms
Quick, quivering hearts in hecatombs."

And suddenly, the less than human creatures are being gazed at with the nature-lover's old intimacy, sharpened by contact with clamorous disaster into finely pointed pain:

> *" The mole's tunnelled chambers are crushed by wheels,*
> *The lark's eggs scattered, their owners fled,*
> *And the hare's hid litter the sapper unseals."*

Hardy considered it his misfortune that the philosophic rather than poetic outlook should have been so scrupulously hunted for in his works. And certainly the labels " atheism " and " immorality " look now like fashion's twins. His attitude, in so far as it is reasoned out, is an effort to cope unflinchingly with a phase in the scientist's encroachment on religion. It was bold, through his refusal to be comforted by the illusion of an interested First Cause. To-day we might grant him a measure of deism for his belief in an external Cause at all. The next step, after abandoning the individual, and denying a fatherly God, is Communism. In Hardy the cosmic processes entangle man, who is to be pitied. The outlook is still tragic. It is typical that his astronomer in *Two on a Tower* finds " impersonal monsters, namely, immensities " in the universe. This was in the 'eighties, before anthropomorphic godhead could be banished, even from the scientist's outlook, without creating an appalling void. Now we are told our universe is expanding. But there are no monsters in it. Nor, in our relativistic world of warping lines, is pity to be bestowed on man. He is neither helpless nor heroic, bound nor dominant, but, faced by a wan choice of mathematical, mystical, and political deities without function, lives in bewilderment and uncertainty. Little wonder that popular novelists are turning back to present Dr. Pangloss and the Song of Pippa in an environment of travelling circuses.

> *" Breezily go they, breezily come; their dust smokes*
> *around their career,*
> *Till I think I am one born out of due time, who has no*
> *calling here."*

The more complex and inexplicable man's predicament becomes, the more will he crave escape into some reassurance that his earthly pains have ample compensation. And since the highest level in the many and the hours of relaxa-

243

tion in the few admit this craving, the man who insistently
denies it must always feel himself born out of time.

For all that, the title of pessimist thrown at Hardy has
excuses. A writer who is totally creative cannot easily be
labelled. Lost in his vision, he has that lack of fixed identity
which Keats bewailed as "unpoetical" in a poet. It is
the uninspired stretches that too often display remnants of
a fiery ardour damped into cold habit. As Browning tends
to end a verse by a swift turn to God, so Hardy haunts the
churchyard. A rhymer so prolific, so habitual, must inevitably produce more verse than his poetic muse can
answer for. His bastard products have a way of falling
into graves along a well-worn track of fate and weariness.
Roused to alertness, he can do something more vital even
with corpses. Look at *Friends Beyond* for a fine and satisfying expression of transcendence:

> " *We have triumphed: this achievement turns the bane*
> *to antidote,*
> *Unsuccesses to success,*
> *Many thought-worn eves and morrows to a morrow*
> *free of thought.*"

Or those who still miss Hardy's humorous irony and light-
hearted satire might be converted by *The Levelled Churchyard*, with its late-lamented "mixed to human jam":

> " *Here's not a modest maiden elf*
> *But dreads the final Trumpet,*
> *Lest half of her should rise herself,*
> *And half some local strumpet!*

> " *From restorations of Thy fane,*
> *From smoothings of Thy sward,*
> *From zealous Churchmen's pick and plane,*
> *Deliver us, O Lord! Amen!*"

When an author has adopted a wide patch of England,
renamed it, made his fiction so entirely its reality that
pilgrims gaze at spots his imagination used as at historic
sites, there is no question of his ultimate popularity.
The sage of Max Gate, bestriding the Victorian distance and
the Georgian foreground, became a legendary figure while
he lived. Fashion at last grew cold to him as "a survival,"

veneration overwhelmed him ; and there was little discrimi-
nation in either attitude. The following notes of visits to
Max Gate have therefore a double value, as coming from
so sensitive an observer as Mr. Edmund Blunden, and as
giving an impression of the actual T. H. of later years.

II

Saturday, July 15th, 1922.

Reached Max Gate about four ; Mrs. Hardy immediately
introduced me to T. H. An artist, Mr. Hill, was present,
commissioned to make a portrait for John Lane's new
edition of Lionel Johnson's book on Thomas Hardy. T. H.
had been sitting all day, but did not appear fatigued. The
pleasant, large sitting-room was dominated, grandfather-
clock and all, by a small portrait of Shelley. Tea and war
reminiscences. T. H. recalled his visits to the commandant
of a local camp for German prisoners. Said (with enjoyable
gravity) that the commandant and he moved freely among
the thousands of prisoners, " and yet they might have
turned on us at any time and neither of us had arms."

After tea Mr. Hill took his leave. Mr. Hardy proposed
a walk. Mrs. H. could not come. T. H. thereon took up
his dog's lead (he was a rough-haired " sheep-dog "), remarking that the dog had two dishes, which he evidently
supposed to possess feelings ; for if anyone's foot touched
them, up jumped the dog with a complaint. (This pleasure
in characteristics one soon saw to be usual in T. H.) We
walked uphill and down to Winterbourne Came at a fine
pace. T. H. spoke, not very favourably, of modern reviewers : he urged me to write on the stupidity of hasty
reviewing. If he were meditating an essay on Shelley
he would give a month to it, but the present reviewers
disposed of a new volume in a day or so. He thought none
of the reviewers of his *Late Lyrics* had read the volume
through ; said they had chosen for quotation only pieces
which he had included with doubts—had indeed put in only
to lighten the volume as a whole.

Through Came Park and its avenue we reached William
Barnes's little but beautiful church ; stood by Barnes's
grave, and also by that of a lady whose portrait was there
on a medallion. T. H. : " She had many lovers." He
mentioned Louis Napoleon's visits to the great house a
short way from the church. (Any Napoleon would have

245

done.)   Leaving his dog tied up outside, he entered
the church (though " no doubt the dog is as good as many
of those that go in "). Something made him recall to me
Hawker of Morwenstow and his six cats, which occupied
a front pew. I was admiring as a piece of calligraphy a
black-letter inscription over the rood-screen. T. H., with
technical and indifferent eye: " Yes, it's a correct church
text."

On the way home I asked if he did not like Barnes as a
poet, not only in dialect, but in common English as well;
this made him break in with enthusiasm, " There's another
great wrong done by the critics—they checked Barnes."
And he continued praising Barnes's volume of *Poems in
Common English*, and deploring the dull criticism it received.

He amused himself over an absurd notice of his poems
in the *Spectator*. On my naming the author, he replied,
" I *said* a woman must have written it." He added, the
notice was friendly enough (it was not!), but he feared its
incompetence, as a piece of writing, might unfortunately
injure the *Spectator*. He had, he said, debated much
whether to publish his new poems, but had done so in
order that they might appear with his own corrections of
the press. He had already suffered enough at the printers'
hands. In a poem of his on Sappho, he had written:

> " *Whose very orts our love incarnadine* ";

it had been printed

> " *Whose very arts . . .* "

three or four times under his nose, till one day he referred
to the original MS.

In a sonnet by Keats, he went on, there was a line with
a meaningless ending—" a diamond Jar." He would
amend this to what he was certain Keats wrote, " a
diamond Tiar." (It seems that he was proud of this very
neat discovery, for it appears in other places in print.)

An article by Maurice Hewlett had troubled him,
especially because it styled a poem " irreligious "—on the
burning of wooden crosses from the battlefield—which
T. H. thought religious to a fault.

By this, we were almost at Max Gate. It had rained
a little. He urged me to change my suit: " You're younger

than I am, as I said before." Dinner in another comfortable room, with leafy light around us; solid sets of books
here, and one oil portrait of T. H. Afterwards there was
earnest talk round the fire—although it was July, a fire
was welcome! T. H. acknowledged himself a book-hunter;
in the pre-Kingsway days he had haunted Bookseller's
Row, which he would have properly named, Holywell
Street. The name Grub Street, too, he said, he had long
wished to see perpetuated, even though only in the form
" Milton Street, formerly Grub Street."

His intense regard for Shelley was obvious. He had once
visited the church where Shelley and Mary were married,
and the varnish of the vestry looked so ancient that he
believed it must have been there when Shelley and Mary
signed the register. The sexton showed him the entry,
and said in response to T. H.'s question, " No, nobody
seems to come and ask to see it." Such neglect reminded
him how once, needing a particular edition of Shelley, he
visited a good bookseller, who, not having it, declared,
" It's not worth our while to stock Shelley—he's gradually
being entirely forgotten."

Sunday, July 16th.

Cloudy and chilly. I took myself off to Dorchester in
the morning. The afternoon we spent at the fireside. With
allusion to my having been a Bluecoat boy, T. H. said,
" It's a great wonder that I didn't go to Christ's Hospital."
His mother knew a Governor of the school, and a nomina-
tion was the natural prospect for him; but the Governor
died when he was still very young. He remarked on the
presumed attitude of the Coleridges towards S. T. Coleridge
—" Probably ashamed of his blue coat "; said that an
enthusiast visiting the family at Ottery St. Mary had
spoken of S. T. C., and found " an icy silence." On my
noticing the architect Pugin as a Blue, T. H. praised him
warmly. Mrs. H. observed that if she had a son she would
as readily send him to school at Christ's Hospital as anywhere.

T. H. conversed in most animated style, smiling, and
often developing towards the close of sentences a tone of
sounding emphasis; losing himself now and then in his
thoughts.

He said he could not understand why Browning's admiration for Shelley had waned in his old age. He had met

247

Browning at the house of Barry Cornwall's widow (Mrs. Procter). (He did not mention that he presented one at least of his early books to Browning.) Mrs. Procter had given him reminiscences of most of the heroes of the nineteenth century: she had been introduced by Leigh Hunt to a slackly dressed youth named Keats, who had left no impression on her otherwise. Of Lamb: she told T. H. that, after their wedding, Procter and she called on Lamb, and he, somewhat embarrassed, did not dare to take her into his untidy bedroom to wash her hands, but instead led the way into the kitchen. T. H. was sorry he didn't take the chance to visit Claire Clairmont.

He produced a noble copy in 4to of Godwin's *Political Justice,* frequently annotated in a hand which he hoped was Shelley's, and looked " very like." (The annotations affected only Vol. I !) He showed me on one title the initials, in pencil, B. S.; one before these couldn't be made out. The notion that this was Shelley's copy gladdened him. I thought T. H. took a delight in going up to his study and bringing down books to display. His notes in them were written clearly, and those in his " Golden Treasury " Keats were very copious. " Diamond Tiar " was noted, and a reference to Milton added. He produced an Otway, suggesting that out of the plays one might arrange pieces worthy of succeeding the " Beggar's Opera," and Young's " Night Thoughts " with funereal embellishments by a Frenchman, on which he lingered. Cowley's Works, too, he showed me in a handsome copy.

He advised me to write a history of old wars in the light of experience gained in the new one, and soon pitched on Marlborough as a fruitful subject. In zeal he hurried upstairs for the required volume of the *Dictionary of National Biography,* and explored the bibliography there given to ensure that the work had not been forestalled.

I kept the plan before me, but not long afterwards a work on Marlborough appeared and prevented me.

He also ran for another volume of *D.N.B.,* in order to find out who Ebenezer Jones was. He had been reading aloud with great happiness the lyric, " When the world is burning," and afterwards I spoke of the author as a Chartist and unhappy genius; this set T. H.'s imagination off. Reading in the *D.N.B.* that Jones was a mounting spirit crushed by public apathy and critical clumsiness, T. H. was moved, and brooded for some minutes.

The Queen's Doll's House Library being at that time in preparation, I spoke of it. T. H. was not exactly pleased with the way in which it was being collected. He said that at first "a Tradesman" had written requesting his contributions, but he ignored the letter. Then some months after "a Princess had, with her own hand, written and turned the request into a petition," proposing to have a copy of one of his poems made, which he might sign. He consented, but had heard nothing more.

Presently I ventured to say how irritated I had been at a lunch party where someone had boasted of his owning two Hardy MSS., one being *The Return of the Native*. Mr. Hardy, more amused than angry, explained. The collector in question offered to have a collection of his MSS. bound, if he were allowed to keep one of them. T. H., in the unthinking "first thought," agreed. Then the other wrote, "You said I could have *The Return*." T. H. did not recall saying this; but he didn't argue. When the MSS., less *The Return*, returned, they were bound very shabbily, and in some pages the edges had been cut. His benefactor now demanded that Hardy should write in *The Return*, "To ——, from Thomas Hardy"; but T. H. declined, pointing out that it was a matter of payment, not gift.

And afterwards the MSS. had to be rebound!

What the other MS. might be T. H. did not know: perhaps it was a ghost of my own.

Mr. Hardy, speaking of fraud, said that a drawing had been sold in New York over his name, but never done by him.

Notes of Sunday, July 29th, 1923.

At Max Gate.

Wessie barks in the drive.

S. Sassoon, T. E. Lawrence in private soldier's uniform, E. Blunden.

Mrs. Hardy enters, doesn't shake hands.

Tea, small talk.

Lawrence, marked politeness.

T. Hardy enters, "brushes" hands, re-seats the assembly.

Lawrence is seated on the sofa—"for once."

T. H.: "No sofas at the camp?"

Lawrence asks question about Tollerdown.

T. H.: "Often bicycled there." He then talks about

local geography—Chard, Crewkerne; anecdote of the " flitting " of an innkeeper (Wynyard's Gap), and of two failures to find a night's lodging.

T. H. recalls an adventure on an embankment at night: " I suddenly found I was looking down on my brother ! "

S. S.: " Were you walking ? "

T. H.: " No, we were bicycling."

S. S.: " Was it steep ? "

T. H.: " No—about six feet."

S. S.: " What happened ? "

T. H.: " Oh, I worked my way down again. The embankment joined the road again."

This simple episode, to T. H., seemed quite " a moving accident."

Lawrence discloses to Sassoon the whereabouts of his tribesmen.

Mrs. H.: " My husband wants to hear you speak some Arabic."

L.: " Can only speak kitchen Arabic."

L. translating a book on the life of a Californian pine-tree from the French, in order to pay for his motor-cycle.

T. H.: " Why don't you translate something from the East ? "

Lawrence: " I have the strongest feeling that there is nothing in the East. . . ."

I think this must have been the occasion when L. and T. H. discussed *The Iliad.*

T. H.: " I've always thought it was as good as *Marmion* " (quite seriously).

I noted that T. H. pronounced *The Dynasts* with a short *y*.

Lawrence, talking to us, expressed a poor opinion of T. H.'s novels, except the descriptive parts; did not recognize the " homegrown quality " in T. H.'s poems; was astonished at " the spectacle of Hardy " as a poet in his old age.

" Afraid of tiring T. H." No great danger of it.

This year the *Pink 'Un* reviewed T. Hardy's Poems (or O. Sitwell had an hallucination !).

THOMAS HENRY HUXLEY

1825-1875

**BY
H. J. MASSINGHAM**

THOMAS HENRY HUXLEY

"SCIENCE," wrote the terrible Infant Samuel, in an age that cut him dead, "is being daily more and more personified and anthropomorphized into a god. By and by they will say that Science took our nature upon him, and sent down his only-begotten son, Charles Darwin or Huxley, into the world, so that those who believe in him, etc.; and they will burn people for saying that Science, after all, is only an expression for our ignorance of our own ignorance."

St. Thomas did unquestionably help to found a new religion, and with a fervour of conviction that built temples to the Principle of Doubt. But his fountain of devotion was the Scientific Method. "I come," he said, "to forward the application of scientific methods of investigation to all the problems of life"; and elsewhere he declared himself without "faith in any source of truth save that reached by the patient application of scientific methods." Thus an historical study of comparative religions in post-Pagan Britain reveals a modification by descent, from the infallibility of the Church to that of the Bible to that of the Scientific Method. The strata of successive beliefs return an unbroken record.

But Huxley is not to be understood except as a disciple in what he himself called the "New Reformation." He had the perfect discipular mind and temperament. Before '59, when the *Origin of Species* appeared, he believed as fixedly as nearly all the rest of the world in the fixity of species, though hardly in the Pentateuchal succession. His four years in the Pacific on board H.M.S. *Rattlesnake* made no difference to his denial of evolution, nor did his

253

subsequent academic appointments, while he stoned the teleology of Lamarck with such derisive shots as hardly troubled to take aim. But in '59 a blinding light fell upon him, and he became a convert to Antichrist, passionate, single-hearted, lifelong, and with a zeal which at his death was to leave the new faith as unrecognizably transmuted as was primitive Christianity by St. Paul.

So long as mind and effort were conceived by Lamarck, Buffon, and Erasmus Darwin to be the dynamic of evolutionary variation, Huxley was as hostile to the theory of evolution as the Church Militant itself. It was when Charles Darwin substituted chance for the will to change as the cause of organic development and labelled the process as a chapter of accidents that the Saul who denied became the Paul who proselytized. Throughout the immense range of his interests and energies it is a disciple we pursue, never the conceiving and originating mentality of a Buddha, a Mahomet, a Darwin. Like all true disciples, he was an exemplary warrior, a Bussy d'Amboise of a swordsman, with muscles of steel, incredibly agile footwork, eye like a basilisk, thrust like a stooping peregrine. His enjoyment in " smiting the Amalekite " was at one with the crashing inevitability of the stroke, and the best tribute to his metal is our disagreement with his own words that " few literary dishes are less appetizing than cold controversy." The vitality of the disciple still makes the dusty field of battles long ago ring with the ghostly hurly-burly, just as it made a novel out of Palæontology and a Labyrinthodont, " pottering like Falstaff in his old age among the coal-forests," the actor in a breathless drama.

In many provinces of thought this proselytizing dynamo driving so lucid an intellect, encyclopædically equipped and expressed with such uncommon force and freshness made the new religion a genuine instrument of liberation Its cutting edge went through Victorian sentimentality and make-believe as though they were soft cheese. In education, Huxley's ideal of experiment superseding authority and of making " a ladder from gutter to University along which any child may climb," flashed a gleam of the Promised Land. His lectures to working men threw a vision of universals across the mean and dismal landscape of their serfdom, of wide worlds of being disclosed in a grain of sand, a piece of chalk, a blot of floating scum

As Darwin's Grand Elucidator, Huxley was the perfect Civil Service embodied in one man. He carried the Darwinian theory no farther in discovery than did its creator, but the conquered territory was controlled and administered with the efficiency of a whole Jesuit Order. He could preach the gospel with the tongue of a ratiocinative angel. The new method of verification by logic and evidence was indeed a destroying angel in the dark corners where the grubs of inertia, pretension, and traditionalism thrived.

His was a name of terror, alike among General Booth's " roaring mystagogues of Corybantic Christianity," the Positivists who mixed " bad science with eviscerated papistry," and the discreet folds of credal orthodoxy, and there is no doubt that he exterminated for ever the claim of Biblical supernaturalism to rest upon rational thinking. When Huxley returned from the crusades of the new religion, faith in the Hebrew cosmogony and in all the magical apparatus of the sacred books had henceforward to part company with reason. The scientific method blew the miraculous element in the Scriptures into dust so long as the apostle of the new faith demanded the verdict of evidence to justify our belief in it. To Newman's " as if evidence were the test of truth," he could bring silence by replying that miracles professed to be historical events. Poor Gladstone's rhetoric was burst like a paper bag. To a certain limited extent Huxley did succeed in identifying the scientific method with freedom of thought. Only a student of religions will express no surprise that this most pious pioneer of the experimenting spirit bequeathed to man in the end one of the cruellest of dogmas and the most idolatrous of formulæ that have ever plagued him.

And yet there is a sense in which this prophet of a novel principle did more than to sanctify the scientific method. Just for the moment, before the vision faded into the common path of disciples, he did marry that method with a true religion. When the miracle-controversy with Gladstone took the form of a discussion as to the illegality of pig-keeping and the Greek or Semitic nationality of the pig-keepers, the twentieth century smiles a sardonic—plague on both your houses. It is not tempered by our view of the one believing he was saving God from the heathen, and the other truth and right thinking from arbitrary superstition. Yet Huxley reached the frontier of a conception of God more intelligible than the invasion of the whole Gladstonian

255

army accomplished. As the spokesman of Darwin, he made one living substance of all the phenomena of life, a single Joseph's coat of the flesh of all living things. If, according to Samuel Butler, the real heretic of his age, the real builder of a new age, we cannot conceive life without soul, so we cannot conceive one Protean life, ever perfecting itself and clothing itself in more radiant form, without one Protean soul—or, as the theologians say, the Word was made flesh. Here Huxley approached the door of the sanctuary, and here, with his hand on the latch, he stopped.

It is an odd experience steadily reading through the nine volumes of the *Collected Essays*. All is clear as a metallic sunshine, a hard-edged daylight over an illimitable arid tableland like the Persian plateau. And suddenly the mists stalk into the scene as over English water-meadows. If Huxley had been the founder rather than the disciple of a new idea, it could never have happened. That is why, I think, half his work was an exposition and glorification of the scientific method and half a contradiction of and blasphemy against it. For it is usually the disciple who in his master's name undoes his master's work. Step by step the end is lost in the means, new idols are pieced and patched out of the *disjecta membra* of the old, and triumphant man enters the service of the new Sabbath. As the god of science rose in the heavens, his minister forgot in rite and worship to do his will.

In his analysis of Hume and Berkeley, and others of his philosophical writings, Huxley began to elaborate a proposition so eccentric that the other half of him, which made a holy war of taking nothing for granted, might well have confused him with a Wilberforce. He believed that in the end we should reach a purely mechanical equivalent of consciousness. For consciousness is a " function of nervous matter," and the brain secretes thought much as the liver secretes bile. All the same, he told us, this amazing hypothesis is compatible with the " purest idealism," because Berkeley shows us that we only perceive phenomena through the mind. Granted, says Huxley, so long as the mind be recognized as a product of molecular changes. In the light of this quaint evolution of the new scientific faith, Huxley's acceptance of Berkeley's subjectivism is as unscientific an evasion as his escape from materialism into agnosticism, word of his own coinage. He may say (rather irritatingly), " How do I know ? " about the ultimate problems of existence, but what he asserts he does know as a physical fact is that it is our bodies not our minds which think, and that our bodies are machines. Donne said, " You might almost say her body thought." In Huxley's opinion, this has come to mean that a motor or engine of mechanical parts is able to drive itself, feed itself, repair itself, reproduce itself, and finally make love or write poems. Into what tortuous thickets of thought was Joshua leading the people of Mosaic Darwin when the sceptic of the occurrence of miracles affirmed his faith in so monstrous a miracle as this ? Almost he speaks with the voice of the theologian, " Credo quia incredibile." It is, indeed, impossible for us to imagine at all that soul and being are born of a mechanical process, the to and fro and up and down of an automatic thing, and we only did so for a while because the force of Huxley's logic acted as a narcotic to our minds. What life is we do not know, but that our bodies live is the elementary knowledge of all mankind. And to say that our bodies are machines is for us to reply that a machine is an inanimate thing, and that if we say that our bodies in life are inanimate we are talking nonsense, and worse nonsense than the belief in Genesis as an infallible scientific statement of the origin of species.

It is quite plain that in such physiological speculations Huxley was talking not science but absurdities, fairy-tales which without scientific doubt or the intellectual scrutiny of his own bounden faith he had derived traditionally from the ridiculous Descartes' idea of animals as " reasoning machines." What Huxley did therefore in his sacred office of propagating the scientific method was to substitute one set of fantastic beliefs for another. The same integrity of mind, logic of exposition, and clarity of expression which had demolished Gladstone's religious mythology adopted this Cartesian myth as his own.

But it was by his interpretation of the Darwinian " Struggle for Existence " that Huxley finally took leave of Darwin, the scientific method and the inward guidance of the fiery cross he had used both as a sword and a beacon. *Evolution and Ethics,* the Romanes lecture of 1893, was the whiff of grape-shot that dismembered the Revolution. The rebel, Lucifer, who had mingled among men, lit up new worlds for them, and was teaching them to think thereby to live, now bundled the old gods out of heaven

L   257

and took a throne there more arrogant than theirs.   It was
that ascent which made a devil out of him.

The kind of gangster film that Huxley manufactured out
of the " Cosmical Process," both in the Romanes lecture
and many others of his essays and lectures, needs no re-
capitulation.   We have all sucked in his idea of universal
nature with our mothers' milk.   Hardly a politician, professor, or pundit of one denomination or another but
repeats it as part of a convention of knowledge which
abides no question.   Had Huxley's dualism of the self-
assertion of nature as opposed to the self-restraint of
civilized human society been drawn deductively out of
a mass of cumulative evidence, weighed, sifted, and
measured, it could never have disseminated itself among
and impressed itself upon all men as a form of unconscious
memory.   Only bare statements can do that, and Huxley's
story of the evolutionary process, which he compared to
the passage of the Beresina in the retreat from Moscow,
and in which he pointed to egoism, rapacity, and a bloody
despotism of the strong over the weak as the qualities of
survival-value in the transmutation of species, rests upon
a series of statements. These statements violate his own
scientific method so flagrantly and crudely that to read his
words, " There is no falsity so gross that honest men,
anxious to promote a good cause, will not lend themselves
to it without any clear consciousness of the moral bearings
of what they are doing," is to realize a mental transmutation of his own, impossible without that distortion of the
original text to which discipleship is so liable.   For there
is nothing, either in Darwin or A. R. Wallace, Darwin's
co-discoverer of the principle of natural selection, to justify
Huxley's sensationalism.   His marginal reading of the
evolutionary text was his own.   Wallace had preceded his
" myriads of generations of herbivores tormented and
devoured by carnivores " by—

> " the popular idea of the struggle for existence entail-
> ing misery and pain on the animal world is the very
> reverse of the truth.   What it really brings about is
> the maximum of life and the enjoyment of life with
> the minimum of suffering and pain.   Given the neces-
> sity of death and reproduction—and without these
> there could have been no progressive development of
> the animal world—and it is difficult even to imagine

a system by which a greater balance of happiness could have been secured."

Darwin said much the same thing:

" When we reflect on this struggle, we may console ourselves with the full belief that the war in nature is not incessant, that no fear is felt, that death is generally prompt, and that the vigorous, the healthy, and the happy survive and multiply."

Besides expressing kindred sentiments elsewhere, Darwin shot out visionary gleams of insight into the deeper issues of the evolutionary fugue not dissimilar from Francis Thompson's. All that his disciple could see was " the wicked flourishing like the green bay tree," Ahriman rampant. Thus was verified the prophecy: " Soon I expect to have shot past you and to find you pitching into me for being more Darwinian than yourself."

This moralization of the natural process is bored with so many logical and scientific fallacies that the private evolution of new presbyter into old priest had become complete. Ajax, standing darkly up against a savage and hostile universe, pitting the microcosm of the " ethical process " against " the unfathomable injustice of the nature of things," Victorian man against a " gladiatorial " cosmos, is apparently unaware that the part is inseparable from the whole. If the " cosmical process " is thus the villain of the piece, then ethical and contemplative man, its latest product, must be the super-Tamerlane. He cannot in any case be radically disjoined from the illimitable process that gave him birth. Huxley's argument, again, in identifying the cosmos with its " lowest attributes," involves what I believe is called a " hysteron proteron." The true nature of the antecedents, that is to say, are only discoverable by reference to the consequents that follow, whereas Huxley, in explaining the higher by the lower, reverses the meaning of both. From Huxley's point of view the Church was right to call attention to " the monkey damnification of mankind " and " the godless world " it made, though what the Church objected to was the descent of man, not from fiend-like universals, but from an ape-like ancestor.

One of Huxley's most famous phrases—" For his successful progress man has been largely indebted to those

qualities he shares with the ape and the tiger "—is a
pregnant illustration of that unscientific special pleading for
which the saint of Science damned the *Quarterly Review.*
It " deals with Mr. Darwin," he said, " as an Old Bailey
barrister deals with a man against whom he wishes to
obtain a conviction, *per fas aut nefas,* and opens his case
by endeavouring to create a prejudice against the prisoner
in the minds of the jury." Lecturing as an evolutionary
anatomist, Huxley uses the term " the ape and the tiger "
in such a way as to convey a figurative significance to it.
Ethical Huxley drags in the tiger by the tail to join the ape
as a symbol of ferocity and self-seeking, while scientific
Huxley gets the best of both worlds by the suggestion
conveyed that the tiger *alike* with the ape stands in ancestral relation with man. But what is the tiger doing in
this galley; where does Stripes come in? A babe in comparative anatomy knows that the Felidæ are as remote
from the humanoid and anthropoid stocks as the Cetaceans.
But if Huxley had used the term " the ape and the whale,"
he would have conveyed no terrors, while if for the cat he
had said " the ape and the mouse," he would, as a matter
of fact, have been true both to science and symbolism, since
the tree-shrews lie along the main phylum of the human
lineage. How strange is the psychology of advocacy, even
of the blackest pessimism, when it can drive the most
honest of men into the tricks of a showman ! It is one of
the most singular ironies of history that the unlawful substi-
tution of the cat for the mouse drove European civilization
along the wrong turning the Victorian Age had pointed out.
It was the inventor of that phrase who wrote about " plas-
tering the fair face of truth with that pestilent cosmetic,
rhetoric."

That it was not an isolated phrase is revealed by the
curious dark obsession of early man's instinctive tigerish-
ness which disfigures all Huxley's political writings, and is
solely responsible for the peculiar asperity of his attacks
upon the Physiocrats and Encyclopædists, Rousseau and
Charles Booth. Once more Stripes bounds into the arena
to the crack of the whip. The reply to the philosophers of
the *droit naturel* was disarming in its simplicity—" All
tigers have an equal natural right to eat all men." The
student of Huxley's mental progress, discovering five
deadly sins committed against the scientific method in one
page, is again led to reflect upon the unfortunate likeness

between destroying angels and their diabolic foes. Had these fallacies—the analogy between tiger and man, that tigers represent the animal kingdom in general, that the young of tigers are consciously ferocious, that men are the natural food of tigers, and that man-eating tigers are symbols of natural right—been voiced by a bishop, what leaping learning, incisive wit and iconoclastic logic would have sprung at his throat!

But the disciple had now ceased to rely upon his native dæmon: the sacred books had become his authority. The whole of his argument as to the nature of primitive man is based upon one sentence from Hobbes, and that only—" The natural state of men before they entered into society was . . . a war of all men against all men." So to secure peace they delivered their natural rights to one supreme authority. The *a priori* methods he denounced so often in his adversaries govern his brief exclusively; he gives no examples of primitive society in being, only of the Aryan paterfamilias declaiming *l'état, c'est moi,* and he invariably confuses the primitive with the savage. This is the reason why Huxley fails to impregnate his political thinking with a single constructive idea. It is vitiated from top to bottom by the untested and derivative dogma that government exists for the purpose of restraining the free play of man's native viciousness, the heritage of " Ishtar " (a name he gives to the " Cosmical Process ") who " drove Œdipus to slay his father and marry his mother "—which is the very last thing Œdipus did consciously, or to which nature would unconsciously urge him or any man. All pain, oppression, savagery, greed are Ishtar's fault, so that Pandora is not in it beside this burdened pseudo-primitive goddess of the Babylonians.

Huxley's polemics upon the cosmic process, whether applied to man or nature, were as unscientific as Thomas Hardy's impersonation of a pitiless First Cause in the novels whose philosophy is of the Huxley persuasion, was inartistic. The argument, that it is in our stars not ourselves that we are underlings, was so literally devoid of even a vestige of deductive reasoning, of evidential value, of scientific analysis, and of impartial judgment that one enquires in wonder how so fanatical and bizarre an illusion crept into his intellect and arrogantly usurped it. There can be but one answer, and that is, that the conditions of Victorian society itself fathered upon him so

261

grotesque a gospel of universal evil and terror. If we make a simple transposition of the pieces on the board, and set up Ishtar to represent that Victorian world of fierce competition, pitiless appetite for wealth, and idolatry of material things bred of Industrialism's prime and sheltering under the cloak of gentility, there in his own society and in his own time is Huxley's reading of the natural struggle for existence. The "Cosmical Process" was a gigantic Victorian age extending to the farthest star, a continuum enough to daunt even so stout an Ajax as the author of *Evolution and Ethics*. By an odd forgetfulness of his theme, Huxley himself in one place expressly likens Victorian society to a gladiatorial show, unconsciously repeating the very phraseology he had applied to poor pelted Ishtar. Again, the belief in automatic progress was all in Macaulay before science sanctioned it. And how exactly was that society's view of life Huxley's own! Was it not the unexpressed reason for the cloistered life of the Victorian miss that *Homo ferox* prowled without? Confessedly, Huxley drew the main lines of his indictment of the universe partly from Hobbes and partly from Malthus, whose economic views expressed the philosophy of Victorian materialism to a hair. In describing the moral nature of primitive man and the evolutionary movement as "a continuous free fight," he was in fact writing an historical survey of the acquisitive society of his own time, that was to become Big Business, and then in one great industrial nation "Big Business without the tall hat," according to the phrase of no less an authority than Al Capone. Uncharitableness does, after all, begin at home, and to us to-day it seems a little hard, not to say grandiose, that the cosmos *in toto* should have had to bear the brunt of the morality of a social organism whose form was confined to a speck of time in the history of life. Huxley's essays are in brief the record of how the primitive Tasmanians were blamed for the ideas and methods of the ethical society which exterminated [1] them, man, woman, and child.

The story of Huxley's intellectual life is certainly a drama on the cosmic scale. He was so powerful a force, a giant though not a great man, that the history of an epoch and the psychology of its ideas were mirrored in his mind. His scientific Calvinism, filled with the "generous new wine" of truth-seeking, and inspired

---

[1] *N.B.*—By putting out poisoned meat for them.

by the glowing fringes of enlightenment, ended in a deterministic nightmare parted from science, in which nothing was left of faith but fetters. The " New Reformation " had failed even more dismally than the Old. I have dwelt at some length upon the Satanic vision into which a genius of clear and narrow thinking had led him, because that is what the world remembers him by. Huxley's horrors were not superfine thrillers like Poe's: they captured the idolatry of three generations because they presumed to be based on the infallibility of the scientific method. By a major irony of history this enormous perversity, by which Huxley shattered his own ideal of the investigating spirit, acquired a European momentum from the scientific authority of the man who stood behind it. A theory which did virtually bestow a cosmic sanction upon all the baser, more vulgar, and predatory forces of society derived its power of diffusion from the honesty and zeal for righteousness of the mind that hatched it. Had Huxley been a lesser figure whose intellectual *bona fides* and scientific warranty had not been taken for granted, it is probable that his desertion of science for a doctrinaire obsession devoid of it would have been quickly detected. But it is only the layman who is pleased to regard the Church of Science as free of dogmatism, and no dogma that ever came out of the clerical citadel that Huxley bombarded was quite so pernicious or barren of concrete evidence to its truth as Huxley's own.

The incalculable mischief that it did is a measure of how much evil in the world is due simply to wrong conceptions. The old gods may have been dotards, the new were certainly demons. Like Atlas, Huxley bears upon his shoulders the world-weight of the delusion that man is instinctively a fighting animal. Neither the invariable association of war with complex social organization both in savage and civilized society, nor the plain and unanimous records of primitive peoples who know neither war nor organization, moved him from the fixed traditional faith of the Hobbes-Malthus school, that unquestioning faith he called " the one unpardonable sin." He, the father, brought despair upon all the children of the new century, since, if our nature be organically corrupted and the shadow of the cosmos towers darkling over this *damnosa hereditas,* no institutional policeman can jail either of them. The evil that a man of Huxley's calibre left to live after him will never be measured. That he destroyed our faith in creeds and religious formulæ was as nothing to his ruin of an intuitive belief in the elements of human nature. He made us turn in disgust from our own honest earthiness either to a sickly spirituality or a coarse glorification of get on or go under. But the worst thing he did was to take a foremost mental part in the greatest revolution the world has ever known—the discovery of evolution—and then to vulgarize the process by which, through an infinitude of intricate and gracious forms, each more perfect than the one that preceded it, a speck of protoplasm resolved itself to man.

Huxley was a Briareus in an age of giants. His humour, his force, his learning and integrity, his illustrative brilliance and unexampled quality of exposition were employed in a hundred fields. Yet it would undoubtedly have been better and happier for mankind if he had never been born.

LORD
MACAULAY

1800-1859

BY
D.
WILLOUGHBY

L*

D. WILLOUGHBY

LORD MACAULAY

WHEN Thomas Babington Macaulay was alive, and for a generation afterwards, he was called a " modern " man. That epithet is, as a rule, an epitaph. Men cannot eat their cake in time and have it in eternity. The spirit of the age may lead its followers to graves in Westminster Abbey, but it is a case of so far and no farther. Had Macaulay been as wholly of his epoch as he was, and is, commonly assumed to be, neither his mastery of the picturesque, nor his skill to tell a tale, nor the brazen resonance of his prose, could have saved his works from a morrow of derision, ending in the mercy of oblivion. Where he was most conspicuously modern, there he is at his stalest, flattest, most unprofitable. Gaping in ecstatic satisfaction at the miracles of the industrial revolution, he was quite simply the bumpkin come to town, and his exclamations are so many warnings that modernness is but provincialism transferred from map to calendar.

The third chapter of the *History*, with its comparison between Victorian England and England of the Stuarts, is a monument to an able man's fatuity. Everything, he says, has changed, and, it seems, immensely for the better. His rhetoric takes a note of high-piping journalese. " Populous and opulent hives of industry " are found on what had once been " desolate moors inhabited only by grouse and wild deer." Proofs of progress leap to the eyes. On the site of " the gayest and most crowded part of Regent Street," the parade of prostitutes in Macaulay's day, woodcock had been flushed when Anne was on the throne. Around the coast, from the " docks and quays " of Liverpool, inevitably described as " endless," to the front at

267

Brighton, which our guide accounts "fantastic" as well
as "gay," it is the same story. If mere size and growth
please and awe him, it may not be for us others to complain.
The virtue of bulk is, indeed, now pronounced axiomatic.
But among the tokens of headway and betterment which
Macaulay catalogues, there are some to which we may
demur. After statistics on the rise of Birmingham, he adds
triumphantly that, though Birmingham buttons were beginning to be known in the reign of Charles the Second,
nobody had then heard of Birmingham guns. Manufacture
of those weapons had been reserved for the era of enlightenment in which Thomas had the luck to flourish.

And it is by no means surprising that Macaulay was
satisfied, and more, with the times in which he lived, and
looked backward from them with contemptuous pity.
"People," he wrote on the margin of one of Swift's bitter
essays, "speak of the world as they have found it. I have
been more fortunate." Fortunate in most things, he was
peculiarly fortunate in his time of birth. Though one of
his grandmothers was a Campbell, putatively a daughter of
Diarmed of the Wild Boar and kin to the Mac Cailean Mhor
himself, Thomas was, at least by English standards, of the
middle class. The war with France ended in his boyhood
at Waterloo, and, with it, the age of unquestioned patrician
domination. Thenceforward, as all except benighted Tories
sensed, the aristocrats, if they were to rule at all, would
rule in partnership with the middle orders, and, though the
fact might be hidden by a variety of face-saving subter-
fuges, the controlling voice in the national concern would
no longer be aristocratic. In the near future, hereditary
status was by itself to count for little save in theory, whereas
wealth and vendible talent were in every effectual way to
carry weight.

Only during a short interlude were the commercially
amassed fortunes of the Macaulay family in the least uneasy, and of the talents of the son who mattered there was
from childhood no doubt whatsoever. Father, mother,
adoring younger sisters, were resolved that Thomas should
be a great man, and Thomas was a complacently consenting
party. Before many years of manhood were behind him,
the greater world was forwarding the clan's conspiracy.

The Whig nobility never lacked acumen. Young
Macaulay, having contributed some clever articles to the
Edinburgh Review, was offered a salaried appointment as

Commissioner in Bankruptcy, and, next, a seat in Parliament. A borough in the Lansdowne gift enabled him to be in the thick of the struggle for Reform. His first speech for the Magna Carta of his class made him, in his own words, " a sort of lion." As index to the prevailing temper, it is still worth reading right up to its highly ornamented yet animated peroration. As argument for making right of suffrage depend on a " pecuniary qualification " it could not be improved. Among its results, and perhaps the chiefest of them, were an order from Lady Holland for introduction of the orator, and a command to dine at Holland House.

The sequence of events throws a light on Whiggery that should not be missed. *Imprimis,* a man of promise, is admitted to the House of Commons. When he has there proved his abilities beyond a peradventure, he is told to enter the holy of holies, a private mansion to which the sole passport is established rank, or, in lieu of it, something uncommonly like genius.

For such as the Macaulays, the years of the last William and of Victoria were, in all material respects, a golden age. Territorial lords might regret their ancient privileges, and manual workers be tempted into dreaming their forbears had better cheer under legendary King Lud, but the *bourgeois* had ample reason for contentment. Long before Darwin had formulated his theory of evolution, the middling English were ready to receive it in the rough. Half Macaulay's writing testifies to his belief that man had risen, not in thousands of years, but in a couple of hundred or less, from a brutish to a godlike state. Without much immodesty, he might have adduced his own career as a not insignificant link in the chain of evidence for humanity's steady and continuous ascent. His ancestors had gone trouserless in the Hebrides. He had been bred at Clapham. Later, his tribe had moved to Bloomsbury. Anon, he was " to quarter himself in a commodious set of rooms on a second floor in the Albany," and, in the end, " with many grateful and respectful expressions," he was to accept a peerage.

Lecky's saying that speculative opinions prevail, not by weight of argument, but by predisposition to receive them, contains the truth. At the start of the Victorian era, augurs were preparing the public for the " upward and onward " doctrines of the later scientists. Macaulay's importance in

269

the band is due mainly to his vehemence. " I wish," said
Melbourne, " that I were as sure of anything as Tom
Macaulay is sure of everything." A spirit of certitude,
wonderful to us who live in an age which has taken the note
of interrogation as its emblem, impregnated the great Victorians. It is precisely because of their certitude that they
still appear great even when absurd. But, while it was
common form to exhibit confidence, Macaulay's cocksure-
ness was remarked as passing bounds. Strangely, however,
one does not gather an idea of positiveness from Grant's
portrait. There are the " homely features " which Carlyle
noted as characteristic of the Western Isles, and one knows
why Carlyle called him " an honest, good sort of fellow,
made out of oatmeal " ; yet, if there is aggressive obstinacy
in the nose, there is more enquiry than assurance in the
eyes. Melbourne, it may be, had been partially deceived
by Macaulay's emphatic, rattling wordiness. On the ground
he believed to be his own, Macaulay would have rated
an open mind as equivalent to moral and intellectual flabbi-
ness. From that area, covering the whole wide surface of
practical politics, he strayed rarely. As a result, his speech
and writing do breathe a dogmatic arrogance which is tempered only by his native amiability and occasional regard
for Victorian etiquette.

Beyond the prescribed limits, he was, and knew himself,
the most bewildered soul on earth. The essay on Bacon
betrays his secret. " The multiplying of human enjoyments
and the mitigating of human sufferings " is to him the
purpose of all philosophy. His care is for the things one
can touch and see ; those who have different interests irk
him. They would, as he discerns, lure him into regions
where his trust in sturdy common sense might be insufficient. He who was the unhandiest of mortals, who
could never tie a neat bow, or shave without inflicting
wounds, exalts the shoemaker above the author of the
books *On Anger*.

> " It may," he writes, " be worse to be angry than to
> be wet. But shoes have kept millions from being wet ;
> and we doubt whether Seneca ever kept anybody from
> being angry."

More is to be said for this point of view than those allow
who slight Macaulay as a prince of Philistines and themselves gorge upon the fruits of Philistinism. But his burst

of sarcasm does reveal the frightened mind of the Victorian who is in dread lest some wind blow out of heaven to shake the new and seemingly solid residence in which he lives so comfortably. Because Seneca has said that the object of philosophy's lessons is to form the soul, and not to improve a plough, a ship, a mill, Seneca must be pilloried as a varlet and charlatan. The rogue had praised poverty with millions out at usury; had raved about liberty while fawning on the minions of a court. Seneca, then, is a person to whom no decent individual will pay heed, and the worthy Macaulay, being for once in a temper, forgets how he has just contrived in one breath, albeit a prolonged one, to condemn Bacon as a corrupt judge, and to laud him as the teacher of fruitfulness.

Macaulay's vehemence on all that he considered in his compass hints his timidity about all he felt to be beyond it. His dislike of the supernatural, from the Cock Lane ghost upwards, was eminently Victorian. Yet his aversion from religious enthusiasms, though widely shared, was exceptionally strong. Snug and pleasant as his childhood and youth had been, his memory of them contained a disagreeable streak. From birth to death Tom Macaulay was never stinted of worldly jam, but he could not forget the otherworldly powders that had once been administered to him with it. He had been brought up according to the strict rule of the Clapham Sect of Evangelicals. Lest the Sabbath should be profaned by walking in the sunshine, the Macaulay children had been forbidden to worship at churches more than a certain distance from the parental abode. As an undergraduate, he had been censured for reading novels. In adolescence, he was reprimanded for contributing to a magazine which published light as well as serious matter. Some, after comparable trials, revolted violently, but Macaulay was "a lump of good nature," and from such substance there is no hewing a downright rebel. Partly for ease, partly in filial piety, he conformed, more or less, while under his father's roof. Afterwards, quite quietly, he put aside religion as something with which he preferred to have no personal contact. Though the *History,* the *Essays,* the *Lays,* all show a boyish love for taking sides, an insatiable zest for joining in the brawls and combats of the dead, his partisanship falters at theological dispute. Then, and then only, he is ready to avow both factions wrong. He is for Parliament and plutocracy against King Charles, and for all and sundry against King James; yet he had no more sympathy than had David Hume with the fanaticism which nerved the Roundheads at Naseby and kept the Cameronians steady at Dunkeld. When the Puritans are allies against a civil tyrant, he pays them a respectful tribute, but it is lacking in the cordiality which comes of comprehension. In all the conflicts between the jarring sects, he is above the *mêlée*, or descends into it solely as advocate of toleration. Such impartiality in such a man spells a vexed indifference.

In the essay on Bacon, the shafts are ostensibly aimed at pagan metaphysicians. Every one of them might just as well have been directed against preachers of Christianity who busy themselves about the Kingdom of Heaven to the neglect of sublunary affairs. Scruples of good taste, very characteristic of nineteenth-century gentility, may have decided the writer to let his opinions be read between the lines instead of in them. But, obviously, he is enjoying himself when, without giving too much offence, he can prod at religious excess. His assertion that the Puritan hated bear-baiting, " not because it gave pain to the bear, but because it gave pleasure to the spectators," is the classic sample of his method. Of a Covenanter who " filled his despatches with allusions to Ishmael and Hagar, Hannah and Eli, Elijah, Nehemiah, and Zerubbabel," he is delighted to add that the carl was cruel, selfish, and " not at all the dupe of his own cant." Fervour, anyhow of the mystical variety, even when patently sincere, was more than Macaulay could forgive. The amenities of the age required reticence for their protection, and, after reading the *Confessions*, he dismissed Augustine for having " the style of a field-preacher." His gibe at Exeter Hall's " prescriptive right to talk nonsense " was, of course, a piece of exceptional daring. It was one thing to denounce the sanctimony of the past; another to assail contemporary pharisaism. The outburst from a man who held circumspection to be the better part of courage shows he has been touched upon the raw. Always, if he turned his head, the dark shadow of a Clapham pulpit lay across the way. Half his fondness for Dutch William was response to that monarch's Gallio-like contempt for creeds and churches.

In nearly all this Macaulay was a typical rather than a singular figure. Victorian England of his sex and order believed that *laissez-faire, laissez-passer* was the right motto in religion as well as in economics. On one point, however, he may have had more discernment than the rest. Others assumed that a religion of which the main obligation was hebdomadal politeness to the deity could survive when all the grosser, more inconvenient superstitions had followed the stage-coach in vanishing before the steam-engine. Macaulay, on the contrary, was of opinion that the Protestant compromise in all its shapes was bankrupt. In his article on the *History of the Popes,* he reminded startled readers that Protestantism had made no national conquest since the Reformation, while individual Papists who left their Church now became, not Protestants, but infidels. The historian in him knew, too, the vitality of Rome. Her vigour, he predicted, might be undiminished when some New Zealander of the future should come to sketch the ruins of St. Paul's from a broken arch of London Bridge.

His avowed faith in progress stopped short of things spiritual. Though Protestant Denmark surpassed Catholic Portugal in prosperity, he suspected that tables of trade and revenue were in this one sphere indecisive and actually irrelevant. Macaulay has been derided as a book in breeches, and the *Life and Letters* tells how apt he was, whether at home or in India, to see the world through curtained windows of a library. Of the " condition of England," as known to Disraeli or Carlyle, he was totally unaware. From four years of India he acquired nothing but a notion that lessons in English literature would elevate the natives. Yet none could read, as Macaulay read, without acquiring some elements of wisdom. His reasoning mind, if often insular and time-bound, was logical. The " errors " of Rome did not strike him as more offensive to intellect than were the " truths " of Clapham. Possibly, it occurred to him that to reject purgatory and to conserve hell was to show an unnatural preference for the fire to the frying-pan. Again, since Thomas More had defended transubstantiation, there was no saying that culture and credulity were incompatible.

Discreetly, but in words which none save dullards can think ambiguous, Macaulay prophesied that the future lay between Catholicism and Rationalism. His own inclinations were towards the latter, yet he could see Catholicism as the " most attractive of all superstitions," and he recognized it as by far the best organized. For denying that theology is a progressive science, he has been reprimanded.

If he was wrong, his excuses were abundant. The god of the pious Claphamites was, apart from some humane views on negro slavery, no whit superior to Jehovah of the Jews. The god of the average Victorian had to be ignored, except on Sundays, lest further acquaintance should lead to a discovery that he had the brain of Mammon and the entrails of Moloch.

But Macaulay's freedom from certain current prejudices is most clearly seen when he touches upon morals. The Victorians thought sex of prime moment, and hardly ever mentioned it. Their successors reckon it a feather in the scale and talk of little else. Macaulay, as essayist and historian, was allowed a liberty refused to novelists and poets, and used it cautiously yet to some purpose. Dealing with the indecorum of society on the morrow of the Restoration, he placed the blame on those saints of the Commonwealth who had made felonies of " vices which had never before been even misdemeanours." His essay on the Comic Dramatists has lost nothing of its original value. For the greater part of his century Congreve and Wycherley were banned as rude and ribald, while their few apologists pleaded feebly that the stage was an unreal world where moral laws did not operate. With two or three sharply edged sentences, Macaulay destroyed the briefs for defence and prosecution. The characters of these comedies spoke the modish dialect of their day, mimed with its gestures, strolled in St. James's Park or on the Piazza of Covent Garden with airs of perfect use and wont. Therefore, said Macaulay, it was sophistry to treat them as strayed revellers from Fairyland with claims to plenary indulgence. With the censors who condemned the plays for verbal improprieties he dealt as firmly. " Whether a thing shall be designated by a plain noun substantive or by a circumlocution is," he wrote, " a mere matter of fashion. Morality is not at all interested in the question."

What made the Restoration Drama thoroughly pernicious was, he felt, its cynical and heartless spirit. According to these tests, by the way, an unexpurgated edition of *Lady Chatterley's Lover* is less noxious than are innumerable novels read to-day with sanction of police and magistrates. And to support his case Macaulay might have cited *Romeo and Juliet* for comparison with *The Way of the World* or *The Double Dealer*. In Shakespeare's tragedy, the lascivious chatter is without malice, and nothing better than

274

onventional and idle modesty is scathed. Though Mercutio
ests at Roemo's craving for " that kind of fruit as maids
all medlars when they laugh alone," it is all in fun, and
loes not smirch the beauty of the lovers' tale. Macaulay's
dictum, that there is no spectacle as ridiculous as the British
public in one of its periodical fits of morality, has been
worn threadbare by repetition. Yet no words so much
quoted have been so ineffective. Who remembered them
when " Charlie Dilke upset the milk," or when the Irish
potato cart was upset over Parnell's body? Mr. Chesterton
has dubbed Macaulay the *bourgeois* in Belgravia, and has
noticed that Victorian " prudery " began with that mixture
of classes which dates from the young politician's welcome
into the *beau monde*. But though Macaulay " wore the
white waistcoat of a blameless life," he was not obsessed
by prudery. If the undevout astronomer be mad, the historian cannot be a prude and sane. Now and then, at all
events, some thought of " other times, other manners "
must broaden his judgment on niceties of conduct.

Macaulay's *History* has always been disparaged and
always read. There is, of course, no defending it against
those who demand history without colour. But it was
surely Macaulay's chief service to literature that he did
carry into a drab epoch the colours of a brighter past. To
him, more than to any other single man, we owe it that
qualities in the English tradition, which are at worst gaudy
and at best gorgeous, were preserved under the smoke-
clouds of the eighteen-hundreds. To the boy of that century
who opened any of Macaulay's volumes before its close,
the page that was not a burst of sunlight was at least a
cheering show from an astonishingly magical magic lantern.
Being practically tone-deaf, their author had in compensation such extraordinarily vivid visual imagination that time
and space dimmed nothing for him. This faculty, if it
possess a human being, may be a monstrous curse, but the
well-regulated Macaulay possessed it rather than was possessed by it. There is no evidence that it ever disturbed
the even tenor of his even, upward way. As a writer he
utilized it constantly. Of what was below the surface of
historical events, or in historical characters, he knew no
more than any dull student can learn by diligence. As
writers of to-day are cinematographic, he was panoramic.
The outward spectacle was ever before him, and he had the
art of setting his visions graphically on paper. One must

not look to him for any of Michelet's penetration or delicacy of touch, but no third historian has rivalled these two in power to endow the past with semblance of a flush and glowing life.

Some critic, probably the late Lytton Strachey, has suggested there would be more interest in Macaulay's works if the author had not persisted in considering the world across the floor of the House of Commons. Others have deplored that he gave to politics time which should have been reserved for letters. Others again have condemned him for Whiggish partiality. The last charge is the least easy to refute; yet, accurately speaking, Macaulay was not a Whig. The true Whigs were a caste, and, as Thackeray once observed, there were very few of them. Macaulay, who sat, spoke, and voted in their select company, thought and wrote as a member of that Liberal Party which had its birth as he was arriving at maturity. As a Liberal he had his bias; only, as the essay on Horace Walpole indicates, it was not uniformly in the Whig direction. Frequently, no doubt, it led him, as every bias must, to be unfair, but unbiased history is pure chimera. Even Acton had his *penchant* for respectability. Moreover, there are advantages in a historian's foibles being plainly marked. Knowing Macaulay from the start to be a Liberal, you know when and where to allow for Liberalism. You know, for instance, he will be quick to brand a king as " bloody " and a priest as " lying," and quickly liable to gloss the fact that bloodiness and lies are not kingly and priestly monopolies. It is the writer with the cross-bench mind who bemuses and deceives everybody, for his verdicts must be taken as much on trust as are the solutions of a cross-word puzzle in which half the words can be read in half-a-dozen ways.

For the rest it is surely well that Macaulay did from time to time quit arm-chair and writing-table. Among the most immediately admirable things he wrote are his battle pieces and the parliamentary sketches which are so much more than sketches. But, if you examine those *chefs d'œuvre* after a lapse of years, you are sensible of some monotony. There is no change in the style of narrative when he leaves the Boyne or Killiecrankie for Westminster and Fenwick's Bill of Attainder. There is the same ding-dong, the same hum of hot excitement, in his treatment of both subjects. Then, it may be, you will jump to two conclusions at once. You will guess that, the most vivid imaginative powers being fallible, Macaulay, who had never heard a shot fired with homicidal intent, was somehow wrong about the battles. And you will divine that he was meticulously and gloriously right in his reconstructions of scenes in bygone Parliaments, because personal experience had helped imagination to guide his pen. To Macaulay the politician working with Macaulay the visualist we owe the best left us by him whom *The Times* named Thomas Babbletongue Macaulay.

JAMES CLERK MAXWELL

1831-1879

BY
J. W. N.
SULLIVAN

JAMES CLERK MAXWELL

THE most significant feature of Maxwell's work, seen from our present perspective, is that it freed the human mind from the assumption that the ultimate nature of the physical world must be described in mechanical terms. As Einstein has said of him, he changed the " axiomatic basis " of scientific thought—obviously the greatest possible achievement in science, as it would be in any other branch of thought. The difference between modern science and pre-Maxwellian science lies precisely in the different axiomatic basis assumed. In this aspect of his achievement Maxwell may be likened to Newton: each of them founded a dynasty.

The mathematicians up to Maxwell's time had achieved a great measure of success in working out in detail the Newtonian conception of a mechanical universe. (I call it the " Newtonian conception," because that is what it is generally called, although Newton held it with certain reservations that were not shared by his followers.) So far as the phenomena of motion were concerned, the explanation was practically complete. The behaviour of colliding bodies, the paths of projectiles, the motions of the planets, and innumerable other phenomena, could all be deduced from Newton's three laws of motion and his theory of gravitation. In the hands of the great mathematicians who followed Newton, the mathematical methods involved had reached a superb degree of development. The success of the Newtonian method had been so prodigious that it is not, perhaps, so very surprising that it began to be regarded as the key to—everything. Laplace went so far as to say that a sufficiently great mathematical intelligence, given the dis-

tribution of the particles in the primitive nebula, coul(
deduce the whole future history of the world.

Nevertheless, there was one set of phenomena for whicl
the mechanical explanation was not yet complete. This wa:
the phenomena of light. Newton had favoured a curiousl\
hybrid theory that light consists of little corpuscles accom
panied by waves, but this was so far in advance of hi:
time that it is only as a result of the latest quantum re
searches that scientific men are quoting this theory as ye
another proof of Newton's amazing physical insight. Unti
quite recently, however, the pure wave theory of light wa:
universally accepted. This theory required a medium fo:
the propagation of the waves, and accordingly the grea
ether theory was invented. But the ether, the most in
dubitable fact of our experience, as Lord Kelvin called it
always remained somewhat recalcitrant to mechanical ex
planation. Prodigious feats of mathematical virtuosit\
were performed. The ether became steadily more com
plicated. Space became filled with an incredible comple\
of cog-wheels, gyroscopes, driving bands, and everythin؟
else that engineering experience could suggest. Never
theless, this vast mechanism, although dowered finally witɭ
the most amazing physical properties, even contradictor\
ones, could not be made perfectly to fulfil its function o
accounting for the propagation of light. As a result o
Maxwell's work, scientific men are now relieved from the
boring and laborious duty of constructing mechanica'
ethers, since we now know that light is an electromagneti؟
phenomenon, and that electromagnetic phenomena are no
to be explained in mechanical terms.

Maxwell's electromagnetic theory of light, the greates
of his scientific achievements, is one of the rare instance:
of a scientific theory that is utterly original. The connectior
between light and electricity had remained wholly un
suspected until he appeared. The mathematicians of hi؟
time dealt with these two sets of phenomena by entirely
different mathematical methods. We have already seen
that they explained light as consisting in the vibrations o
a huge jelly " filling all space." They explained electrica[
and magnetic phenomena by an " action at a distance "
theory. This conception was borrowed from Newton's law
of gravitation. In the enunciation of that law time does no
enter. Two bodies " attract " one another instantaneously.
This conception was applied to electrically charged bodies.

,lectricity was conceived, vaguely, as a sort of immaterial
uid, or perhaps two fluids, as there is a positive and a
egative electricity, and this fluid was dowered with
ttractive and repulsive powers which worked instantane-
usly. The mathematicians explained successfully a good
1any phenomena along these lines.

But while the mathematicians were busy with their purely
)rmal development of electrical theory, Michael Faraday,
robably the greatest experimentalist in the history of
cience, was developing an entirely different group of con-
eptions. It was probably fortunate that Faraday was
ompletely untrained mathematically, so that he had
,othing to unlearn. This lack of training prevented him
rom realizing the success that had been achieved by the
ction-at-a-distance theory, and as his strong, pictorial
magination found no nourishment in it, he unhesitatingly
ejected it. He replaced it by his conception of " lines of
orce." These lines of force, rather like stretched elastic
)ands, invisibly attached one electrically charged body to
.nother. The essential point of this conception was that
he space between electrified bodies was made to play a
undamental rôle in electric phenomena. It became a seat
)f energy, of stresses and strains ; it was no longer a mere
nert " separating agency." The genius shown by Faraday
n developing this conception is really wonderful. Although
vithout any technical knowledge of mathematics, Faraday
1ad a very strong mathematical instinct. His lines of force
vere not merely a vague picture of some spatially extended
nfluence, but, on the contrary, a precise, quantitative con-
:eption. They enabled him to understand, in great variety
.nd detail, a large number of electrical and magnetic
)henomena. Nevertheless, the mathematicians continued
o treat his lines of force with indulgence or contempt, and
his fact may a little have disconcerted Faraday. He says :

> " I have been so accustomed to employ them, and
> especially in my last researches, that I may have un-
> wittingly become prejudiced in their favour, and
> ceased to be a clear-sighted judge. Still, I have always
> endeavoured to make experiment the test and con-
> troller of theory and opinion ; but neither by that nor
> by close cross-examination in principle, have I been
> made aware of any error involved in their use."

On the other side Sir George Airy, the mathematician,

speaking of the agreement between observations and calcu
lations based on the action-at-a-distance theory, says: " I
declare that I can hardly imagine anyone who practically
and numerically knows this agreement to hesitate an instant
in the choice between this simple and precise action, on the
one hand, and anything so vague and varying as lines of
force on the other hand."

Faraday seems to have been led to elaborate his conception of lines of force by his great discovery of electromagnetic induction. This discovery, that an electric current may be created in a wire by passing it through a
magnetic field, is the most important of Faraday's researches, both theoretically and practically—theoretically
because it is essential to the creation of Maxwell's Electromagnetic Theory of Light, and practically because it is the
basis of all modern electric technology. It was published
in 1831, and in the same year James Clerk Maxwell was
born. Maxwell's type of imagination was very akin to
Faraday's, and he was drawn, from the very beginning,
towards Faraday's conception of things. In a letter to
Faraday he says:

" When I began to study electricity mathematically
I avoided all the old traditions about forces acting at
a distance, and after reading your papers as a first step
to right thinking, I read the others, interpreting as I
went on, but never allowing myself to explain anything
by these forces. It is because I put off reading about
electricity till I could do it without prejudice that I
think I have been able to get hold of some of your
ideas. . . ."

Maxwell was twenty-five when he published his first
paper on Faraday's lines of force. In this he finds a
mechanical analogy for these lines by likening them to the
lines of flow of a liquid. But this analogy was consciously
employed merely as an analogy—something that his
imagination could work on. Sir James Jeans has accused
Maxwell's successors of constructing imaginary pictures
and presenting them to the world as scientific realities.
Maxwell himself, however, always had a full share of that
philosophic scepticism which is characteristic of the modern
scientific attitude towards scientific theories. He says:

" By referring everything to the purely geometrical

idea of the motion of an imaginary fluid, I hope to attain generality and precision, and to avoid the dangers arising from a premature theory professing to explain the cause of the phenomena. If the results of mere speculation which I have collected are found to be of any use to experimental philosophers, in arranging and interpreting their results, they will have served their purpose, and a mature theory, in which physical facts will be physically explained, will be formed by those who, by interrogating Nature herself, can obtain the only true solution of the questions which the mathematical theory suggests."

Lightly as he held them, however, Maxwell could not yet orgo mechanistic analogies. During the next few years e elaborated a truly extraordinary mechanical explanaion of electromagnetic processes. But out of this jungle f vortices, "idle wheels," and particles, the fundamental Iaxwellian equations emerge. He found that waves could e propagated through this amazing medium, and that they vould be propagated with the velocity of light.

What degree of importance Maxwell attached to this nechanical analogy we do not know. The quotation lready given suggests that he did not take it very seriously. 3ut he had sufficient faith in the *formal* correspondence f his model with the processes of nature to conclude from : that electricity is propagated through space in the form f waves, and with the velocity of light, and that light is n electromagnetic phenomenon. In later versions of his heory he presented it in a purer and more abstract form. \t the present time his mechanical analogy is of interest nerely as an illustration of Maxwell's psychology.

It is probable that, towards the end, Maxwell was wholly mancipated from the belief that the world is fundamentally . machine. In any case, his theory formed a really im-•regnable barrier to the further progress of the mechanistic nterpretation of nature. It became clear that electricity nust be accepted as a fundamental concept, irreducible to nechanical terms. After one more feverish outburst of ther-building, mathematicians abandoned the mechanical xplanation of light, and instead turned their attention to onstructing mechanics out of electricity.

Maxwell was curiously akin to Faraday, not only in his ype of imagination, but in possessing that mysterious,

indefinable sense called the sense of physical reality
Mathematicians have rarely possessed this sense. Faraday
as we have seen, was not a mathematician at all, an
Maxwell himself was not, as a matter of fact, a really grea
mathematician.   Newton possessed both faculties to
supreme degree, and was also, what Maxwell was not,
great experimentalist. But Newton is unique in the histor
of science.   Usually the flair for physical reality is no
attended by a great capacity for mathematical abstraction
The extremely experienced Cambridge mathematical coach
Hopkins, who had Maxwell as a student, said of him tha
he was " unquestionably the most extraordinary man
have met in the whole range of my experience," and goe
on, " It appears impossible for Maxwell to think incorrectl
on physical subjects ; in his analysis, however, he is fa
more deficient."   And Sir James Jeans, speaking of Max
well's deduction of the laws of gases by considering a ga
as composed of molecules moving in all directions with a
velocities, says :

> " Maxwell, by a train of argument which seems t
> bear no relation at all to molecules, or to the dynamic
> of their movements, or to logic, or even to ordinar
> common sense, reached a formula which, according t
> all precedents and all the rules of scientific philosophy
> ought to have been hopelessly wrong. In actual fac
> it was subsequently shown to be exactly right, and
> known as Maxwell's law to this day."

These facts remind us of the eminent German's remar
about Faraday, " He smells the truth."

It was this extraordinary intuition, combined with a so
of philosophic breadth, that made Maxwell's achievemer
possible. Maxwell's ideas sprang from a wider and mor
subtle context than we find in the minds of most scientif
men. His theory was not understood during his lifetime
it assumed too unfamiliar a context of ideas. This qualit
of originality is apparent in almost everything Maxwell ha
written. It is very apparent in his letters, and seems t
have informed his conversation, for people found him th
most delightful and also the most incomprehensible of con
panions. A typical anecdote is the one Sir J. J. Thomsc
tells when he says: " I was told by Dr. Butler that h
remembered going for a walk with Maxwell without unde
standing one word of what he said, though he talked th

whole of the time, and yet, said Dr. Butler, ' I would not have missed it for anything.' " This same quality made him so unsuccessful as a lecturer. He had no real understanding of the difficulties experienced by the ordinary mind. In his review of Maxwell's little book on Heat, supposed to be intelligible to " artisans," Professor Tate begins by saying: " One of the few knowable things that James Clerk Maxwell does not know is the difference between what is hard and what is easy." This is the less astonishing when we remember that Maxwell was a boy of thirteen or fourteen when his first paper was read before the Royal Society of Edinburgh.

As a child Maxwell was fond of knitting elaborate pieces of wool-work, drawing complicated diagrams, and constructing solid geometrical figures. This was all part of his need to *realize* an abstraction by embodying it in as concrete a form as possible, and this need seems to be intimately associated with that mysterious " insight into physical reality " that characterized him. But combined with this was a great interest in abstract speculation. Maxwell was one of the few scientific men of his time who made a genuine study of metaphysics. And he seems to have had a strong vein of what can only be described as mysticism. This was probably associated, as is usually the case, with some definite period of crisis in his life. This is borne out by his remark: " Long ago I felt like a peasant in a country overrun with soldiers, and saw nothing but carnage and danger. Since then I have learned at least that some soldiers in the field die nobly, and that all are summoned there for a cause." The state of inner illumination that accompanied this conviction is perhaps described for us in his " nostrum ": " An abandonment of wilfulness without extinction of will, but rather by means of a great development of will, whereby, instead of being consciously free and really in subjection to unknown laws, it becomes consciously acting by law, and really free from the interference of unrecognized laws." And his letters to his wife, dealing with passages from the Bible, abound in interpretations which are indubitably mystical.

All these elements in Maxwell conspired to make a completely harmonious whole. This very unusual quality of homogeneity is immediately apparent to any reader of his life and letters, and seems to be responsible for the curious affection, verging on reverence, with which he was regarded

by those who knew him. He was expressing a real difference from himself when he said that some men seemed
to have water-tight compartments in their minds. The
diversity of Maxwell's studies does not strike one as the
different "interests" of a restless curiosity. At most they
are different fields for his attention; he brings the same
attitude of mind to them all. We feel, indeed, that they
are all connected in his mind in some unusual and personal
web of implications. His "context of ideas," to which
we have already referred, was one of the richest and most
subtle that any man has ever had. And for this reason
platitudes acquired an extraordinary wealth of meaning in
Maxwell's hands.

During his lifetime Maxwell was comparatively unknown. His reputation with his scientific contemporaries
was, of course, a high one, but by no means so great as
it has since become. At the time of his death, it may be
safely said, there was no one in the world who realized
what he had done in his electromagnetic theory of light.
Nearly a quarter of a century elapsed after its publication
before Hertz obtained experimental proof that electricity
was propagated through space in the form of waves with
the velocity of light. Amongst the practical consequences
of this discovery are wireless telegraphy and telephony.
The world became pregnant with these things when Maxwell wrote down his equations. But, to the scientific man,
the theoretical consequences of Maxwell's theory are even
more important. As we have said, Maxwell was led to his
theory by a mechanical model. But in deducing his theory
from the model, as it were, Maxwell had made jumps.
These jumps were sheer flashes of genius, but, in relation
to their mechanical setting, they were without rhyme or
reason. But the jumps are absolutely essential to the
creation of Maxwell's equations and, as Hertz said, "Maxwell's theory is Maxwell's system of equations." Thus,
although the theory had been suggested by a mechanical
model, it lacked a mechanical basis. And it gradually
became apparent that this mechanical basis could not be
supplied. This was a turning-point in the history of science,
for it meant that a centuries-old outlook had to be abandoned. Some scientific men, as Lord Kelvin, found it impossible to make the effort, just as there are still some men
of science who hope that, in due time, Einstein's theory
will be "exploded."

To follow out the train of thought that Maxwell started in the world would take us, without any breach of continuity, into the theory of relativity. Thus, Einstein's first paper on relativity had its origin in his attempt to adapt Maxwell's equations to moving systems. Indeed, the whole conception of what is called field physics springs from Maxwell and Faraday. They turned the attention of science from discrete material particles to continuous fields. This outlook cannot yet be applied to the whole of physical phenomena. Besides the great field theories summed up in the theory of relativity we have the quantum relations, those concerned with atomic and subatomic phenomena. These seem to be the most fundamental processes in nature, and they cannot yet be incorporated in any field theory. It is possible that they will always remain outside any such scheme. In that case the Faraday-Maxwell outlook will exercise but a partial dominance over the region of physical phenomena. But no one can yet say that this bifurcation of physical theory is bound to persist, and it may be, as Einstein seems to think, that the dominion of the field theory will ultimately be complete.

GEORGE MEREDITH

1828–1909

BY SIR
WILLIAM
BEACH THOMAS

GEORGE MEREDITH

I. THE FIRST IMPRESSION

AT the very end of his long life, when his limbs no longer expressed the activity of his brain, George Meredith was asked by a great editor to write a poem for the Nelson number of a weekly paper. Against expectation he consented, and gave his reasons. " I like your paper," he wrote; adding this characteristic sentence and sentiment: " Most journalism is either brandy or pap; or both, in execrable mixture." The turn of phrase is pure Meredith. He had real difficulty in saying anything in unaltered idiom. One may confess that often he scarcely distinguished between idiom and *cliché*, disliking one for its likeness to the other. He must make his own tongue; and when the clean, simple, classical utterance found vent in spite of him, it comes with peculiar force and zest, almost like the conclusion of a speech from Cromwell; out of the murky maunderings among obscure philosophies emerges at last the clear-cut phrase: " Gentlemen, I do dissolve this Parliament." This Nelson poem that he presently sent (it is not, I think, to be found in his published works) is made wholly memorable by the chaste and simple line with which it concludes.

" *And victory in his ears sang gracious death.*"

Those on whose impressionable period Meredith burst must always delight in him; and since " the deep power of joy " gives heart to criticism, as well as to more creative activities of life, it may serve truth to preface a colder

calculation of his claim to present and future fame with
some recollection of the original zest that he inspired. It
is right that a later age should add a " sober colouring ";
and perhaps we come nearer truth when we are forced to
lament:

> " And now? The lambent flame is where?
>   Lost from the naked world; earth, sky,
>   Hill, vale, tree, flower, Italia's rare
>   O'er-running beauty crowds the eye—
>   But Flame? The bush is bare."

Nevertheless, the trailing glory was once there; the flame
was God-sent; and the mind that lit the clouds and fired
the Bush must have known true inspiration.

There will always be Meredithians as there will always
be Borrovians and Janeites. He wrote verse and he wrote
prose, he wrote fiction and he wrote criticism that was
certainly not pap, though it may have resembled brandy.
It was not anything that had been produced before;
the genus was new. It was not in succession, and
though it has exerted a more than profound influence on
thought, on the conception of style, on the perception of
the possibilities of language, it has had no lineal successors. The only producer with whom he has suffered
serious comparison is Robert Browning (whom Mr.
Chesterton has called eccentric because of his frantic
efforts to reach the centre), and except for a superficial
roughness and essential obscurity—due in part to intellectual intolerance—two writers were seldom more different in character and personality. Meredith was never
the poet of his day—the man whom every quasi-intellectual
must quote or perish from his circle, as Browning was;
nor was he the Dickens of his day. He never wholly
escaped from the esoteric brotherhood; yet for some twenty
years or more he was one of the few acknowledged masters
of his generation. Hardy and Meredith became in diurnal
criticism as Dickens and Thackeray before them. At home
and abroad they stood for the immortals of the hour, if the
contradiction in terms may be suffered. And they were
more than Dickens and Thackeray in one regard: they
began as poets, and ended as poets of a quality at least high
enough to give excuse for the debate that rages about the
memory of Victor Hugo. Was he greater in prose or
poem?

A charming story is on oral record of a discussion in an Oxford common-room over the poetry of Hardy. Sir Walter Raleigh, the king of critics, was present, but remained mum till his verdict, his casting vote, was imperatively demanded. Then he pronounced judgment. " I like my poetry good," he said. " If I cannot get it good, I like it *rum* ; and Hardy is *rum*." Meredith too was always " rum," sometimes very rum. But rumness which issues from a rum character, being honest rumness, is an unquestionable virtue, whether in an Aloysius Horn or a Carlyle, though it may be felt and condemned as affectation by the majority. If anyone wishes to see a proof of the genuineness of Meredith's style, let him go to the journalism that he wrote in the days when he was pouring out his vigour into the glorious hilarity of *The Shaving of Shagpat*. There is a leading article on the scandal about Palmerston and his octogenarian amours that might have come from the core of *The Egoist*. The personification of scandal with her " restless battledore," the allusive satire on popular morals, the air of an Olympian observer, too objective to be petulant or petty or even partisan, the good-natured demand for essential decency, are characteristic Meredith. They are also good, even very good, journalism. Meredith could not help being himself ; and determined very proudly not to make the attempt. " I give," he said, " I do not sell," a boast we may put alongside the sad, yet, beneath the sad humility, the proud plea of Francis Thompson :

> *" For gold*
> *He was not sold."*

Those who read their Meredith at the height of his fame felt this genuineness, and perceived that it was the gift of a poet, a creator. You cannot sham what you do not copy. So at first we read Meredith for his newness, intensely stimulated by both matter and manner, wrestling proudly with his abbreviated obscurities, his robustious gymnastics, his satiric energy, his sustained intellectuality. And when the bout was over, what was left of solid gain ? Negatively he killed sentimentality. The poignant, devastating pathos of the conclusion of *The Ordeal of Richard Feverel* is carried through without a moment's surrender, in so much as a single sentence, to softness and self-pity, just as the hot and unhappy fate of the two lovers—a theme peculiarly

M*   295 liable to sentimental excesses—comes to a climax in the last splendid sonnet of *Modern Love* without the suggestion of a moral. In Dickens of course sentiment is a sort of Bright's disease; and when the patient eats starch or other substance convertible into sugars, his case becomes grievous. But this excess of feeling, which spoils a Little Nell or a Dora, renders possible the human gusto of a Pickwick or a Mrs. Nickleby; and is the obverse perhaps of a Pecksniff or a Uriah Heep. So Meredith fails most signally where Dickens most triumphantly succeeds. Mrs. Berry is altogether below the aristocratic class of Mrs. Gamp. But when we come to the lovers, to Richard and Lucy, to the Egoist and Clara, to Sandra and Wilfrid, to Janet Ottilia and Harry Richmond, we are vouchsafed the spectacle, hitherto almost denied to fiction, of an equal contest. Atalanta may or may not win the race. It is open. If her second name is Clara she will refuse to pick up the golden balls, and will feel no pity for the conquered victim left to the euthanasia of Laetitia. These combats were rewards enough; but they were not the only rewards for young readers. Meredith, even in his most hilarious rhetoric, has a trick of condensation. He hates dull verbal interludes, even in the course of a moderate period; and one result is that he gives you phrases that belong not to prose but to poetry. The young men who adored Meredith, reading him for the tissue of the stuff as well as the drama of scene and character, savoured the poet in him on every page. They tasted the ambrosia of epigram as well as description. It was reward enough for the slow reading of a difficult tale to remember that the lady's eyes responded " as the ripple rocks the light "; and it was worth a thousand tracts or spiritual exhortations to be told that " the flame of the soul burns upwards; but we must allow for atmospheric variation."

Meredith himself was too consciously aware of this. A neighbour of his on Box Hill called at the hermit's cottage just after reading *Beauchamp's Career*. Meredith asked him just one question. He did not want to know what he thought of the tragedy of the hero, the rival merits of the many fine ladies, the virtue of the wild doctor's political maxims—he asked, with the eagerness of a young poet: " Did you notice my phrase for a *tête-à-tête*? " To have invented the English equivalent, " a-you-and-I," was his special pride at the moment!

He loved vigour of phrase and condensation of meaning as Conrad loved the long rhythms of coloured periods. He could not help experimenting again and again, in verse as in prose. Many of these experiments irritate and bother us. He was so intolerant of a popular world which " never uses one word where ten will do," so enthusiastic of the first half of the Horatian maxim that he quite disregarded the second: *Brevis esse laboro*, he could say so much, but the *obscurus fio* was a confession beyond him. In a quite appropriate passage, though it is no more than a description of the manner and style of *Sartor Resartus* (which he dramatized in *Evan Harrington*), he calls Carlyle's a wind-in-the-orchard style. His own was a kangaroo-in-the-bush style. The track often consists only of the greater hops ; the intermediate pedestrianism is quite omitted ; and like the kangaroo, he changes direction with unforeseeable suddenness. The difficulty of keeping step is real ; and is a nuisance. He does not mix his metaphors ; but they succeed one another at close quarters without any sign that the one suggested the other. His head is a conjurer's hat of similes. Rabbit, handkerchief, potato, and the rest are pulled out at baffling speed, a feat made possible less by his conjurer's skill than the size of the head.

Hence to many readers, even among the zealots, he was " like something out o' nature," as said his Mrs. Berry, " a woman of mixed essences, shading off from the divine into something considerably lower." Mr. Bernard Holland once said that Meredith's work gave him the impression of the cinema screen, which at that date so sparkled and shook that you could not enjoy the pictures as you would if the technique were smoother: Meredith's style wobbled. I quote from distant memory of a private conversation ; but have never been able to read a long piece of Meredith since without appreciating the singular fitness of the comparison. The defect is there, and will remain ; but it will not drive the world from Meredith, as it did not kill the cinema ; and there were always gorgeous intervals—may one say lucid intervals ?—when either the wobble ceased or the picture was so beautiful that you disregarded it. And, after all, the original meaning of that phrase " lucid interval " is flash of inspiration.

Most of us in our traffic with writers, who touch us at all, read them ravenously when first we succumb to their influence. And this eager reading, if not necessarily un-

critical, is coloured by the prejudice of the moment. We
are a little in love; and first love, at any rate, is apt to be
blind: the younger we are, the blinder. If a personal confession is allowable, I read Scott through from end to end
in the space of a few school holidays; and when the fit was
over, could not have given an examiner any reasonable
account of any one of the novels. A sense of romance—
greater in extent than in content, as the logicians say—was
all that remained. Later comes a period when you " remember in tranquillity " and re-read in another mood, to
see if you can " recapture the first fine careless rapture."
Was your hero divine or "something considerably lower "?
Have " the clouds of glory " retained even a sober colouring? We revalue. We find ourselves almost in the shoes
of posterity. Some prejudice may survive from the early
zeal, but *corruptio optimi pessima*: disillusionment in-
creases the severity of later criticism. What shocks we
have all received in our time! *The Old Curiosity Shop,
Middlemarch, Lalla Rookh, Alton Locke*—it seems a sort
of sacrilege not to be able to respond to the vanished appeal.
Even if we half-approve, we must sadly confess, " But
Flame? The bush is bare." We are a little like the dis-
illusioned wife in *Anna Karenina,* who noticed for the first
time and with horror, after an absent interval, what big
ears defaced her husband.

II.   THE SECOND VERDICT

What will be decided in the final court of appeal will be
known only to a later posterity; but till then the second
verdict is what matters. If it corroborates the first, all is
likely to be well. When we return to books of our affection
in more critical mood, the pleasure may be less, though
the admiration more. In coming back to Meredith it is best
to begin with *The Ordeal of Richard Feverel,* for a number
of reasons. It was published in the same Olympiad as
David Copperfield, Pendennis, In Memoriam, and *Scenes
of Clerical Life.*

Its date announces the claims of Meredith to be a Victorian of the first water. His literary life extended—an
unrivalled span—from 1851 to 1901, and though later
readers, who found out his qualities only when Dickens,
Thackeray, and George Eliot were no more, are apt to
regard him as the anchorite of Dorking—as remote almost

from companion influences as the early Gaelic poets—such chronology is wrong. He was one of the great Victorian company, son-in-law of Peacock (himself a Peacockian), well praised by Tennyson, gloriously defended by Swinburne, editor of a weekly paper, *Once a Week*, established to rival Dickens in his famous *All the Year Round*. *The Ordeal of Richard Feverel* was published in 1859. It is his earliest novel, if we except *Shagpat;* and, whatever we may decide to be the best, it is the most important. It announced the challenge. It proclaimed the name and nature of the challenger, who bore a strange device, and fought with weapons of his own manufacture. See him come prancing into the lists. Long ago we were merely interested in the novelty of the champion's appearance. Now we are afraid of his affectations.

To drop metaphors—into which his contagious presence compels and tempts—the opening chapters are spoilt by a certain awkwardness. The boys, the farmer, the claret supper, the as yet unexplained Systematist, the jaunty introductions of queer guests, the over-crammed maxims, hurt the eyes a little, to go back to Bernard Holland's comparison. But as the eyes grow used to the flutter, of a sudden appear pictures and a tale that must remain in the mind's eye for all time. " Magnetic youth," spurred into a gallop of romance by the sight of Sir Julian's discreet love gesture in the arbour, touches the very peaks of retributive justice. Greek dramatists might envy the irony. The sequel for the spurred youth is one of the loveliest lovers' meetings in literature. Ruthlessly, but never without the gusto of full-blooded humanity, the thesis is carried through to the heart-rending climax. The comedy moves us as sentimental tragedy could not; and the unspoken moral bites into our perception beyond the power of rod or sermon.

The story, with its wealth of characters and really lovely scenes—though none so good as the waterside wooing—is sufficient in itself. The essence of all fiction is the human drama. All else is subordinate; but the new thing in our literature was the exposure of the silliness of perverted egoism. It is Olympian, a story filmed from above, not by one of the gods, but by a more than half-human giant, who would pile Pelion on Ossa for a better view of the humanity to which he belongs.

The book magnifies the more you read it; and you consciously perceive why it is great if you read with it *An Essay on Comedy,* written at a later date. It is among the greatest critical work of our literature; and no writer—certainly not Wordsworth in the critical prefaces—has so illuminated the canons by whose measure he has worked. Wordsworth was at his best when he was farthest from his theories. He blazed into splendour when he forgot to be commonplace. Meredith is best when he conforms most closely. When he diverges most widely, he rough-and-tumbles into burlesque, as in the youngest piece of old man's work in the language, *The Amazing Marriage.* Fitzmaurice, meeting him first as a young man, said that " he never walked. He strode." He did that when he was confined to his chair, when, as he said to a young interviewer: " I have not climbed the steps of eighty years to use them as a pulpit." And listen to the rising emphasis of scorn as he reached the " pulpit," a place of all others that he most detested.

What then was this critical theory, this philosophy, not so much of art, as of *his* art? First, that Comedy needs, indeed must have, an audience of both live and learned minds. Unlike poetry, unlike fiction as such, it can only work in an intellectual medium. Leaven will not raise putty. It needs the dough of grain. Second, Comedy displays the ways of men and women for social history's sake. To draw morals is not its business. The comic spirit is without either rancour or sentimentality. It arbitrates in the battle—especially between men and women—but leaves the cause to others. The occasion and the issue are its chief concern. So it differs from satire, from irony, from wit and humour to which, if one may say so, it acts as wholesale distributor. Comedy itself may be comic, tragic, or romantic, according to the events in which the dramatis personæ are involved.

Apart from verse, and the hilarious, unrelated burlesque of *Shagpat,* Meredith gives us comic Comedy in *Evan Harrington,* the son of old Mel, the livest dead man in fiction. He gave us tragic Comedy in *Richard Feverel*; finally he careered into the burlesque comedy of *The Amazing Marriage.* He gave us every sort of Comedy except the dry, desiccated comedy of our most famous eighteenth-century dramatists. Comedy has not flourished in the literature of the English, perhaps because they are essentially a sentimental people. Byron (among the greatest of comedy writers, though, as his chief admirer Goethe said, a baby when he philosophized) has still a much greater reputation abroad than at home. We look for the Moral Purpose; we like even the drawn Moral. Some, but not the greater part, of Meredith's verse is in the domain of Comedy, though his poetry and prose must be tested by different canons.

The sonnet sequence itself, in many details, at any rate, is true comedy; and nothing in the annals of literary criticism is more characteristic than the duel between the *Spectator* and Swinburne over this *Modern Love*. The reviewer was upset before he came to serious criticism by the extension of the sonnet from 14 to 16 lines. The classic form is unquestionably the better, but, after all, Meredith managed his own stanza with consummate skill, and the extra two lines are a real symptom of the vigour and wealth of his mind. He overflowed. Having surmounted the tiresome novelty of the metre, the reviewer found no recognition of the most highly treasured of the Matthew Arnold criteria. A hot and unwholesome situation was expressed and refined without the passing of a distinct moral judgment; indeed, without any certain evidence of what the author thought of the goings-on and imagined goings-on of his dramatis personæ. In short, the critic did not recognize Comedy, or like its appearance. He wanted satire or sermon or romance. He was given something different. Whether he knew anything of Meredith's parentage and training is beside the point, but the work of this writer, brought up abroad, deriving in part from Welsh and Irish stock, setting himself to a form of expression that acknowledged little influence from the great English classics, this bold, bad analyser of sexual difficulties seemed un-English, and therefore unacceptable.

Meredith, of course, it must be repeated, had great faults of style, which in themselves have warned off, and always will warn off, a great many readers. His stride was uneven, he stubbed his toe against all sorts of snags, as happens to those who career over untried country. His intolerance of the commonplace in idiom, his desire to keep the wits of his intellectuals busy at every moment, his breathless vigour, set him to the wholly impossible task of composing rhetorical epigrams or epigrammatic rhetoric. It will not do, as the most intolerant of critics said; and a more important point, it cannot be done. The preface to *The Egoist* (which Andrew Lang to his disappointment

failed to translate into Latin prose) is as condensed as any
of Sir Austen Feverel's maxims in *The Pilgrim's Scrip*;
and much harder to comprehend. He was always experimenting and failing. All this and more may be granted,
but any honest man, who will acknowledge the essential
truth of the *Essay on Comedy,* cannot but feel, when he
reads the better of Meredith's novels, that his place is
assured as one of the few great makers of Comedy in our
literature.

Let no one suppose that, even at his most intellectual
pitch, Meredith was ever abstract. He had a trick, indeed,
of personifying the abstraction itself. Though they differ
by the poles, we may say of any novel of his, as of any
novel by Dickens, that it abounds in lively characters. If
women are more human than men, as doubtless they are,
he is the most human of our writers. Feverel's Lucy,
Wilfred's Emilia or Sandra, the Egoist's Clara, the Prime
Minister's Diana, and Richmond's Janet or Beauchamp's
Cecilia, each playing her game among a bevy of equals or
nearly equals, were created at or about the same date as
Dobbin's Amelia and David's Dora. They had intellectual
contemporaries, it is true, in Dorothea and Romola, but
they excel this heroic pair in the quality of flesh and blood
by as much as they excel the sentimental pair in personal
dignity. No single woman, whether rare or vulgar, in
Meredith's gallery, is quite the equal of Becky Sharp, or
Sarah Gamp, or even Mrs. Poyser; no man of the individual humour of Andrew Fairservice, Lord Steyne, or Joe
Willett. Meredith did not perhaps climb to such peaks of
genius in individual creation, though his *Egoist* has rightly
become a very type; and Roy Richmond is a flesh-and-
blood megalomaniac that has virtues as great as Aristotle's
disembodied megalopsych. This may be granted; but
when we consider the aggregate, his vision of fair women
and of strange gentlemen is various beyond parallel; and
if sometimes we have a little trouble in recognizing their
essential naturalness in their fantastic or mannered dress,
they are even as Becky Sharp in the judgment of Lord
Steyne. "She does not bore me," said that complete nobleman.

Meredith's conception of true comedy and his vocation
to supply it can be traced even in incidental epigrams, and
these stolen from their context. The most characteristic
has been already quoted: "The flame of the soul burns

upwards; but we must allow for atmospheric variation." It begins with what, after all, was the most essential article in his creed: that life was worth while. Like Shakespeare, he thought greatly of man, and like Shakespeare wrote his best prose (almost as good as his best poetry) when directly inspired by the theme: "The flame of the soul burns upwards;" and the excellence is disturbed by a thousand failings, which it is the special task of Comedy to point and illustrate, not for the sake of censure or moralizings or to gratify a taste for satire, but because—

> "My dear, these things are life;
> And life, some think, is worthy of the Muse."

So with humour and good humour, the manly (and Victorian) creed is qualified with the honest confession: "But we must allow for atmospheric variation." The merry metaphor, in its condensed neatness, is the best Meredith, the Epiphany of a vital truth.

Meredith wrote and published, for a continuous fifty years, fifteen novels, bound and interleaved with verse, short stories, journalism, and one supreme critical essay. The best of the novels must belong permanently to our literature. *The Ordeal of Richard Feverel* (published in 1859) for every reason; *Sandra Belloni* (first called *Emilia in England*) for the sake of the heroine and the Pole family. It contains also an incidental conversation on the novel that is as full of meat as the *Essay on Comedy*. It should be known as a *locus classicus*. Suppose that, for the sake of the critics, we omit the next two novels, *Rhoda Fleming* and *Vittoria,* and stop at the *Adventures of Harry Richmond*. It was a portent for its vigour and sweep. The opening scene, with its quick declaration of characters, each giving himself away, its drama, its essential art, its painting of a scene, stands as an ideal of the technique as well as the stuff of fiction. Is there any better opening in the history of the novel? *Beauchamp's Career* is a great political novel, moving and compact of wisdom, though some find Dr. Shrapnel, the seer, difficult to stomach; and its English women, specifically praised as the best, are supreme. *The Egoist* (published next in 1879) is perhaps the only novel that has quite definitely fixed itself in a niche. It queens the company of fair women; it is truer to its thesis than any novel in existence, without losing the sense of human Comedy; it is sprinkled with gems, though

303

some are stones of stumbling: it has enlarged our perception of human nature. The rest of the novels, not excepting
even *Diana of the Crossways*, do not touch these heights
though we must allow Diana (Mrs. Norton) a place beside
Beauchamp (Admiral Maxse). But we may so far dogma-
tize that five novels, to which three others might well be
added, are worth an abiding-place in the history of the
novel; and challenge even *Don Juan* as possessors of the
true spirit of Comedy.

George Meredith wrote verse before—and after—he wrote
prose. He was like his contemporary Thomas Hardy in
that, if in nothing else whatever. It is curious that the
same theme evoked their later Muse; and Meredith would
have been a great poet indeed if his Napoleonic odes had
equalled in breadth and scope Hardy's *Dynasts*. The verse
of the two is as unlike as the prose, except perhaps that
both on occasion are " rum," that is, unlike those who
went before. Meredith did not write a *Dynasts,* but his
mind was essentially a poet's mind in one vital respect:
he could not open his eyes without seeing likenesses. The
poetic phrase set the flourish on his prose in the eyes of his
early admirers, and the poets of the time were his first
champions. Swinburne's letter to the *Spectator* is, or
deserves to be, a *locus classicus,* comparable with Dr.
Johnson's letter to Chesterfield. Swinburne defended his
friend (for he and Rossetti and Meredith had all lodged
together for one brief period), and founded his defence on
the essential beauty of Meredith's work rather than on his
right to try experiments in metre, and his refusal to mount
unnecessary pulpits. What Swinburne quoted with admiration we must still quote with admiration for its own
sake. If a sonnet of 16 lines was an abomination of presumptuous novelty, and the theme was " not quite nice "
(what of Shakespeare's sonnets?), much of the diction was
pure and classical, rising to phrases and lines and stanzas
in the purest tradition of high poetry. The 29th, 47th, and
concluding sonnets are to be remembered only after Michael
Drayton's *Since there's no help* or Shakespeare's *Two loves
have I!*

> " *Love that had robbed us of immortal things*
> *This little moment mercifully gave,*
> *When I have seen across the twilight wave,*
> *The swan sail with her young beneath her wings.*"

or

> " *A kiss is but a kiss now! and no wave*
> *Of a great flood that whirls me to the sea.*
> *But, as you will! We'll sit contentedly*
> *And eat our pot of honey on the grave.*"

He had a talent for last lines as Shakespeare a genius for
first lines; and the series ended supremely:

> " *Ah, what a dusty answer gets the soul*
> *When hot for certainties in this our life!—*
> *In tragic hints here see what evermore*
> *Moves dark as yonder midnight ocean's force,*
> *Thundering like rampant hosts of warrior horse*
> *To throw that faint, thin line upon the shore.*"

Even *Love in the Valley*—a lyric that has no close parallel
in the language—has no simpler, more memorable end
than—

> " *All seem to know what is for heaven alone.*"

There are many who say that Victor Hugo was a great
poet but no novelist. Incidentally they do not include
Swinburne, whose panegyric (in the *Encyclopædia Britannica*) has not the restraint of his claim for Meredith.
Meredith's verse varies in merit almost as widely as Wordsworth's; but the claims of the best of his poetry to immortality are of much more general acceptance than any of
his novels. *Love in the Valley, The Lark Ascending, Dirge
in Woods* (curiously like Goethe's tritest lyric *Ueber Allen
gipfeln*, and quite as good), *Melampus, The Thrush in
February, The Appeasement of Demeter*, and its companion
piece *Earth and a Wedded Woman*—these, to give no more,
do not " abide our question: " they live.

One of the most eloquent passages in praise of Meredith
was written in the *Manchester Guardian*, probably by C. E.
Montague, who laid stress on his supreme descriptions of
London; and the fitness of his characters to the metro-
politan spirit of London. But if Meredith's prose characters
are of the town urbane, the creatures of his verse are of the
country, angelic, " half angel and half bird." Every other
bird, beast, flower, constellation, fleck of breeze and light,
join to make such a chorus for the lady of the mill as never
greeted poet's lover. For its images alone, *Love in the*

305

Valley would not stand among the great lyrics of the world
That witty, if shallow, epigram—" Meredith was a prose
Browning. So was Browning "—is less true than its oppo
site would be—" Meredith was a poetic Browning." Ye
though a good many critics feel that a small bundle of his
verse is more sure of survival than his best novels, he mus
be judged as novelist first. Bulk is of the essence of the
question. Momentum matters as well as speed of flight
But the poesy in him sets the flourish on all he produced
and widely though his prose and verse vary, even in tem-
peramental quality, the core of his artistic creed is to be
found in both. And it is this.

First, he thought life essentially worth while. Second,
he thought all perception worth while for its own sake.
The harvest was enough in itself, before it was turned to
bread. *Love in the Valley* competes with *The Lark Ascending* as his best poem. Most will prefer the first. In richness, in metre, in humanity, it is supreme; but the Lark
is also a creed: it contains the real Meredithian philosophy
of art; and its philosophic, though not artistic, climax is
found in the lines—

> " *And you shall hear the herb and tree,*
> *The better heart of men shall see,*
> *Shall feel celestially, as long*
> *As you crave nothing but the song.*"

Mere description (in which all poets delight) is lifted to a
new plane. It becomes possessed of the insight of thought
itself. Meredith's lark has conquered Arnold's nightingale;
and the false moral criteria, that were the chief flaw of the
great Victorian age, disappear into a larger synthesis.

JOHN
STUART MILL

1806-1873

BY
SIR ARTHUR
SALTER

JOHN STUART MILL

A MERE catalogue of the main activities in which John Stuart Mill achieved eminence is a sharp reminder of the difference between his century and that in which we live. In Logic, in Psychology, in Political Philosophy (or Political Science as we now call it), as well as in Political Economy, he was, and historically still is, in the first rank. He was also one of the greatest of publicists who have brought the wider outlook of the philosopher and the student with practical effect into the realm of actual political problems. His actual presence in Parliament as a member is, indeed, no more than a brief interlude, or epilogue, to his main work; but his writing had a profound effect upon the body of political thought which underlay and determined practical action both in his own day and in later times. And behind all this mass of high achievement it is usually forgotten, and is, indeed, hard to remember that there was the background of an eminent official's life at India House.

We are, it is evident from this almost Aristotelian range and variety of achievement, in a less specialized age than our own. In our time, indeed, Lord Bryce has had a comparable range, but he was obviously a great Victorian who continued his work into a later age, rather than a typical representative of our own century. Specialism is the instrument of advance, but it exacts a heavy price in destroying in the mind of man the unity of what is essentially related. This disruptive effect of specialism, which we now see in practical and disastrous operation in the sphere of economic activity, is no less visible in the universe of knowledge. One of the great attractions of Mill's works is that as we study each subject dealt with, we are reading (almost for the last time) what was addressed equally to the specialist in that subject and to the intelligent layman, and at the same time are admitted to the intimacy of a great mind ranging over a great variety of the fields of inquiry of chief interest to man.

If we now think of John Stuart Mill mainly as an economist, it is for a number of reasons which are independent of the intrinsic value of his positive achievement in this sphere as compared with the others in which he worked. Since his time, Logic has extended farther into metaphysics on the one side and into psychology on the other. Psychology has become empirical and experimental to an extent which has entirely transformed it. Political Science, especially when related as closely as in Mill's treatment to the current constitutional problems of his own age and century, naturally changes rapidly with political evolution. We should, for example, now have to look away from our own country to find the Subjection of Women, which his eloquent treatise and untiring efforts did so much to end, though there is much in his essay on Liberty that may soon become more, and not less, relevant to our current problems than it has been.

His *Political Economy* " dates " less than any of his more elaborate work. True there has been a great development of man's economic activities, and of the forms which they take, since Mill's time. This does not, however, vitally affect that part of *Political Economy* which—having cleared the ground by its abstraction of the " economic man "— approaches most nearly to the character of an exact science ; and, within that sphere, Mill's analysis retains its validity. Moreover, the system which grew out of the Industrial Revolution had already developed sufficiently, when Mill wrote, to be the basis of his analysis. This system, though now in course of transformation, is still that with which any modern student must start. And to a surprising extent, indeed, many of the problems of transition to a more regulated economy were already visible to Mill and discussed by him. Moreover, the lucidity, the exactness and precision of the reasoning, and the ordered sequence of the argument, are unsurpassed among the writers on this difficult subject. They are capable of producing an intellectual ecstasy which, by any young man who has experienced it, is an unforgettable experience.

What manner of man was this great Victorian ? In what

qualities does he best represent his century in contrast to our own, and in what is he chiefly distinguished from his own contemporaries? We shall perhaps best answer these questions by tracing his life and work in brief outline, with appropriate comments.

John Stuart Mill was born in 1806, the year in which Charles James Fox died, three years before the birth of Gladstone. He was one of a large family, but neither his mother nor any of his brothers or sisters seem to have exercised any considerable influence upon him. The impress he bore—and it was one of the most remarkable that any son ever received from a parent—was that of his father, James Mill, the friend and principal disciple of Bentham. This astonishing man is certainly one of the most striking personalities in English history. He had an industry and a vitality, and a relentless and unsparing devotion to the public cause to which he was attached, which have rarely been equalled. In pursuit of his purpose he spared neither himself nor others, least of all the son selected as his successor in the task. He was exacting, domineering, opinionated, and intolerant of all differences of opinion. The consequence was that he subjected the son chosen for the onerous honour of continuing his work to perhaps the most severe and painful discipline which any great mind has ever survived. He directed his education himself, and a remarkable education it was. Greek began at three years old, and before eight John had read the whole of Herodotus, and much of Lucian, Isocrates, and the *Dialogues* of Plato. By the age of twelve his classical reading covered more than most of those who take a first in the classical school of a university can boast of. Succeeding years extended the same standard of study to the higher mathematics, some foreign languages, history, logic, political philosophy, political economy, and certain branches of the experimental sciences. Nor was this immense mass of reading "crammed." The indefatigable teacher took infinite pains to see that the pupil understood as well as learnt wherever possible by the exercise of his own faculties. The classical authors were ultimately read "with ease," the learning digested. The discipline was exacting and relentless. "No holidays were shared lest the habit of work should be broken, or a taste for idleness acquired."

There were, however, occasional alleviations in this iron

311

régime. In 1813, for example, John was taken on an excursion with his father and Mr. Bentham to Oxford, Bath, and the West of England, when he acquired his first taste for natural scenery ; and for the next three years he lived a part of each year in a mediæval mansion of Mr. Bentham's in Devonshire. A few years later, in 1820, he had another stroke of good fortune, for Mr. Bentham's brother, General Sir Samuel Bentham, took him on a tour to the South of France. Here he learnt French and attended courses at Montpelier in chemistry, zoology, metaphysics, logic, and the higher mathematics. This visit to France marked a decisive stage in Mill's development. He was then fourteen years old, as the reader will only realize by recalling continually the date of his birth, for the precocious maturity resulting from his education gives the impression throughout that he was about five years older, at every stage of his early life, than his real age. He now breathed, as he says, " the free and genial atmosphere of Continental life," and acquired an admiration for the French general culture of the understanding, carried down to the most uneducated classes, and the frank sociability of French personal intercourse. The appreciation of these French qualities was only deepened by his fuller acquaintance later with the " English mode of existence in which everybody acts as if everybody else (with few or no exceptions) was either an enemy or a bore."

On his return to England, his education continued no less assiduously but under a somewhat relaxed discipline ; he passed gradually to a period of " self-education." He studied Roman law under John Austin, and studied the English philosophers, Berkeley, Hume and Dugald Stewart. Above all, however, Bentham's great work now came to him with the force of a revelation. The words in which he describes this event of his adolescence indicate an experience curiously like that of conversion. " When I laid down the last volume I had become a different being. The ' principle of utility ' gave unity to my conception of things. I now had a creed, a doctrine, a philosophy; in one of the best senses of the word, a religion." Bentham's creed was rationalistic, materialistic, utilitarian, insisting on the supremacy of reason not only as sovereign but as a tyrant not content to rule the emotions but repressing them, and discouraging the arts by which they are fed. But a religion divorced from these customary aids and associates can yet

312

be a true religion, as Puritanism has also shown. Mill was destined to be, as Gladstone well described him, " a saint of rationalism." But his nature, unlike Bentham's, included deep wells of feeling and tenderness, and a love of music, poetry, and natural beauty, which " expelled from the window, returned by the door." Wordsworth became a means of salvation to him in the worst period of his life, and all the rigour of his creed and training could not destroy, though it long repressed, an almost feminine quality of tenderness and sensitiveness of feeling which later found expression in his intimacy with Mrs. Taylor.

In adolescence, personal influences became of more importance to Mill. He made the acquaintance of Macaulay, Grote, Charles Villiers, and (among those more nearly his contemporaries) was deeply influenced by the brilliant Charles Austin (younger brother of John), Eyton Tooke, and Roebuck, who became his intimate friends. In 1822 (when he was sixteen) his entry into a wider life of personal relationships was marked by his formation of a small society of young men agreed on the principle of Utility as their standard in ethics and politics. He called this the " Utilitarian Society," and it was in this way that the term " Utilitarians " entered the language as the title of the whole school of thought to which Mill belonged.

This year may be taken as marking the end of Mill's education, since, as we shall see, he entered on an official career in the following year.

It is easy—only too easy nowadays—to see the inevitable defects of this kind of education, and to trace their results through much of John Stuart's subsequent life. He realized them clearly himself in retrospect, and describes them very clearly. " I remained inexpert in anything requiring manual dexterity ; my mind, as well as my hands, did its work very lamely when it was applied, or ought to have been applied, to practical details." His education was more fitted for training him " to know than to do." His separation from other boys developed in him the habits of a recluse, and throughout his life prevented him from easy and natural personal relationships except with a few intimates. The character of his training is perhaps responsible for a deficiency in that faculty so valuable within its place, in giving charm and ease to personal intercourse, though so often over-valued and perverted in English opinion—the faculty of humour. Mill was saved by an

N

inherent modesty, delicacy, and sensitiveness of temperament from pedantry or priggishness, but the escape was a narrow one; and to many Englishmen, who often think they have compounded for an irresponsible and frivolous attitude to life and public affairs by the virtue of " not taking themselves seriously," the escape will perhaps seem not to have been complete. Mill, in the better sense, certainly took himself and everything seriously; he was in every aspect of life *sérieux*, as the French say. The consequence is that he made on some men something of the same impression as that left by the Prince Consort, though the warmth and passion of his feeling for freedom and for the oppressed modified this impression.

As serious as these psychological effects was the danger which such a training involved to his physique. When he was twenty years old he passed through a period of depression in which it is probable that he narrowly escaped a complete and permanent breakdown. All the savour went out of life; his creed and all the objects of his effort and ambition became dust and ashes, and he came to the conclusion that he could not endure the resulting agony for more than a year. Gradually, and in part under the new inspiration of Wordsworth's poetry, he returned to a normal outlook on life. Characteristically he himself diagnosed his trouble as a purely mental and psychological one, resulting from the destructive effect upon the emotional life of the analytic process. It is probable, however, that the main cause was nervous exhaustion resulting from the intolerable strain of his work and the iron discipline under which his education had proceeded. It is possible that, in some degree, the results of this crisis were permanent. It is difficult to escape the impression that something of the original force of his nature was deprived of its full potential development. Passion, as a spring of action, became repressed into duty and an iron resolve; and as an element in personal relations became diluted into tenderness and delicacy of feeling.

All this is true; but if it is urged to disparage the method of Mill's education in comparison with what was then, or still more what is now, customary, it is less than half the truth. If any defects in John Stuart Mill's mind and character—and how few and slight, after all, they are—are ascribed to his father's influence and instruction, credit must be given for the immensely greater merits and virtues.

The " hard fibre " of the mind, its exact discipline, the
orderly precision of all his mental processes, his lucidity,
his range of knowledge and interest, his unremitting devotion to the public interest, his integrity and political
courage clearly owe much both to example and to training.
And if Mill lost something of his youth, it is something, after
all, to have added ten years or so to the short span of adult
life. To preserve boyhood to about the age of twenty-two,
as so often happens in a modern school and university,
would be more appropriate if nature gave us a century
instead of a precarious seven decades. However much may
be done by eliciting and satisfying an innate appetite for
learning—and this is, of course, essential—there is enough
of original sin in human nature, and especially the commonest of all serious sins, laziness, for more to be needed.
Vigour of mind will rarely be acquired except under the discipline of mastering painfully, and usually under penalty,
unliked tasks. Knowledge must be attacked as an enemy
before it can be embraced as a friend. The problem is, of
course, one of measure. The rigorous climate of Scotland
gives a hard fibre to the minds and bodies of its natives;
with a little more severity the climate of Iceland starves,
contracts, and destroys. Southern climes please, give perhaps a richer flowering to races more hardily bred elsewhere, but in the end relax and enervate. At most periods,
and in our century more than the last, the danger in
education of a " southern " excess, with its softening of
fibre, is greater than that of any Icelandic extreme of
rigour.

In 1823 Mill entered India House, in which his father
had for some time occupied a post of responsibility, and
during the next thirty-five years took his part in the
administration of India under the régime of " John Company." It was a singularly happy appointment; and in
this era of the harassed clerk it is impossible to read without regret and envy his description of the advantages of
such an official position to one who " not being in independent circumstances, desires to devote a part of the
twenty-four hours to mental exertions." It gave him an
income which rose gradually to £2,000 a year, with a
pension of £1,500 from his retirement at fifty-two till death.
He found his office duties an actual rest from the other
mental occupations which he carried on simultaneously,
finding them " sufficiently intellectual not to be a distaste-

ful drudgery without being such as to cause any strain upon the mental powers." In these happy circumstances he combined official duties with the writing destined to be his enduring title to fame as Samuel Pepys had done before, and as Trollope, Matthew Arnold, and Charles Lamb did in his own century. We should make a grievous mistake, however, if we assumed that for him his official work was (as certainly it was to Lamb, and perhaps Trollope) a mere convenience. It is only too easy to forget that Pepys was an industrious, able, and devoted Secretary of the Admiralty, and that half of Matthew Arnold's life was that of a singularly able and valuable education officer.

Mill's official work was perhaps rather less to him in comparison with his published writing, but he was a loyal and devoted servant of the Company, who at the end passionately regretted its suppression by the State; and, in spite of the centre of gravity of his interest being outside, he probably still had enough industrious ability available for his office to raise him above the average of his fellows. Moreover, he felt that his experience as an official was of definite help to him as a theoretical reformer. It gave him the

> " opportunity of learning by personal observation the necessary conditions of the practical conduct of public affairs. As a speculative writer, I should have had no one to consult but myself, and should have encountered in my speculations none of the obstacles which would have started up whenever they came to be applied to practice. But as a Secretary conducting political correspondence . . . I became practically conversant with the difficulties of moving bodies of men, the necessities of compromise, the art of sacrificing the non-essential to preserve the essential. . . . I have found, through life, these acquisitions to be of the greatest possible importance for personal happiness, and they are also a very necessary condition for enabling anyone, either as a theorist or as practical man, to effect the greatest amount of good compatible with his opportunities."

The disabilities of official life were the necessity of residence in London, instead of the country which he preferred, and exclusion from Parliament and public life. The first was undoubtedly a loss. The second is more doubtful. Mill would certainly not have had a successful parlia-

mentary career of the orthodox tone. The habits of the
recluse, the constraint in personal contacts, the imperfect
aptitude for practical affairs, and (perhaps fortunately for
his real work) the uncompromising quality of his mind,
which both his nature and his training had given him, were
too little modified by his official or other experience to make
it likely that he would ever have fitted happily into Westminster, as his brief three years there in later life tend to
show. And parliamentary life, if prolonged and successful,
would very probably have robbed his work of some of its
chief merits. Nevertheless, he certainly regretted the exclusion, and it is, indeed, possible that he might have been
a great " back-bencher and cross-bencher," and have exercised a great influence, as others have done, in that position.
The disabilities of his office, however, did not include a
prohibition against a free publication of his opinions, and
here, indeed, the modern civil servant may well envy him.

With the generous freedom so allowed, he preached his
political creed in the *Traveller* and in the *Westminster
Review,* both in its original form and as revived later in
the form of the *London and Westminster Review.* He was
one of a young band of philosophers devoted, with the
attractive fanaticism of youth, to their political creed, and
somewhat doctrinaire in its expression. The description so
often given, unjustly he thinks, of a Benthamite, as a
mere reasoning machine, was, he admits, not altogether true
of himself. By later, but not necessarily by better, standards, this charge may perhaps also be made against the
Mill of later years. Throughout his life, certainly reason
was firmly seated on the throne. He lived, perhaps not
unhappily, before Freud and his followers liberated the
proletariat of the mind, the passions, the emotions, the
unreasoning idiosyncrasies; made them not only articulate
but presumptuous, till too often they are no longer content
to press their claims for recognition and legitimate satisfaction, but presume to unseat the monarch and substitute
a soviet of themselves or anarchy. Mill kept reason on the
throne, but increasingly as his character mellowed and his
nature expanded, it was a firm rule (allowing few, though
some, exceptions) but no tyrannic repression of all else.

This mellowing and humanizing of his character Mill
owed to an acquaintance beginning when he was twenty-
five, and ripening a few years later into an intimacy which
became the chief event in his personal life. Till he was

forty-five as a friend, and thereafter till she died seven
years later as a wife, the lady who was Mrs. Taylor when
he first knew her gave him the best that any woman can
give a man. She helped him to recover all that side of his
nature which had been stunted and repressed by his early
training; revived his love for poetry; made his work both
practical and humane by insisting on its constant contact
with the realities of human life and experience to which it
related. She evidently had a quick and penetrating intuition, which enabled her mind to play round, dart ahead,
and illumine the sure and steady logical processes of his.
In time there was a real fusion of the two minds, and his
later work in particular bears much of her impress. He
moved far, under the influence of her personality and of his
own developing experience, from the individualism of his
earlier creed towards State or public control. Sometimes,
perhaps, he failed to distinguish perfectly between the conclusions of his abstract science, based upon the logical
conclusions which follow from the hypothesis of the
" economic man," and the modifications in practical doctrine which are required when the other attributes and
motives of actual man are taken into account, as of course
they must be. This has caused some of his critics to hold
that the quality of his work as an economist became somewhat impaired by his receptiveness to his wife's influence, a
criticism which is somewhat strengthened by the terms in
which Mill assessed her ability.

Nineteen years elapsed between Mill's first meeting Mrs.
Taylor and her husband's death; and nearly two more
before they married. It was inevitable that, in Mill's day,
so intimate a friendship with a married woman, their open
and courageous meeting and travelling together, should
cause some adverse comment and disapproval. The breach
of the ordinary conventions was unconcealed, and even
those who had the wisdom and discernment of character
to know that it was no more, were not necessarily for that
reason appeased. Some discontinued acquaintance, and
Mill, as sensitive as he was courageous, resumed the habits
of a recluse which he had been abandoning.

We now enter the period of Mill's more important constructive work, of which no real account can be given in
a brief essay, whose purpose is to give an appreciation of
the man rather than his achievement. He was already
working on his Logic in 1832, but he was brought to a halt

on the threshold of his account of Induction by a sense of inadequate acquaintance with the whole circle of physical science. He resumed the task five years later, in the year in which he becomes in the literal sense a Victorian, under a stimulus which is illuminating as to the practical purpose of much of even his most theoretical work. Whewell published his *History of the Inductive Sciences,* in which he preached the intuitive doctrine " that truths external to the mind may be known by intuition or consciousness, independently of observation and experience." This was, of course, precisely the opposite of Mill's creed, and it was in his view most pernicious in its practical consequences. It was the—

> " great intellectual support of false doctrines and bad institutions. By the aid of this theory, every inveterate belief and every intense feeling, of which the origin is not remembered, is enabled to dispense with the obligation of justifying itself by reason, and is erected into its own all-sufficient voucher and justification. There never was such an instrument devised for consecrating all deep-seated prejudices."

Under this stimulus, of the belief that false doctrine was fatal to sound reform, Mill braced himself to the necessary study of Natural Philosophy, learnt what he could from Comte, of whom he was for a few years an ardent admirer and frequent correspondent, completed his work in four years, and met with a success far greater than he had anticipated.

The *Principles of Political Economy* was the next important work to follow. It was written in two years, from 1845 to 1847, with substantial interruptions for work on other subjects, especially the Irish Famine. The characteristics which made it an immediate success, and give it enduring interest, are well described by Mill himself. " It was not a book merely of abstract science, but also of application, and treated Political Economy not as a thing in itself, but as a fragment of a greater whole ; a branch of Social Philosophy." " Political Economy," he adds wisely, " has never pretended to give advice to mankind with no lights but its own ; though people who knew nothing but political economy (and therefore knew that ill) have taken upon themselves to advise." Success resulted in a considerable number of editions in later years, and the changes made in these editions illustrate the development of Mill's thought in his middle life. He had started as a " democrat, but not the least of a Socialist." He became less of a democrat, at least in the sense that he recognized more and more the necessity of intermediate institutions and limiting safeguards, and more of a Socialist. The welcoming of factory legislation, the repudiation of his first theory of the " wage fund," his interest in co-operation are among the stages in which he passed very far from his first individualism to a conception of very extensive State regulation and control. But however much he wished to control those of man's activities which were proving destructive to each other, his ultimate ideal of personal human freedom, with individual personality as the final thing of value in the universe, remained intact.

Mill's political writings are dominated by this ultimate ideal, which is translated both into a theory of government (*Representative Government*), political tracts or treatises (*Liberty* and the *Subjection of Women*), and many interventions into current political questions, of which we may note in particular his support of Lord Durham's Report on Canada, his passionate defence of the Northern case in the American Civil War, and his continued interest in Ireland.

Lastly, we have to note the fact of his contribution to Philosophy, on which I am not qualified to comment, beyond remarking that Haldane considered his *Examination of Sir William Hamilton's Philosophy* (1865) the greatest of all his works.

At the age of fifty-nine an opportunity at last occurred of satisfying his early ambition to enter Parliament, and he sat at Westminster from 1865 to 1868. Nothing in his life is more illuminating as to his quality and character. He refused on principle to spend any money in his constituency, while subscribing elsewhere. He frankly stated his personal views on every current question, and claimed complete freedom to press them in Parliament, without regard to the doctrine of any party or the opinions of his electorate. He refused to represent or press local interests in any form. Questioned by a working-class committee as to whether he had called the working class " liars," he said he had, without apology or withdrawal, and was applauded for his candour. He attended all sessions with an assiduous regularity rarely equalled ; and spoke not on the questions

which engaged most attention for the moment, where reputation was most quickly to be made, but on those he thought
unduly neglected. It was magnificent, but it was not
politics, as Westminster understood them. To the old parliamentary hand, Disraeli, he was "a political finishing
governess." Nevertheless he was, in a certain sense, a real
success. Some of his speeches made a deep impression,
and Fawcett asserted with truth that his presence was of
definite value in raising the whole moral tone of Parliament.

Five years of retirement followed, spent partly in
England and partly in the South of France, where his wife
had died. He continued his work, especially that of re-
vising his earlier publications, and found consolation, so
far as consolation was possible, for the loss of his wife in
the society of her daughter, Miss Taylor; and in 1873 he
died and was buried, like his wife, at Avignon.

Such was this great Victorian, John Stuart Mill. His
work and his character both represented the best of that
age. Human affairs and human knowledge, however
complex, seemed still within the grasp of a single human
brain, if fortified by continual training and untiring effort;
and he braced himself for the task. Reason, operating on
experience, is our one and sufficient guide to truth; and the
true controller of our destiny; but if it should control, it
should not repress, the rest of man's rich nature and poten-
tialities, his emotions, and his arts. The stern temper and
sense of duty associated with Puritanism and a dogmatic
religious creed remain, detached from both, as the support
of a different creed and an untiring devotion to the service
of man. But this stern temper was allied with strong
feeling, a righteous indignation against injustice—the
noblest passion of man—a burning sympathy with the
oppressed. And it was compatible with a rich emotional
life, and pleasure in the arts of music and poetry. Happiness was not to him, as to his father, a slight thing, though
it was to be captured only on the condition of not being
pursued. James Mill is an adequate name for the father,
but we instinctively prefer John Stuart Mill to John Mill
for the son.

Integrity, honesty, and courage became in him active and
positive qualities, raising the tone of every society in which
he was present. If there was an absence of grace and ease
and humour in personal intercourse, there was that fine
combination of self-respect and respect for those he met,

which by assuming more than the best in men evokes the best they have. As we turn more and more, as we are turning, to the age which preceded our own, with renewed respect and admiration for its best qualities, we shall find no personality of that time in which they are more richly embodied and expressed than John Stuart Mill.

WILLIAM
MORRIS

1834-1896

BY
J. MIDDLETON
MURRY

WILLIAM MORRIS

WILLIAM MORRIS was the perfect Victorian. By that I mean that he was the perfect embodiment of all the awareness that a lifetime passed in the Victorian age might be expected to bring to a perfectly unspoiled and receptive man. In the first place, he was a typically Victorian social product. He was a child of the new plutocracy which had been thrown up by the prosperity of the new Industrialism; he was carried into life on the crest of the wave of one of the great class-movements of English social history—the vast expansion of the bourgeois aristocracy that was the social expression of the vast expansion of English industry in the early nineteenth century. The educational monument of that expansion is the public-school system as we know it now. Arnold of Rugby is still the tutelary deity of that economic upward surge. His great " moral reform " of the English schools was simply the expression, in characteristically English guise, of the thrust made by the new bourgeoisie into the educational privilege of the aristocracy. It was the morally gratifying form assumed by an elemental economic upheaval.

Arnold did not reform public schools; there were none to be reformed; he created them. He led the movement of creating new schools (occasionally on old foundations) for the sons of the new bourgeois aristocracy. And these schools had to be strongholds of the new morality—the morality based on the psychologically inevitable discovery that accumulation of wealth through industry was a moral achievement of the highest order. The new wealth had to be endowed with a certain consciousness of moral superiority over hereditary wealth. The great English public-school system, which was a purely Victorian creation, was the instrument of this necessary illumination.

Morris was born a year or two too soon to be exposed to the full pressure of this mighty, because unconscious, moral machine. The upward surge of the new bourgeoisie was so great that the new schools could not be made fast enough. And Morris's father had to enter William's name some years before—had, indeed, most characteristically, to buy him a shareholder's place—in the as yet non-existent school of Marlborough. Happily for Morris, it was in a state of chaos when he arrived there at the beginning of 1848, and it remained in a state of chaos till he left at the end of 1851. Though I believe that Morris was too big a man by nature to have been successfully moulded by the full blast of the new public-school system, there is no knowing what it might have done to him. And it may be that it was only by the skin of his teeth, or through a momentary gap in nature, that he escaped being pruned into a decorous Anglican welfare-worker or muscular Christian after the pattern of Tom Hughes and Charles Kingsley.

Morris just escaped the new education, which has been the inescapable education of an English boy of his class ever since. He escaped the condescending sense of social responsibility which has been the blight upon the English bourgeois mind ever since. Morris was pure-bred Victorian bourgeois, and he escaped the new insidious bourgeois culture. That is, I think, one of the fundamental facts about him. He roamed the downs of Wiltshire as a boy, not as a prig; and he was spared the fatal diversion of his manliness into organized athletics. Morris never played games; and he never needed to. The devilish division of life into systematic and responsible work, and systematic and responsible play, which was the great and necessary achievement of Victorian education, passed him by. He was left free to make first-hand his great anti-Victorian discovery, that work could be the enjoyment of the total man.

Morris was free to be what we have called the perfect Victorian, precisely because he escaped Victorianism. England is Victorian still. Less cocksurely, less naïvely, less highly seriously, than in the 1840's; but still at heart Victorian. The public-school expansion after the Napo-leonic Wars has repeated itself after the war of 1914–1918.

The vital economic process is the same, though the manifestations (as befits a decaying national economy) are less exuberant.　What Morris escaped has been the destiny of Englishmen now for nearly a century; the destiny which sends men out to be rulers of Empire and sends them home again with nothing to do but chunter on the nineteenth green of golf clubs, which are Arnold's specific contribution to the moral architecture of the country.　The erstwhile pro-consul of a small continent spending laborious days in filing down his golf handicap—that is the crude symbol of what Morris escaped.　Less crudely, but not more truly, what he escaped was ending like Matthew Arnold:

> " *Wandering between two worlds, one dead;*
> *The other powerless to be born.*"

Morris passed into the new world by imagination and adoption; he was the first, and I think still the only Englishman to have done this.

Morris also escaped—though probably in this case we should definitely say he resisted—the pathetic degradation of the great English Romantic movement.　Through the decorous decline (which Keats found so unbearable) of Wordsworth and Coleridge into high Toryism, the Romantic movement had been safely steered into respectability and repute.　Blake and Keats and Shelley were safely dead, and Godwin was a Gentleman Usher.　Romanticism was put into Orders where it could do no harm.　It burned tapers, wore vestments, wrote the Lives of the Saints, disputed vehemently over the Apostolic Succession, was mildly Gothic in its taste for architecture, and was no trouble to anybody.　The very notion that it was related in a cousinly sort of way to Reform, and even to that horrible Chartism, was unthinkable.　And once that was settled, once it was firmly established that no faint savour of a forgotten Pantisocracy was lurking in its incense, the great English bourgeoisie left it to its own devices with a mildly benignant eye, and turned to the real business of becoming wealthier still.　If the new Romanticism helped to make the Established Church more attractive to its sons, well, that was all to the good.　After all, with the tithes of the hungry forties, the Church was still one of *the* professions; and it was still distinctly easier to become a Bishop than to be made a Peer.

327

Young Morris was intended to climb into social sublimity through the Church. His Romanticism was to take Orders. And young Morris had no objection. On the contrary, he was all for Orders; and since Orders of chivalry were no more, he was ready for monastic Orders instead. He adored cathedrals—already they aroused in him he knew not what obscure but profound response—so why not aspire to a cathedral of his own? Or even a parish church would do, provided that it belonged to the period wherein his imagination delighted to wander. Nor was it long before that period was sharply defined. While still a schoolboy he took full advantage of the educational chaos at Marlborough to lay the foundations of that extraordinary knowledge of Gothic architecture that became his second nature. By the time he reached Oxford, fourteenth-century Gothic was his ideal, and he knew as much about it as anybody. He knew so much, indeed, that whatever shreds of a vocation for the Church clung about him were blown clean away. For obviously, when you really knew something about Gothic, and were capable of imagining most of what you did not know, the real adventure was to build a cathedral, not to preach in one. The quite normal, but very rare, miracle had happened: Morris saw Gothic as new, not as old. The romantic antiquarianism which was the æsthetic of the Oxford Movement left him untainted. He did not share the dreams of dreaming spires, he thought about how they were made. He saw and felt the stone raw from the mason's adze.

No conception of Morris is more false, though none more prevalent, than that which makes of him an antiquarian. He loved old buildings because they were beautiful, but he fought for them because they were history made visible; because he believed that a consciousness of the past was necessary to a true living of the present. To destroy our ancient buildings was to annihilate the consciousness of history; to restore them—which moved him to the deeper fury—was to show oneself incapable of the living consciousness of history, to prove that one was too crass to understand that " there is no going back." Had Morris been the sentimental antiquarian that current superficiality would make him, he could never have been the Socialist that he became—not at all a gentlemanly, sentimental, antiquarian Socialist, but a brand-new, red-hot, revolutionary one: a far more revolutionary Socialist than has appeared in this country since his death.

That is to anticipate. But few men have been more grievously—I sometimes think, more deliberately—misunderstood than Morris. For him the past was the past: infinitely valuable if a man had the strength to face it and yet be unconsumed. But if the past were not a means to living in the present, Morris had no use for it. His real belief was original and profound. It was that, when men have reached the degree of consciousness that they had reached in the nineteenth century, then no right action in the present is possible without an awareness of the past. Once men have become historically minded, then they must go through with it. They can no longer live naïvely in the moment; the childhood of the human race is over. It must then become adult or perish. It must then learn to act both spontaneously and in accordance with consciously recognized historical necessity. A new kind of man, a new kind of society is demanded.

This crucial realization in Morris was largely instinctive; only slowly did it become fully conscious. But it was there from the beginning. Hence it was that in his final period he found Marx completely congenial. Marx's achievement in rooting the necessity of the social revolution in the historical process, in making his revolutionary appeal primarily to those who had achieved " a theoretical consciousness of the movement of history as a whole," was one which found a whole-hearted response in Morris. In fact, Morris, so far from being naturally alien to Marx's revolutionary philosophy of history, was the one man in England really capable of understanding it. Marxism was the philosophy of his own life-experience.

Yet more anticipation. But Morris was one of those ever-growing men in picturing whom anticipation is inevitable. He was an organic whole; his end is implicit in his beginning. The Morris who naturally and inevitably glided away from the Anglican priesthood, because Gothic was a reality and not a ruin, was the man who glided, just as naturally and inevitably, into Marxism, when through his own direct experience he had learned the necessity of a social revolution. He did not need Marx to teach him that necessity; he found in Marx the complete ratification of his own conclusions. His former desertion from the ranks of respectability was merely the consternation of his mother; his later the consternation of his friends. Before as after, he was simply the rare man to whom history is real.

At Oxford he discovered that the Oxford Movement had been for him merely the guise of respectability beneath which he could pursue his imaginations. His love of churches, he realized, was not love of the Church; and for him henceforward churches were holy—and to no man were they holier—because they were the creation of Man, not because they were the habitation of God. God did not trouble him much thereafter. He was fully occupied with being a man; and probably that is the only way of doing God's real business in the world at any time.

Simply and suddenly he found himself a poet. The point at which he picked up the tradition immediately before him was Keats's "La Belle Dame sans Merci." Morris wrote nothing as good; nor was it possible that he should have done. Behind Keats's poem was the anguish of a life-experience which Morris was happily spared. But in so far as the imaginative atmosphere of a poem wrung from an alien experience could be captured, Morris captured it. But from the beginning he had the splendid sanity not to take himself very seriously as a poet. He wrote poems because he enjoyed writing them; but some swift and subtle instinct warned him that poetry-writing had ceased to be a man's business, as indeed it had. We can see pretty clearly now, what Morris felt intuitively, namely, that poetry of the first order had come to an end in Keats. In Keats's great Odes the voice of the individual man touches a supreme agony of beauty. There is no more to be said; and nothing more has been said. Since then poetry has existed, simply because it has not known that it is dead.

But Morris, who adored Keats all his life, was a poet who did know that poetry was dead. And because he was big enough to know it, it did not matter to him. He set about living in other ways. In putting it thus, we are of course making Morris more conscious than he was, or could have been. The question, as it shaped itself in the minds of Morris and his friends, was different. In actual fact, in the days of which we are speaking, Morris still admired Tennyson. Rossetti's "Blessed Damozel" seemed to him a very beautiful thing, as indeed it is. It seemed to him, at the end of his Oxford days, that the voice of poetry was being naturally prolonged from Keats. It was the discrepancy between the splendour of the poetic word and the daily growing squalor of the world of men, which perplexed the Brotherhood. "Was no beauty but the beauty of words to be produced by man in our times; was the intelligence of the age to be for ever so preposterously lopsided? We could see no reason for it, and accordingly our hope was strong."

But Morris was a poet. Why did he not remain a poet, like Tennyson? We may put it down if we will to his overbrimming vitality that demanded not one outlet, but many. But the simple explanation is, as so often, the superficial one. As a schoolboy Morris had, through the working of his own simple genius on the architecture he loved, conceived the architectural ideal. It had been vague; it had been mixed up in his mind with the religious movement; but it had already enough independent existence to prevent him from being turned aside into ecclesiasticism. He had sensed that the real meaning which the cathedrals of the fourteenth century brought to him lay not in the supernatural theology which they symbolized, but in the natural religion which they expressed. They were the work of human hands; and—more essential still—they were the work not of men uplifted into some remote condition of religious or æsthetic "inspiration" by the final purpose of their task, but of simple, ordinary human beings doing the job in front of them. "This talk of inspiration," he said later, "is sheer nonsense . . . there is no such thing: it is a mere matter of craftsmanship."

It took some years for Morris to become certain about this. The famous and beautiful little tale of "The Unknown Mason" belongs to the time of hesitation between a religious romanticism of "inspiration" and the clear recognition of the ordinariness out of which the magnificence of Gothic had arisen. And the mist was finally dissipated from Morris's vision by one man—John Ruskin. Ruskin's essay "On the Nature of Gothic, and the Office of the Workman therein" came as the crucial revelation to Morris; and the revelation was crucial precisely because he was prepared for it, because already unconsciously his own. It liberated him from the last lingering traces of ecclesiasticism. It confirmed him finally in his surmise that it was not the monasteries which had built the great churches, but the guilds; not the priests, but the workmen; not the religion of God, but the religion of Man.

Now this illumination of Ruskin's was not a strictly historical discovery. It was an act of direct imaginative penetration. It might be challenged by pedantic historians. But Morris, by his own imagination, and his now considerable first-hand experience of handicraft, knew that it was true. His imaginative and his actual experience were made one, by Ruskin's discovery that art is the natural pleasure of a man in his work. It gave Morris a final and satisfying explanation of the depth of his own delight in Gothic. The great cathedral had moved him from a boy because he had unconsciously recognized that it had sprung naturally from the simple and harmonious co-operation of many men finding each an individual pleasure in his work. It was the greatest achievement of art, because it was, in the true sense, the most popular art that has been.

Now, Morris had the key, not merely to history, but to life itself, and to the perplexities of his own life in particular. The attempt in which he and his friends of the Brotherhood had been engaged, namely, to re-create the total pervasive beauty of mediæval art in the industrial nineteenth century was radically misconceived. They had been schoolboyish dreamers, ignorantly tilting against the necessity of history. The art of any epoch was, in reality, the expression of its social life. The omnipresent beauty of mediæval art—and the perfection of the cathedral arose simply from its including more of that omnipresence—was due to the fact that the social life of the Middle Ages was such that it allowed the workman to take pleasure in his work, and to find in it the freedom for individual expression. The effort to re-create such an art in the absolutely changed social life of the nineteenth century was therefore doomed to failure. They were building their cathedral without a foundation. The economic basis of their work was itself a dream.

Once again the scope of a brief essay compels us to represent the resolution as more sudden than it was. Morris, in his efforts—which were in the main single-handed—to re-create an architectural art, was compelled to demand of the industrial system products which it was no longer capable of producing. Since, in his business of decorative artist, he could not make everything himself (though probably he learned to make, and made, more things than any craftsman in England had made before him), he had to seek things that were not standardized from the industrial machine. It could not supply them. Thus he was involved, by the mere day-to-day practice of his craft, in an incessant battle against the competitive industrial system. Furthermore, though he himself was happy enough in his incessant making, he was compelled ruefully to recognize that only the rich middle-classes could afford to buy his products, and that as often as not they bought them from essentially vulgar motives. In fact, by his craft he was mainly gratifying the taste for luxury of those classes who were indirectly or directly enriched by the system against which his craft was directed. And, after all, was he himself not, by origin and maintenance, the privileged child of the system he loathed?

Hard practical experience had taught him that a living art could only arise out of a surrounding body of living crafts, and the crafts could not be made to live again while the system remained what it was. He was on the brink of Socialism, of genuine revolutionary Socialism, of complete Socialism, which, as he said, is always Communism. But for a moment something withheld him from the final plunge. Nor was this the simple personal reluctance which any convert to genuine Socialism must feel. It was a significant and symbolical dilemma. For Morris was, primarily, a craftsman. He had deliberately and joyfully devoted his life to a revival of the handicrafts. In one sense, as he now clearly saw, his work was ultimately futile, since, in order to become the complete, the historically conscious artist, he must needs abandon art itself. That was the inexorable logic of his now complete realization: he must devote himself to the cause of social revolution. Yet where, in the England of the late 1870's, would he find men to understand the nature of the revolution he demanded? Between the sordid squalor of the poor and the vulgar squalor of the rich, what was the essential difference? What chance had he of awakening men to the necessity of a new *kind* of life? Unless they could see with their eyes the fundamental distinction between beauty and ugliness, what change would even revolution bring? Surely his task—since he was only a man, after all—was to labour away at making articles of common use beautiful once more, at educating men by word and deed into the knowledge of what they had lost. Which was his business—to teach Art, or to preach Revolution?

Morris made the heroic answer. He to whom Art had

meant far more than to any man of his generation, found the courage to say, Let Art go !

> " The absence of popular art in modern times is more disquieting and grievous to me for this reason than for any other, that it betokens that fatal division of men into the cultivated and degraded classes which competitive commerce has bred and fosters ; popular art has no chance of a healthy life, or, indeed, of a life at all, till we are on the way to fill up this terrible gap between riches and poverty. *Doubtless many things will go towards filling it up, and if art must be one of those things, let it go*. What business have we with art at all, unless all can share it ? I am not afraid but that art will rise from the dead, whatever else lies there."

That was Morris's final sacrifice, and it was a prodigious one. He made it not merely in imagination, but in act also. Not merely did he accept as a necessary immediate consequence of the social revolution he desired the disappearance of such genuine art as still remained ; but he devoted the vital substance of his remaining days to arduous propaganda for the Socialist cause. And when at last he left the active movement, it was because he could do no more within it. He was too complete a Socialist for Socialism. It was beginning to pass into Labour politics and Fabianism—historically necessary phases, no doubt, in which the bankruptcy of Socialism that is not revolutionary and " religious " should be made plain to all seeing eyes—but phases with which, though he saw them to be inevitable, the necessities of his own nature forbade him to compromise.

Hence the apparent failure of Morris's life. The conviction in which it culminated, the sacrifice with which it was crowned, seemed to have been wasted. For fifty years the bourgeoisie and the proletarians alike have turned away from Morris's Socialism. The middle-class have accepted his art and ignored his revolution ; the working-classes and their leaders have turned away from his vision to barren practicality. The Labour movement has become a mean-souled combination of sectarian Trades Unionism and renegade Radicalism. And even those within its ranks who have been most deeply discontented with its feeble achievement have been inclined to put the blame not on the Socialist desertion of Morris, but of Marx. The distinction cannot be made. If the Socialist movement in this country could have remained faithful to Morris, it would have remained faithful to Marx also; if it could have remained faithful to Marx, it would have remained faithful to Morris also. For Morris was the truest Marxian Socialist this country has ever had.

Both men alike were possessed by the historical vision. Morris read history through art, Marx read it through economics; and since it can be as truly read through one sign as the other by the man who has the greatness of soul to accept the truth even though it be to his own undoing, they both found the same story there recorded. The same essential imagination was in both; both reached the same inevitable conclusion. Both were big men. They were succeeded by little men, in action and in theory; by men who did not want a social revolution, and were themselves no less afraid of it than their nominal enemies. Middle-class culture—and there is no other to-day—took what it wanted from them both. Academic historians filched Marx's theory of the economic determination of history and made their reputations without even a passing tribute to his compromising name; æsthetic snobs seized upon Morris's artistic achievement and made their reputation by emasculating it. Both classes alike shunned the revolutionary basis of the doctrine like the plague.

For Morris and Marx were both alike in this: that they had a complete doctrine, and it was the same doctrine. They reached the same final unity by different ways, but it was the same unity. Both Morris and Marx were historical materialists, and because they were genuine in this they were revolutionary materialists. They saw that they were history, and they resolved to be it. Marx's historical materialism was philosophical in origin, Morris's was æsthetic and instinctive: the materialism of the man who loves material, and knows by direct experience that when a man is happy in his work of shaping the material of the world, he needs no religion, because he is fulfilled.

" What other blessings in life are there save these two, fearless rest and hopeful work? Troublous as life is, it is surely given to each one of us here some times and seasons when, surrounded by simple and beautiful

335

things, we have felt really at rest; when the earth and
all its plenteous growth, and the token of the varied life
of men, and the very sky and waste of air above us,
have seemed all to conspire together to make us calm
and happy, not slothful but restful. Still oftener be-
like it has given us those other times, when at last,
after many a struggle with incongruous hindrances,
our own chosen work has lain before us disentangled
from all encumbrances and unrealities, and we have
felt that nothing could withhold us, not even ourselves,
from doing the work we were born to do, and that we
were men and worthy of life. Such rest and such
work, I earnestly wish for myself and for you and for
all men: to have space and freedom to gain such rest
and such work is the end of politics; to learn how best
to gain it is the end of education; to learn its inmost
meaning is the end of religion."

There is no more to be said.

Morris's Socialism is often called Utopian, naturally, by
those who have never troubled to understand it; or by
those who think of the means towards Socialism as the end
of Socialism. Of whom there are perhaps more than ever
to-day. Morris's Socialism was completely realistic, as
realistic as Marx's Socialism, for the simple reason that
it *was* Marx's Socialism. If Socialism is to be called
Utopian because it shrinks from political chicane, then all
genuine Socialism is Utopian: Marx's and Morris's and
Lenin's. Morris did not invent a new kind of Socialism.
The fact that he came to Marxian Socialism by his own
way; that he had an ideal of human social activity; that
when he tried to realize this ideal in practice, he discovered
that the social revolution alone would make it possible;
that he became a Socialist for that end—this does not make
his Socialism different from Marx's. Marx also had his
vision of the Communistic society, and it was not essentially
different from Morris's. It was Marx's Socialism which
Morris accepted, not some different doctrine of his own, and
he accepted it in the full knowledge that the period of revolutionary transition to complete economic equality might
mean the complete destruction of Art. Knowing what Art
really was, he was not afraid for it. He accepted the death
of the art of luxury as the price to be paid for the rebirth
of the art of work.

The idea was far too revolutionary for his friends. They did not know, as he knew, that in a capitalist world his own art, which they admired, was an art of luxury. It has been far too revolutionary for the bourgeois intellectual since Morris's day. The artist has gone on creating ever more esoteric art for the solace of middle-class *acedia* and has been unaware of his own degradation. And even when, in rare cases, the gifted artist has been forced to the recognition of his own futile and unworthy position, he has as often as not sought refuge from responsibility in that very ecclesiasticism from which Morris broke free at the outset of his career. On every side, in every aspect, Morris's vision has been proved true by events. Not only has art become steadily more sterile; but his prophecy of the immediate future of the Socialist movement has been justified in detail. Six years before his death, in saying good-bye to the movement, he wrote these memorable words:

" The whole set opinion amongst those more or less touched by Socialism, who are not definite Socialists, is towards the new Trades Unionism and palliation. Men believe that they can wrest from the capitalist some portion of their privileged profits, and the masters, to judge from the recent threats of combination on their side, believe also that this can be done. That it can only very partially be done, and that the men could not rest there if it were done, we Socialists know very well; but others do not.

" I neither believe in State Socialism in itself, nor, indeed, as a complete scheme do I think it possible. Nevertheless some approach to it is sure to be tried, and to my mind will precede any complete enlightenment on the new order of things. The success of Mr. Bellamy's Utopian book, deadly dull as it is, is a straw to show which way the wind blows. The general attention paid to our clever friends, the Fabian lecturers and pamphleteers, is not altogether due to their literary ability; people have really got their heads turned more or less in that direction.

" Now it seems to me that at such a time, when people are not only discontented, but have really conceived a hope of bettering the condition of Labour, while at the same time the means towards their end are doubtful; or rather when they take the very beginning of the

o   337

means as an end in itself—that this time when people
are excited about Socialism, and when many who
know nothing about it, think themselves Socialists,
is the time of all others to put forward the simple principles of Socialism regardless of the passing hour.

" My readers will understand that in saying this I am
speaking for those who are complete Socialists—or let
us call them Communists. I say for us to make
Socialists is the business at present, and at present I do
not think we can have any other useful business.
Those who are not real Socialists—who are Trades
Unionists, disturbance breeders or what not—will do
what they are impelled to do, and we cannot help it ;
but we need not, and cannot heartily work with them,
when we know their methods are beside the right way.

" Our business, I repeat, is the making of Socialists,
i.e. convincing people that Socialism is good for them
and is possible. When we have enough people of
that way of thinking, they will find out what action
is necessary for putting their principles into practice.
Therefore, I say, make Socialists. We Socialists can
do nothing else that is useful."

They are the words of a man too great to be a politician.
Since they were written, Fabian Socialism has come and
gone ; the new Trades Unionism has created a new bourgeoisie and a new aristocracy no less vulgar than the old ;
the first Prime Minister of Labour has become the chosen
Prime Minister of the united bourgeoisie. Yet Morris's
words are as true to-day as when they were written.

As he was at the end, so he had been at the beginning
of his connection with the active Socialist movement. In
1883 he wrote concerning Hyndman :

" He is sanguine of speedy change happening somehow, and is inclined to intrigue, and the making of a
party : towards which compromise is needed, and the
carrying people who don't really agree with you as
far as they will go. As you know, I am not sanguine,
and think the aim of Socialists should be the founding
of a religion, towards which end compromise is no use,
and we only want to have those with us who will be
with us to the end."

Unless Socialism is a religion, it is nothing. Morris was

338

one of the great men to whom it was a religion. Like all true religions, it demanded of him a great surrender; when he had made it, the world of his experience was unified. A final simplicity descended on all his thinking and doing. He had but followed his life where it led, and when it brought him to the realization that he must lose his life to save it he accepted the destiny with the same simplicity, the same generosity which had brought him face to face with it. He, whose life had been devoted to making art real, accepted the necessity of the destruction of art. It also must die to live again. That acceptance was possible for him because of his faith in art. Because he knew that art was necessary to man, he was willing that it should die. "I am sure," he said, "that it will be but a temporary loss, to be followed by a genuine birth of new art, which will be the spontaneous expression of the pleasure of life innate in the whole people."

The depth of Morris's faith in art, which was his faith in man, made the sacrifice possible for him. It is the feebleness of their faith in art, and in man, which has turned his artist-successors aside from the path along which he led them. Because they have been afraid for *their* art, they have declared that they are afraid for art. They have been merely afraid for themselves. And because they have been afraid for themselves, they have suffered the great Socialist movement to be degraded. They have withdrawn from it in fear, and left it to the fearful. Because of their cowardice, it has been cowardly. And what have they gained? They too have gained the world and lost their souls.

Had I been writing a book, instead of an essay, about Morris, I should have lingered affectionately over many things which have no record in this brief description. I have insisted on what I believe to be the essence of the total man. He was one of the greatest of all the Victorians: in the age, united, it seemed, by every possible bond to its inmost body, bone of its bone, flesh of its flesh, yet from the beginning outside it. Outside it by chance hap as a schoolboy; outside it perdurably by his final surrender to the future. Because he was outside it, he was able to understand it; because he was of it, he was able to live it. *Fortunatus nimium.*

I have insisted from the beginning on the inevitability, and naturalness, and significance of Morris's Socialism. It is the message of the whole man. It was not a doctrine he embraced, but a discovery he made. Had Morris been the only Socialist in all England, still he would have been a Socialist. If he had been the only Socialist in all the world, still he would have been a Socialist. That is, in its simplest form, the difference between Morris and the thousands of others who, by this time, have adopted and profited by the name of Socialist. It is also the reason why it would have been not merely impossible to treat of Morris save in his growth towards Socialism, but dishonourable even to attempt it. Unless we are prepared to regard Morris's Socialism as the consummation of all that he did, or failed to do, in other more comely and respectable provinces of human endeavour, we must leave him alone. It takes a man many years to discover what he ultimately and irremediably *is*. Most men go to their graves without knowing it. Morris was the kind of man to whom that destiny was impossible. He had the genius of experience, of experiencing. He at least was doomed to discover what he was. And he *was*—a Socialist.

The signal honour of being that essence Morris shares with very few. With Robert Owen, with Marx, with Engels, with Lenin, perhaps with St. Simon. But among all Socialists Morris stands apart, with Marx and Engels, by the profundity of his approach to his own final and irrevocable discovery. That this is unrecognized, or openly denied, is merely another proof of the superficiality of Socialist and Communist thought in England. Incapable of thinking for itself, it takes its thinking at second-hand from the Continent. It mistrusts Morris because he was not Marx; just as now it mistrusts Marx because he was not Lenin; just as, a few years hence, it will mistrust Lenin because he was not Stalin. But, in simple fact, Marx and Morris are fundamentally at one, precisely because they are different. Marx came to his Socialism because he was a man to whom the philosophy of Hegel had been real. There are very few men at any time to whcm any philosophy is real. Marx was one of them. He believed in Hegel; and, since he was a great man, he believed in precisely that in Hegel which was worthy of belief, because it was true: namely, the vision of history as the working out of an almost wholly unconscious process. Marx made it his own mission to become completely conscious of the unconscious process of history. It was at once a revolution in thought and a revolution in his moral being.

Just as Marx was the final outcome of the great idealistic movement of philosophy, which was the nationally perfect form of Romanticism in Germany, so Morris was the final outcome, in an equally perfect national embodiment, of the English Romantic movement, which was poetical and artistic. What Marx had passed through as the conscious philosopher of history, Morris passed through as the unconscious artist of history gradually compelled into consciousness. Morris directly experienced the impasse of which Marx had grasped the historical necessity. Morris flung himself into the effort to live the life which Marx had apprehended as the ideal. Morris proved upon his pulses, in the characteristically English way, the truth which Marx had formulated. Hence the shallowness of those superficial theorists who represent the Socialism of Marx as opposed to the Socialism of Morris. They are the precise counterparts of one another. They represent simply a typically German and a typically English discovery of a universal truth: they converge, and are distinct, are one, and yet themselves, in the catholicism of the future.

JOHN HENRY
NEWMAN

1801-1890

BY
M. C.
D'ARCY, S.J.

JOHN HENRY NEWMAN

THE influence of Newman at Oxford, we are told by Principal Shairp—and his evidence is corroborated by other contemporaries—was something unlike anything else. " A mysterious veneration had by degrees gathered round him, till now it was almost as though some Ambrose or Augustine of older ages had reappeared." This reputation won so early in life was never completely lost. After his conversion to the Catholic Church and retirement from public debates, it became shadowy, but it was the shadow of a great name. Had this not been so he could never have recovered his fame so quickly when he descended into the lists against Kingsley. Memory had already enshrined his name, and by the end of his life he had become almost a legendary figure, the silver-tongued saint and Englishman clothed in the red of Cardinals.

Inevitably a reaction set in. The theological writings proved too hard a nut for the teeth of the young to crack, and by the time many of us came to manhood new interests and tastes were taking us far from the Victorian ideals. A style modelled on Cicero seemed over-rhetorical, and to judge from the titles of Newman's books they were concerned with topics of his day, and could not but smell of the sacristy. Nevertheless, it was impossible to forget him. Time and again his name cropped up, his voice could be heard in the tones of new preachers and prophets, his authority was enlisted in the defence of novel opinions, and sayings of his kept their freshness. And then interest was quickened again by the definitive life of Wilfrid Ward, with its revelation of his weakness as well as of his strength. The rhythm of his life was seen to possess a curious

o*

dramatic quality, starting with the picture of a boy, shy and awkward, with an inward conviction that the world was but a show hiding the unseen, the image not the substance of truth, dangerously sensitive to the words and regard of others, and upheld by a somewhat Calvinistic assurance of vocation and destiny. It was this boy who, after coming up to Oxford, the seed-plot of Anglicanism, callow and shy, was in a few years to make all England ring with the tidings of the greatness of its national religion. From obscurity he passed rapidly into the position of a leader, and his vocation seemed clear and settled. It is strange to find him at this time conscious of more to be accomplished, of a life to be led whose end he could not see. Then came the cloud no bigger than a man's hand, and in a few years duty to God was to send him back to a self-chosen obscurity and bring on him misunderstanding, and, what he least of men could bear, the resentment of friends and the charge of evasiveness and disloyalty. This phase ended in agony in 1845, and was succeeded by a new peace and the joy of good repute. Once more the sense of a vocation seized him at the prospect of a life led in truth, in the defence of the Christian religion amid the goodwill of new companions and against that spirit of Liberalism which from the beginning he had marked down as the most dangerous enemy of Christianity and of all that he held dear. And yet once more all seemed to go amiss. He had indeed the peace of the truth, but nothing else. One after another of his undertakings came to nothing—a series of the lives of the saints, a Catholic University in Ireland, his editorship of the *Rambler*. He felt that he was not *persona grata* with his ecclesiastical superiors, that their policy was different from his, and with the customary exaggeration of an introspective mind he complained to his friends of his uselessness.

And yet once again a period of his life closed with a triumph, and a new scene opens with the same hopes of a vocation to be fulfilled. This time the change was due to no new revolution in his mind. It came when his honesty was challenged by Kingsley, and the opportunity was given to him to vindicate his life. The *Apologia* brought him once more before the public, restored all his old prestige, and gave him a position in the Catholic body which he was never to lose. But if the change was immense, the fortune of his life continued to be woven in the same pattern as before. Discouragement set in again when his scheme for the entry of Catholics into Oxford suffered a reverse, and some of his old friends grew more and more estranged from him. The ascendancy, too, of Manning meant a victory for those whom he considered to be a party of reaction and intransigeance, and, as he thought, Rome viewed him with suspicion for his reported opinions on Infallibility. He was an old man now, and he wrote, " I have so depressing a feeling that I have done nothing through my long life, and especially that now I am doing nothing at all." So he began to prepare for death in a mood in which resignation was mixed with disappointment. And then Providence intervened once more, and after a last small but bitter test, when Manning misinterpreted his reply to the offer of a Cardinal's hat, he was able to say that " the cloud is lifted for ever," and his life closed in a quiet splendour with his work done.

This revelation of Newman's character in Ward's biography, especially through the letters, does undoubtedly make it more dramatic, but there are those who fear it has removed the halo and made him all too human. It would not be too difficult, indeed, to fasten on certain tendencies and traits in his character and make them responsible for his misfortunes. He had a very thin skin, and was upset by trifles; he took offence easily, hugged criticism when a more robust character would have gone on his way unheeding; and whether through shyness or excessive sensibility, he found it difficult to straighten out misunderstandings, even at times to make up quarrels. In his early portraits he looks strait-laced, and some of the stories told of him remind one of an Oxford don with whom it is forbidden to take liberties. Fortunately, it is impossible to deny him a sense of humour, but to expansive people he was apt to appear punctilious and lacking in warmth. As Wiseman and others discovered, one could not get round him with soft words. This typically English coldness of manner was possibly a cloak, but more likely it was due to his early training and to the Oxford whose spirit he had imbibed. Such a culture had its disadvantages: it cut him off from the hurly-burly life of the cities and the countryside, and made him smile tolerantly, as so many other Victorians did, at the habits and ways of foreigners. He was never thoroughly at home in Ireland, and he has been accused of attempting to foist an Oxford education on a youth straight from the soil with far different cultural and national needs. It limited also the range of his thought; he was content to be a Tory without investigating too closely the democratic movements on the Continent; he knew little or nothing of German thought, and preferred to move within the circle of ideas which had appealed to him in his youth.

Such criticisms have their truth, but as always happens with a rich and complex character, almost opposite impressions can be formed of him. His face and head were compared, by a contemporary of his at Oxford, to the well-known bust thought to be Julius Cæsar, and another says of his conversations that they had a very wide range, and that his talk could be animated and fascinating. All his life he had to check enthusiastic followers from swearing by every word he uttered. It is not easy—indeed, it is frankly impossible—to reconcile the charge of womanishness with the authority he wielded, and so, if at times his voice sounds shrill, we have to ask whether this be not due to its range and variety, whether the flexibility of his character be not the sign of a great if delicate strength. Wilfrid Ward relates the well-known story of his walk with his friend Christie shortly before the crisis at Littlemore, how Newman never said a word, but at the end Christie's hand was wet with his friend's tears. Almost as famous is the incident which occurred at Ambrose St. John's death. He was the dearest of Newman's friends, and Newman threw himself on his bed, and lay there broken in sorrow the whole night. These are not the actions of a man who can be judged by the standards of ordinary men. So delicately responsive a constitution was made for high issues and also for suffering. It equipped him for greatness, and at the same time caused him to be misunderstood.

But this sensibility might have been his undoing had it not been for two thoughts or motives which dominated his life. At times he was, I shall not say on the verge, but in some slight danger of becoming a frustrated genius, one whom friends would have sorrowed over for his surrender to cynicism and a joyless and morbid satisfaction in hard fate. That this did not happen is due to his sense of a vocation and the strength of his conscience. These two were closely allied. He tells us that from early childhood the spiritual was more real to him than the material world of appearance and changing shadows. For this reason, when a student he had felt a sympathy with the philosophy of Berkeley. This sense of finer issues, of an ineffable spiritual reality, he never lost, and it made him indifferent to much that attracted others, indifferent to dress and food and natural comforts. Both at Littlemore and as an Oratorian his manner of life was very austere. It gave him also that vision of the soul's orbit and destiny which is the privilege of a rare class of men, the Augustines, the Pascals, the seers. Despite vast individual differences, Newman is of the family of these two just mentioned. He broods over predestination like Pascal, and like Augustine he turns constantly to conscience for light and truth. His language about it has often puzzled his readers, for it clearly meant more to him than it does to most of us. It is in his experience almost the direct voice of God, certainly the communicating chamber between the soul and its Lord. It will seem less strange if we read what he says in connection with his profound belief in the immaterial and his own vocation, and also with what St. Augustine writes on the same subject. They have the same experience and the same doctrine. In the deep place of the soul God gives audience. " Everywhere, O Truth, dost Thou give audience to all who ask counsel of Thee.". . . " Truth is near to all, is eternal for all; it prompts from without, it teaches from within." It is interesting to find this fellowship of mind across the ages. Newman's interests from student days lay with the Early Church and the Fathers, and the background of his philosophy of life is not so much Berkleyan as Neo-Platonic. Augustine, however, was an African, whereas Newman was a nineteenth-century Englishman, and the one had lived the life of a pagan and the other had been brought up a strict Protestant. The training of his childhood left Newman with a deep conviction of sin. In the *Parochial Sermons* his doctrine is severe, even harsh at times, and in them he resembles Pascal more closely than in later life. After his conversion the atmosphere noticeably lightens; he becomes more human and tender; he gives play to his affection for his dear St. Philip and the Mother of God. But he does not change his language about conscience. His sense of vocation grows only the stronger, and he becomes more and more persuaded of the authority of God within as well as in the teaching of the Catholic Church without. This is the explanation of his influence over others and of the impression he made. From the time he began to preach his listeners felt that here was a personality, a leader who drew his thought from some secret inner communion with unseen powers. He was one of those whose lot it is to be alone with the Alone, to be aware of only two realities, God and the soul, " amid the encircling gloom." And this is why, though Pusey and Keble were his seniors, and Pusey at least in a better position to lead the new movement, people turned instinctively to Newman as the one divinely anointed.

There were many prophets in the nineteenth century, moral, artistic, educational, and social. Newman shared few of their convictions. He preferred Trinity Chapel at Oxford to the Pugin gothic and the Venetian designs of Ruskin; he had no liking for Carlyle's heroes, and he was too much of a Tory to have sympathy with the social theories of Mill. Where he ceased to be conventional was in the realm of ideas, and as in his prose, so in ideals he stands apart from others by the pure quality of his thought and rich simplicity. Carlyle and Ruskin may have had a more robust sense of the immediate needs of the time ; Newman is less conversant with social or economic necessities, but ever so much more alive to the interests of the soul, and no one can equal him when he sets out to explore the labyrinths of the spirit with its strange forces and half-formulated desires and its burden of destiny. The subtlety of his thought might have been wasted had not conscience and the sense of a mission enlisted and marshalled all his interests. As it was, he was inclined to see complications where more simple minds thought that all was straightforward; his hesitations before any enterprise, his long delay before conversion, his slowness to accept terms with would-be friends were due to this elaborate sincerity. When Kingsley accused him of dishonesty, he had as his real ground the unjustifiable but intelligible suspicion that Newman was too subtle to be straight, and we must be thankful that the charge was made, as it enabled Newman to set out with such almost uncanny skill the workings of his conscience many years before. We see, as he tells his story, the extreme delicacy of his mind, his habit of revolving many thoughts, the constant self-examination before the tribunal of his conscience, and his horror of untruthfulness.

Such extreme sincerity, it may be said, is seldom wholesome, and is often the mother of delusion. Gladstone is

cited as having a conscience which told the hour he wanted,
and no doubt the passage from introspection to self-deceit
is easy. But not to one who like Newman deemed that he
dwelt by conscience in the presence of the God of truth,
the Judge of the living and the dead. "General conscientiousness is the only assurance we can have of possessing it
(a spiritual mind); and at this we must aim, determining
to obey God consistently with a jealous carefulness about
all things, little and great." The same thought is developed
in some of his sermons, where he is summing up his view
of life with its consequent trials and joys. "He goes by a
law which others know not; not his own wisdom or judgement, but by Christ's wisdom and the judgement of the
Spirit, which is imparted to him by that inward incom-
municable perception of truth and duty, which is the rule
of his reason, affections, wishes, tastes, and all that is in
him, and which is the result of persevering obedience. This
it is which gives so unearthly a character to his whole life
and conversation, which is ' hid with Christ in God; ' he
has ascended with Christ on high, and there ' in heart and
mind continually dwells; ' and he is obliged in consequence
to put a veil upon his face, and is mysterious in the world's
judgement, and ' becomes as it were a monster unto many,'
though he be ' wiser than the aged,' and have ' more
understanding than his teachers, because he keeps God's
commandments.' "

All the principles of Newman's own life are set forth
in these words—the law of conscience and of Christ, the
inward spirit, the dwelling apart, alone with the Alone,
the consequent misunderstanding, and lastly the law of
obedience. No estimate of Newman's character and point
of view would be complete were obedience not included.
Obedience was not easy to him, as he found it more natural
to lead than to follow, and he was a thorough individualist
by temperament in his preference of experience to scholastic
logic and theoretical principles. But like Augustine he was
so conscious of the majesty of God in conscience and of his
lowliness by comparison that his one object was to live out
his life in obedience to the overruling and living truth.
Within this divine providence he was to find himself and
have a mission. He assumed at first that that way of life
was to be found within the communion in which he had
been brought up, in work for the renovation of the Anglican
Church. That Church stood for him as the embodiment

of the divine presence upon earth which with its heel crushed underfoot the rebel tendencies in man. There, too, lay the spiritual kingdom which kept the absolute sanctions of God before man unchangingly amid the shifting values of human culture in the shadow world in which man lived. The best that man could do was Liberalism, that compound of criticism and expectation which preferred progress to stability, and self-made religion and philosophy to obedience. These two contrasts were ever before him in the forms of orthodoxy and liberalism; they turned his mind to the problem of belief, inspired the subject of his sermons, and led him to watch the future with ever-increasing anxiety.

The convictions thus formed drove him out of the Church of his baptism into another, which, despite cross after cross, became for him his home. Here was " the pillar and ground of truth; " conscience within and the will of God as externally manifested were thus reconciled. This gives the reason why irritation at methods adopted by the Catholic Church in England never upset his faith. The certainty of his belief did not, however, lessen his disappointment. His task, as he thought after his conversion, was to develop the forces within the Church against the menace of Liberalism. He foresaw that it would make rapid strides, and in the name of knowledge and progress beget religious unbelief. Herein he showed himself a true prophet. He may have been unfair in giving the name of Liberalism to the movements he viewed with such apprehension; but he was not in my opinion wrong in diagnosing what would happen, in foretelling a Waste Land and a Brave New World. This power of divination is of itself sufficient to dispose of the charge that his mind was preoccupied with parochial and passing scenes. He knew too well the trade routes of human ambition, and what is conservative or corrosive of belief. It is not surprising, therefore, to discover in his writings much that is relevant to present problems, and to learn that both in Germany and France he is becoming more and more accepted as one of the master-minds of the nineteenth century.

In England during his lifetime he failed, in his own opinion, to persuade his fellow-Catholics of the truth and importance of what he wished to say. Herein he minimized the effect of his teaching, but it is true that he met with opposition. In his policy he was perhaps too fearful of the opinion of his countrymen, whereas the Church being cosmopolitan was harsh when he wished it to be conciliatory, dogmatic when he thought it more opportune to be silent, and remained apparently supine or indifferent about what he considered urgent. If Newman were alive to-day he would probably modify his criticism, for the Church's treatment of him, as of other ardent reformers such as Lacordaire, looks from afar much more sensible than it must have done to those who suffered from it. He was in so many ways ahead of his time. In his *Development of Christian Doctrine*, for instance, some would say that he did for theology what Darwin was doing for science. For years theologians took little notice of it; now it is part of the accepted teaching. Similarly with his *Grammar of Assent*. It was greeted with criticism because it lacked the precision of the trained scholastic philosopher. Newman was never a professional philosopher; he had found the basis for much that he wanted in Butler, and he had that distaste, which goes so often with religious and prophetic genius, for logic and metaphysics. Defects of this kind prevented many from seeing the vital importance of the ideas contained in it. What Newman had done was to put his finger on the most relevant problem of the day and to work out an answer in the very terms in which men actually thought. Now we can see that it is a work of the greatest originality, and that he blazed a new way, this time within the country of the mind.

Both, then, as a thinker and as a man Newman deserves the reputation he won during his lifetime. The criticisms that have been passed on him serve but to remove the halo which unwise admirers assigned to him. If he was not a saint, he was, at any rate, a highly sensitive genius whose lips were touched by an angel with a burning coal. The delicate strings of his character were habitually strung up by an inner passionate conviction of what cannot be called so much duty as God in his conscience. Because of this, because he dwells so familiarly with the unseen, and is the interpreter of the soul's language with God and with itself, he does not grow smaller as the nineteenth century is left behind. It is true that the memory of him is linked with certain scenes, as walking down the High, alone and absorbed, a figure of awe to the passing undergraduate, or reading from his manuscript in silvery tones from the pulpit of Oscott or Edgbaston, or with his spiritual and worn face clothed in the robes of a Cardinal. But to give colour and locality to genius is not to rob it of its immortality. He chose for the inscription on his tomb, "From shadows and images into truth"; I think that amid much that has grown shadowy in the last century his name will shine with a steady, perhaps even greater, light.

FLORENCE NIGHTINGALE

1820-1910

BY
LAURENCE
HOUSMAN

FLORENCE NIGHTINGALE

AN iridescent medallion under glass, of a red cross sur-mounted by a crowned monogram of crystals, in a bed of lilies, and encircled by a blue band bearing the words ' Blessed are the merciful,' drew me in early years to the name—already sacred in legend—of Florence Nightingale. This medallion, the central ornament of a drawing-room table, formed the chief and most attractive art-object of my young days. It combined in its gaudy setting—a brass tazza of florid scroll-work—beauty, religion, and patriotic sentiment; it also had the flavour of Royalty, for the Prince-Consort himself had designed it.

The original, then made popular by reproduction, sym-bolized the heroic service of a woman (still living, I was told) whose name struck me as more beautiful even than the design.

Has there, indeed, ever been a name more sweetly com-pounded for the lavishing of sentiment than the name of Florence Nightingale? Theosophists tell us that, when the soul reincarnates, it chooses its own time, name, and parentage. If that be true, Florence Nightingale chose her name wisely and well. It may have conveyed little of her character, but as a means of peaceful penetration for the pioneer work she was to accomplish, it could hardly have been bettered.

Another name, as felicitously chosen for the life it was to fit—the name Victoria—had come to its small beginning just a year earlier. And these two lives, so closely con-temporary and so fortunately named, were destined to become symbolic and outstanding examples, in the era which followed, of the opposing forces through whose help

357

or hindrance that great social revolution which is called the
Woman's Movement took shape and grew strong, producing results which, for the present generation, have made
the conditions of those days (so little remote in time) seem
unbelievably far-off and strange.

But though, in aim and temperament, these two, Queen
and Commoner, were so widely divided, each alike had a
power of set purpose and initiative which produced revolutionary results. Victoria, within a decade of her accession,
had revolutionized the social standards of the Regency,
and had made society decent.

This left Florence Nightingale a harder nut to crack; her
revolution took longer; the decency of Victorianism (or
what it regarded as such) took more than fifty years to
undermine. The upheaval, begun by Miss Nightingale,
did not reach its culmination till Queen Victoria's reign had
prosperously ended. For to the Queen must be conceded
that ponderous marking of time which bears her name; for
fifty years she, more than any other woman, moulded the
social history of this country. But while she gave to the
age a static expression by becoming the embodiment of its
conventions, Florence Nightingale, by her own more forceful example, sowed those seeds of revolutionary change
which have made Victorian woman a thing of the past.

Yet Florence was herself a very Victorian character.
Her exceptional powers of body and brain, and the abnormal driving force which lay behind them, merely served
to give anticipatory expression to a problem which already
stirred uneasily beneath the surface in thousands of homes.

We do not consider it necessary to say of certain great
men, however exceptional their powers, that they did not
belong to their age; it is often far more true that by the
exercise of those exceptional powers they brought out the
latent qualities that were in it—that, through them, the
age found itself. It is quite true that the women of the
Victorian age took a long time to find themselves along
the lines laid down by Florence Nightingale; but it was not
because they lacked the strength of character. Strength of
character made them obstinately possessive of the little
world over which they bore rule; and a very strong little
world it was—so strong that it survived absurdly into the
nineteenth century, and put up quite a good fight for itself
when all the conditions on which it was based had become
obsolete.

Some years ago I showed to a friend a set of photographs,
taken when photography was young, of women who had
come to maturity in mid-Victorian days. His comment,
" What tremendous characters ! " was a just summary.
Strength of character was the salient feature, beauty and
fashion the adjuncts. And yet, outside the domestic circle,
those women had not made any mark on the world—they
were unknown, unheard of. They were women who, supporting rigorously the conventions of their day, had
gloried in the limitations of their sex, and imposed them
censoriously on others. Convention formed, indeed, a part
of their religion. And yet—as my mind browses up and
down the records of those past lives—I am convinced that
they accepted convention mainly because they believed
that it gave them power. Victorian womanhood was an
army, well drilled and well organized; yet it was all so
quiet and underground, or so domestically within doors,
that one wonders where the organization came in. Was it
the ' afternoon call,' or was it—the power of prayer?
" Leave then thy sister when she prays," said Tennyson.
Had he spelt the word with an " e," it would have been
more to the point. The religious views of our Victorian
sisters needed no cockering, and no protection from the
assaults of ' honest doubt'; inflexible in quality and
predatory in operation, they had a devastating effect upon
the intellectual progress of the rising generations they controlled. Even to-day the pulpit has not quite rid itself of
the influence of its Victorian mother's knee.

Florence Nightingale herself had, in those early days,
strange views about prayer, and prayed, not according to
the sinner's need, but according to how she liked him. " I
could not," she owned, " pray for George IV. I thought
people very good who prayed for him, and wondered if
he could have been much worse if he had not been prayed
for. William IV. I prayed for a little. But when Victoria
came to the throne, I prayed for her in a rapture of feeling,
and my thoughts never wandered."

In that case one can only surmise that women of less
advanced views were also praying for her, with equal rapture, and, judging by results, with more success.

Florence Nightingale found it hard to believe that in
prayer thoughts could wander. " When you ask for what
you want," she said, " your thoughts *don't* wander." But
the reform of George IV's character lay outside the range

of her desires. Evil, she believed, was a necessary ingredient in the creative scheme; God put it there to teach men what to avoid; it was educative. Law and order were the appointed means for bringing His Kingdom to earth; and God Himself was a Law-giver who believed in corporal punishment.

All of which goes to show that, though she was one of its most tremendous characters, Florence Nightingale belonged to her age; and it was as much her religion as anything, which, in spite of great mental misery, kept her within the confines of the home till her thirty-fourth year. And from that long imprisonment of a body and mind so restless, so resolute, so energetic, we may measure the strength of the bondage she had to break. Her mother, not her father, was the main obstacle. It was from its women that the convention took its strength. In spite of their confined lives of narrow outlook and poor, scrappy education, they had as much force of character and power of will as the generations of women who have come after; and whether they put down their foot to maintain convention or to break it, it was with an equal will of their own that they did so.

Queen Victoria and Florence Nightingale were both masterful characters; and it was perhaps by a mere accident of circumstance that the one stood for the old order (with a difference), while the other stood for the new. Victoria became her own mistress at seventeen, Florence not till she was twice that age. It made a difference. Seventeen years of continuous contact with the 'sleeping ignorance,' which the social conditions of her day imposed on women, had caused the iron to enter into her soul. After she had made her escape into a life of active service, she wrote—but did not publish—a bitter commentary on the case as she then saw it. Under the sub-title "Cassandra," it strangely forms part of an appeal to the artisans of England for the recovery of "religious truth," at a time when the falling away from faith of the working-class was becoming noticeable.

> "Why [she asks in her first paragragh] have women passion, intellect, moral activity—these three—and a place in society where no one of these can be exercised? . . . Men are angry with misery. They are irritated with women for not being happy. They take it as a personal offence. . . . In the conventional

society (which men have made for women, and women
have accepted) ' women must have no passions.' They
must act the farce of hypocrisy [and teach it, she goes
on to say, to their daughters]. Society forbids. . . .
The family uses people for what it wants them for—
for its own uses. The system dooms some minds to
incurable infancy, others to silent misery. . . . In
society men and women meet to be idle. Is it extraordinary that they do not know each other, and that
in their mutual ignorance they form no surer friendships? Did they meet to *do* something together, they
might form some real tie. . . . The woman who has
sold herself for an establishment, in what is she superior
to those one may not name?"

[An interesting sentence that—combining the new
woman's revolt against the expedient of respectable marriage, with acceptance of the Victorian convention that the
prostitute must not be named—not even when the actual
parallel was being drawn.]

" And marriage being [she goes on] their only outlet in life, many women spend their lives in asking men
to marry them, in a refined way."

Of the " philanthropy " which women were allowed to
practise, she remarks scornfully:

" Were the physician to set to work at his trade as
the philanthropist does at his, how many bodies would
he not spoil before he cured one? . . . Women long
for an education to *teach* them to teach, to teach them
the laws of the mind and how to apply them. . . .
They long for experience, not patchwork experience,
but experience followed up and systematized to enable
them to know what they are about, and where they
are casting their bread, and whether it *is bread* or a
stone. . . . If we have no food for the body, how we
do cry out, how all the world hears of it, how all the
newspapers talk of it with a paragraph headed in great
capital letters, 'DEATH FROM STARVATION!'
But suppose one were to put a paragraph in *The Times*,
'DEATH OF THOUGHT FROM STARVATION,'
or 'DEATH OF MORAL ACTIVITY FROM STAR-
VATION,' how people would stare, how they would

laugh and wonder! One would think that we have no heads nor hearts, by the total indifference of the public towards them. Our bodies are the only things of consequence. . . . With what labour women have toiled to break down all individual and independent life, in order to fit themselves for this social and domestic existence, thinking it right. And when they have killed themselves to do it, they have awakened (too late) to think it wrong."

This cry of distress was written by a woman who, five years earlier, had achieved an astounding success in the public service, and a popularity greater than that of the Queen herself. She was famous and powerful, and was still carrying on, with quiet efficiency, her work of public usefulness. She did not write it for herself, but for others. Of her two literary advisers, one, John Stuart Mill, wished her to publish it; the other, Benjamin Jowett, advised that she should not. She accepted Jowett's advice; one wonders why.

It was symptomatic of the sincerity of her character that she concentrated her attack, not on what was merely old-fashioned and narrow in the lives of the women of her day —their religion—for that was fairly sincere; but on that which was damnably false—their social and their sex relations. It is now almost unbelievable how false, root and branch, those relations were; and they were false, for the degrading reason that it was what men were supposed to like. Perhaps they did, from having known nothing better. The exhibitionism, called Modesty, which women assiduously practised in those days, was their main stock-in-trade for escape from the home of their parents to a home of their own, where, in a certain measure, they could become themselves. They spent their lives, as Florence put it, "in asking men to marry them, in a refined way"; and intellect being looked at askance and passion forbidden, they laid their modesty on with a trowel. It required a lot of doing and a lot of living-up-to. I am inclined to think sometimes that it was sheer force of character and self-discipline which enabled women to faint, when—according to the conventions they worshipped—they were expected to faint; and that, had they been weaker characters, they could not with such unfailing regularity have performed the task required of them.

But the whole thing was a sham. Early Victorianism was an age of moral cosmetics; and women, who would have regarded the lipstick as lascivious, did not scruple to lard themselves with all the weaknesses which were supposed to appeal to man's taste for mastery. In the social entertainments of the day they sang love-songs to themselves, and to each other without the slightest sapphic intent. Mrs. Norton's ' Juanita,' and Adelaide Procter's ' Message ' were set for the female voice; and with these aphrodisiacs the male heart was to be softened. One of the most popular songs of the day, pursuing femininity to the depth, told of a certain sweet Alice, '' who wept with delight if you gave her a smile, and trembled beneath your frown.'' In the last verse '' sweet Alice,'' happily disposed of, '' lies under the stone.'' Even as recently as fifty years ago, that song could be sung without being laughed at; that could not happen now.

Florence Nightingale was too sick and angry to laugh. She was a practical genius; and the wasting of woman's qualities enraged her. No doubt, in stating the woman's case, it was often her own past that she remembered, and, in certain passages, her own character and capabilities which she described in those vivid and bitter phrases.

> '' Some women [she writes] have an attention like a battering-ram, which, slowly brought to bear, can work upon a subject for any length of time. They can work for ten hours just as well as two upon the same thing. . . . What these suffer—even physically—for the want of such work no one can tell. The accumulation of nervous energy, which has had nothing to do during the day, makes them feel, every night when they go to bed, as if they were going mad; and they are obliged to lie long in bed in the morning to let it evaporate and keep it down.''

'' Like a battering-ram '': here undoubtedly we have self-portraiture; and for seventeen years the battering-ram adopted the device of lying late in bed as a means of escaping from its own consuming energy.

The device failed; at the age of thirty-four, tentatively at first, while out of sight on holiday abroad—then resolutely and completely—she broke the home-ties, and took up the practice of nursing. It was a more shocking thing to do

363

than we can now well realize: hospital nurses were improper characters, they drank, they were suspected of illicit
relations with the medical staff and the students, and had
no training or qualifications worth talking about. And
what they were then, to the Victorian mind, they must
always continue to be. Into this state of affairs the ' battering-ram ' entered. Her first act of organization was to
set up a hospital—for women—in Harley Street: a fairly
decent thing to do. Her committee decided to exclude
Roman Catholics; she presented her resignation, and the
decision was reversed. But honest, direct action like this
was not always, she found, possible; intrigue and roundabout methods which, at the start, she had determined to
avoid, were necessary for getting anything done. She presented her decisions to the Committee as though they came
from the medical staff; while with the medical staff she
talked things out as man to man, and as though such things
as committees did not exist. Within less than two years
she had acquired a proficiency which would have taken
others ten. And then, in the nick of time, came the call to
action, in a great national crisis, which for the rest of her
long life gave her the fame and power necessary for the
practical and efficient employment, not so much of her
great heart, as of her great mind.

  Her offence—for offence it had been—against the conventions of gentility was transformed by national need and
by popular applause into heroic virtue, at the very moment
when it took the jump from the comparative decency of the
nursing of carefully selected gentlewomen (though it did
include Roman Catholics) to the organization of an over-
crowded military hospital where decency, sanitation, and
system were all equally lacking. The happy accident of
a nation badly and blunderingly at war was her opportunity; and the pretence that a modest woman must not
look upon the body of any man but her own husband was
blown sky-high, in the patriotic fervour of the moment—
never quite to return. Military and ministerial inefficiency
had begun to make war dangerously unpopular; and while
Tennyson wrote a famous poem to reconcile the public
mind to one blunder, she, by the wiping out of another,
almost restored to the war its popularity, and saved the
life of the Government. On that figure of revolt, not knowing what they did, the Church, the Crown, and the public
laid consecrating hands. The ' public ' in more senses

than one. Florence Nightingale became, not merely the
heroine of the Nation, but the talk of the taverns ; and it
was approving talk. Tipplers toasted her, and damning
the Government and the War Office, went home drunk in
her honour. Queen Victoria was herself temporarily weaned
from her prejudice against the entry of women into public
life, and though jealous of Florence's popularity, wished
she could have "such a head " at the War Office. Two
decades later the royal mind reverted to type, and declared
that Lady Somebody-or-other, who wanted the vote, also
" wanted whipping."

It was inevitable, under the circumstances, that an
emotional interpretation should be given to the great work
of rescue which Florence Nightingale accomplished, that
heart should be put before head, and the ' Commander of
Genius,' with her calm powers of organization and discipline (subduing even blockheads and fools), should be
hailed as an ' Angel of Mercy,' with pity as her prevailing
motive. But had she been asked to choose her own motto,
it would not have been ' Blessed are the merciful,' with its
corresponding reward, but far more probably ' Blessed are
the masterful, for they shall obtain mastery.' Mercy she
had in abundance, but it was not the incentive and main-
spring of her action ; her motive force was a passion which
she was able to put unerringly into practice, for method as
against muddle. The legendary ' Angel of Mercy ' could
not have accomplished the task which the ' battering-ram '
was able to perform; and if there was in her character
something hard and inflexible and quietly ruthless—to
friends as well as to foes—let us take off our hats to it, and
thank God that it was so.

The mastery which she secured in that time of crisis she
never let go. Her later career, through thirty more years
of activity and over fifty of life, was amazing both in its
methods and in its results. Broken in health, house-bound,
almost bed-ridden, she invented an economy of technique
suited to her condition, by which it is quite likely that she
got more work done than had she remained a vigorous and
active member of Committees where so many wordy battles
have to be fought and so much time lost. Without any
diminution of industry or abatement of mental energy, the
fiery reformer became a recluse ; and we have the astonishing spectacle of this frail invalid exercising, through her
own small band of workers, and sick-room interviews with

selected persons, a greater and more persistent influence on Royal Commissions, Ministers, and the departmental acts of government than any other person of unofficial standing that one could name. To one after another of the departments of public service—hospitals, nursing, barracks, sanitation—she gave her great gifts of organization and common sense; wherever she directed her efforts, she brought health and saved life. Sometimes, as the result of reforms which she inculcated, the fall in the death-rate was as great as that which she had brought about in the hospitals at Scutari. In the barracks and military hospitals in India the diminution of mortality was enormous; and it was mainly her doing.

She did not spare the dull officials, with whom she came in contact, the sharpness of her tongue. In spite of her feeble state of health, she went down to inspect the hospitals at Chatham, and commenting on what she found there, remarked: "Another symptom of the system which in the Crimea put to death 16,000 men. You might as well take 1,100 every year out into Salisbury Plain and shoot them."

And so it is not to be wondered at that with the old military type of mind (slow to move) she was never popular —was regarded, rather, as something which should not have been allowed. Many years after the Crimea, certain retired Colonels and Generals, who had perhaps tried a fall with her and had failed, spoke of her as "a damned nuisance"; the drop in the death-rate at Scutari, from 42 to 2 per cent., not seeming to them sufficient compensation for that un- warrantable intrusion of a woman into the affairs of men.

During the quiet labour of her latter years she became almost a voluminous writer. In the drawing-up of schemes, the compiling of reports, and in contributions to blue-books, her handwork—though anonymous—is constantly to be found. A Royal Commission, set up at her instigation in 1859, and making its report on lines which she laid down, was still the main basis of Government action fifty years later. In the report of the Commission on the Health of the British Army in India, her own contribution formed the most readable part: it was reprinted and sold by the thousand. When a condensed version of the whole report was required for public consumption, finding the official synopsis unsatisfactory, she re-wrote it, and published it at her own expense. Her record and her abilities com- bined placed her above criticism, almost above opposition.

At the age of seventy-two we still find her a driving force—one whose policy was always to be ahead of what those in authority were willing to do. "We must create," she wrote, "a public opinion which will drive the Government." And driving Governments was, in fact, her life's work.

Her name became so valuable that, when she ceased to subscribe to a certain Society, the Society refused to take her name from its lists—her name being worth so much more than her subscription. And so far as the Woman's Movement was concerned, she stood, as a power and as an example, almost alone.

During the last long Suffrage Campaign which secured women the vote, two names of legendary pre-eminence were constantly invoked by the opposing forces—Queen Victoria and Florence Nightingale. Florence Nightingale was in favour of the vote, Queen Victoria was against it; but the approval of the former far outweighed the disapproval of the latter. People smiled when the old Queen's disapprobation was quoted—for had she not already so much more power than any vote could confer? Florence Nightingale, on the other hand, had discovered, not only for herself, but for women in general, the crying need for some public means of striking a balance against the incompetence and indifference of men in certain departments of life which to woman mattered considerably. After Florence Nightingale had come Josephine Butler; and whereas the one had achieved success through great popularity, the other —fighting a longer and harder battle—had won her victory, only after many defeats, through bitter opposition, reproach, and scorn.

Florence Nightingale stands curiously isolated—the one popular figure in a Movement which incurred so much unpopularity, before it became the accepted thing. But though her popularity greatly lightened her task, and made much that she did possible, which might otherwise have remained impossible, it is still probably true that hers was the most towering ability, as it was surely the most unusual in kind, of all those great and varying abilities which, from the sleep of the Victorian age, awoke the Women's Movement into life and strength.

LORD
PALMERSTON

1784-1865

BY
HAROLD
NICOLSON

P

LORD PALMERSTON

THE Muse of English history is, as we know, a woman of marked Whig tendencies, and so apt to define as " progress " what is little more than the way we happen to have gone. Credulous she is, moreover, in respect of the aims and achievements of Liberal statesmen—attributing to the expedients of these gentlemen the dignity of a conscious and consistent purpose.

It is thus significant that our English Clio, when she comes to Lord Palmerston, should so frequently avert her eyes. For Palmerston, although the most showy of our Foreign Secretaries, is not a show-piece in the Valhalla of Liberalism. There is a distinct trend upon the part of our Whig historians to suggest that Palmerston, after all, was scarcely Whig—an unexpressed wish that he had remained an open Tory all the time. Can it be denied that this, their disparagement, proves that in such matters our Whig historians are both honest and clear-sighted?

For, had they so desired, they could (with no violation of patent truth) have pointed to many admirable achievements on the credit side. He created an independent Belgium, neutralized and guaranteed. His efforts to suppress the slave-trade were consistent and indubitably sincere. His opposition to the system of Metternich, although a trifle personal, was sufficiently continuous. He was sound on Catholic Emancipation, and, under the guidance of his son-in-law, was equally sound upon Factory Acts and Child Welfare. His many statements on the rights of small nations and the maternal duty of the Mother of Parliaments were impeccable both in tone and manner. It could be shown even that for a few bright days in 1848

371

he was modernist enough to contemplate a Treaty of
Arbitration with the United States. One could instance
also his manly independence of Osborne, his championship of Kossuth, his breezy vindictiveness against General
Haynau, and above all the fact that he was universally
recognized as being " the people's man."

So much for the credit side of Palmerston's pass-book.
The debit side shows him, when one comes to examine it,
heavily overdrawn. In the matter of Reform Lord
Palmerston was less than lukewarm: he was distinctly
cold; it was his presence in successive Liberal Cabinets
that acted as an obstruction to much reformist legislation.
On occasions, notably in his early career, he had shown
himself a confirmed reactionary: he had approved of
Copenhagen upon the shocking ground that there were
moments when the Law of Nations must surrender to the
Law of Nature. He had, while Secretary at War, consistently defended flogging, and by arguments more
specious still. As Foreign Secretary he exposed his
country to incessant alarums, driving the chariot of
Britannia along the very brink of disaster. He was responsible, during his fifty odd years of public life, for
involving his country in one major, and four minor, wars.
He bullied Greece, China, and Persia; yet in 1848 he tried
to prevent Charles Albert from helping the Milanese; and in
1849 he approved of the Russian intervention in Hungary.
He abandoned Poland as he abandoned Schleswig-Holstein.
And in the end, the bluff and bluster of fifty years left us
marooned, mistrusted, and disliked.

It is not surprising, therefore, that the Whig historians
should hesitate to defend Lord Palmerston upon the
balance of his practical achievement. We may suggest,
moreover, that behind their displeasure lurks an even more
intense resentment. For not merely did Lord Palmerston
fail as a practical statesman, his failure as an idealist was
even more disastrous. To him was given the great opportunity to adjust the Canning formula to the needs of the
middle nineteenth century. To him was given the even
greater opportunity to found upon the ruined system of
Metternich the structure of a truly democratic diplomacy.
Not only did he fail in exploiting these two opportunities:
he secured that similar occasions should not recur for two
generations. In vulgarizing the Canning formula, in
rendering diplomatic diplomacy demagogic, he not merely

missed two great opportunities, but he discredited and
besmirched two great ideas. He committed these errors,
not wholly from lack of intelligence, certainly not from
lack of knowledge, but owing to his essential smallness of
soul. It is thus inevitable that the Liberal historians should
look back upon Lord Palmerston with displeasure and
regret. Let us examine how far this disapproval is justified
by the facts.

The development of Palmerston's character is both
curious and obscure. One observes three distinct periods:
the period of passive diffidence, the period of dynamic
caution, and the period of reckless " sportsmanship."

Although it may seem strange to us, Palmerston, as a
boy, was shy. His relations, while he was still at Harrow,
complained of his " lack of spring "; during the three
years he spent under Dugald Stewart at Edinburgh he was
studious, diffident, and reserved; even at Cambridge he
impressed his contemporaries as determined but dull. True
it is that on coming of age he had the impertinence to
contest the seat vacated by Mr. Pitt, but at twenty-five he
refused, owing to his distrust of his own powers, the post
of Chancellor of the Exchequer. And thus for nineteen
years he remained Secretary at War, designing head-gear
for the Royal Artillery.

Palmerston only began to be Palmerston when he reached
the age of forty-six.

This early diffidence must be discounted by other considerations. If Palmerston remained, during his early
virility, comparatively obscure, he did not remain comparatively unambitious. There are many reasons to
account for his lack of progress in the earlier years. He
was a professed Canningite, and George IV considered
him " proud." In spite of this, however, he was offered,
and refused, not only the Governorship of Jamaica, but a
thrice-proffered chance of India. Moreover, he enjoyed
the War Office, which was not without its patronage, and
in the files of which he could dabble at his ease. " P.,"
wrote Lord Melbourne, " likes his business so much." " I
do not conceal," confessed Palmerston later, " that I
think it is a great bore to go out: I like power: I think
power very pleasant." Apart, however, from the charms
of bureaucracy, there were the charms of being an English
nobleman. There was Broadlands, and the Sligo estate,

and the Welsh slate mine, and the pheasants in Yew Tree Wood, and all those visits to Newmarket. There were Almack's rooms, and Lady Cowper, and Lady Jersey, and Mrs. Petre. There were several highly pleasurable visits to the Continent. Palmerston's advancement may have been slow: it was never monotonous. And as the years passed he acquired much knowledge, some practice in speaking, and many friends.

His second period, the period of dynamic caution, begins with his first term as Foreign Secretary in 1830 and ends with his triumph over Louis Philippe in 1841. Had Palmerston died with the Convention of London, he would have lived in history as the most successful of our Foreign Secretaries. His handling of the Belgian question, his adaptability during that period to Lord Grey, was a masterpiece of temperate and determined negotiation. His handling of events in Spain and Portugal, though at moments eccentric, was in general consistent and reputable. The early stages of the Syrian crisis found a Cabinet unwilling to listen to Palmerston's exhortations, and it was not till July of 1840 that he was given his head. He took it. Beyrout, Sidon, and Acre went up in flames. Ibrahim collapsed, and with him all French hopes of an Arabian protectorate. From this moment Palmerston lost his balance. Instead of sparing the French the discomfiture of humiliation, he ground the face of Guizot in the dust. The Entente crumbled. And four years later Guizot, to the astonishment of Europe, took his revenge. The affair of the Spanish marriages was Palmerston's first serious defeat. It left him with an obsession in favour of diplomatic "victories." He failed to see that no victory is ever diplomatic.

The third stage, the stage of arrogant recklessness, begins in 1841, culminates in the Don Pacifico bluster of 1850, and is interrupted by his dismissal in December, 1851. Is it exaggerated to attribute his unfortunate passion for Napoleon III, not so much to the old friendships of Gore House days, as to an unworthy desire to be revenged on Princess Lieven, Clairemont, and Guizot? It is not fantastic. Palmerston was a supreme egoist, and his views, especially in later life, were coloured and directed by personal animosities. Is it fantastic, again, to contend that we owe the Crimean War to a desire on the part of Palmerston to "score off" Osborne, John Russell, and

always, could best be maintained by the balance of Continental power. Stability by a temperate middle course between the system of Metternich and the disruptive forces of post-war nationalism. He wished, as Professor Temperley has pointed out, to " make the world safe for constitutional democracy." He was not anxious to intervene in the internal affairs of other countries, but he recognized that certain circumstances might (given the policy of the northern Cabinets) render such intervention a " duty." He added the corollary that intervention, if undertaken, should be undertaken with overwhelming force. For Canning understood that *good* diplomacy means *certain* diplomacy: uncertain diplomacy, then as now, was, and is, always bad. Canning understood, moreover, that the major condition of certainty in foreign negotiation is that the negotiator should be backed by the ultimate authority, sovereign in his own country; and that therefore the foreign policy of Great Britain, depending ultimately upon the sovereignty of the electorate, should be " intelligible and popular."

Observe how these excellent axioms were adopted and falsified by Lord Palmerston. To him " self-preservation " became arrogance abroad, and at home the volunteer movement and the hysterical fortification of Portsmouth and Plymouth Hoe. To him the balance of power degenerated into a desire to play off France against Russia without consideration of the shiftings occasioned to that balance by the emergence of Germany and Italy. To him intervention became merely the opportunity for display— overwhelming at moments of sensationalism—claiming a weak alibi when intervention was inconvenient, expensive, or of little news value. For him " national honour " was exemplified by such demonstrations as the Don Pacifico blockade, or by such discreditable expeditions as the Persian and the Opium Wars. In his hands British foreign policy ceased to be either intelligible or consistent: it became " popular " only, and as such it slid down the oiled slope towards sensationalism.

It has been questioned, indeed, whether the expression " democratic diplomacy " is not a contradiction in terms. It has been pointed out that the great democracies are for long periods indifferent to external politics, and that if this indifference is reflected in the Government, a policy of inertia must result. It has also been observed that these phases of indifference are periodically succeeded by phases of sensational interest. Foreign affairs, so soon as they become dramatic, attain to news value. It is almost inevitable to conclude from such premises that popular diplomacy must be either dangerous or inert. That this depressing theory should have taken such a hold upon our political thinkers is intelligible: I should admit myself that it was true to 60 per cent.; yet the remaining 40 per cent. is so important and so essential that its degradation, or at least its retardation, at the hands of Lord Palmerston awakes a protest which accounts for the virulence of our present criticism.

How, then, are we to explain the enigma of Lord Palmerston? He was a man of considerable, if superficial, talent, great energy, dog-like courage, unusual knowledge and experience, and a marked gift for negotiation. Yet he lacked principle. There was in Palmerston no co-ordinating and directive element such as rendered the short dominance of Canning an example to every serious diplomatist of the modern world. Palmerston was spiritually and intellectually shallow. Subconsciously he was aware of this defect, and he therefore essayed the compensations of technical knowledge, recklessness, and popular esteem. Palmerston possessed to an unfortunate degree the spiritual and intellectual indolence of the average Englishman. He was too lazy to envisage the logical conclusions of his own premises. In order to excuse himself he identified such processes of consistency and prevision with the "system" of Metternich; and to his mind Metternich, as we know, was "mostly wrong." Yet the sturdiness of Palmerston was not a mental, still less a moral, but purely a physical sturdiness. He believed that he could navigate the shoals of Continental diplomacy by bluff, a little dexterous opportunism, and frequent appeals "to the English sense of justice and honour." Yet because the gambits of Palmerston could never be referred to any central or directive principle, because it was all too evident that he was manœuvring for a popularity which, as Metternich remarked, "in a statesman is misplaced"—for these reasons, although backed by the plaudits of the multitude and a most efficient fleet, he failed to establish the prestige of England, and succeeded only in perpetuating the legend of her perfidy and cant.

For Palmerston, like all very unpunctual people, was an egoistic man. His attitude to his rivals and his colleagues in the task of diplomacy was both personal and vain. The only two occasions on which he miscalculated the opinion of the man in the street was when he backed Napoleon over the *coup d'état,* and when he backed Napoleon over the Orsini manifesto. In so doing he was governed by his abiding spite against Guizot. On other occasions (Syria, Kossuth, Haynau, even Don Pacifico, the Crimean, even the Opium War) he gauged public opinion to a nicety. " He would," records Greville, " see any newspaper man who called upon him." And thus it came that *Punch* portrayed him as sucking the demagogic straw. And thus it came that he shone for the multitude as " an English nobleman " who stood " for old English truth and feeling." And thus it came that he misled the Court and his own colleagues in the Cabinet. And thus it came that he ended as the prisoner of his own legend.

Palmerston, in his endeavour to shine as the " old English gentleman," became, as the years passed, more and more English and less and less of a gentleman. Deliberately he created the monster of public opinion by which, in 1853, he was himself idolized and overwhelmed. The " intelligible " policy of Canning became in Palmerston's hands merely the " popular " policy, whereby he blackmailed his colleagues and became " hateful and inexplicable " to foreign Courts. His " open covenants " degenerated into press stunts, and when the breeze of popular favour turned for an instant against him, he would not hesitate to fake (as he faked the Burnes reports) the papers which he laid before the House.

" Triumphant and jocund," Palmerston passes down to us in the uncritical pages of *Punch*. We turn again to his earlier statements—to those many pronouncements in which he re-echoed the thoughts of his great master. " Our policy," we read, " is not to intermeddle in the affairs of other countries, but by the legitimate exercise of the influence of Great Britain to support other nations in their struggles to obtain for themselves institutions similar to those which have been described as forming the boast of this country " (June 1840). " The sun," we read again, " never sets upon the interests of this country ; and the individual whose duty it is to watch over its foreign rela-

379

tions would not be worthy of his position if his activity were not commensurate with the extensive range of the great interests which require his attention " (March 1843). " I hold," we read again, " with respect to alliances, that England is a Power sufficiently strong to steer her own course, and not to tie herself as an unnecessary appendage to the policy of any other Government. I hold that the real policy of England is to be the champion of justice and right " (March 1848). " I am aware," we read again, " of the great repugnance to discussion on our foreign relations of many in this House, who think that our duty does not extend beyond an investigation of matters connected with our domestic affairs . . . or who believe that in affairs of foreign politics there is some superior mystery or craft above the comprehension of ordinary men, yet it is high time that such notions should be exploded. . . . There is nothing so mysterious or difficult in our foreign relations as that any man might not grapple with them, who came to the consideration of the subject with an ordinary share of intelligence " (March 1830).

These are high and sensible words ; these are sensible and high-minded pretensions. Had Palmerston lived up to his own rhetoric, had even he lived up to his own demagogy, he might have proved a second and more durable Canning. As it was, he can only be regarded as the first of many Bülows.

WALTER PATER

1839-1894

BY
KATHARINE
GARVIN

WALTER PATER

W HEN Pater wrote that "while all melts under our feet, we may well grasp at any exquisite passion," he declared the ardent purpose of a life devoted to the preservation of beautiful experience. He showed his chosen field of beauty when he wrote that what had interested living men and women could never lose its vitality. Nature he loved, but as a manifold enricher of the human soul. His field was history; in the parts of it that he chose to re-create, in the manner of his re-creation, he indicated two strains of Victorian thought.

He was not so much a great artist as one better than most others of his time. While showing contemporary tendencies, he was not wholly of his time, for he set up a new standard in art. He inherited the happy-go-lucky Romantic treatment of ancient story and art, and he had not lost the inexact love of the past which fires the imagination to original creation. Even more he is of the new academic school which realized the past through detailed reconstruction. Nothing shows this more clearly than his rediscovery of the Renaissance, where he first found the mental qualities that he admired. He found, like Renaissance scholars, a supplementary life in reverent care of the past, and in this he represented the spirit of decadence and rebirth that agitated the thought of his time.

Pater's biographers are oddly half-hearted, as if they were baffled themselves when they tried to discover the man behind his writings. The scant details of his life are less important than his inheritance of history. Jowett is the only person recorded as thinking him remarkable in early life, when he said that his mind might " come to

great eminence;" "bad eminence" he might have substituted, for in Pater's period of flagrant unorthodoxy,
Jowett thought him an unwholesome influence in Oxford.
Scraps of information from his students, lists of distinguished people who numbered him among their friends,
throw no real light on a character evidently difficult of
access.

Enough oddities came out to show his type if not his
real character. He loved cats, and was unself-consciously
sweet to them. He once entered his house with a guest,
picked up his Persian, and kissed it as if it were the most
natural thing in the world. One remembers the white
Angora:

> "With a dark tail like an ermine's, and a face like
> a flower, who fell into a lingering sickness, and became
> quite delicately human in its valetudinarianism, and
> came to have a hundred different expressions of voice
> —how it grew worse and worse, till it began to feel the
> light too much for it, and at last, after one wild morn-
> ing of pain, the little soul flickered away from the
> body."

Of natural emotion his biographies give little trace. He
was so shy that he felt difficulty in greeting people in the
street, and this may have influenced his reserve. He had
some sense of fun, which appears not so much in his laughter
at Gilbert and Sullivan as in his mimicry of Mark Pattison
querulously facing an imaginary burglar; even more in the
dryly caustic remarks he made about lovers and others.
The only trace of wit in his writing is where he says "there
is always something of an excellent talker about the writing
of Mr. Oscar Wilde."

His deference to opinion was natural in a man made
hypersensitive by deformity and a plainness conspicuous
at school. His care for what was thought of him comes out
in many ways, some straightforward, some perverse. A
healthy instinct made him dislike being called a hedonist,
"because it produces such a bad effect on the minds of people
who don't know Greek." It was also rational, though hardly
courageous, to suppress the original conclusion to *Renaissance Studies,* because he thought that it might mislead
young men. But perversity is discernible in the defiant
way in which he delighted in shocking people with his
rejection of Christianity. That he had some religious

instinct is evident from his writings. At first it seems to have been a love of order and ethics rather than a genuine mystic sense; and when he came back to the fold, in later life, he seems to have found it a refuge from the inexorable loneliness of the soul.

The general impression of his character is colourless. People found him a sweet and entertaining companion, his manner affected only before strangers, through shyness. His only concessions to external æstheticism were an apple-green tie, and rooms attractive through rare ornaments. His life showed no signs of great joy or great suffering; and the conception of a timid, effete personality, disturbed by high and right ideals, is borne out by his writings. His judgment is often invalidated by the shallowness of his experience. His comments seldom lead to a deeper insight of his subjects. His treatment of death, birth, love, and religion are usually either sentimental or insensitive; and when he writes pure criticism, whether of Wordsworth, Rossetti, or Michelangelo, he communicates no real enthusiasm because, one feels, half of what these artists express is beyond his little ken.

By far the most interesting phase of his work is that of the imaginary portraits. *The Child in the House* is the earliest essay in which description and meditation centre round a vague yet vividly emotional figure. In it Pater used not historical but semi-autobiographical material. In *Marius* he discovered how to combine psychology with scholarship in the admirable mould of a character working out a perennial problem but placed in ancient surroundings.

The portraits are the climax to Pater's art, his true contribution to literature. Not only do they bear a new form, but they offered a fitting scope to Pater's talent, which was vague and uneasy unless related to a particular mind. His paragraph on *Mona Lisa* feels towards a history of that lady, and his comments are a sort of ghost of an imaginary portrait. He used this vehicle to confess himself, by projecting aspects of his own mind and supplying qualities that he would like to have had as well as physical traits that were denied him. In statement of his own difficulties in historical conditions, he had something to say for which his peculiar wedding of prose and meditation were uniquely suitable.

Like much writing of our own day, Pater's work is

episodic, incapable of sustainment. *Marius* shows how difficult he found it to preserve unity and proportion when dealing with material of more than a certain length. A contradiction between standards and talents is not uncommon; and just as Pater drew characters with something like his own mind, but with the beauty he so sadly lacked, so he, the apostle of beautiful form, lacked structural and architectural form in his writings. Critics are used to acclaiming him in a lukewarm way, reverting to the comforting fact that at least he was a good stylist. It is certainly true that one cannot read his work without becoming drugged or bewildered through the style; but it is not true that he was a good stylist. He had a finicking regard for the euphonious or the obscure word, but he lacked the clarity of mind essential to style. He had no idea how to construct a sentence, and it is odd that, classical scholar as he was, the study of the economy of Latin prose had no effect on his own. His sentences are seldom lucid and their rhythm is jerky. He tried to obtain rhythm without having it in his thought, and without having mastered the technique of English style which is at least as complicated as Latin. A recent student of his technique finds that he is often ungrammatical, using, for example, the horrible vulgarism of " like " for " as "; and that he habitually left rhetorical ambiguities, such as change of subject or tense, awkward parenthesis, false subordination, and non-structural appendages. Confusion and muddle are, after all, defects in one who professed to be a careful writer, and whose style has been his chief claim to admiration. As his method of composition would lead one to suspect, his style has the appearance of being composed of afterthoughts, not unlike Milton's prose in its effect, though without Milton's force. The bones of Pater's work are weak and shaky; and good style cannot be without a fundamentally bold design.

Ornamentation is stuck on as it is so often in Victorian Gothic, whereas in true Gothic the decoration develops out of the utilitarian line. Still, what Pater lacks in structure he makes up for in incident and ornament. He was particular in choosing words. Sometimes indefiniteness prevails, as when he calls a cat " the furry visitor "; and sometimes he is entranced with an unusual word like " mysticity," which he wears to death, and uses incorrectly. More often he conveys admirably definite impres-

sions in small compass by using words that another might
have overlooked, and by suggesting " their first meaning."
He was a dreamer, a meanderer among by-ways of thought
rather than a systematic thinker. So words interested him
more than sentences or paragraphs, and this is another
reason why the portraits give him better opportunity than
criticism or philosophy. His best effects convey a visual
image:

> " On the soft slope of one of those fresh spaces in
> the wood, where the trees unclose a little, while Jean
> Baptiste and my youngest sister danced a minuet on
> the grass, to the notes of some strolling lutanist who
> had found us out."

Such miniatures abound in his work, as false to life as
they would be true to painting, yet with more atmosphere
than painting can give. They are the best of what he had
to say—the crystallization of casual experience.

What stands out most from his thought is a recurrent
theme of lifelessness. Contrasting mediæval art with
Greek, he recalls Fra Angelico's *Coronation of the Virgin,*
where Mary, he says, is " corpse-like in her refinement."
A synonymity of death with refinement pervades his work.
However he may deplore it in particular instances, it is
nevertheless one of his ideals. Greek art, he says, like
death, sets the features free of emotion, leaving more play
for splendid vitality of body. The English kings " seem to
lie composed in Shakespeare's embalming pages." These
qualities give the character of his own art better than they
delineate his subjects. The composure that he has chosen
to see indicates his own peculiar quality of mind.

He combines an extraordinary certitude of style with
restlessness of subject-matter. His own writing is corpse-
like in refinement, in purgation of all that is turbulent or
accidental ; vigour and passion are chastened and em-
balmed. His work is like Snow-white in her crystal coffin,
with the colours of life gleaming through, but the sculptured resignation of death ; or like the Sleeping Beauty,
whose slumbers must have given her features the dignity
of death without its decay. Life absolved from reality is
his gift to literature. He lacked vitality, not the appreciation of it, and his treatment is more concentrated because
he lived almost entirely in the mind.

His preference for death leads him to select the decadent

aspects of civilizations. In *Marius* he shows a Greek system
of philosophy in its Roman survival, but about to succumb
to Christianity. He seldom goes, in the mediæval period,
before the fourteenth century, when the civilizing process
had all but destroyed vigour, and when artificiality with
its adorable elaborations more and more took the place
of Nature. He ignores the vigorous and classic side of
the Middle Ages, and almost apologizes for Old French
assonance as merely imperfect rhyme. From the *Roland,*
he comments only on the "fair, priestly hands of Archbishop Turpin." The friendship of Roland and Oliver,
typical of what was best between man and man in early
Europe, he does not mention; and when he speaks of
friendship, he turns to *Amys and Amile,* where exaggerated
sacrifice for a friend replaces the stronger epic presentation
of love and loyalty. For the weight, the strength of great
art—consider Æschylus, Praxiteles, Chartres—he has no
use, overlooks it when it is there, or dismisses it as
grotesque. One remembers that he called excessive emotion
grotesque, finding an ideal in temperance. Pater represents grace, elegance, and quiet dignity, things needed in
his period of much bad form. His art is admirable for
achieving them in the expression of spiritual disturbance.

His criticism of painting stresses certain aspects in the
same way. He may have been incapable of seeing otherwise, but one gathers that his vision was a chosen one. He
said that he could hardly read a chapter of Stevenson or
a line of Kipling because he felt them to be strong writers,
and he did not wish to be turned by their direction from
his chosen path. His interpretation of art may also be
dominated by wilful blindness to elements that are there
for the ordinary looker. Botticelli's madonnas seem
peevish to him, he finds something "mean or abject" in
them; while of Venus he suggests "that the sorrow in her
face was at the whole long day of love yet to come." He
harps upon an imaginary sadness, for which he mistakes
a tender thoughtfulness that in faces of a sober cast has
the appearance of melancholy.

Pater habitually misread the expressions of women, as
he was sometimes rude to them in life, and this incapacity
for understanding half of humanity is one of his weaknesses. "Women," he said, "can perceive neither truth
when they encounter it, nor beauty where it really exists";
and though he should not be condemned any more than

St. Paul for generalizing about the sex, yet his prejudice damaged his comprehension of men and their motives. The fine portrait of Sebastian van Storck breaks down when the hero is concerned with Mademoiselle van Westrheene, because she is too coldly drawn to give Sebastian's revulsion from her the force that it ought to have. Other comments on men fail because their relation with women is imperfectly understood. Of Gaston he says: " For him, on the other hand, ' the pity of it,' the pity of the thing supplied all that had been wanting in its first consecration, and made the lost mistress really a wife."

A similar lack of delicacy and perception shows throughout his work whenever he touches on human relationships. He sees the pictorial and theatrical side of a situation, and in groping for words for what he cannot comprehend, falls back upon the trite : " The virginal first period of their married life in their dainty house in Paris—the pure and beautiful picture of the mother, the father, and at last the child, a little girl, Jeanne." Neither " virginal " nor " dainty " is adequate ; and it is hardly necessary to add the epithet " little " to a new-born child. The same young mother looks at her husband with " the moist suppliant eyes of some weak animal at bay." The fault is not that the persons described are unreal, for unreal beauty can convey real emotion ; but here there is neither feeling nor knowledge of it.

Pater could see shallow distinctions between characters, but he was too æsthetic to deal with the depth of human motives. Life in blankness, dignity, austerity is the object of his admiration, and in consequence false emotional situations abound in his work. Emerald Uthwart, schoolboy, rose and said to the master, " And now, sir, that I have taken my punishment, I hope you will forgive my fault." Flavian, dying, said that it would be no comfort that Marius should come and weep over him—" Unless I be aware and hear you weeping." Seldom a touch in Pater's characters identifies them as human beings. The truest is Sebastian van Storck, but even he, after vindicating the intellectual fanatic's right to seclusion, must die nobly in saving a child—a sentimental ending typical of Pater.

We must approach Pater, to do him justice, as a pictorial and dramatic artist. He did not, like Swinburne and Rossetti, try his hand at sculpture or painting ; but he was nevertheless meant for a plastic artist. Cinematography, if one can imagine it well coloured, would have been the ideal medium for his mind. The beauty of changing scenes on the films have a true emotional value which is possible in no other art. The beauty of Pater's work lies in certain impressions of character or mood seen pictorially with a grace caused by spiritual motion. In this way certain feelings are treated validly, and are full of meaning. The effect is often as inconsequential as some of T. S. Eliot's poetry, because it moves the imagination through the half-conscious mind.

The stress on lifelessness apparent in Pater's criticism and in his choice of decadent periods of history is an integral part of his temper which he himself recognized and described. A haunting fear of death probably assailed him early, for the *Child in the House* shows a child's pre-occupation:

> "He would think of Julian, fallen into incurable sickness, as spoiled in the sweet blossom of his skin like pale amber and his honey-like hair; of Cecil early dead, as cut off from the lilies, from golden summer days, from women's voices; and then what comforted him a little was the thought of the turning of the child's flesh to violets in the turf above him."

The impressionability of childhood with its clinging fancies is well-drawn; but how false, though lovely, is the sentimental thought of graveyard violets shows up if one compares Sir Thomas Browne's passage about flesh turning to grass. The obsession for mortality persisted in Pater. He found it in the poetry of his time:

> "One characteristic of the pagan spirit the æsthetic poetry has, which is on its surface—the continual suggestion, pensive or passionate, of the shortness of life. This is contrasted with the bloom of the world, and gives new seduction to it—the sense of death and the desire of beauty; the desire of beauty quickened by the sense of death."

And his keen resolution to reclaim moments of beauty must have been due to some such seduction. Sebastian van Storck, in some ways the most like him of his characters, had the same leaning, and the following passage

about him shows the idea tangled up with that of the evan-
escence of beauty:

> " He seemed . . . in love with death; preferring
> winter to summer; finding only a tranquillizing in-
> fluence in the thought of the earth beneath our feet
> cooling down for ever from its old cosmic heat; watch-
> ing pleasurably how their colours fled out of things,
> and the long sand-bank in the sea, which had been the
> rampart of a town, was washed down in its turn."

Even in reviews, Pater chose to quote passages that give
a picturesque aspect of death. From Symonds's *Italian
Renaissance* he selected the lovely Roman dug up in the
fourteenth century " fairer than any woman of the modern
age could hope to be." From another writer he found a
passage about a dead child, where the horror of the conception is mitigated by the sensuous beauty of the suggestion of colour. He quoted another about Flaubert's sister
buried in her wedding-gown amid bunches of roses, violets,
and immortelles. Death was only palatable to him in
sensuously beautiful guise; and many passages of his own
writing describe memorable images of death. Emerald
Uthwart is described in his coffin with a red soldier's coat,
covered with flowers, the peak of his nose emerging, the
wind ruffling his hair. There is the spectacle of Aurelius
with his dying child in his arms; of the white Angora; of
the death of Flavian; and there is that outrage to the
Catholic Faith which compares a church containing the
sacrament to a house where " lay a dead friend," the whole
point of Christianity being that this friend is living.

His usual image of death in fair serenity gives place
sometimes to a more gloomy scene:

> " The storm which followed was still in possession,
> still moving tearfully among the poplar groves, though
> it had spent its heat and thunder. The last drops of
> the blood of Hyacinth still trickled through the thick
> masses of dark hair, where the tonsure had been. An
> abundant rain, mingling with the copious purple
> stream, had coloured the grass all around where
> the corpse lay, stealing afar in tiny channels."

And here another strain shows, Pater's attraction to a

sort of pagan occultism with suggestion of reincarnation
and possession, mingled with crude savagery. The subject
of the essay from which this passage comes is a monk who
reincarnates Apollo, but whose soul is not so much of the
Greek sun-god as of the dark spirit that mediæval popular
theology made of him. Similarly, *Denys l'Auxerrois* is the
reborn wine-god, influencing people and clergy joyfully
and evilly. Atrocities to animals and humans are suggested in both studies; and both men have the fairness of
aspect which seems to have been matter of mistrust to
Pater's mediæval populace, and perhaps to himself. His
attempts to convey a macabre atmosphere are not wholly
successful. The lynching of Denys and the tearing of his
flesh into shreds is described too politely to give the proper
Grand Guignol effect of grim exultance. Algernon Cecil
speaks of an " unwholesome fascination " in the *Renais-*
sance Studies " which few of us are so right-minded as not
in some degree to feel " ; but in the *Renaissance* it is not so
apparent as in these sketches and in parts of *Greek Studies*.
It belongs to the same school of æstheticism, mingled
with unhealthy weirdness, that produced Vernon Lee's
Wicked Voice, and Oscar Wilde's *Fisherman and his*
Soul.

Through Pater's vacillation and morbidity shines a
genuine passion for passion. The tragedy is that he seemed
unable to realize it ; he spent his mental life seeking sensuous stimulants from reading and painting. The best essay
that he wrote, on *Æsthetic Poetry,* contains a full blossom-
ing of feeling for the first and only time. It is, unusually
for Pater, distinguished by complete certainty of thought
and style, without rambling either of sentence or paragraph. A sane ardour shows in majestic and lucid phraseology. He strongly declares here what he suggests in
other places, that the beauty he approved was an emotional
one rooted in physical desire, and harmonious with the
great body of nature. He contrasts William Morris's
manner between *Guenevere* and *Jason,* comparing the two
to twilight and morning phases of life. Incidentally he
introduces an observation of psychological truth which
shows that he could handle the travail of the human spirit
when he was not too ambitious. He says:

" Those, in whom what Rousseau calls *les frayeurs*
nocturnes are constitutional, know what splendour

they give to the things of the morning; and how there comes something of relief from physical pain with the first white film in the sky."

Jason has something of this morning relief; and in it, says Pater, "Desire . . . is towards the body of nature for its own sake, not because a soul is divined through it." Here he is frankly on the side of strength and grandeur; and gives a salutary warning to his age and ours when he says:

> "Complex and subtle interests, which the mind spins for itself, may occupy art and poetry or our own spirits for a time; but sooner or later they come back with a sharp rebound to the simple elementary passions —anger, desire, regret, pity and fear, and what corresponds to them in the sensuous world."

The whole essay moves like Bach's composition, without a false step. Yet he suppressed it for twenty years, published it, and suppressed it again.

If it be true that this essay was "too intimate to be anything but a source of anxiety to himself," its suppression explains Pater's failure of greatness. He knew the magnificence of elementary things and the dangers of subtlety. Yet, like Gaston's, one side of his nature craved the twilight. He portrayed art and humanity as fantastic and neurotic. He deplored the "over-wrought spiritualities" even while he exalted them when he spoke of "that passionate stress of spirit which the world owes to Christianity." The blame for the conflict rests partly on his age, for indecision of ideal is characteristic of his time. He longed for a return to the life of the senses, but he was limited by a gentility which was of his period, and partly (though this is a matter of conjecture) by physical and psychological disabilities accentuated by an academic life. The contention between meekness and savagery, the primitive and civilized, ethics and beauty, explains his love for characters like Denys and Apollyon. He was an artist who found escape, and fulfilment of life in writing; but in him neither escape nor fulfilment was complete, because he was held back by the reserve of his Dutch blood, heightened by inheritance of the conventional rigidities of Victorian England. But in this age, when muddled thought and nonsensical vision are often dignified by the name of

393

poetic genius, it is well to remember Pater's austere pronouncement:

> " The legitimate contention is, not of one age or school of literary art against another, but of all successive schools alike, against the stupidity which is dead to the substance, and the vulgarity which is dead to form."

COVENTRY PATMORE

1823-1896

BY
HERBERT
READ

COVENTRY PATMORE

COVENTRY PATMORE was recently described as " the most neglected of our notable poets ; " [1] even his grave we were told, is untended, and fit to illustrate one of his best lines :

> " *The darnell'd garden of unheedful death.*"

And this would seem to be all the comment which time has made on the proud words which Patmore placed in front of the collected edition of his poems : " I have respected posterity ; and, should there be a posterity which cares for letters, I dare to hope it will respect me."

Perhaps we have not lived long enough to earn the name of posterity ; perhaps we do not care sufficiently for letters to honour the grave of a poet who made no compromise with the public of his own day, and can therefore expect none from the public of ours. But that is not the real truth. Whenever a critic of faithful conscience recalls the poets of this period—Tennyson, Arnold, Clough, Patmore, Browning, Rossetti—it is on the name of Patmore that he lingers with a still lively sense of wonder. The rest have been fully estimated, and their influence, if not exhausted, is predictable. Patmore is still potential ; but to what extent, and whether purely as a poet or more likely as a mystic, are questions which must be answered in this general stock-taking.

That arrogance which dominates all contemporary accounts of Patmore's personality is the first quality we must dwell on, because it is a reflex of the man's relation

[1] By Mr. Clifford Bax, in *The Times Literary Supplement*, May 12th, 1932.

to his age. No poet—indeed, no personality of the whole period—stands in such direct opposition to all its beliefs and ideals—perhaps we should say, finally stood in such opposition, for Patmore's settled attitude did not develop until middle age. He began his career with family circumstances which explain a good deal—a harsh, unsympathetic mother, and a father who, though sympathetic to the extent of spoiling him in every direction—particularly in the direction of a literary career—was regarded by the world at large as a cad and impostor, till he finally fled the country to escape his financial entanglements. Such circumstances are bound to produce in a sensitive nature " defence " compensations which take on the appearance of self-assertion and intellectual arrogance. And these are perhaps the very factors which, whilst they explain the " drive " of a personality like Patmore's, also give us a clue to its creative limitations.

Patmore once declared that he was the only poet of his generation, except Barnes, who steadily maintained a literary conscience. This is perfectly true. He was a *clerc* who never betrayed that tradition of intellectual integrity of which every poet should be the trustee. Everything he wrote was written with a great sense of responsibility, not only to the public, but to his own inner light or inspiration. Though his first considerable work, *The Angel in the House,* won an immense popularity, he deliberately turned his back on this success, to pursue a path implicit in his faith which led him to intellectual heights where no considerable public could then follow, and which will always be reserved for the select. In politics he was bitterly opposed to all parties. Gladstone he abhorred so thoroughly that he could write of him :

" *His leprosy's so perfect, men call him clean* " ;

and his scorn of Disraeli and " the false English Nobles " was equally vitriolic. In contrast to the prevailing economic and political optimism, he adopted views of unrelieved pessimism. He saw himself (alone with Barnes !) as the last classical author of a civilization on the verge of extinction :

> " Unpalatable and unacceptable as the suggestion may be, it cannot be denied by persons who are able and willing to look facts in the face, that there are already strong indications of a relapse into a long-

protracted period of social and political disorganiza-
tion, so complete that there shall be no means of leisure
or even living for a learned class, nor any audience for
what it has to impart. Such recrudescences of civilization have occurred, and they may occur again, though
the prospect may be as incredible to most Europeans
at the present moment as it must have been to the lieges
of the Eternal City at the height and sudden turning-
point of its popular glory and seemingly consolidated
order."

In religion he became, again in opposition to the intellectual trend of his period, a Catholic of the most mystical
type ; and even in his religion he was so little in sympathy
with its temporal vessels that he continually murmured
against the priesthood and even against the Pope.
This attitude was maintained with courage and absence
of reserve. " Plain-speaking," he says in one of his
essays, " does not vitiate. Even coarseness is health
compared with those suppressed forms of the disease of
impurity which come of our modern undivine silences."
And it was one of his first principles that there existed
an absolute incompatibility between genius and any kind
of insincerity. This belief is stated with great force in an
essay in *Religio Poetæ,* the purpose of which is to distinguish the intellect from the understanding (or discursive
reason) and the memory as the peculiar faculty of genius :

"The intellect is the faculty of the ' seer.' It discerns truth as a living thing ; and, according as it is in
less or greater power, it discerns with a more or less
far-seeing glance the relationships of principles to each
other, and of facts, circumstances, and the realities of
nature to principles, without anything that can be
properly called ratiocination. It cannot be cultivated,
as the understanding and memory can be and need to
be ; and it cannot, in the ordinary course of things, be
injured, except by one means—namely, dishonesty,
that is, habitual denial by the will, for the sake of interested or vicious motives, of its own perceptions.
Genius and high moral—not necessarily physical—
courage are therefore found to be constant companions.
Indeed, it is difficult to say how far an absolute moral

399

courage in acknowledging intuitions may not be of the very nature of genius : and whether it might not be described as a sort of interior sanctity which dares to see and confess to itself that it sees, though its vision should place it in a minority of one."

This courage Patmore himself possessed in the highest degree, and certainly he did not shrink from finding himself in a minority of one. Admitting this, it only remains for us to consider critically the quality of his vision and his ability to make this vision objective.

Perhaps we might consider the more technical question first. By this I mean Patmore's whole conception of poetry as an art, and then his own particular style. Both aspects of the question give rise to the most searching doubts. The problem is simplified for us by the compactness and cohesion of Patmore's verse. It can without loss be reduced to two parts—to two sequences of poems distinct in style if not in matter. *The Angel in the House* was one of the most characteristic and certainly one of the most successful poems of the whole Victorian age : it had sold over a quarter of a million copies before the author's death. The first part was originally published in 1854; the final part in 1863. It belongs to that bastard type of literature—the novel in verse—and has much of the atmosphere and, for those who like it, the charm of the domestic fiction of the period. It was fairly characterized by Edmund Gosse as "humdrum stories of girls that smell of bread and butter."

Defect of presentation explains why *The Angel* is not read to-day; and I can imagine no posterity which will reverse our present inclination in this matter. This poem has become and will remain a literary curiosity, not justified by any remarkable beauties even of texture or expression. For it has to be admitted that Patmore, at this stage of his inspiration, was no inevitable poet. He chose a simple metre for his simple subject—iambic octosyllabic—and laboured hard to make it smooth. But as Tennyson said, some of his lines seemed "hammered up out of old nails," and though such lines were pointed out to him, he was often incapable of seeing anything wrong with them, and there are plenty left in the final version. That would not matter so much if there were corresponding jewels of highest light, to outshine these defects; but actually the texture is sustained at an even level of apt but uninspired expression. It is wit-writing of an extremely competent and felicitous kind, but it is not, and perhaps never pretended to be, lyrical poetry of any emotional intensity.

Yet no poet since Wordsworth and Coleridge, not even Matthew Arnold, had such a clear conception of the poet's function. In that essay, extremely compressed with sense, which gives the title to the volume *Religio Poetæ,* we find the best expression of Patmore's views. The Poet is compared with the Saint: he is above all the *perceiver,*

> " nothing having any interest for him unless he can, as it were, see it and touch it with the spiritual senses, with which he is pre-eminently endowed.
>
> " The Poet, again, is not more singular for the delicacy of his spiritual insight, which enables him to see celestial beauty and substantial reality where all is blank to most others, than for the surprising range and alertness of vision, whereby he detects, in external nature, those likenesses and echoes by which spiritual realities can alone be rendered credible and more or less apparent, or subject to ' real apprehension,' in persons of inferior perceptive powers. Such likenesses, when chosen by the imagination, not the fancy, of the true Poet, are *real* words—the only real words; for ' that which is unseen is known by that which is seen,' and natural similitudes often contain, and are truly the visible *ultimates* of the unseen. . . .
>
> " He gives the world to eat only of the Tree of Life, reality; and will not so much as touch the Tree of Knowledge, as the writer of Genesis ironically calls the Tree of Learning that leads to denial of knowledge. He is the very reverse of a ' scientist.' "

This emphasis on the realism of words is in advance of anything suggested by Coleridge. It is to be found in Vico, whom Patmore could hardly have read, but only receives its full development in the present-day theories of Croce, Vivante, and Mr. I. A. Richards. It was his firm faith in this theory which reconciled Patmore to the intermittency of his inspiration. When a poet *knows* what poetry is, he cannot be false to his genius. It would be a spiritual betrayal which could only end in spiritual death. Patmore had genius enough to perceive this, and I think that it was this very concentration on the nature of poetry which led

Q

him towards the wider mysticism of the Catholic faith. In another essay in *Religio Poetæ* he says:

> "The most peculiar and characteristic mark of genius is insight into subjects which are dark to ordinary vision and for which ordinary language has no adequate expression. Imagination is rather the language of genius: the power which traverses at a single glance the whole external universe, and seizes on the likenesses and images, and their combinations, which are best able to embody ideas and feelings otherwise inexpressible; so that the 'things which are unseen are known by the things which are seen.'"

And elsewhere he says:

> "Sensible things alone can be expressed fully and directly by sensible terms. Symbols and parable, and metaphors—which are parables on a small scale—are the only means of adequately conveying, or rather hinting, supersensual knowledge."

Patmore's own poetry, in its final and most important phase, was to become just such a hinting at supersensual knowledge. But this change of spirit was dependent on a change of form.

Patmore's poetic technique received an immense impetus from his invention of what was virtually a new verse-form —the "Ode," which he began to use about 1865. A certain degree of originality in formal structure has perhaps been a condition of all exceptional poetry—novelty of means acting as a spur to any kind of individual attainment. Edmund Gosse was of the opinion that Patmore found the analogy for his "Ode" in the *Canzoniere* of Petrarch. Patmore himself tried to find a sanction for his form in the historical development of the Ode in English poetry, but these pedantic notions of his are not very convincing. The form, in fact, developed under the stress of a particular mode of feeling. To quote a comparatively simple example:

"A FAREWELL

> "With all my will, but much against my heart,
> We two now part.
> My Very Dear,
> Our solace is, the sad road lies so clear.

> *It needs no art,*
> *With faint, averted feet*
> *And many a tear,*
> *In our opposed paths to persevere.*
> *Go thou to East, I West.*
> *We will not say*
> *There's any hope, it is so far away.*
> *But, O, my Best,*
> *When the one darling of our widowhead,*
> *The nursling Grief,*
> *Is dead,*
> *And no dews blur our eyes*
> *To see the peach-bloom come in evening skies,*
> *Perchance we may,*
> *Where now this night is day,*
> *And even through faith of still averted feet,*
> *Making full circle of our banishment,*
> *Amazed meet;*
> *The bitter journey to the bourne so sweet*
> *Seasoning the termless feast of our content*
> *With tears of recognition never dry."*

It will be seen that the Patmorean ode is, in short, an iambic measure (like that of *The Angel in the House*), which, however, breaks away from the regularity of the octosyllabic couplet or quatrain to indulge in what Patmore himself called " the fine irregular rock of the free tetrameter." The verse in these Odes moves " in long, undulating strains " which are modulated by pauses and irregularly occurring rhymes, the rhymed words determining the length of the lines which vary arbitrarily from two to ten or even twelve syllables. It is therefore a metre of extraordinary freedom and impetuous force—which only needed the freedom of stress introduced by Patmore's friend Hopkins to give us all the constituents of modern free verse. " The beauty and incomparable variety of the metre," wrote Patmore in a letter published in Mr. Champneys' *Memoirs,* " opens up quite a new prospect to me of the possibilities of poetry " ; and again: " I have hit upon *the* finest metre that ever was invented, and on *the* finest mine of wholly unworked material that ever fell to the lot of an English poet."

The Odes, begun about 1865, represent Patmore's output for the rest of his life—about thirty years ; and yet they only occupy a hundred pages in the collected edition of his works. This comparative paucity may be explained by the high standard of literary morality which Patmore set himself. " Every one of my books," he wrote, " has been written after many years of reflection on its subject—reflection for my own benefit, not primarily with a view to the book—and has been merely the easy and rapid overflowing into words of the fullness of thought at last attained." And as a corollary to this we find him saying: " My best things were written most quickly. ' Amelia ' took four days; ' Deliciæ Sapientiæ de Amore ' two hours; several of the best Odes even less." Perhaps it was a mistake thus to wait for thought voluntarily to move harmonious numbers —perhaps it is always a mistake to conceive poetry as a species of divine visitation—Hopkins was of that opinion. But Patmore made this attendance on inspiration almost an article of religious faith, and though he worked in preparation for a poem with solemn deliberation, he never once forced his muse to unwilling expression.

Possibly an explanation of the intermittency of his inspiration is to be found in the nature of Patmore's personality. He himself was fond of making a distinction between the masculine and the feminine mind in literature. For instance, in his essay on " Mrs. Meynell," he says:

> " A strong and predominatingly masculine mind has
> often much to say, but a very imperfect ability to say
> it; the predominatingly feminine mind can say any-
> thing, but has nothing to say; but with the double-
> sexed insight of genius, realities and expressions are
> wedded from their first conceptions, and, even in their
> least imposing developments, are living powers, and
> of more practical importance than the results of the
> highest efforts of mind when either of its factors greatly
> predominates over the other."

He found Mrs. Meynell too deficient in this " *ultimate* womanhood, the expressional *body*," to give her a right to be counted among the classical poets. The same charge might, I think, be made against Patmore himself. Edmund Gosse [1] records that—

> " during the debatable period between his first wife's
> death and his second marriage, Patmore's ideas with

[1] *Coventry Patmore*, by Edmund Gosse (1905), pp. 124-5.

regard to poetry underwent a very remarkable change. In later life he was accustomed to insist on the essential oneness of his work, and to point to its uniform features. But setting his eloquent casuistry aside, the reader cannot fail to see a very broad chasm lying between what he wrote up to 1862, and what he wrote after that date. In the first place, the appeal to a popular judgment, to a wide circle of amiable readers, entirely disappears. Patmore, with the removal of so many earthly ties, and with the growth of what was mystical and transcendental in his temperament, became haughty in his attitude to the world. His conscientiousness as an artist was quickened, and at the same time he gave way to a species of intellectual arrogance which had always been dormant in his nature, but which now took the upper hand."

This intellectual arrogance represents a certain settling of his fluent feminine personality, the psychological condition of his poetic force, along firm lines of masculine character inhibitive to this force, and there can be little doubt that this tendency was immensely accelerated by the decision he had to make about this time—he had not only to compromise in some degree with his doctrine of the inviolability of nuptial love, but concurrently was impelled by his conscience to make the final act of submission and become a member of the Catholic Church. The complex strands of this psychological development cannot be unravelled here (they are explicit enough in the faithful account of his conversion which he wrote in 1888), and I am far from suggesting that this individual case reveals any general rule; but in plain fact Patmore did emerge from this mental turmoil with his masculine arrogance intensified, and with the frequency (but not the intensity) of his poetic impulse in consequence impaired.

It is time now to consider the substance of Patmore's poetry. Mr. Arthur Symons once described Patmore as "a poet of one idea and of one metre," and it is indeed amazing to see the alacrity with which he first adopted his central idea, and the tenacity with which he developed it and intensified it. Already in the more philosophical parts of *The Angel in the House*—in those Preludes and Devices which interrupt the narrative and in "the Wedding Sermon" with which it concludes—Patmore had outlined his

405

conception of love. Incidentally, these Preludes often display a complex fusion of fantasy and wit which put them on the highest level of English metaphysical poetry: I quote "The Amaranth" as an example of this type:

> *"Feasts satiate; stars distress with height;*
>   *Friendship means well, but misses reach,*
> *And wearies in its best delight*
>   *Vex'd with the vanities of speech;*
> *Too long regarded, roses even*
>   *Afflict the mind with fond unrest;*
> *And to converse direct with Heaven*
>   *Is oft a labour in the breast;*
> *Whate'er the up-looking soul admires,*
>   *Whate'er the senses' banquet be,*
> *Fatigues at last with vain desires,*
>   *Or sickens by satiety;*
> *But truly my delight was more*
>   *In her to whom I'm bound for aye*
> *Yesterday than the day before,*
>   *And more to-day than yesterday."*

As for the philosophy which underlies the whole structure of *The Angel*, and which was to be developed into rarer mystical concepts in the Odes, it has never been better summarized than by Patmore himself in an essay on "Love and Poetry" which appears in *Religio Poetæ*:

"The whole of after-life depends very much upon how life's transient transfiguration in youth by love is subsequently regarded; and the greatest of all the functions of the poet is to aid in his readers the fulfilment of the cry, which is that of nature as well as religion, 'Let not my heart forget the things mine eyes have seen.' The greatest perversion of the poet's function is to falsify the memory of that transfiguration of the senses and to make light of its sacramental character. This character is instantly recognized by the unvitiated heart and apprehension of every youth and maiden; but it is very easily forgotten and profaned by most, unless its sanctity is upheld by priests and poets. Poets are naturally its prophets—all the more powerful because, like the prophets of old, they are wholly independent of the priests, and are often the first to discover and rebuke the lifelessness into which that order is always tending to fall. If society is to survive its apparently impending dangers, it must be mainly by guarding and increasing the purity of the sources in which society begins. The world is finding out, as it has often done before, that it cannot do without religion. Love is the first thing to wither under its loss. What love does in transfiguring life, that religion does in transfiguring love: as anyone may see who compares one state or time with another. Love is sure to be something less than human if it is not something more; and the so-called extravagances of the youthful heart, which always claim a character for divinity in its emotions, fall necessarily into sordid, if not shameful, reaction, if those claims are not justified to the understanding by the faith which declares man and woman to be priest and priestess to each other of relations inherent in Divinity itself, and proclaimed in the words, ' Let us make man in our own image ' and ' male and female created he them.' "

The mystical developments of this philosophy received a perfect prose expression in that lost masterpiece, the *Sponsa Dei*, which Patmore destroyed when Hopkins warned him that it was " telling secrets," and that he ought to submit it to his spiritual director. Edmund Gosse, who had read the manuscript, says that " no existing specimen of Patmore's prose seems to me so delicate, so penetrated by quite so high a charm of style." And the subject, he says,

" was certainly audacious. It was not more or less than an interpretation of the love between the soul and God by an analogy of the love between a woman and a man; it was, indeed, a transcendental treatise on divine desire seen through the veil of human desire. The purity and crystalline passion of the writer carried him safely over the most astounding difficulties."

One cannot help regretting the destruction of this work (as we regret the poems which Hopkins, for similar scruples, himself destroyed), but actually I doubt if much of the substance of Patmore's doctrine has been lost. It is all implicit in the Odes, and in that book of maxims which is one of the greatest of Patmore's achievements, " *The Rod, the Root, and the Flower* " (an English work which it is not

Q*   407

wholly ridiculous to compare with Pascal's *Pensées*). The
following Ode, "To the Body," may be given as an example of the daring, and the impetuosity (there are only
three sentences in it), and the final intensity of Patmore's
poetry:

> " *Creation's and Creator's crowning good;*
> *Wall of infinitude;*
> *Foundation of the sky,*
> *In Heaven forecast*
> *And long'd for from eternity,*
> *Though laid the last;*
> *Reverberating dome,*
> *Of music cunningly built home*
> *Against the void and indolent disgrace*
> *Of unresponsive space;*
> *Little sequester'd pleasure-house*
> *For God and for His Spouse;*
> *Elaborately, yes, past conceiving, fair,*
> *Since, from the graced decorum of the hair,*
> *Ev'n to the tingling, sweet*
> *Soles of the simple, earth-confiding feet,*
> *And from the inmost heart*
> *Outwards unto the thin*
> *Silk curtains of the skin,*
> *Every least part*
> *Astonish'd hears*
> *And sweet replies to some like region of the spheres;*
> *Form'd for a dignity prophets but darkly name,*
> *Less shameless men cry ' Shame!'*
> *So rich with wealth conceal'd*
> *That Heaven and Hell fight chiefly for this field;*
> *Clinging to everything that pleases thee*
> *With indefectible fidelity;*
> *Alas, so true*
> *To all thy friendships that no grace*
> *Thee from thy sin can wholly disembrace;*
> *Which thus 'bides with thee as the Jebusite,*
> *That, maugre all God's promises could do,*
> *The chosen People never conquer'd quite;*
> *Who therefore lived with them,*
> *And that by formal truce and as of right,*
> *In metropolitan Jerusalem.*
> *For which false fealty*

> *Thou needs must, for a season, lie*
> *In the grave's arms, foul and unshriven,*
> *Albeit, in Heaven,*
> *Thy crimson-throbbing Glow*
> *Into its old abode aye pants to go,*
> *And does with envy see*
> *Enoch, Elijah, and the Lady, she*
> *Who left the roses in her body's lieu.*
> *O, if the pleasures I have known in thee*
> *But my poor faith's poor first fruits be,*
> *What quintessential, keen, ethereal bliss*
> *Then shall be his*
> *Who has thy birth-time's consecrating dew*
> *For death's sweet chrism retain'd*
> *Quick, tender, virginal, and unprofaned."*

Even at its best Patmore's poetry is spoilt by ugly inversions and elisions, inexcusable considering the freedom of the form. But in these last Odes we are hardly aware of such faults: the thought is irredeemably fused in the expression, and the result is true poetry of the rarest and perhaps the highest kind—metaphysical poetry such as has been written by Lucretius, Dante, Donne, Crashaw, and Wordsworth. Those who limit poetry by a narrow lyrical conception of the art will find little to charm their indolence in Patmore. But those who are braced to the highest levels of the art, where the flowers are few and fugitive, where Nature and Humanity, to adapt a saying of Patmore's, are beautified and developed instead of being withered up by religious thought, will find in the best of the Odes a fund of inspired poetry for which they would willingly sacrifice the whole baggage of the Victorian legacy in general. And they will find this poetry amply supported by Patmore's prose, to which justice is not often done—prose which has " the virile qualities of simplicity, continuity, and positiveness."

Of the fundamental faith to which all Patmore's writings are finally related, it would be presumptuous to do more than point out quite dispassionately its vigour, its broadmindedness, and its essential freedom. It was a faith opposed to the whole trend, literary and scientific, of Patmore's period. Patmore was not afraid to scale his isolated peak, but in this he had the good sense to abate some of his usual arrogance. His last word is given in the Preface

to *The Rod, the Root, and the Flower*, written in 1895, the
year before his death:

> " Far be it from me to pose as other than a mere
> reporter, using the poetic intellect and imagination so
> as in part to conceive those happy realities of life which
> in many have been and are an actual and abiding
> possession ; and to express them in such a manner that
> thousands who lead beautiful and substantially Catholic
> lives, whether outside or within the visible Church,
> may be assisted in the only true learning, which is to
> know better that which they already know."

ROBERT PEEL

1788-1850

BY
H. J.
LASKI

ROBERT PEEL

I

"A CONSTITUTIONAL statesman," wrote Bagehot, "is in general a man of common opinions and uncommon abilities." It would be difficult to find a better description of Sir Robert Peel. In the forty years of his political life, he was responsible, neither in discussion nor in legislation, for any single idea which had not become almost a platitude of social thought. He opposed almost every constructive measure of his time until it was obvious that its passage was inevitable. He never displayed Disraeli's power of seeing with the sudden insight of genius the essential problems of his time. He had none of Mr. Gladstone's genius for growing with the growth of his age. He was always one with his generation; there is no single theme upon which he can be said to have become its leader. On all the great questions of his time his perception of necessary action came, almost invariably, at the eleventh hour. Other men sowed; he reaped the fruits of their sowing in the face of his own life-long convictions.

Yet if ever there has been a supremely useful man in English politics, Peel can lay claim to the title. He made possible, as no other man could have done, the peaceful and effective transition from the England of Lord Eldon to the England of Victoria. He transformed the Tory Party from a body of men committed to the legendary reaction of the Napoleonic epoch to one prepared to act upon the foundations of that silent economic revolution symbolized in the Whig triumph of 1832. He did not do so from a desire for change. He commended himself to the Tories by his power to resist it. But, as befitted the son

413

of the new magnates of industry, he had a power of adaptation lacking in the majority of his colleagues. He possessed the art of knowing when to give way. He had an eye for reshaping the front of battle. When he came to high place in the counsels of the Tory Party there was grave danger that its blind hostility to change might make the necessary reformation of political structure impossible without catastrophe. When he left office, in 1846, the scene was laid for the peaceful and prosperous evolution of the Victorian epoch. Without his leadership in those difficult years, it is hard to see how revolution could have been avoided.

The achievement is the more remarkable, because it was not one that its author deliberately willed. We think of Sir Robert Peel to-day as the author of a great currency reform, and the man who carried Catholic Emancipation and the abolition of the Corn Laws. It is difficult to remember that he was also the stern defender of Peterloo and the Six Acts, that he was second only to Croker in his hostility to the Reform Act, that he laboured with all his power to make the Orange interest in Ireland impregnable. He showed no spark of interest in any of the great social problems of his day—law reform, municipal reorganization, educational improvement, ecclesiastical reconstruction— save as an administrator prepared to lend the skill of his efficiency to the planning of other men. As befitted his father's son, indeed, he did something for the Factory Acts; and the formation of the police force was a social change of the first order. Yet the impression left upon the student of his career is that of a man who accepted change he could not avoid rather than of one who willed it, realizing its desirability. His heart was always with an England that was already an anachronism when he came to high place; we can pay tribute only to his mind.

And it is a tribute the more remarkable when the circumstances of his effort are remembered. Though he had loyal and devoted coadjutors in Wellington and Graham; though in 1841 he was the head of probably the ablest Conservative Government there has ever been in this country, Peel was never driven forward by a spontaneous insight from his colleagues that corresponded with his own. The original realization of inevitability came always from himself, and the documents make it clear that he won his colleagues painfully to his side by a slow process of educational conversion. He never saw the necessity long years ahead;

he was never able to prepare himself and his party for its admission. Perception was always for him a long and only half-conscious conflict, between inner desire and almost sudden intellectual realization. He arrived at his convictions by what Wordsworth called a "wise passiveness." There was always a slow and cumulative pressure of facts, the general bearing of which he never permitted himself to see until their conclusion was irresistible. But when the moment had come he met its challenge with a determination and a courage it is impossible not to admire.

Peel, in a sense, is the first of modern English statesmen. No one had amply realized before him the implications of the modern State. He saw that a continuance of government by connection was incompatible with the necessities of administration. He realized more completely than any of his predecessors that collective Cabinet responsibility could alone secure the passage of necessary legislation in a modern Parliament. He embodied, for the first time, that conception of the Prime Minister as a *primus inter pares* among his colleagues, supplying the co-ordinating power and motive force to the whole. He was, too, perhaps the first great statesman to abandon the rotund and classic eloquence of the eighteenth century for the plain and unadorned debating methods in the Victorian Parliament; Peel was the bridge between the organized complexity of Burke and Pitt and the business-like simplicity of Lord Oxford. He was, once more, the first modern statesman plainly to conceive the significance of administration; and, in this sense, his careful and scrupulous use of the patronage may well be said to mark an epoch in the history of the civil service. And it is, finally, of real significance that— save for the brief and exceptional instance of Perceval— Peel was the first essentially middle-class Prime Minister of England. Neither Harrow and Christ Church nor great wealth could conceal the fact that his position was due to trade; there was conceded to him a power of direction which, in the past, the aristocracy had shared only with legal eminence. With his arrival in Downing Street was foreshadowed the effective end of the *ancien régime*. His career symbolized the acceptance of the new men made by the Industrial Revolution—the tacit recognition of their right to a full share in the State. And his arrival at power —as the correspondence of Cobden makes plain—gave commercial England a new confidence in the régime by

reason of his place in it which no other Conservative leader
could have secured. He meant the replacement of a class
born to rule by men whose own effort constituted their
title to place; and it was justly assumed by business men
that the change involved a new spirit in the direction of
affairs.

II

No one has ever denied great personal qualities to Sir
Robert Peel. Sterling common sense, remarkable powers
of application, the gift of finding his way through great
masses of business, a high sense of personal scruple, intense
devotion to what he conceived to be his duty—not even
the most hostile of his critics has denied him these. From
his earliest days in the House of Commons he took his place
as what may be termed an indispensable man. Inferior
to Canning in the arts which dominated the pre-Reform
House of Commons, he had a stability of opinion, a
soberness in judgment, a power of winning trust from his
followers and subordinates which have rarely been equalled
in English politics.

It is clear that he had a complex nature. Aloof and
reserved, he lacked altogether the power to unbend. He
had no gift of familiarity. He never seems to have made
men easy with him. Proud, sensitive, and cold, he rarely
had intimates who penetrated within the inner recesses of
his mind. He shrouded himself within a cloak of aloofness
which probably multiplied his difficulties for him. The
note of his correspondence is almost always formality and
stateliness. There is nothing in him of the man who
enjoys the luxury of ample colleagueship. He seems to
have met men invariably on the footing of business to be
done rather than of friendship to be enjoyed. He had no
talent for encouraging the young. He never cultivated
men from an interest in winning their discipleship in the
fashion of which men so different as Disraeli and Mr. Lloyd
George have possessed the secret.

It was said by Disraeli that Peel seemed to have no life
outside the House of Commons, and that remark is the clue
both to the qualities and the defects of his mind. It was a
mind incapable of imagination or foresight. It had gravity
and dignity, the power to see all round the immediacies of
a subject. But it was a mind of narrow sympathies and
range, interested invariably in the technique of application

rather than the discovery of principle. It was the mind which
captivated a supporter by stating a known case supremely
well, rather than one which convinced an opponent by
drawing attention to new or forgotten aspects of the problem. There was no humour or wit in Peel; there was never
sublimity, and perhaps once only the appearance of sentiment. He had a power of grasping detail which perhaps
only Mr. Gladstone has surpassed; but, as is so often true
with that type of mind, the passion for perfection of detail
tended to make him more interested in the way in which
a thing was done than in the larger aspects of the thing
he was doing.

A great Parliamentary leader he undoubtedly was; and
it is worth while to reflect for a moment upon the causes of
his success. There have been leaders like Mr. Gladstone
whose outstanding superiority made an alternative choice
unthinkable; and there have been those who, like Disraeli,
grimly drove his party step by step to the realization that
there was no alternative. Leaders with qualities more
brilliant, like Lord Rosebery, have been unable to maintain their command; while others, with a character not
less remarkable, like Mr. Asquith, have never attained the
same instant recognition. Yet from the Reform Act until
the split of 1846 Peel exercised over his party a predomin-
ance as great as Mr. Gladstone's, even when he had at his
side men who, like Wellington, Graham, and Stanley, were,
in their different ways, hardly less notable than himself.
What was the secret of his power?

He was, in the first place, a great Parliamentary debater.
No speech of his, it may be, ever reached the supreme
heights; but no speech of his was ever unworthy of the
occasion for which it was made. He had not only a distinguished presence, but a voice which Disraeli declared
to be one of the two perfect things he had ever known. He
knew the House of Commons as a great violinist knows his
instrument, and in his forty years' membership of it his
judgment of its temper was not mistaken half a dozen times.
He had the kind of self-confidence in speech which puts
heart into a man's side. He had the gift, if not of making
friends, of training followers; it is significant that men so
different as Graham and Sidney Herbert, Cardwell and
Gladstone, Hardinge and Dalhousie, all served their apprenticeship to him. While he conveyed the invariable impression of loftiness in objective, he was never out of his party's

distance. What he was doing could always be understood, and, save on the two famous occasions when he changed his policy, men followed him because of the confidence they feel when they know and understand their leader's direction. Indeed, there is a sense in which his very arrogance and aloofness were a help rather than a hindrance to him. It enabled him to impose his will, simply because his manner did not invite discussion or disagreement. His obvious industry and his known conscientiousness were of great importance to him. The first gave him the position which always comes to a leader who invariably meets his opponents on the basis of equal knowledge; the second preserved him from the formation of cabals against him within his own ranks. Peel, it was clear, might be avid of power; but it was also obvious that his desire for power was an ambition instinct with high purpose.

His powers of work were extraordinary. No Prime Minister in our history has ever dominated so completely the process of administration. His care about the details of measures was even a matter of complaint by his colleagues, since it made him hostile to amendments from the floor of the House. And so complete was his control in Parliament that Stanley, then the first debater of the day, actually proposed his own removal to the Lords on the ground that no field was left for the exercise of his powers in the Commons. No small part of Peel's authority must have come from his remarkable capacity for persuasion. A minister who really knew, down to the minutiæ of public business, what each of his colleagues was doing, must have been a tower of strength to them. He was not only invaluable to them in debate; he brought to the discussion of their problems, as his correspondence makes plain, a knowledge of their bearing full of that common sense which comes from intimate acquaintance with detail as well as principle. No doubt the attention he gave to public business would be impossible in our day, for the increase in the volume of departmental affairs has increased at least tenfold. Yet Peel's manner of attacking the Prime Minister's function of co-ordination is a masterly example of the administrative art; and Lord Haldane, no mean judge of such matters, paid Peel a well-deserved compliment when, in 1924, he presented Mr. MacDonald with the *Peel Papers* as the best account available of what the Premiership essentially involves.

III

Yet there are grave weaknesses in Peel which, at this distance of time, we tend to forget in the dramatic finale of his last five years. He was always a man of limited views. He never foresaw the emergence of great issues, or made preparations to deal with them. He thought the obvious commonplaces of his party, without ever leading them to new ground. Nothing that he did suggests essential inventiveness of mind. His career, for the most part, is an illustration of the power to do the obvious thing in the grand manner. He never thought ahead. He was content to proceed by the cumulative effect of small actions rather than to attack the problems he confronted at their root. He seems, both in his speeches and his letters, wholly devoid of the speculative faculty. Like the late Lord Oxford, he was always direct and lucid; but he never, like Lord Oxford again, allowed his mind to play around the hinterland of a great theme.

He was, perhaps, rather the agent of other men's thoughts than the maker of his own. His speeches are rarely illustrations of principle. He hurries at the first opportunity to the question of its application, where, like the great administrator that he was, he seems more comfortable. He rarely seeks to build up a case on general grounds. There is a lack in his thinking of anything that may be termed a general philosophy. Disraeli's complaint that no one knew, like Peel, how to " dress up a case " is not an unfair charge. And there is about his discussion a certain unctuousness of temper, a complacent self-rectitude, which suggests a grave lack in him of imaginative power. Like most great debaters, he confined himself to the truths that were valuable for the occasion rather than the truths really essential to his theme. He persuaded men less by the quality of his argument than by the brilliance of the manner in which he stated it.

It is not improbable that he was himself the victim of the illusion the debater is able to produce in his hearers, that a point scored in tactic is a truth discovered in argument. Sensitive though Peel was, jealous almost to a fault of his reputation, he does not seem, unlike most sensitive people, to have been an introspective person. He had a remarkable confidence in his own judgment, a tendency, born of that confidence, to believe that if a thing was to be done, he was

the best man to do it. In a large degree, no doubt, his
immense powers entitled him to that self-assurance. But
they also blinded him to the significance of other men's
opinions, and they tended to make him feel, as in 1829 and
1845, that he had almost a natural right to power. Convinced, no doubt quite fairly, of the purity of his own
motives, he could never understand why his change of
front should give rise to criticism among his fellows. There,
no doubt, his aloofness, and its consequential autocracy of
temper, led him astray. After 1829 there was really no one
among his own followers, save the Duke of Wellington,
who could really talk to him on equal terms; and the
Duke's sense of discipline was so complete that, once Peel
was the acknowledged leader of the party, his prerogative
of equal criticism was never used. It is, doubtless, a mistake for a political leader to be one with his followers on
every occasion; but no political leader can permanently
maintain his authority who is not accessible to them on the
vital occasions. Peel's manner to lesser men seems always
to have been that of a monarch towards his courtiers; he
was always in the full robes of State. He never learned the
essential lesson, that friendship means something more than
a dignified condescension.

Two other aspects of Peel are important. His instinct
was autocratic, and that made him distrustful of other
classes save those he knew at first-hand. The mind and
wants of the working class he never really grasped until
Cobden and the potato famine forced him to attend to them.
He understood well enough the vulgarity of demagogues
like Cobbett; he never understood the things in English
life which gave them their immense influence. The wrongs
which made Dickens shrill with anger, the abuses which
turned Bentham into a radical reformer, seem to have been
wholly unperceived by him. He accepted the era of reform
as inevitable, and persuaded his party to accept its implications; but these, for him, were always minimum
implications. He sought to fight a rearguard action against
social and political change, so that, at any given moment,
the least surrender should be made. And it is curious to
note how low he estimated the motives of his opponents
once they did not belong to the governing classes of Great
Britain. For him, the agitator like O'Connell was invariably outside the pale; and only long and bitter experience
persuaded him to give his full attention to the case made

by Cobden and his allies. There is hardly a note in his long Irish correspondence which does not suggest that Ireland, for him, was simply a territory to be administered rather than a wrong to be righted. That sudden almost poetic insight of Burke into the sufferings of other men, which makes his strongest Conservatism reach out hands to the Liberal temper, was a quality of which Peel was wholly devoid.

And, save in his remarkable power over administrative detail, Peel was in no sense a constructive statesman. Most of his essential achievements were by way of repeal. He knew how to clear the ground; he had little faculty for building on the ground he had cleared. Constructive power in a statesman implies the qualities of imagination and generalization; and neither of these did Peel possess. From the latter, indeed, he may almost be said to have shrunk. He preferred the immediate adjustment to broad re-organization. No doubt, in some degree, that preference was the outcome of the material with which he had to work. Men who had cheered Eldon and Liverpool would not have supported a Tory democrat within ten years of their disappearance. But, even granted the limitations of his party, it is difficult not to feel that Peel was really unconscious of the volume of reorganization that was required. He could be brought to admit that Catholic Emancipation was inevitable; he would never have attempted the equally inevitable disestablishment of the Irish Church. He could insist that his duty was to use his patronage honourably; he would never have risked Gladstone's great Order in Council of 1870. Peel's mind was throughout a deliberately negative mind to which change is in itself abhorrent; and he was persuaded to the acceptance of other men's innovations less by the realization of their value than by suspicion of the cost of reversing the new order.

IV

So long as men are interested in the history of English politics, they are certain to debate Peel's famous changes of front over Catholic Emancipation and the Corn Laws. No one is likely now, in the light of the available material, to impugn the sincerity of Peel. It is obvious, in each instance, that he reached his decisions only after long searchings of heart and with the full conviction that the facts left him no alternative.

But sincerity in politics is not enough of itself. A states
man cannot be deemed to have acted rightly merely because
his motives are not open to question; he must not merely
will what is right, but know, also, what it is right to will
And in each case, it may be argued, while the document:
offer proof of Peel's courage and sincerity, they condemn
and condemn seriously, his judgment. The determination
to resign on Catholic Emancipation in August 1828 was
taken with the full, if reluctant, acquiescence of the Duke
of Wellington. The decision to withdraw the resignation
was made in a letter of which all the assumptions appear
to be dubious, and which could in fact have had no other
possible alternative but his continuance in office. As late
as January 1829, Peel thought that twenty years of
opposition to the Catholic claims made it unsuitable for
him to be the minister to promote their acceptance. Then
episcopal obstinacy made him feel that, without his aid as
a member of the Cabinet, Wellington might find things
difficult, especially from the side of the King. He argued
that if George IV was to sacrifice his convictions, the least
he could do was to sacrifice his also.

But it is surely obvious that a constitutional minister is in
a wholly different position from that of the Monarch. The
latter may encourage or warn; it is not his function to resign
if his advice is disregarded. A minister is in a wholly different position. By promoting a measure to which he had
been invariably opposed, for which he had so recently
sacrificed Huskisson and Anglesey, he could not fail to give
the impression that office came first and conscience afterwards. Nor does he explain why, out of office, he could
not have given the measure the full weight of a support
which would have been all the stronger from the independence of his position. His argument that George IV
might have abdicated can hardly carry serious weight; a
man of Peel's insight must have known full well that there
was no martyr's courage in the King's composition. The
fact seems to be that, with the highest possible motives,
Peel was the victim of the politician's common delusion
that he is indispensable to the government of the country.
He clearly loved office, like most able, and many commonplace, statesmen; he had the consciousness of great powers;
he saw the urgency of action. He doubted whether any
man could as well frame, and as skilfully carry, the necessary measure as himself. He was, in fact, unconscious of

422

he complicated motives which in reality underlay the decision that he made.

His case over the Corn Laws is a stronger one; for his
authorship of the Repeal was due to Lord John Russell's
failure to form a Government when Peel resigned. But
even here there is a process of self-delusion. From
Graham's letter of December 1842, it is clear that the
inevitability of free trade in corn was present to the mind
of his closest political associate. It is difficult not to feel
that some such view, also, must have been Peel's own. It
then becomes a problem of grave importance to understand
why, in the next three years, he took no steps to acquaint
his party with the necessities of the position. He knew that
his followers were overwhelmingly protectionist, that the
Corn Laws was for them a sacred article of faith. He must
have had an overwhelming self-confidence—not to use a
stronger word—to believe, particularly after 1829, that he
could blot it out from their creed at a moment's notice.
His own view that, on other terms, he would have failed
to carry repeal, seems to repeat the error of 1829; it contains the implicit view that he was, in fact, the most suitable
person to be in charge of the crisis when it occurred.

Nor can it be said that he did all for Lord John, in the
latter's difficulties, that might have been expected. The
latter failed to take office through a personal quarrel between Grey and Palmerston. Peel did nothing to emphasize
to Russell how urgent it was that repeal should be effected
by the party committed to it. He did not emphasize the
impossible position his own resumption of office would
obviously create. He did not offer those safeguards of
whole-hearted support in a grave crisis which would have
led Russell to overcome his difficulties. Without hesitation
he resumed office on Russell's failure, and, with his support, carried repeal in the teeth of his own party. Is there
not something to be said for the Prince Consort's judgment
that Peel believed, no doubt unconsciously, that " the
minister who settles the Corn Laws is not so easily turned
out " ? Is it not possible that he counted on being forgiven
in 1846, as he had been forgiven in 1829, on the ground
that he was indispensable to his party?

His own defence, of course, was the simple one that he
owed a greater duty to the nation than he owed to the party
he led. But on this, surely, there are two things to be said.
The abstract proposition is without meaning except in the

423

context of its concomitant circumstances. A Pope who proposes to change a basic dogma of the Roman Church owes it at least the duty to make the faithful aware that the change is desirable. The leader of a constitutional party cannot have a lesser obligation; and on this head Peel, effectively, did nothing at all. It is, moreover, a dangerous maxim that a leader historically associated with one set of principles may take over those of his opponents whenever he thinks national necessity requires it. The opening here given, not merely to opportunism, is wide indeed. Men support their political leaders on the basis of some well-defined and established expectations. The whole groundwork of confidence in public probity is cut away if the leader's desertion of those expectations proceeds without regard to the conversion of his followers. In Peel's case, no doubt, the conscious motive was high; but the example of 1846 was followed by Disraeli in 1867 in a fashion which admits of no defence. Political sincerity needs its special technique; and it is difficult to avoid the conclusion that Peel's retention of office in the two great crises of his career was a violation of the rules upon which it needs to be founded.

Yet no estimate of Peel can be just which concludes upon a critical note. No student of his career will be tempted to forget the unwearying passion for the public good he displayed in the last half of his political life, especially in its four final years; nor is he likely to withhold his meed of profound admiration for the immense abilities he brought to his self-imposed task.

CECIL
RHODES

1853-1902

BY
CLIFFORD
SHARP

R

CECIL RHODES

FEW probably of the younger generation of Englishmen possess in their minds any adequate picture of Cecil Rhodes. Fewer still can have had a chance of realizing the true moral dimensions of the man who not only laid the foundations of the modern Anglo-Dutch Union of South Africa, but, by efforts that were almost single-handed, added to the British Empire the vast and fertile territories to the north which now and for ever bear his name. He did not give them his name: they took it; and perhaps it is only amongst Rhodesians that his memory enjoys at the present time the fame and the affectionate admiration that properly belong to it. To be able, indeed, to have any personal recollection of the tremendous position that Rhodes once held in the eyes, not only of South Africa or even of Great Britain, but of all the world, one would need to-day to be of an age nearer sixty than fifty. Yet Rhodes was a younger man than Asquith, younger, too, than, for example, Mr. Justice Avory or Mr. Augustine Birrell or Sir Oliver Lodge.

The reason for the comparative—but certainly only temporary—obscurity into which Rhodes's name has fallen is no doubt mainly the fact that there exists at present no really first-class record of his life. And the reason, again, for the absence of any such record is, with equal certainty, to be found in the unfortunate episode which threw a cloud over the last six years of his life—Dr. Jameson's tragic and farcical " Raid " into the territory of the Transvaal Republic.

The Raid was the last event in Rhodes's career as a public servant, but it must be dealt with first, because until

427

his connection, or rather lack of connection, with it is understood, it is impossible to appreciate in due perspective either the ideals or the policy of the man who accepted responsibility for it, yet whose whole life-work it seemed to ruin. Rhodes was a man to whom Fate allowed no second chance. A career of astonishing and ever-accumulating success was broken by one serious mistake which he did not live long enough to retrieve. For once he trusted the wrong man.

The full inner history of the Raid has not even yet been written in any official or easily available form. But the facts have all been printed disjointedly, and about the broad outlines of the episode there remains no mystery. The situation in the Transvaal in 1895 was extremely critical. President Kruger's patriarchal régime seemed tottering to a fall. It was threatened not only by the European immigrants at the gold-fields (the " Uitlanders "), to whom Kruger refused any form of franchise, but by a large proportion of the younger Boers themselves. Some sort of internal revolution seemed inevitable and imminent —a matter of weeks rather than of months. Presumably by Rhodes's orders and certainly with his full approval, Dr. Jameson organized a small force on the frontier which, at the proper moment, *after* the outbreak of the insurrection, was to be ready if necessary to lend assistance to the anti-Krugerists, with whom, by the way, practically all the Dutch population of Cape Colony were in sympathy. The issue was not at that time a racial one: it was an issue of enlightened progressivism and commercial union versus one of the most hidebound systems of oligarchical and reactionary separatism that then existed anywhere in the world.

Dr. Jameson, however, got tired of waiting. Acting altogether without instructions, he " invaded " the Transvaal with his ridiculous force, and within less than a week had made England the laughing-stock of the world.

Actually Rhodes had no responsibility at all for this preposterous exhibition of tragi-comic futility. But morally and officially he accepted full responsibility. He stood by his friend without reserve ; he never even admitted in public that Jameson had acted without instructions, still less that he had acted in a manner contrary to the whole tenor of his own policy and aims. He knew that he himself had made two genuine and serious mistakes. While holding the office of Prime Minister of Cape Colony he had no business, in

his wholly separate capacity of Chairman of the Chartered
Company, to authorize the organization of an armed force
for such a purpose even outside Cape territory. That was
his gravest mistake. His lesser mistake was his choice of
the leader of that force. So he faced the music without
seeking to excuse himself either in public or in private.

There is a certain absurdity in the association of Rhodes's
name with the blunder of the Raid, or, indeed, with any
other imaginable exhibition of practical stupidity. His
powers of foresight and his immense practical capacity
made it necessary for him to gamble with Fate. It
was never his way to strike until he had made success
certain. The Dutch leaders of Cape Colony never suspected
him of complicity in the Raid. They knew him far too
well. When the news first arrived, their attitude towards
him was one of simple condolence, not upon the failure of
the Raid, but upon the manner in which an ill-advised, not
to say hare-brained, subordinate had let him down, and so
given a new lease of life to the Kruger régime which they
hated almost as much as he did.

Later their attitude was modified. The intense racial
feeling aroused, or rather created, by the Raid, forced them
in the end to renounce their sympathy if not their private
friendship. They drifted away from him, and the main
object of his political life, which had always been the complete obliteration of racial differences throughout the whole
of South Africa from the Cape to the Zambezi, seemed for
a time to have been defeated. Until the very last moment
in the autumn of 1899 Rhodes not only hoped but believed
that the war would not come. He hated the stupidity of
force from the bottom of his soul. But the war came, and
before it had ended he was dead. Had he lived but a few
years more to see the establishment of the Campbell-Ban-
nerman constitution he would have died in peace, for
beyond all doubt that great stroke of Imperial statesmanship would have appeared to him to ensure the fulfilment
and the crown of all his own policies and ambitions.

Since those days—so short a while ago—the minds of
men have changed. The quarrel between " Imperialists "
and " Little Englanders " has ceased to exist. The latter
name, indeed, has disappeared from the language since
the " Empire " of the great Queen became a " Commonwealth," whose unity in freedom every sane and sensible

subject of the Crown wishes to preserve and to increase.
And so perhaps the time has now come when the dreams
and deeds of Cecil Rhodes may be discussed without political passion, and above all without reference to that
blunder of a subordinate which, although it ran counter to
the essential spirit and purpose of his public life, has been
allowed to overshadow—almost to obliterate—the whole
story of an illustrious career.

By common consent Rhodes was the arch-Imperialist of
an Imperialist age. Yet of that crude, bombastic, Rule-
Britannia sort of "Imperialism" which made the word
stink in the nostrils of so many patriotic and sensible folk,
he had not in him a single touch. From the very first his
dreams were of race union, never of race ascendancy, and
frequently in South Africa itself he was accused of being
far too pro-Dutch. Had he not been the richest as well as
the most powerful man in the country, he would certainly
have been suspected of having actually been bought by the
Dutch.

A life cannot be described in a brief essay. A strictly
judicial examination is still more impossible. The most
that can be attempted is the first rough outline of a portrait.
Fortunately, this is not so difficult in the case of Rhodes as
it might be in that of a smaller man. For both his character and his career were large; their finer shades are not
of very serious account. His understanding of men and
their motives was universal rather than particular, profound rather than subtle. The quality of his mind showed
itself at the very beginning. He arrived from England at
his brother's farm in Natal as a mere schoolboy not yet
eighteen. But within a few months he was beginning to
dream his practical dream of the Union of South Africa and
the "open road to the North." He saw that to realise his
dream he must have money, and so he went to the new
diamond-fields to get it. He saw also that he would need
more education, and so he planned to go to Oxford as soon
as he was financially independent.

In 1871, at the age of eighteen, he migrated to the
Kimberley area with a Greek lexicon amongst his kit. In
1873 he went to Oxford where, having been rejected by
University because he had not time to read for an Honours
degree, he entered his name as an undergraduate upon the
books of Oriel College—whose hospitality he subsequently
recognized by a gift of £100,000. But he had kept only

one term, when he was obliged to go back to Africa.
He returned again to Oxford in 1876, 1877, and 1878 (when
he was Master of the Drag), spending, however, each long
vacation in Kimberley. When he kept his final term at
Oriel (Michaelmas 1881), and took his degree of Master
of Arts, he was already Chairman of the de Beers Mining
Company and an active member of the Cape Parliament,
wherein he had outlined the native policy to which he
always subsequently adhered, and (just before sailing for
England and Oxford) had been mainly instrumental in
forcing the resignation of the Cape Ministry upon an issue
relating to that policy.

Rhodes then returned to South Africa to stay. Eight
years later, having meanwhile gained full control, not only
of the diamond industry and to a large extent of the gold-
fields, but of the Chartered Company which was seeking
to pacify and settle the territories north of the Transvaal
and south of the Zambezi, he became Prime Minister of
Cape Colony. Largely owing to the unswerving political
support of the Dutch, he held this position of triplicate
authority for six years. Then came the miserable Raid and
his resignation from all his offices.

Few men—perhaps none—in any country or in any age
can have wielded power so complete and so far-reaching
as Rhodes did during those six years, political power,
financial power, and the virtually unfettered direction of
Imperial expansion into unmapped regions. He exerted
those powers almost faultlessly as well as to the full. When
he retired he had really accomplished all that he had set
out to accomplish. The spirit of Union was everywhere
the dominant force throughout South Africa (in those pre-
Raid days), save on the *stoep* of President Kruger's residence in Pretoria and in the lonely farms of the Calvinistic
backvelders of the northern half of the Transvaal Republic.
Farther north, Salisbury and Bulawayo were well-established British settlements, and the bridge which was to carry
the railway across the Zambezi at the Victoria Falls from
Southern to Northern Rhodesia, and on to Tanganyika and
the Congo, was in course of construction. Smaller men
could do, and have since done, all the rest.

Very little of the story of Rhodes relates to the gaining
of money. He cared nothing for money itself, save as an
instrument of freedom and power, and he seems almost

R*   431

to have left both the making and the management of it to his spare time. When he had made what he wanted he left it to grow, and when he thought about it at all his mind dwelt less upon its magnitude and increase than upon the purpose to which it should ultimately be devoted.

He was always on good terms with the Dutch. He was inclined both to like and to trust them from very early Kimberley days. These sentiments were mutual. They recognized his fundamental honesty and he theirs. With his Dutch political allies, the Afrikander Bond, he was always perfectly open. They wanted Union and he wanted Union, and that was a sufficient basis for common action in those critical years. If their ideal was a United South Africa under its own flag, whilst his included the acceptance of the Union Jack—well, that was a matter for free choice in the future after Union was accomplished. Rhodes for his part was ready enough to postpone the decision, since he was fully convinced that when the time came the advantages of membership of the British Commonwealth (for it was in the guise of some such phrase that Rhodes, twenty or thirty years ahead, as usual, of the political ideas of his time, always thought of the " Empire ") would be so obvious as to be irresistible.

Rhodes sat in the Cape Parliament, from his first election until his death, for a constituency which was predominantly Dutch. Even after the Raid his Afrikander supporters in Cape Colony did not cease to trust him. As late as 1897 the leading members of the Bond—though they could not officially co-operate with him—admitted publicly that Rhodes would head the poll in any Dutch constituency in the Colony. And well, indeed, he might ! The Dutch knew that he was English to the bottom of his heart, but they also knew that his opposition to any sort of racial prejudices or distinctions was equally genuine. When General Sir Charles Warren, some years earlier, having established a British Protectorate in Bechuanaland, had sought to restrict grants of land in that province to settlers of English descent, Rhodes's intervention had been instant and decisive.

" I raise my voice," he declared in the Cape Assembly, " in most solemn protest against such a course, and it is the duty of every Englishman in the House to record his protest against it. The breach of solemn pledges and the introduction of race distinctions must result in bringing calamity on this country, and if such a policy is pursued it will endanger, not only the whole of our social relationships with the Colonists of Dutch descent, but endanger the supremacy of her Majesty in this country."

The natives also trusted Rhodes completely, and from first to last he exercised a strong personal influence over them, whether they were soft Cape Hottentots or the war-loving Matabele of the north. He had a natural and unfeigned sympathy with their point of view and always championed their interests when they were threatened. He was once questioned by the coloured community as to the real meaning of his favourite slogan of " equal rights for every civilized man south of the Zambezi." His reply, scribbled on a scrap of newspaper, was unhesitating and unambiguous. " What is a civilized man? A man, whether white or black, who has sufficient education to write his name, has some property, or works; in fact, is not a loafer."

With loafers of any colour or description Rhodes had no patience. He even went so far as to provide in his Will that no male descendant of his own family should be qualified to inherit his English estate unless he should have spent, or being under age would agree to spend, at least ten years in the active pursuit of some useful profession or business—the Army not being allowed to count for this purpose as work! Rhodes always hated fighting and disliked military officers. That he should be held responsible, even in the remotest degree, for the tragic war which broke out five years after he had resigned office is one of the ironies of modern history.

It has sometimes been suggested that Rhodes was somewhat lacking in physical courage. That he shrank from physical violence is certain. He never hunted big game. Once, and once only, when on trek he shot a zebra and immediately hated himself for having done it. Of lions he was quite frankly afraid, and more than once took to his heels to avoid an encounter. But beside this simple timidity must be set such incidents as his famous meeting with the Matabele chieftains in the Matopo hills. The war against these descendants of the Zulus had been protracted, and he was sick of it. So—in spite of the opposition of General Carrington, commanding the British

433

force—he arranged to go with a small party of seven to meet the chiefs in the hills four miles from the British camp. Both sides were to be unarmed. He arrived safely at the appointed place, and found the men he sought waiting for him, but the next moment his party was surrounded by several hundred natives fully armed with guns and assegais. His chief companion, Colenbrander, shouted, " Keep on your horses "—contemplating perhaps some desperate deed of valour with a forlorn hope of escape. The party obeyed him, all except Rhodes, who jumped off his horse and ran straight towards the chiefs and their advancing ring of spears, upbraiding them in their own tongue (of which, by the way, he was no master) for their breach of faith, and saying that he would speak no word to them as long as one man had a gun in his hand. In three minutes the guns had disappeared, and in three hours the essentials of peace were agreed upon. From that moment onwards he became in effect the hero and suzerain chief of the Matabele. They named him Lamula'mkunzi—" Separator of the Fighting Bulls "—and by that name he was called until his death and long after. Evidently, if he lacked physical courage he possessed a substitute for it good enough to deceive a great fighting race. Probably if he had been asked about the matter he would have said: " I understand Matabeles ; I do not understand lions."

Abruptly Rhodes's mind always passed from the particular to the general, and here the transition must be equally abrupt. Rhodes was perhaps one of the most consistent men who ever lived. At the age of nineteen his purpose in life was fixed, and thereafter, though it grew and expanded with the growth of his own knowledge of men, it never changed. It was a purpose, moreover, which was related to the future, not merely of his own adopted country, but of the whole world. His central and most persistent dream was of the Federation of Man under the inevitable leadership of the Anglo-Saxons. When in later years he gained some knowledge of Germany and the Germans, both at home and abroad, his faith in the special qualities of the Anglo-Saxons was broadened into a belief that the world was destined to be led by the Nordic races as a whole—as witness the final form of his Will.

It needs particularly to be emphasized that Rhodes dreamed and thought in terms always of co-operation and

434

leadership, never of strife and dominance. No doubt he believed that the Anglo-Saxons—with or without the Germans—could dominate the world by force if they wished, but that was not at all what he wished. To him all strife was waste or worse. Dominance, which might require force to support it, neither came within his definition of " leadership " nor in his eyes could hold any promise of stability and progress.

This attitude was plainly exhibited in his single incursion into the sphere of home politics. He was wholly in favour of Home Rule for Ireland, and he gave Parnell £10,000 for campaign purposes; but he gave it upon condition that Parnellite Home Rule should not involve the complete withdrawal of Irish members from Westminster. At the same time he gave £5,000 to the Gladstonian Liberals upon the same understanding, plus a further condition that there should be no policy of " scuttle " out of Egypt. These two gifts define the quality of his Imperialism in a manner that hardly needs further comment—the greatest possible local autonomy, plus an unchallengeable Unity.

Rhodes's Will is the most complete as well as the most authentic and well-considered documentary exposition of his world aims that we possess. It expressed, not the last wishes of an old man, but the living and deeply rooted hopes of a man who was young until he died. It offers, moreover, the plainest possible illustration and proof of his rare capacity for turning dreams into action. In his early days, Uganda was not then even a British Protectorate, the Sudan was in the hands of the victorious Mahdi, Rhodesia did not exist save in the mind of the great dreamer.

But the dream which was embodied in the Will was a much greater one than that. The Will was in the most literal sense a life-work, and by that document, and that alone, Rhodes might fairly claim, if such claim were necessary, to be judged by posterity. In it he combined two of his strongest beliefs, firstly, his belief in the great future awaiting the Anglo-Saxon peoples, and secondly, his faith in the inestimable power of a common education to draw men together. Thus he conceived the idea of founding international scholarships on a magnificent scale. Few people perhaps realise that there are now always resident at Oxford in term time no less than 200 undergraduates drawn half from the Dominions and half from the United

States; and each scholarship is sufficient (£400) to cover the cost of living as well as of tuition.[1]

It is usual, in biographical literature, to speak of the "personal magnetism" of the subject. In Rhodes that quality—whatever it may be—excited an extraordinary measure of love and loyalty from all with whom he came into personal contact. He could always fire the imagination of youth, even in the middle-aged and the elderly. He combined the far-gazing imagination of a H. G. Wells with the driving force and negotiating ability of a Lloyd George and the intuitive understanding of other races of a General Gordon. He had besides the personable lovableness of all three. And to these distinguished qualities he, pure Englishman as he was, added a business capacity with which even the Jews of Kimberley and the Rand learned that they could not successfully compete.

Rhodes lived his life in a hurry and in the shadow of death. He had known from his 'teens that he could hardly expect to reach, and certainly not to pass, middle age. When he was twenty a London doctor gave him only six months to live. The last intelligible sentence that he muttered, an hour or so before he died, is authentically recorded: "So little done, so much to do." When he resigned all his public offices he was forty-two; when he died he was forty-eight.

[1] The similar Scholarships which Rhodes provided for German students were annulled by Act of Parliament during the Great War. To this step Rhodes, had he been alive, would no doubt have consented at the time, but it is certain, if anything is certain, that he would never have agreed to the annulment being permanent. The Trustees of his Will have revived the German Scholarships on a small scale since 1930, out of funds at their disposal, but the Act of Parliament has yet to be repealed.

GABRIEL CHARLES DANTE ROSSETTI

BY LORD DAVID CECIL

1828-1882

GABRIEL CHARLES
DANTE ROSSETTI

THERE is no doubt that the nineteenth century, which witnessed progress in almost everything else, witnessed a decline in poetry. It began, indeed, with a great outburst of it, the Romantic Movement. But that very Romantic Movement bore within it the seeds of poetic decay. For it marked the beginning of a fatal division between poetry and life. A poet, like anybody else, is not a completely self-dependent individual: he is also a member of a society. And like any member of a society, he must partake of its general life if he is fully to develop his talents, must draw nourishment and stimulus from its common interests and enthusiasms if he is to maintain the vitality needed to make him create. But he can only do this in a society that appeals to his sympathies, one whose institutions and preoccupations and underlying values have that ideal justification, and can be regarded in that romantic aspect which can give them significance or attraction in the eyes of one whose ultimate standard of values is æsthetic.

Now the life of England up till the nineteenth century did have such an aspect and such a justification. The religious questions which dominated the interests of the average man of the seventeenth century were also some of the dominating interests of Milton and Herbert; the social and political causes which stirred the enthusiasm of the average man of the eighteenth century stirred equally the enthusiasm of Addison and Swift; Addison was even a Minister of the Government. But by 1800 the advance of rationalism and the Industrial Revolution between them had broken up the fabric of common belief and institutions, and put no other new one in its place; so that in order to find that background of moral and intellectual values necessary to stimulate them, the poets had to turn to the unorganized certainties provided by their own experience : Wordsworth to his own personal response to nature, Keats to his personal response to sensuous beauty, Shelley to his personal response to the calls of love and liberty, and to construct from these a moral and intellectual background of their own. But though in varying degrees they succeeded in doing this for themselves, they did not do it for anybody else. And their failure meant that rationalism and industrialism, growing daily stronger, gradually shaped an order of society and standard of values, material, sceptical, empirical, practical, irreligious, relative, incapable of awakening any sort of æsthetic response at all. With the consequence that artists grew steadily more indifferent to the religious or political questions that agitated the men of action of their day ; till to-day they are two nations which hardly know each other's language. One would as soon expect a poet to be an engine-driver as a member of the Cabinet.

Abstracted from that soil of common life which alone could generate the sap necessary to keep it alive, it was inevitable that the flower of creative inspiration should wither. And it has. There is no living tradition of major poetry to-day : such genuine poetry as there is can be divided into fragmentary and plaintive dreams of a never-never land of poetic fancy to which the poet escapes for a moment from the prosaic reality which imprisons him, and fragmentary and incoherent imprecations against his chains.

But before this happened, when the flower torn up was still freshly blooming, its colours vivid, its petals unshrivelled, an attempt was made to replant it in a new and artificial soil. It is the historical importance of the æsthetic movement that it attempted to create a new intellectual and moral background for the artist, when that provided by the ordinary life of his day no longer had power to stir him. This background had a purely æsthetic basis. Like those of all artists, the standards of its exponents were founded on æsthetic impressions ; they valued things because they appealed to their sense of beauty or glory. Since the civilization around them no longer stirred these senses, and since its inhabitants did not respect standards that referred to them, the artists felt driven to

construct a philosophy which dissociated these values from
any connection with anything else. They felt with Keats
that beauty was truth, and therefore they considered that
truth could only be attained through æsthetic experience.
Man should make himself constantly aware of beauty; his
life should be a consistent succession of impressions of
beauty, a glittering diamond chain of exquisite moments,
with not one drab thread showing between each separate
gem. Further, the practising artist argued from this that
his aim should be, not to instruct or uphold any special
moral, political, or social cause, but simply to create
beauty, to add to the stock of objects which could stimulate
æsthetic impressions. It is a narrow philosophy, as was to
be expected from the circumstances of its inception. And
it was too inconsistent with the prosaic, squalid, chaotic
facts of human nature to be carried out successfully in
practice. Nobody has got a vital enough sensibility to be
unceasingly susceptible to æsthetic impressions all the time,
even if he has the time or the health or the money. This
its exponents found. Their lives were all disappointing to
them because they could not maintain themselves in the
ecstasy which in their view was the only right condition in
which man should live. But though impractical, it is an
elevated philosophy; a strenuous, athletic, chaste self-
dedication to what it conceived to be the highest; utterly
different from the sensual self-indulgence that its enemies
represented it. And its exponents were among the great
English writers. The greatest of them is Dante Gabriel
Rossetti.

He is not the most typical; he is not so typical as Walter
Pater. Pater is the pattern as well as the prophet of
Æstheticism. For his deepest emotional experiences were all
evoked by actual works of art. Some of Rossetti's too; but
not all. He was also a lover. And he looked to love as
much as to art to provide him with a standard of value
and a source of inspiration. But he is a more considerable
writer than Pater; his genius was more creative, built on
a grander scale. He is indisputably the representative man
of the Æsthetic Movement. And, as a matter of fact, he is
so, even when he is writing about love. For he approaches
love from the æsthetic standpoint; he values it, as he values
art, because it provides him with his most exquisite experiences. When he writes about it he does not, like most
poets, celebrate the charms and virtues of his beloved or

lament the sufferings caused by her coldness or cruelty, but rather illustrates the quality of the varying phases of his emotion. He seeks to communicate to the reader the peculiar flavour and beauty of love's first yearnings, say, or its consummation, as he might seek to communicate the special flavour and beauty of Leonardo's "Virgin of the Rocks" or Botticelli's "Spring." Love and art were to him the two windows through which the celestial light of the truth which is beauty alone is mystically apparent to mortals.

> " *Under the arch of Life, where love and death,*
>   *Terror and mystery, guard her shrine, I saw*
>   *Beauty enthroned; and though her gaze struck awe,*
> *I drew it in as simply as my breath.*
> *Hers are the eyes which, over and beneath,*
>   *The sky and sea bend on thee,—which can draw,*
>   *By sea or sky or woman* [1] *to one law,*
> *The allotted bondman of her palm and wreath.*

> " *This is that Lady Beauty, in whose praise*
>   *Thy voice and hand shake still,—long known to thee*
>   *By flying hair and fluttering hem,—the beat*
> *Following her daily of thy heart and feet,*
> *How passionately and irretrievably,*
> *In what fond flight, how many ways and days!* "

So considered, an intellectual position is not likely to be held by an instinctive poet, who sings thoughtlessly and spontaneously as the bird sings. Nor was it. Rossetti is a highly conscious artist. For one thing, he deliberately limited himself to subjects he thought the right subjects for poetry. He could write well, about quite different subjects. " A Last Confession " is an effective character-study in the Browning manner; " Jenny " a brilliant achievement in the realistic-pathetic. But he never attempted to repeat them. Love and Beauty, he thought, were the true subjects for the artist; so he wrote about Love and Beauty. And the main bulk of his poetry can be divided, in the first place, into poems about love and beauty; and further, into those poems in which he philosophizes on these subjects, and those in which he, as it were, shows them in action, describes the sensations of some moments of love's bliss, or,

[1] The emphasis on this word is mine.

as in his narrative poems, explores the picturesque possibilities of legend and fairy-tale.

This deliberate self-limitation of subject-matter is the
most significant fact to be taken into account in any attempt
at understanding Rossetti's genius, or estimating his place
in the hierarchy of poets. It reveals him, more than anything else, as the true representative of the æsthetic point
of view, for it shows it in action. And this has meant that
he can only be fully appreciated by that minority of human
beings who, to some extent, share the æsthetic point of
view. If Rossetti had given scope to the less purely
æsthetic, more human side of his talent, he would certainly
have been a more popular poet; and he might have been a
greater one.

His method of writing is as conscious as his choice of
theme. He deliberately chooses different manners for different subjects; his narrative poetry is in the simple,
coloured, concrete, angular style of the Pre-Raphaelites;
his sonnets in a majestic, polysyllabic, abstract, Latinized
diction, which rather recalls Milton. But both styles
are conscious styles, with the charm of the improviser;
the dew is not fresh on its petals; it is often over-
elaborate; if it is simple, it is with an artful simplicity;
we are never unconscious of the artist vigilantly at work.
Nor have his epithets and similes, though always well-
chosen, the heaven-sent felicity of Shakespeare's or Keats's.
We feel his language clothes his thought admirably,
but not that it is its incarnation. His rhythms, too,
lack the irresistible lilt and rush of the natural singer;
his lyric flights are those of the aeroplane rather than the
bird. In fact, we must admit that his writing never gives
us the authentic thrill of the finest first-hand inspiration.

But with the conscious artist's limitations he has his
merits. The sense of form, for one thing: with a thrilling
concentration his narrative poetry proceeds from opening
to climax; severely his sonnets maintain that unity of tone
and theme which is the distinguishing mark of their form.

" *Once more the changed year's turning wheel returns;*
　　And as a girl sails balanced in the wind,
　　And now before and now again behind
　Stoops as it swoops, with cheek that laughs and burns,—
　So Spring comes merry towards me here, but earns
　　No answering smile from me, whose life is twin'd

With the dead boughs that winter still must bind,
And whom to-day the Spring no more concerns.

"*Behold, this crocus is a withering flame;*
This snowdrop, snow; this apple-blossom's part
To breed the fruit that breeds the serpent's art.
Nay, for these Spring-flowers, turn thy face from them,
Nor stay till on the year's last lily-stem
The white cup shrivels round the golden heart.

This is what a sonnet should be: not a string of jewels, but a single, shining, faceted diamond.

It reveals a second virtue, his command of metre. For if he is not over-successful with the lyric forms, of the more deliberate elegiac he is a triumphant master. Whether in his sonnets or the intricate stanzas of "Love's Nocturn" and "The Stream's Secret," they move with a peculiar, charged, slumberous, orchestral plangency, unlike anything else in English literature.

Above all, the fact that he is a conscious artist makes him consistent. Reading him we have that delightful sensation so rarely permitted us by the reckless poets of England, that we are safe. As with Milton and Spenser and Gray, and with how few others, we can start a poem of Rossetti's sure of a smooth and steady flight, unbroken by bumps and jolts into the prosaic, the ridiculous, and the irrelevant. He is never patchy; the golden glaze of his beautifully finished style harmonizes his whole picture in the same level glow. And it does more than harmonize, it dignifies it. Rossetti's conscious craft is not that of the *petit maître*; it is a lofty speech adopted in no irresponsible spirit for lofty themes.

"*Follow the desultory feet of death.*"

"*Sleepless with cold, commemorative eyes.*"

"*And whom to-day the Spring no more concerns.*"

"*What shall be said of this embattled day,*
And armèd occupation of this night?"

These are in that highest achievement of conscious art, the grand style.

The outstanding representative of the Æsthetic Movement in English literature, the perfect example of the capacities and limitations of the deliberate artist—to say this is yet not to say everything about Rossetti. Indeed, it is to leave unsaid the most important thing, for it omits that aspect of talent which is not typical, those individual qualities which make his work unique. Like all creative geniuses, Rossetti can do some things in a way no one else can: tell a story, for instance. As a matter of fact, the power to tell a story in verse is a very rare one. Some of the greatest poets cannot do it at all. Keats's *Isabella,* Tennyson's *The Princess* are treasure-houses of poetic phrase and fancy, but they are very badly told stories. None of the characters is alive; there is no dramatic tension; we never want to know what is going to happen next. Rossetti's narrative poems contain nothing like as beautiful poetry; but we long to know what is going to happen next. Thrillingly, and with a slow, compelling effect of fate, the dramatic tension rises; vividly the wild, ballad-like figures emerge from the background; irresistibly the author casts the spell which transports us to the peculiar atmosphere of the story, the wild mediæval Scotland of "The King's Tragedy," the sinister witch-chamber of "Sister Helen," the luxurious southern palace of "The Bride's Prelude," heavy with intrigue and sultry noontide sunshine, the tragic moorland castle of "Rose Mary."

Closely associated with this ability to create an atmosphere is Rossetti's visual power. He was a painter as well as a poet, and some of the best parts of his poetry are his pictures. How exactly does he bring the still sick-room of "My Sister's Sleep" before our inner eye?

> "*Her little work-table was spread*
>   *With work to finish. For the glare*
>   *Made by her candle, she had care*
> *To work some distance from the bed.*

> "*Without, there was a cold moon up,*
>   *Of winter radiance sheer and thin;*
>   *The hollow halo it was in*
> *Was like an icy crystal cup.*

> "*Through the small room, with subtle sound*
>   *Of flame, by vents the fireshine drove*
>   *And reddened. In its dim alcove*
> *The mirror shed a clearness round.*

> " *I had been sitting up some nights,*
> *And my tired mind felt weak and blank;*
> *Like a sharp strengthening wine it drank*
> *The stillness and the broken lights.*"

Even the celestial landscape of " The Blessed Damozel "
he can make concrete for us. As clearly as his sister's
bedroom, we see the gold bar laden with lilies, the
earth millions of miles below spinning " like a fretful
midge," " the curled moon " above it " like a little feather
fluttering far down the gulf," the souls mounting up
to God " like thin flames." Even the granted prayers,
" melting each like a little cloud," are made visible to
earthly eyes. Nor does he evoke the impressions of the
other senses less vividly than those of the eyes; the rain
pattering on the windows of the firelit hall where King
James of Scotland awaits his death; the cadence of magical
music that precedes Rose Mary's first gaze at the crystal;
the stifling summer heat of Aloyse's wedding-day.

> " *Although the lattice had dropped loose*
> *There was no wind; the heat*
> *Being so at rest that Amelotte*
> *Heard far beneath the plunge and float*
> *Of a hound swimming in the moat.*

> " *Some minutes since, two rooks had toiled*
> *Home to the nests that crowned*
> *Ancestral ash-trees. Through the glare*
> *Beating again, they seemed to tear*
> *With that thick caw the woof o' the air.*

> " *But else, 'twas at the dead of noon*
> *Absolute silence; all*
> *From the raised bridge and guarded sconce*
> *To green-clad places of pleasaunce*
> *Where the long lake was white with swans.*

> " *Amelotte spoke not any word*
> *Nor moved she once; but felt*
> *Between her hands in narrow space*
> *Her own hot breath upon her face,*
> *And kept in silence the same place.*"

Finally, Rossetti can communicate to us a unique quality of emotion. His later sonnets are charged with peculiar passion. It is not the direct, ardent, natural man's passion of Burns or the argumentative, sharp, dynamic passion of Donne; but a brooding, complex emotion, at once static and troubled, voluptuous and intellectual, sumptuous and mystical. It has the splendour and fullness of autumn with its ripe fruits and its spilt scarlet leaves; and it has also autumn's melancholy. It is a passion that is conscious of its own mortality, that feels the decay implicit in its very magnificence. Its melancholy, indeed, is not less intense than its abandon. The one seems the child of the other. Rossetti's life had been dedicated to the pursuit of beauty in art and woman, "passionately and irretrievably." He had learnt that it was a vain pursuit; that, in this wearisome condition of mortality, followed exclusively without regard to any other sort of consideration, it ends in shame and disappointment, dust and ashes. Although its compelling attraction was as strong to him as ever, he realized that in this world, at least, it could never be satisfied. And fired by mingled desire and despair, his genius glowed to a new and dusky intensity. Solitary amid the ruins of the palace of art and love that he had built for himself, its sculptured reliefs lying broken and overturned in the rank grass, the November wind wailing though its desecrated halls, blowing the withered leaves down its roofless corridors, he gave voice to his sorrow, in words far more poignant than any that issued from him when it was standing in the pride of its beauty:

> " *Look in my face; my name is Might-have-been;*
> *I am also called No-more, Too-late, Farewell."*

What, then, is our final judgment of Rossetti? He cannot be put among the very greatest English poets with Shakespeare and Milton, or even with Spenser and Wordsworth and Shelley and Coleridge and Keats. For, apart from anything else, he came too late. The point of view from which he took his inspiration was too artificial, too remote from the primary impulses and aspirations of humanity. He is a poet of the silver age; and silver, however beautifully worked, can never be as precious as gold. Moreover, it must be repeated, his work, even at its very best, does not breathe that quality of divine, inevitable inspiration which

447

is the hall-mark of the very highest flights of poetry. Yet the very facts which prevent him being one of the greatest poets make him a great one. The point of view for which he stood, in spite of its narrowness and its ultimate failure, has a nobility not to be expressed by a mere shallow talent, however skilful: a worthy representative of it must be built on the grand scale. And Rossetti was a worthy representative. He adorned it with the grace of a consummate craftsmanship, a coloured imagination, and a sombre passion.

JOHN
RUSKIN

1819-1900

BY
R. H.
WILENSKI

S

JOHN
RUSKIN

". . . One had pleasure in making some sort of melodious noise about it. . . ."

"Praeterita," i. 139.

". . . the words on the scroll of a crest must be always a declaration of the bearer's own mind . . . I changed on my seal, the 'Age quod agis' into 'To-day.'"

"Praeterita," ii. 160.

"It is the vainest of affectations to try and put beauty into shadows, while all real things that cast them are left in deformity and pain."

Preface to a Catalogue of Works of Art.

"I have seen and heard much of Cockney impudence before now; but never expected to hear a coxcomb ask two hundred guineas for flinging a pot of paint in the public's face."

"Fors Clavigera," Letter 79.

THERE was a good deal of Cockney impudence in Ruskin; he was vain, conceited, and arrogant; and, judged by modern standards, he was inadequately educated in most of the fields in which he worked. But he was a great man all the same.

He is commonly regarded as a sentimental, moralizing æsthetician. He was nothing of the kind. He was a man of action, who was condemned by an unlucky accident to act for the most part by means of words and sentences,

451

and who largely failed in his life's endeavours for the simple reason that he *could not write.*

When I say that Ruskin could not write I do not mean, of course, that he could not produce literature, or strike out an arresting sentence, or charm, interest, and stimulate his reader. Everyone, who has ever opened any volume of his writings, knows that he could do any of these things, and that it would scarcely be an exaggeration to say that he never wrote a page in which he did not do them all. But it is, I think, accurate to say that he could not write, because all through the years of his maximum activity he was incapable of using language as a precise means of communicating ordered thought. For thirty-five years, from 1843 to 1878, he played a part of consequence in the life of his day, in spite of this inability to write; when finally he arrived at real control of language he was an exhausted organism with nothing to communicate but the gossip of a tired old man.

The trouble was that he was the victim of a vice. He was addicted from childhood onwards to a drug which he was forced to take in daily doses in the nursery until he acquired the taste for it. In youth and maturity he fought against the abuse of the drug; but he fought in vain; when at last he was immuned by satiety, his power of action was all spent.

The drug, of course, was the emotive language of the Bible. Ruskin, as everyone knows, was made to read the Bible *aloud* every day in childhood and early youth. He was started at the beginning, taken through to the end, and then taken back to begin again. He was also made to memorize long sections of the text. This continued till he went to Oxford. He then knew *by heart*:

Exodus, chapters xv. and xx.
Deuteronomy, chapter xxxii.
2 Samuel, chapter i. from 17th verse to the end.
1 Kings, chapter viii.
Psalms xxiii., xxxii., xc., xci., ciii., cxii., cxix., cxxxix.
Proverbs, chapters ii., iii., viii., xii.
Isaiah, chapter lviii.
Matthew, chapters v., vi., vii.
Acts, chapter xxvi.
1 Corinthians, chapters xiii., xv.
James, chapter iv.

and he had thousands of other phrases in his head. He
continued to read the Bible as long as he read anything.
He was always obsessed with the emotive rhythm, the
sonority, the obscurity, the archaism, and awful associations of this living text within his brain. We shall never
know to what extent the obsession impeded his power of
thinking, but no one who has really studied his writing will,
I am convinced, deny that this obsession fatally impeded
the precise externalization of his thought. The remembered
language continually intervened between the thought
and its expression, and often side-tracked the thought
itself.

Ruskin, it is quite clear, struggled to use language as a
means of precise communication. He fussed about the
derivations of words in an effort to persuade himself that
he was learning to use words with scientific care. But, in
fact, he continually failed to achieve sustained control of
his vocabulary. Again and again he began by making
sentences in which the words exactly represent the thought;
and then some remembered emotive words and phrases
would rise to his mind's surface, and he would take first one
sip of the fatal drug, and then another, till, finally, he
would abandon the hard task of precise externalization of
thought, and yield to the pleasure of making "some sort
of melodious noise about it." Again and again a paragraph
begins as precise writing and ends as emotive rhetoric
recalling the Bible. In book after book the words on
the first few pages have no power themselves, but sub-
missively obey the thought; then gradually the words
become more Biblical, and so emotive, till, in the end, the
thought is dancing to their tune.

The generation to which I belong—the generation which
was of military age in the German war—is very suspicious
and impatient of emotive rhetoric, because it suffered from
the effects of that rhetoric in the war. Most of my contemporaries are so "put off" by Ruskin's addiction to this
drug and his shameless distribution of it that they dub
him "a master of prose style," and leave the thirty-nine
volumes of the Library Edition uncut upon the shelf.
They thus know little or nothing of Ruskin's action because
that action cannot now be apprehended except by reading
the thirty-nine volumes. Moreover, they frequently assume
that Ruskin, as would appear from the outsides of the

thirty-nine volumes, was mainly a prolific writer of long books with emotive, obscurantist titles.

But, in point of fact, only a small proportion of Ruskin's writings are, properly called, books at all. Apart from *Modern Painters, The Seven Lamps of Architecture,* and *The Stones of Venice,* which were all written by the time he was forty, and *Praeterita,* the incomplete autobiography written when he was approaching seventy, he hardly produced anything which was planned and executed as a book. It is important to remember that the thirty-nine volumes consist for the most part of the texts of lectures, of essays and pamphlets, and of journalism, and that the effect of these productions at the time was reinforced (*a*) by personal contacts, (*b*) by local and topical interests, and (*c*) by the author's reputation first as the champion of Turner and the Pre-Raphaelites, then as " The Professor " in Oxford, and finally as " The Master " of St. George's Guild. Ruskin would not have played the part he did if he had done nothing but write long books. He acquired his power and influence by miscellaneous word-action reinforced by these three factors; and it was also mainly by the sale of his miscellaneous pronouncements, collected into volumes with the emotive, obscurantist titles, that he derived his income in his later years. There was no prejudice against emotive rhetoric in the nineteenth century, and, as a result, thousands at that time sipped the drug as administered by " The Professor " or " The Master," and having once sipped wanted to sip more.

But when Ruskin's miscellaneous productions encounter my generation they are in a different position altogether. They have not only to break down the hostility to emotive rhetoric but also to achieve their effect without the former reinforcements; moreover, they experience a third difficulty because much action which Ruskin then paradoxically declared to be necessary and inevitable has now taken place, and we have already learned to take it so much for granted that we find it difficult to realize the former paradoxical character of Ruskin's pronouncements, and we are apt to forget the courage which the making of those pronouncements involved.

For my own part, it is now seven years since I bought the Library Edition and began to cut it. I have found reading in the volumes an exhausting process because I have tried to read behind the writing and to get contact with

the young Cockney, who wrote it, then knew next to nothing about the pictures of the old masters; and, from the point of view of the student of æsthetic, it is manifestly unsound because it suggests that the spectator's own previous experience of nature provides adequate means of testing the content of truth in works of art. But the book nevertheless was of value at the time because it was constructive in character in the sense that the author sought to indicate a way of appreciating certain aspects of the work of a living artist whose later manner was misunderstood. Ruskin made a name as an art critic of consequence with this publication; and he deserved to.

But the next stage in his career was far more difficult, as he found out when, two years later, he travelled in Switzerland and Italy to collect material for the continuation of the book. For now he really began to learn something about the old masters. On this journey he worked in the Louvre, and he discovered Fra Angelico, the frescoes in Florence and Pisa, and Tintoretto in Venice. These experiences placed him in an awkward position. He had somehow or other to reconcile his new knowledge with the emphatic judgments in his first book. This situation was to occur again and again in his career as an art critic. He coped with it each time empirically as best he could. As a result, though everything he wrote about art is interesting, his art-criticism as a whole is an appalling muddle. One of the editors of the Library Edition told a friend of mine that for every emphatic statement in art-criticism made by Ruskin, there was another in some other part of his work, equally emphatic, in the opposite sense. This is hardly an exaggeration; and it was probably inevitable in the case of a man who, at twenty-three, had " got away with " the remarks on the old masters which appeared in the first edition of the first volume of *Modern Painters*.[1]

But it was not only ever-increasing knowledge which caused the inconsistencies that abound in Ruskin's art-criticism. There was another and a profounder cause—a conflict in aim which began on this tour and continued all his life.

On the 1845 tour, Ruskin travelled by carriage with a guide and a valet (he was always liberally supplied with

[1] In the revisions of his writings, which Ruskin carried out in later life, he removed many passages from the earlier books.

funds by his father). At Chamouni he had supper of
forellen, woodcock, and *omelette soufflée,* with a half-bottle
of wine " in fine condition." Before he had finished, he
went out to look at the sunset, and after supper he wrote
to his father: " As I came back to my *soufflée* and Sillery, I
felt sad at thinking how few were capable of having such
enjoyment and very doubtful whether it were at all proper
in me to have it all to myself." He was twenty-six when
he wrote this letter, and he was to become more and more
doubtful whether it was at all proper for him to spend his
time in the study of sunsets and works of art, and in the
production of drawings and writings, and more and more
doubtful if he was justified in spending his money in the
ordinary enjoyments of a gentleman, an artist, and a
scholar. More than twenty years later, when he had just
inherited the greater part of his father's fortune, he wrote
to his mother: " I am quite unable to judge what is best
for me to do. There is so much misery and error in the
world which I see I could have immense power to set
various influences against, by giving up my science and
art, and wholly trying to teach peace and justice ; and yet
my own gifts seem so specially directed towards quiet investigation of beautiful things that I cannot make up my
mind, and my writing is as vacillating as my temper."

He vacillated in this way all his life. He would be
peacefully drawing a Venetian palace when a newspaper
statement that a London seamstress had died of starvation
would come into his mind, and, throwing down his brush
in an attack of conscience, he would rationalize this dissatisfaction into a theory that there can be no justification
for art when there are people who live and work in terrible
conditions and have insufficient food. On another day he
would find himself in Manchester or Sheffield and take
refuge from the squalor of the half-developed industrial
world by burying himself in botanical study among the
flowers and minerals and Turners in his home, and he
would rationalize this retreat into a theory that no squalor
would be tolerated in a society where the ruling classes
loved flowers and minerals and art. Much of the confusion
in his art-criticism can be traced to mental processes of this
kind.

But all the time, we must remember, Ruskin was a man
of action. The second volume of *Modern Painters* was not

an action of much consequence. His defence of the Pre-Raphaelites was more important. *The Times* had described the Pre-Raphaelite pictures in the 1851 Academy as "mere servile imitation of remote antiquity," and had said in conclusion: "That morbid infatuation which sacrifices truth, beauty, and genuine feeling to mere eccentricity deserves no quarter at the hands of the public." Coventry Patmore drew Ruskin's attention to this criticism, and Ruskin wrote a vigorous letter to *The Times*, pointing out that what the Pre-Raphaelites were attempting to imitate was "not Pre-Raphaelite *art*, but Pre-Raphaelite *honesty*." He followed this by a pamphlet in which he tried to reconcile his old praises of Turner with his new praises of the Pre-Raphaelites, and by material help to the artists—purchases of their works, introductions to collectors, and general encouragement. His championship was effective, and after his action the Pre-Raphaelites were taken seriously in many quarters.

This encouraged him to further action, and he began the publication of yearly pamphlets called *Academy Notes,* to draw attention to other painters who seemed to him honest. The pamphlets were sold near the Academy and many visitors used them instead of catalogues. But Ruskin discontinued them after five years, partly because he found that artists whom he knew personally were offended when he damned their pictures, and partly because the detailed study of the Academy exhibitions had strengthened in his mind two steadily growing convictions: (*a*) that the regeneration of English art could not be accomplished by art criticism, but only by the regeneration of English life; and (*b*) that the regeneration of English life could not be assisted by the kind of activity which the Royal Academicians described as "art."

Ruskin wrote his last Academy pamphlet in 1859. He had published the second volume of *Modern Painters* in 1846, the third and fourth volumes in 1856; *The Seven Lamps of Architecture* had appeared in 1849, the three volumes of *The Stones of Venice* in 1851 and 1853. By the time the final volume of *Modern Painters* appeared in 1860 he had completely lost faith in art-criticism as worth-while action in itself; and, indeed, from 1855 onwards he had begun his social action properly so-called.

His first social work was at the Working Men's College

459

in Red Lion Square. This College had been founded by Maurice in 1854, and Ruskin lectured and taught there and provided easels, pictures, and so forth. In 1855 he delivered in Manchester the lectures on "The Political Economy of Art," which he afterwards reprinted as "*A Joy for Ever and its Price in the Market*," with the line from Keats on the title-page. From that date he was more and more disposed to lecture and to contribute to reviews and newspapers in order to get personal contacts and to reach a wide public; and he studied social problems and social economy with the full power of his analytic mind.

By 1860, when he was forty-one, he felt equipped, as a result of these studies, to make an elaborate statement of his economic attitude and convictions. He went to Chamouni (where fourteen years before he had those qualms of conscience about the sunset and the Sillery), and there he now wrote the essays afterwards reprinted in *Unto this Last,* which were followed by the essays afterwards reprinted in *Munera Pulveris.*

These essays on social economics were first published in the *Cornhill Magazine* and *Fraser's Magazine*; and, as is well known, they were received with derision. They also much distressed Ruskin's father, who could not bear the thought that his son (who " would have been a Bishop ") was now becoming suspect as a crank with subversive social and economic views. Ruskin was always parent-ridden to an astonishing degree. He had allowed his parents to marry him, and he allowed his mother to bully him to the very end of her life. He had designed the essays as the beginning of a campaign of social action. But, though his guns were loaded, he stayed his hand to please his father and practically suspended his social action during his father's life.

His father died in 1864. Ruskin was thereby transformed from a man of forty-five living on an allowance equivalent to something like £3,000 a year in present money, to a man of forty-five in unrestricted possession of a fortune equivalent to at least £300,000 to-day.[1]

He was thus equipped and ready for direct social action. But still he did not consider himself free. He still thought

[1] His father left him £120,000, various leasehold and freehold properties, and pictures valued at £10,000. He left his mother £37,000 and the house at Denmark Hill for life.

it necessary to please his mother—the stupid tyrant who
had forced the daily dose of the Bible-drug into his infant
brain. Ruskin's mother was still stupid and tyrannical;
but she was now eighty-three; he decided that it might be
possible to work a little behind her back—if he restricted
himself to articles in reviews and newspapers which she
would not read, and to the publication in book form of
inoffensive lectures like *Sesame and Lilies*; with this and
a little botany, a little geology, and a little drawing as
recreations, he might be able to wait and appease his desire
for action till the hour of release. And wait he did, with a
good deal of fretting, till the old lady's death in 1871, which
brought the equivalent of another £70,000 or so into his
exchequer, and would have brought complete freedom if
only he had been wise.

But, alas! he had not been wise. He was now fifty, and
at the height of his strength; his name was widely known;
and he had the equivalent of £370,000 to do what he liked
with. For years past, he had been preparing for this
moment of freedom and power, for the moment when he
would be free, not only to talk and write conspicuously
about social improvement, but to act conspicuously also.
And when the moment came, he had himself already
destroyed his chance.

Two years before, he had been offered the Slade Profes-
sorship of Fine Art in Oxford and (as he wrote himself
about twenty years later) he had "foolishly accepted it."
He had accepted it partly out of vanity: he was flattered
at the invitation which gave him a new status. He had
also partly accepted it to please his mother and partly to
have a good excuse to get away from her. He had persuaded himself that he accepted it because he believed that
the social work which he had at heart could only be accomplished by means of the upper classes. But by accepting
it, he was undertaking to become a regular lecturer in art-
criticism—a field in which he had long ceased to have
continuous interest; he was undertaking, as he wrote to
the Dean of Christ Church, to do "nothing intemperate or
mischievous," and he knew that he was expected to avoid
discussion of social economics in his lectures. He was
undertaking this in the frame of mind in which he wrote:
"I simply cannot paint, nor read, nor look at minerals,
nor do anything else that I like, and the very light of the

461

morning sky . . . is hateful to me because of the misery
I know of and see signs of where I know it not. . . . I will
endure it no longer quietly." On the threshold of a real
opportunity for direct social action on a large scale, he had
become—" The Professor."

The first Oxford lecture was delivered in 1870. In the
next eight years he made desperate and despairing efforts.
He was not a man to perform his academic duties in a
perfunctory way. He took enormous pains with the preparation of his lectures and the arrangement of the exhibitions by which he illustrated them; and he did much
extra work unofficially with admiring students—many of
them young women—which was perhaps pleasant but took
time. He also maintained all his previous activities. He
drew, he studied, and wrote about geology, botany,
Italian art, and anything else which chanced to interest
empirically his analytic mind.

He did all this, and embarked *at the same time* on the
use of his powers and resources for the translating into
action of his social attitude and convictions—a full-time
occupation in itself. This action included some celebrated
minor enterprises like the street-sweeping in St. Giles's, the
Hinksey road-making, and the tea-shop in Paddington.
But its main features were the invention, foundation, and
launching of the Guild of St. George and the publication
of a monthly sociological pamphlet—*Fors Clavigera*—
addressed to the Workmen and Labourers of Great Britain.
He allocated his fortune to this social work. But he did
not finance his enterprises in a constructive way. Here,
as elsewhere, he reacted to immediate stimuli. His generosity was empirical. He gave, but he did not co-ordinate
his gifts. He frittered away his money in a series of
impulsive benevolent gestures—until in his old age he had
nothing but the income from his books.

No one could have kept up the activities which he carried
on for these eight years; in 1878, when he was fifty-nine, his
brain gave way; and he had periodic mental breakdowns
for the remainder of his life.

Till recently, Ruskin's writings on social economics were
generally regarded as Utopian literature and his social
experiments as comic failures. We have all been told,
amid laughter, that the Hinksey road was a very bad road,

that the Paddington tea-shop did not pay, and that the British Constitution was not shattered by the St. George's Guild. But *Unto this Last, Munera Pulveris,* and Ruskin's other economic writings, whatever they may have turned out to be as a result of his inability to write, were not designed as literature or as academic exercises in economic theory, but as a programme of action; and if it be realized that his social experiments were fundamentally *gestures,* they will be seen not really to have failed at all.

Ruskin had looked at conditions around him and seen that they were unsatisfactory. He had sought the causes of those conditions and traced them to the stupidity, insensibility, and greed of the business world, and to the absence among the poorer classes of a willingness to submit to discipline. He had examined the official social-economic creed—the so-called Law of Supply and Demand based on the postulate of an Economic Man—and found it to be the rationalization of the stupidity, insensibility, and greed on the one hand, and the indiscipline on the other. He had analysed the most powerful material factors in the unsatisfactory prevailing conditions—the increased use of machinery and the increased production of gold; and he had come to the conclusion that, without a change of spirit in the business world, and with the persistence and continuous increase of the power of these factors and the continued acceptance of the official social-economic creed, the unsatisfactory conditions would *inevitably and steadily grow worse, until a situation would arise when there would be thousands of unemployed people who would have to be fed by the workers or allowed to starve.* He had set himself to indicate to his country that *therefore*: (*a*) the stupidity, the insensibility, and the greed of the rich and the indiscipline of the poor must be altered; (*b*) the creed rationalizing the conditions must be abandoned; and (*c*) the use made of the increased and increasing machinery and the increased and increasing gold must be different. He had done this, before he came into his father's fortune, by talking and writing; from 1871 to 1878 he did it by talking and writing, and also by the major gesture called the Guild of St. George and the minor gestures of the road and the tea-shop. Ruskin never expected that the Guild would change the British Constitution, and he was not trying to reorganize transport when he set the Undergraduates to make a road.

463

Events have shown that Ruskin was not only right in his analysis of the conditions which he saw around him, but also right in his realization of what would *have* to be done if those conditions were allowed to develop. He has been shown right not only on general lines but in a great many details. When he began his social-economic studies there were, for example, no free State elementary and technical schools as we understand them; there were no minimum wages in industry, and there were no old-age pensions. In the Preface to *Unto this Last* (1862) he proposed them all —not as Utopian ideals, but as *necessities demanded by elementary justice in the conditions of the modern world.* He hated machines and the gold standard and the Law of Supply and Demand because he was certain that the use which was being made of them would lead to more misery and starvation; and time has shown that he saw accurately and advocated nothing but social services that were bound to come.

The temptation to speculate on what Ruskin would say and do if he reappeared among us is irresistible. We might expect him to throw emotive rhetoric at the heads of our modern artists, to congratulate us on our social services, and to look on the Soviet Republic and the Fascist organization as enlarged versions of the Guild of St. George. But, of course, he would do none of these things. He was a man of action with a brilliant independent mind, and his motto was *To-day.* He would see, not what we see, but something that escapes us, and urge us to undertake *immediately* something that in 1980 will be done. And we should pay no heed to him because, presumably, he would still have the language of the Bible in his ears and be still unable to call a spade a spade or think of one without the associated ideas of Eden and Adam.

But one thing, I believe, is certain. He would be pleased —though not surprised—to observe that, though the professional artists of 1932 find it impossible to read what he wrote about art, the professional economists find it useful to know what he wrote about economics.

Mr. Wilenski is engaged upon a full-length study of John Ruskin, which is to be published shortly by Messrs. Faber & Faber, Ltd.

LORD
SALISBURY

1830-1903

BY
HUGH
MASSINGHAM

LORD SALISBURY

ROBERT, third Marquis of Salisbury, and four times Prime Minister of England, is not at all the kind of statesman one expects to find in the Victorian age. With the exception of Disraeli, the important figures in Victorian politics were whigs or radicals, who devoted their time to putting forward with great sincerity and much repetition the humanitarian ideas of the eighteenth century. But Salisbury was not of this train, and he regarded with cynical detachment the radical idea that man was ascending ever upwards on the ladder of Progress—towards a Paradise which by the end of the century Bradlaugh and Morley had made nice and airy by sweeping out all the religious paraphernalia. What was to happen at the end of the journey—what, in other words, we were going to *do* when we were all thoroughly emancipated—was not quite clear.

It is this contrast between impoverished intellectual life and emotional frothiness which makes the Victorian radical seem so immature to the modern generation. The appeal was so often to the heart and so rarely to the head. Disraeli is an exception, but then, Disraeli, like Bolingbroke and Burke, was a man of first-rate genius, and his appeal is not primarily emotional. He is one of those men who do not come right out of the age in which they live, as Machiavelli does out of mediæval Florence or Bolingbroke out of the eighteenth century. The Jew in Disraeli enabled him to stand a little apart, to see all round the smug English character, and he does not in the least belong to the generous but cocksure Victorian England that came into being with the enlarged franchise.

467

The problem that these new voters set the Conservative statesman was how to get their confidence without becoming a Liberal in the process. Disraeli solved it, partly because he was a man of genius, partly because, like Randolph Churchill, he was a picturesque personality. Salisbury had not Disraeli's gifts or Disraeli's personality, and even in his later years, when his slouch and his beard became electoral assets, he was not a great popular figure. Gladstone's admirers felt that, even as they listened to him, a squad of recording angels was taking down his words in a mood of breathless ecstasy: no one felt the same glow when listening to Salisbury. And yet, if he never exerted the same moral authority as Gladstone, he had many of the qualities that might have made him popular. He was a fighter, and he spoke and wrote in one of the most vigorous of styles. It is true that he is not a great stylist, if by style we are thinking of a Clarendon or a Burke, or, to come nearer home, if we are thinking of Salisbury's own contemporary, Bradley. His prose is too metallic, too hard: its very directness becomes monotonous. There is no subtlety in it. But it seems pure water after the muddiness of some of his political contemporaries. Take Gladstone, for instance. Gladstone was considered the greatest orator of his day; but no one, not even those interested in the history of the times, reads him now for pleasure. It is not only that there is a bad Ciceronian flavour about Gladstone's prose. What makes him so irritating is that his matter is so rarely equal to his manner: there are times, even, when the matter seems on the point of vanishing altogether:

> Is it not wonderful to those who are freemen, and whose fathers have been freeman, and who hope that their children will be freemen, and who consider that freedom is an essential condition of life, and that without it you can have nothing great and nothing noble in political society, that we are led by an administration . . . to march upon another body of freemen and against their will to subject them to despotic Government?

Some of us would have thought it very " wonderful " if we had discovered " nothing great and nothing noble " in the Middle Ages. Of course, Gladstone is not always so silly as this, but even when he is addressing a

more intellectual audience—as in his periodical tilts at
Huxley—his argument never seems to move surely from
one step to another. He is so busy qualifying, with saying
that black is not always black but sometimes (for who can
tell?) may even be grey, that his argument, instead of
advancing, appears actually to be on the retreat.   Salisbury's method is quite different.   When he has anything to
say he says it right out and makes no bones about it:

> Englishmen were, perhaps, never very popular on
> the Continent. Satirists and wits have always amused
> themselves with caricaturing the somewhat angular
> peculiarities that mark our national character, and the
> portrait was seldom flattering. But still, the reproaches
> expressed or implied were of a kind that is not very
> difficult to bear. Pride, uncouthness, foolhardiness
> form the staple of the criticism levelled at us by
> foreign writers. Undue roughness and violence were
> the mark at which they were aimed. They were
> derogatory rather to our claims to the polish of civiliza-
> tion than to any more sterling qualities. Sometimes
> other blots were hit—our supposed perfidy, our selfish-
> ness, our shopkeeping propensities. But whatever else
> was said of us, no one ever thought of impugning an
> Englishman's courage. If the Great War had done
> little for our popularity, it had at least left deeply
> graven on the minds of Continental populations that
> we could fight. But all this is changed now. All the
> respect for our national character, which was founded
> on a belief in its bull-dog characteristics, has dis-
> appeared. Our courage is not only disbelieved, but it
> is ridiculed as an imposture that has been found out.
> English bravado and English cowardice are the com-
> mon staple of popular caricatures. The Englishman
> furnishes to Continental wits the same sort of standing
> butt that the Yankee presented to us three years ago.
> The estimate of the English character that is felt in
> every circle and class of society abroad, and expressed
> without reserve in the Press, may be summed up in
> one phrase, as a portentous mixture of bounce and
> baseness.

The quotation shows how different in temper Salisbury
was from his radical contemporaries. The principles he
stood for seem equally strange in the atmosphere of Vic-

torian Radicalism. Salisbury was an aristocrat and an intellectual, living in a democratic and emotional age, and it is not surprising that he left no measure of reform upon the statute-book. Salisbury's career is thus of great interest. The last aristocrat makes his bow upon the English political scene, and the account of his stewardship seems not so much a judgment upon a man as upon a caste and a habit of thought.

It is extraordinary to find such a man in such an age. In fact, the puzzling thing about Salisbury's career is not the policy he pursued; it is the question of how so negative a person, who was frankly sceptical of democracy, ever came to be the Prime Minister of a place like Victorian England that believed so strongly in political democracy. The reason is that he was carried along by a series of remarkable events with which he had nothing to do. When Disraeli died, the choice of a Conservative leader was between Salisbury and Sir Stafford Northcote, and Salisbury—although considered reactionary—was obviously the better man. But with the radical tide running so strongly he could not have hoped to be Prime Minister for any length of time had it not been for a sudden departure in Liberal policy. In 1886 Gladstone declared for Irish Home Rule, and the uncemented structure of the Liberal Party fell to pieces. The Conservatives swallowed the Whigs without irreparably ruining their digestion, because Hartington and his friends were in reality Conservatives who objected, not to Tory principles, but merely to the party name. The arrival of Chamberlain turned out to be quite a different matter. He not only became the eyes and imagination of the Conservatives: he made the new voters think of Toryism as something more than a policy for dukes and squires. In short, Chamberlain, as much by the magic of his name as by his ideas of social reform, reconciled the working man to the Conservative Party. Salisbury had nothing to do with it. With his scorn for popular judgments, his critical intellect, and his epigrams, he was the last man to bridge the gulf between eighteenth-century Toryism and nineteenth-century democracy.

But had the late Victorian electorate deliberately chosen an aristocrat, it could not have done better than Salisbury. He was a realist with a fine intellect and a tremendous sense of public duty. All sham moved him to impatient scorn. He shunned society, despising it for its shallowness and its

borrowed opinions, and from the start he decided that to be
" stewed and bored at dinners and parties " was the " usual
destiny of us unfortunate white slaves." Hatfield groaned
with his protests, though he could, when cornered, be the
most charming of hosts. Even as late as 1889 he could
write to the Duchess of Rutland: " In our modern Church
we have abolished fasts and penances, and we are quite
right in doing so, because they would be quite superfluous
and excessive, now that we have invented evening parties
and Court ceremonies."

The Church, however, had his unswerving loyalty. Salisbury was a Christian and a devout member of the High
Church party of the Church of England. Like Gladstone,
he believed that Christianity implied a Church, and he
would have approved of the inversion that the " spirit
killeth but the letter giveth life." Yet the difference
between Salisbury's spiritual life and Gladstone's was
profound. Gladstone, a Nonconformist in High Church
clothing just as he was a Conservative in Liberal clothing,
lost his bearings altogether. The Nonconformist, wander-
ing about in an unfamiliar mystical forest, was never quite
sure when the voice was the voice of Mr. Gladstone and
when it was the voice of the Lord God Almighty. Perhaps
there was no difference after all—and another tree and
another sin fell in the quiet of Hawarden. But Salisbury
was never guilty of self-deception. You could not know
the truth simply because the ways of God were hidden in
impenetrable mystery. Lady Gwendolen Cecil says, in the
biography of her father, that " all his life he found a difficulty in accepting the moral teaching of the Gospels." Or,
in Salisbury's own words, " God is all-powerful and God is
all-loving—and the world is what it is ! How are you
going to explain *that*?" And, to quote his daughter
again: " When it was urged against the truth of some
Christian doctrine that it was morally unsatisfying, or
rationally incomprehensible, his only comment used to be,
' as if *that* had anything to do with it.' " You go your way,
then, and " it is precisely an even chance whether it takes
us with God or exactly against Him." Even a mystical
interpretation of the drama of life—man's fall and existence
as men and his restoration by grace—these and similar
speculations would have seemed to him of no practical
importance.

It was hardly a philosophy that was likely to be very

clearly understood by the thousands of Victorian chapel-goers who liked their religion neat and without any mystical dilution; and it remained throughout his life a definite barrier between him and the emotional, earnest democracy of his day. There was between Bright and his audiences a reassuring sense of affinity which came from looking at things in the same way. Salisbury, on the other hand, remained aloof, regarding man's unprofitable journey with cynical detachment. And where was it to end? Salisbury did not know, was not prepared to guess. One did one's duty and was not responsible for the results.

Salisbury was undoubtedly a Christian, but mixed up with his religious convictions there was a queer blend of cynicism and fatalism. He was intellectually and psychologically quite incapable of joining the various movements of reform that filled the Victorian age with so much tumult and colour. By nature he was a solitary, and just as in his private life he resented the efforts of society to interfere with his privacy, so in his public life he profoundly disbelieved in the growing tendency of the State to interfere with the individual. His daughter says that he " carried respect for the liberty of the subject to a reckless extreme, and on one occasion protested seriously against his wife's infringement of it in the person of a child of ten." And she adds in a passage that indirectly brings out Salisbury's real personal charm :

> There were few decisions of juveniles in which, when left to himself, he was not prepared tacitly to acquiesce: " N. has been very hard put to it for something to do," he wrote of a schoolboy who happened to have been left for a short time under his sole care at Hatfield. " Having tried all the weapons in the gun-cupboard in succession—some in the riding-school and some, he tells me, in his own room—and having failed to blow his fingers off, he has been driven to reading Sydney Smith's essays and studying Hogarth's pictures." " He may be able to govern the country," was his wife's comment on such occasions, " but he is quite unfit to be left in charge of his children."

It was undoubtedly very pleasant. " ' My father always treats me as an ambassador,' was the murmured reflection of a youth in his teens, ' and I do like it.' "

No doubt; but when the principle was applied to politics

it did not have such happy results. Is the individual never to be interfered with? Salisbury's answer was not at all satisfactory. He was against the Liberal policy of extending the franchise, and here undoubtedly he was on firm ground. Gladstone had the word freedom always on his lips, but when you examine his speeches it turns out that he does not mean intellectual or spiritual freedom but merely the right to use the vote. The Conservative objection was that by giving the vote to everybody you did not necessarily end oppression, if oppression there were: what you did was to exchange one set of oppressors, who were the most cultured class of the community, for another set of oppressors who were as yet untried politically and without a sense of responsibility. Salisbury was in the vanguard of this opposition, and it says a great deal for his integrity that when Disraeli in 1867 coolly took over the Liberal policy, as a man might borrow the petty cash in a temporary emergency, he very promptly resigned: he was not in the least afraid of being numbered among the " extra stupid section of the stupid party." He was still firm in 1885, and in his negotiations with Gladstone's Government he insisted that the boundary commissioners " should have due regard to the pursuits of the population." It was not the perfect means of minority representation, as Salisbury well knew, but it was the best that could be done in the circumstances, and it protected business quarters of a town, for instance, from being swamped by the working-class elements.

The criticism that can be made against Salisbury in this connection is a criticism that can equally be applied to the whole of his career: he had no alternative policy to offer. One expects something more from a statesman than sheer negation. In the controversy over the Corn Laws there was a great deal that was shoddy in Disraeli's talk about the " gentlemen of England," for Disraeli far too often " pities the plumage and forgets the dying bird; " but the strength of his position was that he was not only offering an alternative policy but also an alternative way of life. And this is precisely what Salisbury never did. When Disraeli opposed the Repeal of the Corn Laws, he was insisting that there was something more important than mere wealth: over and above his economic objections to Free Trade was his argument that a flourishing agriculture was essential to the well-being of a nation; in short, that it

was part of the " good life." Salisbury seems to have no
moral background to his actions: you cannot relate his
opposition to an enlarged franchise to any definite, creative
philosophy. The voters in a nation, he said, could be compared with the shareholders of a company, and it followed
that just as the biggest shareholders had the largest number
of votes at the company meeting, so too the largest holders
of property should be given more votes than the Tom,
Dick, and Harry of the unpropertied classes of the community. Even from the point of view of what passes for
practical politics, the argument is indefensible. Can anybody think of a worse thing to say to the god-fearing people
of England? And his inability to realize this earnest streak
in his countrymen had very important practical results. It
allowed the Liberal Party to make a corner in " sweetness
and light"—an asset that the present Labour Party has
quietly appropriated. The Conservative Party became
even more identified with property than it had been before,
and when Randolph Churchill sprang his silly ideas about
Tory democracy on an open-mouthed electorate, it suddenly occurred to some people that the Conservative Party
might stand for a way of life. No one could have thought
so from a casual glance at the massive figure of Salisbury,
with the hand impatiently tapping the knee. Was there a
God? asked the waiting multitude. Yes, said Salisbury,
but He was a very great personage, an aristocrat, not given
to particularly humane impulses. And what, then, ought
we to do? Your duty, replied Salisbury. It is not surprising that the electorate preferred the more comforting and
precise advice of the Liberals, which could fortunately be
so often carried out at the expense of the Turk.

If Disraeli was the imaginative thinker, Salisbury was
the negative one, and this conclusion is inevitable, whether
you consider their records in domestic politics or their different ways of handling foreign affairs. When the two were
working in harness the result was excellent. In the negotiations over the Berlin Treaty, Disraeli supplied the constructive policy and Salisbury filled in the details. Disraeli's
objective was perfectly clear. Looking upon England as
an Asiatic Power just as much as a European one, his aim
at Berlin was to bolster up the Turk and thus to prevent
an enemy from getting hold of the Dardanelles and closing
the road to India. But loyally as Salisbury worked at Berlin
he never believed in the Eastern policy: good, honest

Englishman that he was, he distrusted the "rococo atmosphere" that surrounded it, and he prophesied the fall of
the Government. His heart was in "intelligent inaction,"
and this was the policy he pursued when he became responsible for foreign affairs.

Within the limited field that he marked out for himself
he was undoubtedly successful. Foreign diplomatists
found him a pleasant relief after being lectured by Liberal
statesmen, and for a time he raised Britain's price in the
diplomatic market by showing Europe that her support was
worth having. Europe never really understood either
Gladstone or Disraeli; but they understood Salisbury and
respected him. There is, too, no doubt about his skill as
a diplomatist; he showed great dexterity throughout his
career at the Foreign Office, and especially during the Boer
War, when there was a danger of a European combination
being formed against us. But his skill was intellectual not
psychological. There is no evidence that he ever understood the *unreif* German mentality that showed itself just
before the War: Salisbury went to France when he went
abroad, and he refused to see, or to go and see, anybody.

Had he lived earlier in the century, say during the
period when Palmerston was mainly responsible for foreign
affairs, his qualities might have made him the supreme
statesman of his age. The old Europe had been a picturesque place where a man like Salisbury, with his cautious
realism and his exact understanding of England's immediate interests, could have played the game of isolation
without storing up dangers for the future. Moreover, for
all its martial music and its amusing trumpeting about
emancipation and liberty, the Europe which existed between the fall of Napoleon and the rise of Bismarck did
not possess the particular fatal elements—the forces of
organization, coupled with immense wealth—that made a
general world war on the scale of 1914 possible. The notion
that democracy is more pacific than other forms of government is the merest moonshine; for by its popular education,
which enables its leaders to whip up instantaneous passion
through the Press, and its industry, which supplies the
necessary wealth, it is all the time creating a military
machine more powerful than any autocracy ever dreamt
was possible. Sedan showed that the new forces were
already at work. The war of 1870 was very much more
than a private fight between two great nations, and more,

even, than the announcement that a new nation had now
to be reckoned with: when Napoleon III fell, the last of a
happy-go-lucky civilization toppled over with him. From
that moment a new era began. Henceforward Europe
might be a worse place, or it might be a better one, but it
certainly was not going to be the same, and Salisbury had
no constructive policy in his bag.

When he formed his second administration in 1886, the
loose structure of the old Europe had already hardened into
the new. Salisbury undoubtedly realized some of the
dangers.

" If in the present grouping of nations," he wrote
to the Queen in 1887, when Bismarck was trying to
draw us into an alliance, ". . . England was left out
in isolation, it might well happen that the adversaries
who are arming against each other on the Continent
might treat the English Empire as divisible booty, by
which their differences might be adjusted, and though
England would defend herself, it would be at fearful
risk and loss."

Exactly. England, bulging with possession, was the
obvious prey, and yet Salisbury's method of dealing with
the danger was merely to postpone it. Picking up the now
traditional policy of isolation, he met the German demands
for an alliance with cautious objections. England could not
commit herself to a future war without knowing the *casus
belli*, and in any case, he could not form an alliance that
was aimed against France. Yet he ventured to put a timid
foot into the stream. He very wisely came to an understanding with Italy on the question of the Mediterranean,
and throughout his second administration he managed to
work fairly amicably with Berlin. But it must be remembered that, skilfully as he handled affairs at this time, no
other course was open to him. While France remained
" generous by fits but permanent in mischief," no understanding or lasting friendship was possible with her. Salisbury might have placated Paris by ordering the evacuation
of Egypt; but he found he could not do so, and protests
and bad temper were continually being blown across the
Channel. Nor was Salisbury, with his cynical detachment,
the best person to calm down the mercurial statesmen in
Paris. " Oui, oui," he said to the French Ambassador at
the time of the Fashoda incident, " vous avez raison, mais

il faut que vous vous en alliez." Disraeli was not the only
person who found that his "noble friend" was not a
"man who measures his phrases."

In fact, those who put Salisbury's statesmanship high
because of his handling of affairs up to 1890 forget that
Bismarck was the real power in Europe, and the only
one who counted. While he remained, the dangers of a
European war were always present, but always under
control. For old, testy, malign, and jealous as he then
was, the man who had summoned up the new spirits also
knew how to keep them in check. When he ceased to rule,
Europe fell to pieces. It was not only that economic
rivalries were added to racial antipathies; that was so
before 1890. The fatal thing was that when Bismarck went,
three of the most inept rulers in history—William II of
Germany, Francis Joseph of Austria, and Nicholas II of
Russia—all were upon the scene at the same time.

Europe under these three men moved inevitably towards
war; and the fact is that Salisbury did nothing to stop it
and had no policy except a hand-to-mouth one. Indeed,
throughout his third and fourth administration Salisbury
showed no sign of fully realizing how serious matters had
grown, and that the policy of isolation, carried out on the
old terms, had become impossible. Even his shrewdest
strokes were but brilliant flashes of insight into a situation
that was rapidly growing beyond him. The Anglo-German
Convention was designed to remove one source of friction,
and at the time seemed to lay the foundation of a new
understanding between the two countries. Salisbury could
not see that it was already too late, and that the cool
diplomacy of Bismarck's time had gone.

How rapidly the European scene was changing must
have become only too clear to him when he formed his
third administration in 1895. Salisbury came back to the
Foreign Office, to find Germany estranged from England.
This was underlined for him by the Kruger telegram and
the German Navy Bill. In the following year the Kaiser
was saying: "The German Empire has become a world
Empire." And in 1897 the Tirpitz Bill, with its proposal
for an automatic naval programme, was a direct challenge
to England that could not be ignored.

These successive hammer blows made Salisbury's problem quite clear. His prophetic warning of a European
combination against England seemed about to be fulfilled.

477

In 1899 there was an attempt to form an alliance between Germany, France, and Russia, and it only fell through because the Kaiser, unable to sacrifice anything even for the prize of the British Empire, refused to give up Alsace-Lorraine. The Queen had seen what might happen long before. " She cannot help feeling that our *isolation* is dangerous," she wrote to Salisbury. But the man at the Foreign Office changed not. " Isolation," he wrote to her, " is a much less danger than the danger of being dragged into wars which do not concern us."

The argument would have been unanswerable in Palmerston's days: it had no application to the Europe which then existed. The German Navy Bill was aimed at Britain, and the group of inept mediocrities in Berlin were daily making it more obvious that they were bent on a trial of strength. Salisbury might have met the situation, either by an alliance or by putting England into a state of defence. By going on with a negative policy of inaction he did not solve anything, he merely postponed everything; and although he played his cards with the hand of a master, the decisive trick was always in the other hand. To do nothing at all was to run an utterly unjustifiable risk, and when the Boer War came, the danger was patent to everybody.

Indeed, Salisbury, like Gladstone, lived beyond his time. But there is a difference. Gladstone was always catching up with events, and had he lived for another decade he might have understood the new social forces that were at work; and no doubt he would have led them. Salisbury, with a far less flexible mind, remained stationary throughout his career, and he drifted—like an inanimate barrel—into a crisis that he never understood, and therefore never knew how to control.

ROBERT LOUIS STEVENSON

1850-1894

BY
H. M.
TOMLINSON

ROBERT LOUIS STEVENSON

I WELL remember the day in Leadenhall Street when a youth saw a fresh newspaper placard coming along, and how his indifference abruptly changed when he read its news of the death of R. L. Stevenson. Some light went out of that day; he felt even a little lonely. But it was only a Victorian day, and that is his only excuse; it was not his fault he was in it. The horse-buses were there, and the hansoms and top-hats, though he was not of the age to remember how the ladies were dressed; however, they were not habitually in Leadenhall Street, all that time ago. But he can see the corner plainly enough where the placard struck him, though he will never again see it in reality. It was by the old office of Devitt & Moore. That puts a plain year to the incident, for the building has vanished, and not everyone to-day remembers who once owned such famous clipper ships as the *Collingwood* and *Sobraon*.

A great number of young people felt the same as that youth, without a doubt, and for a similar reason, when they heard that Edgar Wallace had gone. It is not an unworthy, if it is not a critical tribute. We are never exacting over what gives us joy until the day comes when joy seems rarer than it used to be, and we are critics at last. That youth, for instance, was heartily enjoying a serial yarn, *The Ebb Tide*, then running in a periodical called *To-day*, edited by Jerome K. Jerome. We had solemn enjoyments then, I know. That was the time when *The Story of an African Farm* was said to be an addition to great literature, and Mrs. Humphry Ward was being discussed as gravely as she wrote; Grant Allen's *Woman Who Did*, the very next year, was to be a striking landmark in

T

our moral and intellectual progress, so now we may judge
our distance from it, as it is out of sight. We had to climb
iron cleats to the upper deck of the Blackwall bus, and sat
hunched up back-to-back along the middle of it. Nor did
we laugh at ourselves because of all this. So much of the
fun of those days was unconscious. It was bequeathed, its
signal merit unknown to us, to this generation, which
cannot help smiling when the oddities happen to be
noticed. Maybe there is a cheat in the fun; it may hide a
warning also, though this generation, unaware of its own
solemn acceptances, will note only that the oddities are
comical.

Mr. Havelock Ellis, whose erudition and critical opinions
command our respectful attention, once said that Stevenson
was " the hollow image of a writer; a man who, having
laboriously taught himself to write after the best copybook
models, found that he had nothing to say, and duly said it
at length." It seems to me that whenever I see a contemporary reference to Stevenson it disparages him; and
though we may pay no more attention to that idiosyncrasy
of latter-day literary opinion, as a substitute for the Delphic
oracles, than we give to a Parliamentary debate, yet when
Mr. Havelock Ellis disparages it becomes a serious matter.
We have to look then to where we stand, and ask ourselves
why we are there. Some years ago I was inclined to agree
with the veteran writer and scholar. That was easy,
because other lively interests and compelling events kept
the dust flying, and it settled fairly thickly on what was in
repose, on what was bright and surprising, once on a time.
It settled even on the memory of that sad placard.

But perhaps worse than the distractions of time and
change, there had arisen a discussion of Stevenson, very
prolonged, and on a plane higher and nobler than most
subjects could sustain; it was more like adoration than a
discussion. It embarrassed many admirers of R. L. S.,
who suspected, we may suppose, that rapt star-gazing,
though good for us occasionally, is indiscreet in daylight's
busy hours. We noticed plenty of harsh daylight fall
presently on our romantic hero of letters, and that is apt
both to dishearten the rapture of worshippers and cheer
the ribald. When that occurs it is the ribald who win
attention, for their comments are more entertaining. The
worshippers become silent and disappear; as faith is unarmed, it puts up a miserable show before mockery. And

thus we find Stevenson to-day, still as popular as most of our present story-tellers—ask at any free library—yet rarely mentioned when serious literary estimates are being made. He has joined Scott, Thackeray, and Dickens, only it happens that as they are so tall they cannot be conveniently hidden; no matter what we say or do, there they still are; and Stevenson is of lesser stature. But a writer may be of considerable importance, if not immediately noticeable when well back in the past with Dickens. We might judicially remember, now and then, that there is a probability that our admiration for some obvious contemporary names may puzzle the next generation as much as an old serious worship of Stevenson puzzles us.

Though Stevenson taught himself, "a sedulous ape," to write after the best copybook methods, one thing he had in him: he could tell a story. He did not have to copy from models for that. The drive of his spirit was not as incontestable as Kipling's; he paused to consider words, and Kipling, one guesses, never had to do that; so the spell Stevenson casts, as a story-teller, is not so compelling as Kipling's. But then, as an Ancient Mariner, Kipling is the most hypnotic we ever had. You can, if you will, deny Stevenson; but though you may be armed against Kipling, and know precisely what he is going to say, for you have heard it before, once he begins you surrender. Few of us would deny Kipling's extraordinary power, yet few of us will admit now that Stevenson had a similar gift, and in a high degree. Yet try over again the fight in the round-house in *Kidnapped*—in fact, try over again other passages from Stevenson that you can recall, and you may find that you are caught and held, as you were when first you read them.

The story-teller appeals to the child in us. As to that, Stevenson could disparage himself. He confessed sadly, in his last year, that he had written for "boys." We know he had. But who are the boys? The spinner of a yarn addresses himself to what is primal in his audience. When we wish to chill the youth in us, and make him feel sadder and wiser, we rebuke him with some advice on the "literature of escape." Yet what is that? Is there no escape through *Pickwick* or *Robinson Crusoe*? Are we not released by H. G. Wells's *Mr. Polly*? The category may be sound, but we note in regret that literature, if the pleasure it gives is any clue to its virtue, means more to a

boy lost in *Treasure Island* than it does to his seniors who
are doing their best to believe what they are told about the
latest developments in English prose, and are struggling to
enjoy them. However important those late developments
may be, the story-teller and his way with us is as old as
the drawings in the caves of Altamira, and he is never
likely to lose his power while there is leisure and a fireside.
The boys who attend to him are as old as those caves.
Stevenson, late in his day, shook his head in regret over
his work—and he had just completed *The Ebb Tide*, too
—as though he had wasted his life. He had been writing
for boys.

Well, so had Kipling. Dare we say one word against
that? And if we dare, that takes nothing from his magic.
The story-teller is like the man who could go beyond
killing a mammoth and supplying the cave with food—
the man who could, while telling the people by the fire all
about it, make that mammoth the very shape of the lurking terror of night and the glaciers and the forests; they
who listened knew it was true. The cave became their
home; it was a light in the dark, for the bard had come,
and the daily battle was significant. We are never likely
to come out of that cave, not while there is night and
mystery.

The Samoans, who knew Stevenson, called him Tusitala,
which we are told means " teller of stories." They seem to
have gone to the heart of the matter at once, and no
further. They were satisfied. The did not know R. L. S.
had been a " sedulous ape " of the best literary styles, but
they recognized his signal merit, because they were un-
lettered, and expected no more from him. They were good
instinctive critics. They did not look for what was not
there. Had they been able to read *Virginibus Puerisque*
they would have wondered what it was about.

It would have been easy to tell them. Light-hearted
comments on life and letters by those who will know better
presently are not likely to be more valuable than would be
those of a Samoan on psycho-analysis, and hardly as entertaining. We should not expect a youthful writer to do as
well as a sage when discussing life and art, whatever his
instinct for story-telling. Who would read *Virginibus
Puerisque* when *Notes and Comments* was at hand? But
Stevenson's letters are different. Did any of his critics ever
condemn his work with the candour he himself shows in

484

his letters to Sidney Colvin? *The Ebb Tide* is his " Blooming Error." There is no doubt he thought it was. Which one of us, with that to his credit, would declare he was " pretty nearly useless at literature "? And, " I am a fictitious article and have long known it." The letter in which that sentence appears was written near the end of his life. I do not think that men who so search their own hearts are major prophets, but at least they are different in nature from the confident fellows who really have nothing to say, and say it at length.

I find *The Ebb Tide* as good now as when I was reading it serially on a Blackwall bus. The letter in which Stevenson confessed he was a fictitious article must have reached Colvin while I was first enjoying that yarn. We may still be glad he wrote for us boys. So what is success? And what is reality? And who shall judge? The writing of that story apparently gave Stevenson a deal of trouble. He misnamed it frequently in his letters. And Attwater of the story, we know, is a difficulty with some readers, who cannot allow him to pass. But let them try to imagine what is likely to happen to an austere religious fanatic fated to isolation among primitives. I do not think Attwater is too grim and fantastic a figure to anyone who has heard tales on the beach, and who may even have noticed the conviction of original and other sins at its corrupt work on a soul condemned to brood in solitude. The consequences of that are ugly. I fancy Stevenson knew of an Attwater. Compare, too, now we are at that book, Stevenson's Huish with Conrad's Donkin. Certainly there are Cockneys who are Donkins, but so there are men like him everywhere in civilization. He is only a weakling, malicious in his ineffective resentments and suspicions. Huish is different: he is a scoundrel, depraved and malignant, but he can cheerfully face his fortune. Stern authority never intimidated him: it only kept him quiet while he was watching for its weak points. I do not know where in Hackney that name Huish was found for him, but except for that strangeness he is a native. Huish shows the mettle of his pasture throughout the story, and the consequence of the social poison he took with it. Donkin is only a literary exercise to relieve a repugnance his creator strongly felt for incompetent seamen who whine over food and discipline. The Londoner of the Tower Hamlets or the South Side has native characteristics which distinguish him from

485

the rest of his race as readily as a Devonian is seen not to be of the Clyde. His speech, his equable temper, his sardonic humour, his affectation of indifference to good or bad fortune, his easy lapses into luscious sentiment, and his discomfort, which is quickly loud derision, before heroics, are fairly constant traits. When he is wicked his logical ruthlessness can be horrifying. Huish is a surprisingly good portrait of a Cockney ruffian, of the 1870's, for a Scot to have made.

Huish was more like life than Stevenson's women; but R. L. S. agreed with his critics that his women somehow are lacking. It is true, too, that not one of them could cheer a chapter of the fiction to which we are now accustomed with a promise of fulfilling her soul later in the book. It is tedious to watch her. She disappoints. You see almost at once she will never venture to integrate herself; no expectations are roused. She will keep to the accustomed path for reasons deemed to be reasonable with her own sort.

A young poet, naturally dishevelled by these reforming years of peace and revolution, once roundly swore that Stevenson was no better than imitation flowers. It was extraordinary to him that Stevenson used to be highly respected as a writer. What had he written? Oh yes, of course (the poet confessed), *Treasure Island*—he read that when a boy! But it was plain to me that poet would have thought it no crime to spell the name as Stephenson.

It is hard for some of us elders to agree with that view, though it is easy to understand it; as easy as to agree that R. L. S. troubled too much to refine to a hair, and that his women are as tasteless as coloured wool-flowers to busy bees. It is easy to sympathize with that view. We ought to know what passion this generation must feel to get abolished the lumber of the past. Something ugly and violent, or at least bleak and destructive, is what we must expect of our younger writers, who turn in iconoclastic hate on the precedents of the world as they see it. They want to change all that, and I have nothing much to oppose to their desire, yet will continue to feel nervous when the books to which oldsters are accustomed go flying by the undiscriminating armful into the desolate gutter. Stevenson, quite properly, means little or nothing to them; it is their fate to be more seriously occupied. Yet I wonder whether there are any male characters in the strong fiction of these later years able-bodied enough to polish the belt-buckle of Alan Breck?

It is curious that in our later fiction, though its women are lively, attractive, and problematical enough, and keep us watching closely for what they will do next, the men seem to be nameless servitors, listless in their subjection. Biologically—for machines now do the work of the world —that may be right. Our fiction reflects its day. What else have the men to do but serve the women? They have no need of names. It should not surprise us that a boy will still turn to Alan Breck in joy, for he loves a quick adult male who owes allegiance to none but a prince; to any sort of prince. Why not write for that boy, as he is as old as humanity? Let us try to imagine that strange meeting, when a bright iconoclast of to-day called Alan Breck to his face a sedulous ape! A pleasing interlude! After witnessing it we might find a ballad of the old sort to flow with a new promptitude.

The man who wrote *Kidnapped* perhaps would not have jollied himself aloud about the ape learning to write had he guessed what would have been made of his unlucky metaphor. That ready-made gibe at his reputation has been thrown at him because it was easier than finding offensive missiles of our own. But I should have thought, after all, that the writing of English is a craft to be learned. We know that most of our great prose works have been written by men above forty years of age. The right vocabulary and habitual ease with it, and the urge of long reflection releasing itself through a comfortable theme, are not likely to come together before middle-age. No poet arrives from the blue instantaneous and complete, like Apollo. What could any one of us do, except eat and drink and all that, if others had not lived before us, and left evidence of their labours which prompted us to go on with it? Perhaps Stevenson wrote as he did because he had a tender literary conscience, even an over-weening sense of his duty to give his public only the best he knew. He spoiled himself, some of us say, because he gave more work to arranging his words than some other writers give to their subjects; yet it is hard to blame him for that, while his books remain so fresh for boys. They are lucky boys, when a writer spent for their sakes a long apprenticeship at his craft. It is not the way we do it now, but then we came after Stevenson. We have that advantage. We are not so interested in tradition and its continuity. We know of something which is called a new rhythm of life, and that, without doubt, demands a new measure of literary expression; therefore we cannot turn to the past for our new prose forms, but to the future, where nothing exists. This makes things difficult for us. We are forced to look within ourselves for what we want; we must be our own classics.

Then again, it is evident that Stevenson had no philosophy of life, or only a cheap sort, altogether inapplicable to our problems. He had very little to say, though certainly what he did say included the description, in *The Wrecker*, of the voyage of the *Norah Creina* to Middle Brooks, and the first sighting of the mysterious wreck. That is excellent writing, though innocent of new rhythm. If he spent more time than is usual with us in studying the ways of the seventeenth- and eighteenth-century authors, evidently he did not lose anything by it, except the time in dalliance with obsolete measures. He had no philosophic background; but he did have the experience of a man beset by circumstance that was not always sunny and friendly, and that gave him—though there was enough of artifice and the poser in him to make us look at him sideways—humility before great works, and pity for the fallen and oppressed. He could become, let us remember, even a redoubtable champion, when good men and unarmed folk were attacked. I do not know whether Stevenson is a writer who, as the saying goes, will live for ever, but he will live long enough for me.

ALGERNON CHARLES SWINBURNE

1837-1909

BY W. J. TURNER

T*

W. J. TURNER

ALGERNON CHARLES SWINBURNE

NOBODY living to-day—and I deliberately choose the word *living* and not the word *surviving*—has much sympathy with the Victorian age. Some ascribe to it all our present evils, others would take away even that achievement from a period whose confidence and prosperity they regard as diseases worse than our own diffidence and bankruptcy. But in no sphere is the reputation of the Victorians worse at present than in literature, and since poetry is the quintessence of literature, it follows that Victorian poetry is, to the present generation, more contemptible than any other literary product in the history of England.

It is perhaps natural, even if not inevitable, for every age to turn away in boredom or dislike from the practices of its predecessor; but how are the boundaries of a period to be defined? It seems to me that the only sure basis is that of the generations. Here, at least, we have something fixed and certain. Most men and women are active from the ages of twenty to seventy. Thus we have a period of fifty years, during which a country's population of adults is the same, but growing gradually older. Every twenty years, however, there is a fresh crop of men and women beginning to mature. It is likely, therefore, that a change in spirit will take place about every twenty-five years. The new generation may follow mostly in the steps of their fathers; or the new generation may be hostile, and move as far as possible from the ways of its predecessor. It might be permissible to consider that, during the period of the reign of Queen Victoria, from 1837 to 1901, a period of sixty-four years (which is very little more than the fifty years I estimated as the life of every generation), there was such a strength of tradition and stability of environment that the crop of young men and women coming about every twenty years changed very little in type. Considering what unity the Victorian era seems to have in our contemplation of it, this hypothesis seems plausible. It only means that the three generations of grandfather, father, and son, from 1837 to the end of the nineteenth century, were of one definite, strongly defined character; all cast in the same mould, but with the features becoming softer and more blurred as the mould wore out. This we may call the Victorian tradition. This tradition does not, to the present generation, need defining.

I must, however, give a description of it in order that we may consider Swinburne's relation to his own period; for whether we read Swinburne or not to-day, we have inherited him as one of the major poets of the Victorian age, and we must first of all consider how far he is representative or not. A few dates will help to focus for us the dawn of the Victorian era. Keats died in 1821, Shelley died in 1822, and Byron in 1824. These three poets are the last in our history to which " greatness," or poetical genius of the first order, is commonly ascribed,[1] and each of them would serve as an antithesis to all that is meant by the epithet " Victorian." By no effort of imagination can we force Keats, Shelley, or Byron into a Victorian framework; they simply will not fit. On the other hand, no three poets could differ from one another more than these three. What is it, then, they have in common which is incompatible with Victorianism? I doubt if any convincing answer can be given to this question. It is not some common principle in Keats, Shelley, and Byron which is alien to the Victorian age, but some common principle in the Victorian age which is alien to Keats and Shelley and Byron. What is this principle? Is it possible to discover it, or does any simple statement of it amount to a distortion or falsification?

Dangerous as it is, I will state a principle and proceed to explain and illustrate it, since by so doing it will be exposed to criticism, and we may discover how far it offers a genuine explanation. The principle of Victorianism is

---

[1] It may be objected that this is not true of Byron, but we are not assuming these three to be of equal genius, and I cannot see how we can admit *Don Juan* among the masterpieces of literature, and deny genius of the first order to its creator.

the principle of permanent enjoyment and satisfaction. To
say that the Victorians were satisfied with the world they
lived in and with the way they lived in it would be to deny
that they were human at all; but to say that they made it
a principle to take the world as it was and to be satisfied
with it, subject only to imposing their will upon it, would
not be inaccurate. Everything subsequently depends upon
the nature of the will that is to rule the world. Now, the
Victorian will was a will for physical and mental comfort,
for a permanency of satisfaction. They discovered that
one of the surest methods by which this state of blessedness
could be achieved was by a strict limitation of the desires
requiring to be satisfied. This was the whole secret of their
intensive and passionate cultivation of a system of inhibitions. What was inhibited was not what was, in itself,
necessarily undesirable, but what was so difficult to satisfy
as to endanger individual and social equilibrium. Now we
can see why Shelley, Keats, and Byron is each in his own
way utterly un-Victorian. I would also draw attention to
the fact that they all belonged to a period of chaos following the French Revolution, and that we may perhaps find
a certain likeness common to the Augustan age which
preceded them and the Victorian age which followed them.
Both periods are characterized by stability and uniformity,
and the principle of moderation is as strikingly Augustan
as the principle of limitation is Victorian. The inhibitions
of the Augustan age were prescribed by good taste, the
inhibitions of the Victorians by good form, but whereas
the Augustans' love of moderation was a pure love—a love
of the thing itself, intellectual and æsthetic—the Victorian
passion for limitation was based on fear, and was therefore
moral and impure.

The world of the Victorians became increasingly narrow
as they cautiously proceeded to confine themselves to passions which could be satisfied without undue disturbance.
They were so successful in their effort that they created an
everyday reality which seems to us of an almost incredible
solidity. Out of the artificial warmth of this reality the
notion of everlasting progress sprang like a fantastic orchid.
Nobody saw how strange a thing it was. But this was not
the only strange and exotic manifestation of Victorianism.
The whole activity of Victorian artists was turned to the
creation of a dream-world which would contain all that
had been rigorously excluded from the world about them,

but in an innocuous form. The job of the artist in the Victorian age was to provide harmless replicas of all the wild beasts of nature, all the passionate fauna of the imagination which the will had shut out. Hence the sentimentalizing, the prettiness, and general emasculation of Victorian art. It followed necessarily that, for the first time in our history, a low conception of the artist and his function prevailed. The real business of life was elsewhere. For a man there was only one serious occupation, and that was to extend and make more durable the comfort of humanity. All that was necessary to man's comfort was known. The conception of comfort was fixed—since that was the indispensable condition of obtaining it—and anybody who tried to change the conception of comfort was a social danger and a public enemy. How could any man enjoy well-being if his idea of his being well was liable to alteration? Not to have fixed principles was to be a prey to every fancy that blew in with the wind; it was, indeed, to be in the state in which we are to-day, when no man can lay his hand upon his heart and declare that he knows what he wants. The Victorians knew what they wanted, and went on wanting it with the fanaticism of those who have found one reason for living and fear to lose it, lest they fail to imagine another. Under the whip of this fear it became the moral duty of every member of society to have the same wants—whose catalogue was chanted day and night from birth to death on every public and private occasion. To suggest that those wants were illusions, to try to break down the fences of this Victorian preserve, and show that, instead of its containing the universe the bulk of the universe was outside it, was to be not only a criminal endeavouring to destroy society but, worse still, a servant of the devil endangering the human soul.

It is not surprising that, among us who live freely in the wilderness, walking over the scattered fragments of the walls of the Victorian preserve, there should be some who wish they were safely back in that comfortable enclosure. It is among these that we may look for an attempt to reestablish the reputation of the Victorians. There will be many who long for the peace and security of fixed principles, and feel uncomfortable amidst the present chaos in literature and art. The more intelligent of them will declare that a marked enclosure and a code of principles are

494

essential to life and literature. They will maintain that the
conservative and the revolutionary can only exist within
this magic circle, of which they are the complementary
arcs. Now, the best way of testing this theory is to look
at the work of a Victorian revolutionary, and see if it makes
up for the deficiencies of orthodox Victorian art, or whether
it also is as facile and debilitated as the Victorian pseudo-
classics. If the latter is the case, we are entitled, I think,
to consider the whole jargon of the timid and fearful about
" law and order "—whether it takes the form of exalting
academies or of institutions or of churches at the expense
of the individual human being—as a mass of lies.

Among the poets of the Victorian age Swinburne alone
was considered a revolutionary. Swinburne was born in
1837, the year of the accession of Queen Victoria, and he
died in 1909, eight years after the death of Queen Victoria.
His life, therefore, covers the whole Victorian period. It
was in 1866, at the age of twenty-nine, that he published
Poems and Ballads, which were immediately abused with
violence by the critics as licentious and immoral. The rage
and hostility aroused by Swinburne's poems, and their
large circulation for many years, prove that they had a
certain vitality. It is difficult for us to realize with what a
shock the average Victorian read the " Hymn to Prosperine," or to imagine the blasphemous effect of such a
line as—

> " *Thou hast conquered, O pale Galilean; the world
>   has grown grey from thy breath.*"

To us, reading this poem, it seems a piece of rhetoric whose
virtues are essentially academic. There is in it no illumination, no revelation, such as we look for from great poetry;
there is no music or magic to move us, and, finally, there is
no exercise of the intellect to delight us. Speaking for
myself, I can only say that this poem is absolutely dead,
and that such typical lines as:

> " *A little while we die; shall life not thrive as it may?
> For no man under the sky lives twice, outliving his day.
> And grief is a grievous thing, and a man hath enough
>   of his tears:
> Why should he labour and bring fresh grief to blacken
>   his years?* "

495

seem no more than a banal expression of platitude with nothing of that personal intensity which gives life. Some ears may still be tickled by the jingle of these lines, but there is no inner relation between the words and the metre, and it is only by an inevitable inner relationship that rhythm is created. The " Hymn to Prosperine " is completely academic in form, and the appearance of unconventionality is achieved by merely crying down what everybody else is crying up in the fashion of an undergraduate whose present unconformity is part of his future conformity. The very expression of Swinburne's anti-Christianity was a tribute to Christianity as the Victorians conceived and practised it, and, in the absence of orthodox belief, his lines become meaningless. Swinburne, in his first book of *Poems and Ballads*, wrote " A Song in Time of Revolution, 1860," which begins:

" *The heart of the rulers is sick, and the high-priest covers his head :*
For this is the song of the quick that is heard in the ears of the dead.

" *The poor and the halt and the blind are keen and mighty and fleet :*
Like the noise of the blowing of wind is the sound of the noise of their feet " ;

and continues in the same rhetorical style, to say nothing of significance. If we compare this empty verbiage with anything that Shelley wrote on the subject of freedom or revolution, we see immediately the difference between the poet and the rhetorician. To Swinburne " republic," " revolution," " freedom " are stirring words to excite himself with ; for he was so typically Victorian that they frightened him just as they frightened the most ordinary citizen, the only difference being that Swinburne liked the sensation of being frightened. Swinburne had not the power of getting behind words, and in this again he was thoroughly orthodox and academic. The word republic was a blessed word, merely because to the majority of the people around him it was an accursed word. The essential childishness which made Swinburne delight in the word republic has something endearing about it. But one fears that for him a republic could do no wrong, and no crimes could be committed in the name of freedom. One doubts, indeed, whether he would not have helped to deprive mankind of the last vestige of freedom, provided only it were done in the name of freedom. But this is merely to doubt his critical power, and it is arguable that he might have achieved real poetry in spite of this deficiency. I can only say for myself that I can find no poetry in his hymnings of freedom and republics. The famous *Songs before Sunrise* produce on me no effect whatever, except of unbelief and tedium. One of the reasons for this is Swinburne's extreme excitability, which caused him to force his voice from the beginning to the end of every poem, without any modulation. The poem, " The Eve of Revolution," begins:

> " *The trumpets of the four winds of the world*
> *From the ends of the earth blow battle.*"

The second stanza begins:

> " *I hear the midnight on the mountains cry*
> *With many tongues of thunders.*"

And the third stanza:

> " *I set the trumpet to my lips and blow.*"

Any one of these verses alone would be more effective than the poem's twenty-seven stanzas, in which the result of all this blowing of trumpets and thunders is absolutely nil. Another well-known poem on liberty is that entitled, " To Walt Whitman in America." The first stanza is addressed to Whitman himself:

> " *O strong-winged soul with prophetic*
> *Lips hot with the bloodbeats of song,*
> *With tremor of heartstrings magnetic,*
> *With thoughts as thunders in throng,*
> *With consonant ardours of chords*
> *That pierce men's souls as with swords*
> *And hale them hearing along.*"

Along with Swinburne's characteristically ineffective hyperbole, this exhibits another of his radical faults, namely, the frequent complete lack of any relation between the sense and the movement of his verse. This forcing of words into a ready-made metric mould, quite against the natural sense-rhythm of the language, has been acclaimed by some critics as showing an extraordinary mastery of verse. One popular encyclopædia states that Swinburne is " admittedly the greatest British master of metre." I would maintain, on the contrary, that Swinburne, of all our poets of lyrical reputation, had the worst ear. You will search in vain all through Swinburne's poetry to find a single example of sound married to sense in one harmonious rhythmic whole that has the beauty of form we expect from a great poet. Those of his poems which least offend the ear have nothing more than a fluency and smoothness in common stanza forms which is not beyond the capacity of any minor verse-writer. Austin Dobson and Andrew Lang have a virtuosity of this kind that is quite equal to Swinburne's, and I cannot see any metrical triumph beyond their capacity in those poems of Swinburne's generally famed for their virtuosity in rhyme and metre such as, for example, " Itylus," " The Garden of Proserpine," " A Forsaken Garden."

Of all the poets of comparable reputation, Byron is commonly judged to have the worst ear, but in my opinion this criticism is ill-founded. The pedants and prosodists who arraign the bad rhyming of *Don Juan* are writing themselves down as fools ; because the absurd, extravagant, strained, and false rhyming of *Don Juan* is an essential part of its effect. Do these pedants imagine that Byron could not tell the difference between a perfect rhyme and an imperfect rhyme? They might as well imagine that Mozart could not tell the difference between a perfect consonance and an imperfect consonance ! But in fertility, daring, vividness, and imaginativeness of rhyming Byron is as supreme and incomparable a master as Mozart is of modulation. And the variety, subtlety, and swiftness of rhythm to be found in Byron's handling of the *Don Juan* stanza form are just what we miss in Swinburne's rigid pattern-making.

Always it is the form which is important, because nothing exists apart from its form. In this poem, " To Walt Whitman in America," Swinburne gives a description of " Freedom," but we shall find that the description is as vague as the word itself in the mouth of a wind-bag.

> " *The earth-god Freedom, the lonely*
> *Face lightening, the footprint unshod,*
> *Not as one man crucified only*
> *Nor scourged with but one life's rod ;*

> *The soul that is substance of nations*
> *Reincarnate with fresh generations;*
> *The great god Man, which is God."*

Here we have the *Form* of Swinburne's " Freedom." But
who of Swinburne's contemporaries could object to this
unshod footprint of an earth-god? The Victorians were
thoroughly democratic, but a belief in " the great god
Man " did not commit the believer to anything, nor help
the Victorian to decide whether Karl Marx or the Archbishop of Canterbury was the visible representative of the
invisible god-Man which is both God and Freedom.
Swinburne's hymning of freedom and revolution never
could have disturbed the Victorians profoundly. Indeed,
they had much the same admiration as he had for Garibaldi, Mazzini, and other successful libertarians. Political
tyranny has never been popular in England. Where he
really did shock the majority was in his love-poetry. Here
again, however, Swinburne had exactly the same moral
ideas on sex as the rest of his age. He is not free in the
least from any of their superstitions and prejudices, and
his classification—

> *" The lilies and languors of virtue*
> *The raptures and roses of vice "*—

corresponds perfectly to the common man's conception of
vice and virtue in his age, and perhaps in this age too.
All that he does is to pay the homage to " vice " which
others paid to " virtue." This is to be unconventional, but
not original. His rhapsodies on this theme have, however,
a preciseness and genuineness which his rhapsodies on
freedom and revolution lack, and this is the only part of
his work in which we to-day can find any life. Curiously
enough, it is just what is unrepresented in the only available
Selection from Swinburne's Poems, which was compiled by
Watts-Dunton, and by 1894 had reached a fifth edition,
thus giving to all who know Swinburne only from this
selection a totally false impression of his poetic achievement. Seven-tenths of this " Selection " is mere rhodo-
montade, utterly empty and unreadable. But if we turn
to Swinburne's first series of *Poems and Ballads,* we will
find, in poems such as " Laus Veneris," " Anactoria,"
" Dolores," " Fragoletta," and others, a genuine personal
expression. Different people will value it differently, but

no critic, I think, will claim that it belongs to the higher orders of poetry. Some critics may ascribe these poems to Swinburne's revolt against the excessive squeamishness, hypocrisy, and prudery of the Victorians, but to me they seem a wholly personal and genuine expression that belongs to Swinburne and to nobody else. Of course he struck a responsive chord.

Every human being, unless born imperfect, has in some degree the elements of Swinburne's special sensibility. What makes the difference is the proportion. Those in whom the proportions of these sexual elements resembled Swinburne's, and who had some gift as writers, no doubt felt his influence, and imitated him according to their talent. Others, in reaction against the childishly timid attacks on this poetry by people whom we call philistines— meaning thereby people who are not aware of the true origin and significance of their behaviour—made a deliberate intellectual onslaught on the public sensibility. So there emerged what was called by hostile critics the "fleshly" school of poetry. It tells us a great deal about the maladjustments, sensuous and intellectual, of the Victorians, that the noun "flesh" and the adjective "fleshly" had an exclusively bad odour, and were used always as terms of reproach by them.

To this generation—to whom, happily, all Swinburne's Tannhäuser-like revellings in the Venusberg, normal and abnormal (to use two Victorian words which still have a useful but rather misleading significance), are so familiar, and so taken as a matter of course that they have lost all their illicit fascination—Swinburne's poetry is of small importance. It now takes its place with, let us say, the drawings of Aubrey Beardsley as one of the minor curiosities of artistic creation.

If we ask ourselves why such work is so weak in its power over us, surely the answer is that the disproportion of its elements is so great that most of our major passions and the greater part of our sensibility are shut out. We do not feel, when reading Swinburne, extended and enriched, but narrowed and restricted. No doubt this has its value also, and perhaps it is unwise to attempt to assess it, because it might have more value for some than for others and for one generation than another. The Victorians looked askance at the word "pleasure." We who have passed through an epoch of psycho-analysis, in which innumerable

masked inhibitions have been ruthlessly exposed and declared first of all dangerous and the cause of all spiritual
ills and then necessary and valuable if used wisely and in
moderation, regard " pleasure " differently. Our attitude
is: at what point does pleasure become unprofitable? That
is to say, we are more realistic and less superstitious. We
have dared to look pleasure in the face with our eyes open,
watching the results of this encounter. The important point
is, what is our criterion of unprofitable? When does any
pleasure become unprofitable? I think the answer to-day
would be: when it interferes with other pleasures. The
Victorians (and some linger among us) would call this a
materialistic attitude; but surely it depends on what we
class as pleasures? The Puritan conception of the body
as separate from and hostile to the spirit is the source of
all the Victorians' fear, both of pleasure and of God, and
also of their restricted conception of sin.

This conceptual separation of " being " into the body
and the spirit, the flesh and the mind, has necessarily its
physical copy. So we have at one pole of Victorianism
the fleshly school of poetry, and at the other the spiritual
anæmia of puritanism. The sign of a great creative period
is integration, not disintegration, and our final criticism of
Swinburne as a poet is that he is not anywhere an integrat-
ing force working against the disintegrating forces of his
time, but rather one of the by-products of a general disintegration of the human personality during his age. This
disintegration was brought about by the Victorians' narrow
conceptions and ruthless pursuit of comfort.

LORD
TENNYSON

1809-1892

BY
JOHN
COLLIER

LORD TENNYSON

NOTHING reveals more than does a certain sort of bathetic line. There is a protrusion of a secret self which abashes us, and moves us to terror or to a giggling fit, just as if, seeing a well-known face before us, we had stretched out a hand to shake, and grasped some unformed or trotter-like organ.

> " . . . . *But your rough voice*
> *(You spoke so loud) has roused the child again.*
> *Sleep, little birdie, sleep! will she not sleep*
> *Without her ' little birdie?' well then, sleep,*
> *And I will sing you ' birdie.' "*

Some writers never fall into this sort of thing. Their bathos is negative. A Dryden either succeeds, or is nothing. If he makes a bad line, it falls dump, like lead.

> " *A senseless lump of sacred clay* "

is just a flat chord in the symphony. It is not a little phrase from " The Rosary," which has strayed in by accident, out of the writer's heart.

It may be thought, that is because Dryden's heart was not directly connected with his poetry. Chaucer's was. He wrote:

> " *Pees, litel sone, I wol do thee non harm.*"

So was Nicholas Breton, who puts it thus:

> " *Come little babe, come silly soul,*" etc.

Chaucer nods often enough, so does Milton for that matter, and they make us nod too. Donne snores, but such do not blab secrets in their sleep, and in an accent which is other than that of their waking hours.

The positive bathos, the significant and super bathos, with which we are concerned, is first distinguishable in the eighteenth century, growing there in something a clipped and formal fashion; and in the nineteenth it spreads, fattens, thrusts up here and there, and blooms at once beautiful, ridiculous, and disgusting, as befits the complex and poisonous parasite which it most interestingly is.

The primitive form is to be found in such lines as these of Goldsmith:

> " ' *Forbid it, Heaven!* ' *the Hermit cried,*
> *And clasped her to his breast:*
> *The wondering fair one turn'd to chide;*
> *'Twas Edwin's self that prest!* "

and in their innumerable contemporary counterparts, and though they may in themselves seem mere lumpishness, we, who are familiar with later stages, may at once set them down as being of a malignant nature.

In the first years of the nineteenth century we find a higher development of this malady, and when we read certain stanzas of Peter Bell we feel that even positive bathos can sink no lower. Nor can it, but it can drag the poet more closely in its wake. Wordsworth's silliness was silliness in theory: it possessed the man, but it left the poet behind. Wordsworth ceases to be a skilled versifier, even, when he rides his hobby-horse too far. But there was still the Victorian age to come: a generation that had fed on the rank and un-nourishing flesh of the hobby horses of their predecessors, and who had the asses-meat mingled in the very fibres of their being, and whose bathos was no longer dead matter, or alien to their art, but was of themselves, and animated with all their corrupted skill.

Tennyson, who wrote the lines agreeing to sing " birdie," had not a subtle but a super-subtle sense of words. In one respect his best lines exceed Shakespeare's: they have more iris to them. It is better to have written, " *It is a nipping and an eager air,*" or " *The dawn in russet mantle clad,*" than—

> " *Walked in a wintry wind by a ghastly glimmer and found*
> *The shining daffodil dead, and Orion low in his grave* ";

but it is Tennyson's couplet which is palpitating and phosphorescent, almost corrupt, with consciousness and sensibility. It is unwholesome to be as venison-ripe as this is, but it is very lovely, don't you think? And, closer to our point, he who made that unerring stroke, that exquisite lie, *shining*, never set down word numbly or unknowingly.

He was, moreover, vain. Mr. Benson, who is to be relied on, says that " he resented deeply and bitterly any depreciation of his work. Even his most intimate friends did not dare to hint disapproval of his works; the deepest affection would not have stood the strain of such a demand." Mr. Benson gives us also an account of someone bringing to Farringford a school magazine, in which there was a disparaging reference to the poet.

> ". . . It was most painful to see how for days the words burned in his mind like a poisoned wound: no matter what subject was started, no matter how much interested he himself became in pursuing a train of thought, he always came back to the same grievance. No amount of influence with other minds it seemed could atone for what ' these young gentlemen ' had said. Such stories could be multiplied indefinitely."

This superb craftsman, then, was so vain that the censure of schoolboys could fret him into making an embarrassing fool of himself for days. We may be sure that he let nothing appear until he was persuaded that it was good. A man who dreads criticism, and has FitzGerald, with his delicate and candid mind, for friend, a man who is capable of the phrase " the *shining* daffodil dead," does not, unless he is besotted, exhibit such a false and gee-gaw word, and in such a tasteless setting, as " gaily " here:

> " *In her ear he whispers gaily*
> *If my heart by signs can tell,*
> *Maiden, I have watch'd thee daily,*
> *And I think thou lovest me well.*"

Nor, when the austere Arnold waits to read, will he knowingly let this rank matter escape his revision,

" *And the vitriol madness flushes up in the ruffian's head,*
Till the filthy by-lane rings to the yell of the trampled
wife."

507

Or this ignoble realism,

" *And sleep must lie down arm'd, for the villainous centre
    bits*
  *Grind on the wakeful ear in the hush of the moonless
    nights.*"

Why, it is like the worst of Dickens. Neither you nor
even I would write those lines. It seems impossible that
such a poet as Tennyson could be blind to their absurdity,
or, seeing it, let them stand. But they do exist, and scores
like them, and they are the arch examples of positive
bathos, being sporadic eruptions of a poison which pervades the whole system, and whose subtle influence is to be
detected in the super-imposition of incongruous mental
worlds, in the amazing complexity of bright hallucinated
detail, and in the fever that lends its burning loveliness to
the best lines, as it makes hideous the worst.

Nothing grows without seed. There was always this
tendency in Tennyson, even in his earliest and purest
period, but there was so sudden a development of it in the
latter part of his 1842 volumes as to suggest that it had
received some strong stimulus from without. We can
hardly hope to prove such a supposition as this: the real
evidence is intangible, never to be resurrected; but we may
look at the possibilities.

First, though his vanity has been mentioned as a deter-
rent, we should not pass on without noticing that it may
have operated in just the opposite fashion. Unlike pride,
vanity is a gross feeder: it is not much concerned with the
quality of praise, but must have plenty of it. Tennyson
may have so much desired the acclamations of the many,
that in 1840 or thereabouts he began to take a *broader view,*
as we call it when we let go some cruel ideal. I think he
definitely and consciously elected to popularize his work,
determining to become, as Shakespeare was, an expression
of the whole life of his age, rustic, bourgeois, and noble;
the mirror of his age. He succeeded, and reflected the
fancies and sentiments of Victorian England.

It is unlikely to have been his appetite for praise that
moved him, however. The main factor was probably not
vanity. In fact, his vanity was less a desire for praise than
a dread of attack: for all the world as if there were something on his conscience.

About 1840 his outlook was a gloomy one. He had been

in love four years, and there was very little prospect of his ever attaining that income on which it was thought fit for him to marry. It would be unjustifiable to suggest that he therefore determined to win popularity at any price. I think that would have been utterly impossible to him, and, what is more, it is not what happens in such cases.

It is a fact fertile in probabilities, however, that to want anything very much inclines one to very considerate attention to the means by which it may be attained, and that, of all cravings, that of love is the most potent, and the most treacherous as well, inasmuch as it sets up a change in the very fibres which hold out against it. A lyric poet of lovely sensibility, a man in love, and one whose favourite dinner was a beefsteak and a pint of port, he was of heroic proportions, and a handsome man, and yet, if ever a face can be trusted, one with a soft streak somewhere in him (" that man must be a poet," said Thompson on seeing him for the first time at Cambridge), a man who, though he was an Homeric laugher, had little sense of that biting humour which reveals (or he would never have written " Oriana "), a man whose intellect was constantly acclaimed for its richness and range, but one whose mind was really neither keen nor hard nor exact, and whose young life was a vicarage and a sheltered one, and who therefore, between easy thought and easy life, missed both one and t'other of those two sorts of " reality " which are none the less salutary for being named in slap-dash fashion; such a man is not fitted to sustain his values against that long siege, erosion from without, change of substance within, that is effected by years of unsatisfied love. Such is an abnormal condition, and though it swings us to extremes of feeling, whose valuable acquaintance we might otherwise fail to make, it does so quite exactly as an intoxicant does, which alters our values while its influence prevails, and alters ourselves if its influence prevails too long.

Four years is too long in many cases. Surely it was long enough to affect the machinery, delicate in a double sense, by which Tennyson produced his poems. If it affected him deeply enough to produce, or assist in producing, the change that was manifested in his work at this time, that is sufficient. There were still ten years of " weary waiting " to confirm the change, and widen the self-widening angle of deflection. Of course Tennyson was deeply affected: he would have been less than a man if he had escaped the

strain, as he would have been more than a man if he had
survived it unaltered. We are only concerned with its
effects in so far as they relate to his work, so that only
internal evidence is of value to us. Of that there is enough.

First, we may note the large number of themes and
passages concerned with the " poor suitor," which range
from the quite lightly conceived day-dream, " The Lord of
Burleigh," to those inflamed passages in " Locksley Hall,"
" Aylmer's Field," " Maud," and other poems, which, by
the personal quality of their hurt and angry ring, betray
the smart.

Then, what is more pathetic, but moves our sympathy
less, since it is unwholesome, there is that sick breath of
Tennyson's when he speaks of women. Many of his
women are only characters in a tale, as Guinevere was, or
figures in a picture, as was the miller's daughter; these
are well enough; but there are others, all alike, who, one
feels, moved the poet as real women might, and the adoring
submissiveness of these, and their pallor and fragility, have
been frequently commented on.

" Then her cheek was pale and thinner than should be
*   for one so young,*
* And her eyes on all my motions with a mute observance*
*   hung."*

It would seem that he, who in real life was impotent
before his own caution, or his betrothed's, or his world's,
or all, was determined to dominate in fantasy; so much so,
indeed, that he drew himself pictures of invalids, who
might be expected to adore more poignantly, more atten-
tively and mutely to observe, and more helplessly to obey.

To sum up, then: he was vain, and may have wished
for a larger audience; he was told constantly, by many
future deans, that his was a great intellect, and he may have
felt himself wasted on the narrow perfection of his lyrics;
he needed fame for money's sake; he was in love, and may
have consciously and naturally determined to be a deeper
and more significant person because of it; he was in love,
and, it seems, became to some extent a rather maudlin
and sentimental person because of it; he was vain, and his
first departures into sentiment may have received unusual
quantities of praise from all but the rigorous few (it is
eloquent that at this period he ceased all correspondence
with his male friends—perhaps he found their criticisms too

limited); he was twenty-eight, twenty-nine, thirty, at which age a man feels almost a physiological need of coarse success, and will be less severe upon reasonable means of attaining it. With all this intolerable deal of motive, it really seems not entirely unlikely that Tennyson, in 1840 or a year or two before, may have taken the not obviously unworthy aim of being the Shakespeare of his day, not as a dramatist of course, but as a poet who expressed equally the simple heart, the noble soul, manners, and affairs, for, always roaming with a hungry heart, much, he considered, had he seen and known. We might look about for some examples of this, and of the difficulties which awaited him.

Every important poet who has ever lived, is, in his own special sense, the first of the moderns. Tennyson is very considerably so. Who before him wrote of that world in which Mr. Ford and Sir James Jeans thrive, and you and I have the doubtful privilege of living? Compared with Tennyson, Wordsworth and Keats were still happily situated in the centre of a flat and stationary earth, up from whose eastern rim a small obsequious sun climbed every morning at the ordainéd hour. Tennyson was the first poet to absorb the modern consciousness, which has had remarkable effects upon poetry. It began with Copernicus and Galileo, Newton and such, their officious inventions of the roundness of the world, and that about the size and order of the stellar orbs. I hear that certain of their conclusions are wrong after all, but have little hope that the sensible proportion which these men abolished will ever be reinstated. Your scientist, like a jerry-builder, erects structures which serve his doubtful purpose for a short time only, but which deface the beauty which has preceded them, for ever.

Be that as it may, we can note, in the first years of Victoria's reign, the way in which modern thought became coincident with poetical feeling, and how it was Tennyson who was first conscious of it. Shelley and Wordsworth and others assembled its elements in their minds, but without the final awareness. It was as if a room was being furnished (with all too infinite riches) in the dark. The light, when at last it was switched on, revealed ferns collected from haunts of coot and hern in a vicarage boyhood, huge Ammonites and the first bones of time, and on the tables every clime and age jumbled together, pictures of the Alps, a height, a broken grange, a grove, a flower, King Arthur

like a modern gentleman of stateliest port, and, on the other
side of the fireplace, his gracious consort similarly framed.
In the mirror, consciousness was at last complete. Alfred
Tennyson surveyed himself and his surroundings. Both
were impressive. The remoter background, the universe
beyond the window, was less mysterious than ours, but
quite as deserving of popularity:

> " *Regions of lucid matter taking forms,*
> *Brushes of fire, hazy gleams,*
> *Clusters and beds of worlds, and bee-like swarms*
> *Of suns, and starry streams.*"

By a very extraordinary mental gambit, the number of
worlds and suns celebrated in these lines did not at first
reduce the interior we have described to a nothing, but
rather inflated it in the aspect of belonging to a really
large concern. Tennyson was delighted with the size and
enterprise that are to be observed on every hand, just as if
he was an enthusiastic novice in our largest West End store.
" Forward," he cried,

> " *Forward, forward let us range,*
> *Let the great world spin for ever down the ringing grooves*
> *of change.*"

None the less, this great world was to prove one of his
stumbling-blocks. He is indebted to it for one thing, and
that is, for a freshness, or rather a novelty, in his imagery,
and a widening of its scope. But even that is a mixed
blessing. He flounders among the newer terms, sometimes
presenting them in a state of incomplete fusion:

> " *So careful of the type? but no,*
> *From scarped cliff and quarried stone*
> *She cries, ' A thousand types are gone:*
> *I care for nothing, all shall go '*";

and sometimes completely and comically unfused, as in the
prologue to the Princess:

> " *A man with knobs and wires and vials fired*
> *A cannon: Echo answer'd in her sleep*
> *From hollow fields: and here were telescopes*
> *For azure views; and there a group of girls*
> *In circle waited, whom the electric shock*
> *Dislink'd with shrieks and laughter: round the lake*

> *A little clock-work steamer paddling plied*
> *And shook the lilies: perch'd about the knolls*
> *A dozen angry models jetted steam:*
> *A petty railway ran: a fire-balloon*
> *Rose gem-like up before the dusky groves*
> *And dropt a fairy parachute and past:*
> *And there thro' twenty posts of telegraph*
> *They flash'd a saucy message to and fro*
> *Between the mimic stations: so that sport*
> *Went hand in hand with Science."*

Poetry, however, seems to have lagged a little behind.
What a dead expenditure of art is here! It is dreary to see
so much skill produce such a desolation. His expanded
scope is only fruitful when the poet draws on that romantic
science with which he was familiar as a boy, the *fairy-tales
of science*, which, after all, were part of that sweet and
close cleaving to nature which was our Victorians' best
and peculiar contribution to our culture.

They knew birds, the sandy shore, the stars, no longer as
the formal decor of verse, but with a lovely intimacy.

" *'Tis the place, and all around it, as of old, the curlews
     call,*
    *Dreary gleams about the moorland flying over Locksley
     Hall.*

" *Locksley Hall, that in the distance overlooks the sandy
     tracts,*
    And the hollow ocean-ridges roaring into cataracts.

" *Many a night from yonder ivied casement, ere I went
     to rest,*
    Did I look on great Orion sloping slowly to the West.

" *Many a night I saw the Pleiads, rising thro' the mellow
     shade*
    Glitter like a swarm of fire-flies tangled in a silver braid."

There was never before anything like this. Nevertheless,
it was Tennyson's birthright, the product triply of his time,
his genius, and his happy place in life. He did not come
by the best of it in the expansion of his interests: he could
only add to, and, if any thing, coarsen, that perfect gift of
his for making pictures, which, since it was too perfect for

U   513

the old formal material, was forced to go to nature for new, just as Constable's fresh and eager technique demanded oak and elm in place of the classical "brown tree." The essential quality which distinguishes him is apparent in his earliest poems, in "Mariana," for example, in every line of it, though the images are *flatter*, less subtle, than in some of his later work.

> "*All day within the dreamy house,*
> *The doors upon their hinges creak'd;*
> *The blue fly sung in the pane; the mouse*
> *Behind the mouldering wainscot shriek'd . . .*"

It is more complex, more iridescent in "The Lotos-Eaters," but the development is a natural one, a development of technique, a progress towards maturity:

> "*And in the afternoon they came unto a land,*
> *In which it seemed always afternoon.*
> *All round the coast the languid air did swoon,*
> *Breathing like one that hath a weary dream.*"

This, too, owes nothing to the broadened outlook of later years. It is the result of focusing the sense, not of dispreading it. Later on, though, we find phrases as vivid and effective as can be imagined:

> "*There has fallen a splendid tear*
> *From the passion-flower at the gate,*"

in which there is a bravura at once magnificent and shallow, transparent as it were, so that when it is superimposed on a conception in good taste, as in *shining daffodil,* we are finely deceived and justly delighted, but when the taste is at all coarse, as in *splendid tear* (and yet how magnificent!), we become uneasy and understand how, not only these two phrases, but also such as *Queen rose of the rosebud garden of girls,* can co-exist in the same poem.

Another of Tennyson's difficulties arose from his fundamental inability to write of human beings. It is only the fundamental ability that he lacked: he had all the rest to quite an extraordinary degree. In fact, his creatures are so perfectly described, so well furnished with little traits and gestures, so well rounded, well coloured, so all but human, the hateful waxworks, that we cannot but be moved to spite and laughter.

514

Their deficiency is not through a failure of his art, but partly because of its success. His is the wrong sort of art. When he is trivial, and content to make a visual picture, we are delighted, for his vision is unfailing, or was until he began to paint that peculiar series of pictures, from which, one would think, most of the Victorian Royal Academicians derived their subjects.

> " *Melissa, with her hand upon the lock,*
> *A rosy blonde, and in a college gown,*
> *That clad her like an April daffodilly. . . .*"

She, of course, is charming, but the more elaborate figures positively suffer from being so perfectly described. He shows the waxwork in too clear a light : we are engrossed by the wax.

> "*. . . till the maiden aunt*
> (*A little sense of wrong had touch'd her face*
> *With colour*) *turn'd to me with, ' As you will :*
> *Heroic if you will, or what you will,*
> *Or be yourself your hero if you will!* "

As for his Leolins, Lilias, squires and cottagers, they are creatures of the novelette, are rendered repulsive by efficiency.

The fact is, Tennyson, no more than any other naturally lyric poet (how different a lyrist is from a ballad writer !), had no genuine impulse to create characters. His figures are limited, because he had never ceased to see life through the coloured-glass windows of Somersby Rectory, but they are repellent and absurd, because he created them with an averse heart. At the end he was doing so more mechanically than can be described :

> " *She that holds the diamond necklace dearer than the golden ring,*
> *She that finds a winter sunset fairer than a morn of Spring.*"

But here are examples enough ; it is not our business to pillory the poet.

From about the time of " Maud," Mr. Benson notes " a curious ebbing of the spring of inspiration. From that time dates a certain resolute search for poetical material, a certain husbanding of resources ; frequent inquiries among his friends for incidents and subjects—answered in the most conscientious and philosophical spirit by Jowett. . . ."

What a dreadful revelation ! For we can say, as surely as we can say anything of a poet, that Tennyson's original gift, had it been kept pure, would never have died within him. We are still striving, and so far without complete success, to achieve an adequate expression of that iridescent consciousness (one might say, that consciousness in a new " dimension ") that just appeared in the nineteenth century. No one has yet displayed such equipment for the task as did Tennyson. No failure has been so tragic and so absurd as his.

He had definitely undertaken a task too big for him. While all poets, except those who are content to be very small indeed, must find the modern world too much for them, and lapse now and then into the peculiar ridiculous bathos we have noted, which is essentially that of un-digested life, Tennyson had this embarrassment to a greater degree than was inevitable to one of his gift and day. As to whether this followed on any of the possible reasons we have glanced at—that we may conclude as we please,—so long as we are not too definite.

WILLIAM MAKEPEACE THACKERAY

1811-1863

BY
FRANK
SWINNERTON

WILLIAM MAKEPEACE THACKERAY

LITERARY criticism is no longer purely æsthetic. It is, at the very least, what is called "psychological." When Mr. Flawner Bannel, in the epilogue to *Fanny's First Play,* said that if he were told the author's name he would be able to say whether the play was good or not, he was laughed at by the audience. Quite rightly. But if he had said that he must know all about the author's life before he could discuss the author's work, or that he must try and read into that work the secrets of the author's heart, he would have been heard with awe. For the modern analytical mind has no simple pleasures, and a book in these days is not so much a book as an occasion of pathological investigation.

Thackeray is a very tempting subject for this method, not only because his domestic life has been veiled deliberately from the public eye, but because his work is so full of disguised autobiography, and so perplexing in some of its characteristics. The accounts of Thackeray given by his colleagues are contradictory; some of his own professions and apologies do not square with some of our inferences from his writing; there is much in him that is at first blush quite inexplicable. Is it wholly inexplicable?

His father and maternal grandfather were both employed by the India Company; and Thackeray was born at Calcutta in 1811. His mother was then nineteen. The boy was sent at an early age to England (his father having died, and his mother having married again), and to the Charter House, where he apparently spent ten years. At the time they were not happy years. He was "a pretty, gentle, rather timid boy," who "had no skill in games, and, I

think, no taste for them." As Yellowplush says: " If you
were ever at a great school, you must recklect who was
the boy most bullid, and buffitid, and purshewd. . . . I
recklect there was at our school, in Smithfield, a chap of
this milksop, spoony sort."

And Michael Angelo Titmarsh himself enlarged upon
this matter in the words:

> " If papa and mamma (honour be to them!) had
> not followed the faith of their fathers, and thought
> proper to send away their only beloved son into ten
> years' banishment of infernal misery, tyranny, annoy-
> ance; to give over the fresh feelings of the heart of
> little Michael Angelo to the discipline of vulgar bullies,
> who, in order to lead tender young children to the
> Temple of Learning (as they do in the spelling-books),
> drive them on with clenched fists and low abuse—if
> they fainted, revived them with a thump, or assailed
> them with a curse—if they were miserable, consoled
> them with a brutal jeer—if, I say, my dear parents,
> instead of giving me the inestimable benefit of a ten
> years' classical education . . .''

Here, at the Charter House—for although this is the most
vehement cry of all, the condemnation of public school
ways is repeated elsewhere, with gradually diminishing
strength as indignation faded and his manner grew blander
—was first encouraged Thackeray's lack of confidence in
himself, his reserve of manner, his habit, the sensitive
weakling's habit, of quizzing in secret that which he may
not openly condemn. Thackeray saw what went on about
him; he knew that he had no power to resist it; he doubted
the power of others to correct it. Very well, behind that
pale face a scornful and resentful mind meditated with a
kind of trembling calm upon the baseness of human nature
and the vanity of human wishes. Particularly upon his
own powerlessness, and the little worth of those things
which he most desired. " I like pointing morals," he afterwards wrote, " and inventing for myself cheap consolations,
to reconcile me to that state of life into which it has pleased
Heaven to call me."

From the Charter House Thackeray went to Cambridge,
which he left after two years without taking a degree. Of
this period his son-in-law, Sir Richmond Ritchie, unctu-
ously and significantly remarks, in words to which I shall
return later, that " his time was not wasted. Without being

a scholar, he acquired a literary knowledge of the classics, and he gained all those indirect advantages which distinguish Oxford and Cambridge from other seats of perhaps purer learning. For one thing, Cambridge fixed his social status. Though afterwards he was to consort with Bohemians and other strange acquaintances into whose company a man is forced by adversity, he was never a Bohemian, and always faithful to the traditions of the class in which he was born and bred ! "

Thackeray then lived for a time in Germany, and for a longer time with his mother and stepfather in Paris. The knowledge gained upon the Continent served him inexhaustibly for the rest of his life. He used it, not only in direct transcripts or in the embellishment of his literary pieces, but in his major fictions, from *Barry Lyndon* to *The Newcomes*. It was the most interesting and formative experience he had. And at last, at the age of twenty-one, he inherited a little fortune which he lost in disputed ways (by cards, by the failure of an Indian bank, by investment in a ruinous journalistic enterprise). Thereafter, faced with penury, he played with the thought of becoming an artist, but was driven to the use in earnest of the pen to which he had already lightly turned in fun and vanity.

Those were days when several young men had leapt directly into poular notice as novelists. Lytton, Disraeli, Ainsworth, and Dickens, for instance, were all stars before they had reached the age of thirty. But Thackeray's early fiction, when it was not written in deliberate parody of the faults he saw so clearly in the work of these successful writers, took the form of a series of brief sketches, which appeared in various magazines over various pseudonyms ; and he went without fame for more than ten years after the publication of his first little book. Ten years is a long time to wait for fame ; the delay did not increase his self-confidence or the geniality with which he regarded those who were ahead of him. He smiled ; he suffered ; he felt insecure.

Meanwhile, he had married, his wife had lost her reason, and he was left with young children to support. When at length, following in the footsteps of Dickens, who by this time must have outdistanced his rivals, Thackeray began the publication of *Vanity Fair* in parts, he was thirty-seven, was unknown by name to the general public, and at first was threatened with further non-success.

The eventual triumph of *Vanity Fair* was followed by the

triumph of *Pendennis,* and the comparative failure of *Esmond.* It was followed by lecture tours in England and the United States, in the course of which Thackeray made money. It was followed by other novels and miscellaneous writings, the editorship of a successful magazine, and by death at the age of fifty-two. From *The Paris Sketch-book* of 1840 to the *Roundabout Papers* of 1863, the years were full of published work, most of which is still read and re-read to-day, if not by those whose interests are bounded by local horizons, then by their elders and the more humane of their contemporaries. And in the result, if Thackeray's reputation at the moment is lower than it has been, it is securely that of the most typically Victorian novelist of them all.

Typically Victorian, I must explain, in its belief that goodness is preferable to cleverness, in its unobtrusive religious conformity (which is allied with great intolerance and even ribaldry concerning tracts), in its respect for both the solid virtues and the *convenances,* in its humour, its conspicuous gentility, and its incessant concern with conduct. Thackeray had all along been in the habit of observing others rather critically; but in fiction he always held his hand in the matter of their ultimate condemnation. He saw the hypocrisies of his period; but in his novels he defended those hypocrisies as exemplifying " the decency of secrecy." To him, cruelty, meanness, selfishness were the unpardonable sins; avarice, snobbery, and what we should call " swank," were to be loathed; women were children and ministering angels when they were not artful little cats; and the world, like a pair of cricketing teams, was divided into two portions—England and the Rest.

In that England there were three classes—" the great folks," the " decent, comfortable society of the second-best sort," who, " if they were not the roses, lived near the roses, as it were, and had a good deal of the odour of genteel life," and the poor. He is not really uncomfortable about the poor. He can say that " Piccadilly was hardly yet awake the next morning, and the sparkling dews and the poor homeless vagabonds still had possession of the grass in Hyde Park "; but, as Colonel Newcome says, " I am as little proud as any man in the world; but there must be distinction, sir; and as it is my lot and Clive's lot to be gentlemen, I won't sit in the kitchen and booze in the servant's hall."

It was Thackeray's lot to be a gentleman. His son-in-

law has told us as much.　But he did not belong to the
" great folks," and so his books do not deal with the great
folks.　Though aristocrats appear in them, they are not
aristocrats of the first order.　They may have titles ; but
in manners and habits they belong to the Victorian bourgeoisie.　Old Indian Army officers, bankers (ruined and
opulent), artists, spendthrifts, lawyers, and writers form
the bulk of his dramatis personæ.　Being a Victorian gentleman who only lived *near* the roses, Thackeray did not
mention, in mixed company, a great number of things
which our living writers delight to display.　His world was
one which had never heard of Freud.　But even if he had
heard of Freud, Thackeray would rather indignantly have
pooh-poohed Freud, as the Victorians would rather indignantly have pooh-poohed Freud, on the ground that
there were matters in life better ignored.　Dare I say that
this is a view which the world may possibly revive?

Thackeray ignores many things.　His concern is with
what may be described as the superficies of manners and
morals.　When the heroine of *Vanity Fair* marries, he
refers briefly to " the first blushing days of the honey-
moon," but he does not otherwise concern himself with
the institution of marriage.　Children are in fact born, like
little flowers, and if the mother is a good woman she loves
her children, while if she is a bad woman she neglects them.
For the rest :

" There are things we do and know perfectly well
in Vanity Fair, though we never speak of them—as
the Ahrimanians worship the devil, but don't mention
him ; and a polite public will no more bear to read an
authentic description of vice than a truly refined English
or American female will permit the word ' breeches,'
to be pronounced in her hearing.　And yet, Madam,
both are walking the world before our faces every day,
without much shocking us.　If you were to blush every
time they went by, what complexions you would have !
It is only when their naughty names are called out that
your modesty has any occasion to show alarm or sense
of outrage, and it has been the wish of the present
writer, all through this story, deferentially to submit
to the fashion at present prevailing, and only to hint
at the existence of wickedness, in a light, easy, and
agreeable manner, so that nobody's fine feelings will
be offended."

In spite of that reticence, and that simplification of human nature which makes Thackeray's picture of manners appear mild before our greater sophistication, there is, in all his best work, a steadiness of vision not to be found in the work of most of his contemporaries. His field may have been narrow, and his self-imposed limitations may have been rigid under their assumed ease; but the values are consistent, and the genius of the author, in my opinion, not to be questioned. The birth and breeding of a gentleman may not be the ideal preparation for the novelist's art, because gentility hampers the observing mind as well as the recording pen, and Thackeray did not allow himself to recognize all that his perceptions must have suggested. But reserve and restraint are both qualities in the artist. Even on paper, our most outspoken writers draw the line somewhere. Thackeray, being a Victorian, drew it elsewhere. On one side of the line he was deliberately unheroic, and, as his old critics used to say, " realistic "; to the other side of it he turned a Nelson eye.

That other side is the side which preoccupies the gobblers of Freud. These ardent spirits believe that truth lives there. I believe that truth spends part of its time there. Thackeray believed that when truth crossed the line it was in retreat. He drew the curtain. The Victorians agreed with Thackeray. It was one of their strengths. They made stout beds and ornamental chamber-pots, but they did not expose them. They reared families, exalted respectability, built solidly, saved their nonsense for literature, and believed in being moral; but they were vulgar, self-deceiving, and opportunist. Thackeray said all this. He said:

" It is time to begin speaking the truth, I think. Lady Ashburton says not. Our Lord spoke it, and was killed for it, and Stephen, and Paul, who slew Stephen. We shuffle and compromise and have Gorham controversies and say, ' Let things go on smoothly,' and Jock Campbell writes to the Mother-Superior, and Milman makes elegant after-dinner speeches at the Mansion House—humbugs all! "

Thackeray was not a humbug. But, like Erasmus, he was not, by temperament, a martyr. He therefore did not speak the whole truth, and he did not try to speak the whole truth. He had been to a public school, and had learnt there the code of conduct which still governs the upper and middle classes of England. There were certain things which a gentleman did not do—or, if done, that he did not refer to. Thackeray was strict as to that. He was so strict that when a young critic attacked him with venom in a trifling periodical, he brought about that young critic's expulsion from his club. He was likewise so decent, in the schoolboy's sense, that he lent a large sum of money at the instance of a friend to a man who was no more than an acquaintance. But his gentility was a handicap in the writing of great novels, because it restricted their themes.

Two other characteristics restricted the themes of Thackeray's books. One of them was his timidity. He was not only a gentleman; he was sensitive to the point of tenderness. Sensitive to criticism, sensitive to the pain of others, sensitive about his own broken nose (which he never forgot), sensitive to his failure, sensitive to his success, to the greater success of Dickens, to silence, to applause. And, like many sensitive men, he was—ever so little—spiteful. There was, involved with his sensitiveness, a kind of envy of others. On paper he was always offering himself as a genial fellow, laughing tolerantly at the world's follies, shrugging his shoulders and saying, " Well, well ; boys will be boys ; and a good woman is a great hypocrite for our good and the good of the world." Some of these little pictures are among the most delightful things he wrote. But he kept an observant eye upon what other authors were writing, and, having as a boy shown " his faculty of making verses, chiefly parodies," he parodied all his contemporaries without benevolence. He laughed at their faults, not in amusement, but in ridicule. He was not very much liked by those contemporaries.

And yet he wished greatly to be liked, to be loved. It is an extraordinary thing that, apart from Mrs. Brookfield, who collected some of his letters to herself and her husband, no friend has ever contributed to our affectionate knowledge of the man. The memoir-writers of the day are never his friends. Apparently he was too timid and too sensitive to make friends with men, otherwise than at his club, where all were members of a large group. He was also too timid to get the best out of such women as he knew. Although he seems to have been friendly with the Brookfields, he told the lady that he had been too frightened of impertinence to give her a daguerreotype of himself, as he had intended doing. To plan such a gift, to abandon the plan, and then to tell of your abandonment of the plan—is not that very curious and interesting, psychologically, in a great man?

It betrays, at least, a highly sensitive vanity, and a faint-heartedness which must have affected his work. He did not, that is, essay the heights opened to him by his talent. To Conscience, perhaps a regular companion, who had set some such view before him, he says he answered:

> "Madam, because an eagle houses on a mountain, or soars to the sun, don't you be angry with a sparrow that perches on a garret window or twitters on a twig. Leave me to myself; look, my beak is not aquiline by any means."

Trollope, who knew and admired Thackeray with understanding, has an interesting remark as to this sort of defiance to Conscience, which brings me to the second characteristic already mentioned. He says that Thackeray would rarely (apart from *Esmond,* never) use what he calls the novelist's "elbow-grease"—forethought. "Unsteadfast, idle, changeable of purpose, aware of his own intellect, but not trusting it, no man ever failed more generally than he to put his best foot foremost." In *Esmond,* Trollope believes, Thackeray did plot and plan, and change his plan, and reconsider his detail before beginning to write. The result was an ambitious work which is unquestionably Thackeray's finest novel, and one of the finest *tours de force* in English fiction. Elsewhere, being too idle to do the necessary preliminary labouring, Thackeray (in Trollope's view) always did work inferior to the best that was in him. He improvised.

This seems to me to be a most interesting explanation of one aspect of Thackeray. True, it was the fashion of that day to improvise; the publication in serial form, in parts, which Thackeray copied from Dickens, was a temptation to every form of go-as-you-please. But Trollope goes farther. He speaks of that "touch of vagueness which indicates that his pen was not firm while he was using it." It is the criticism of a fellow-craftsman, and as shrewd as we could wish. It tells us why, with all our awareness that we are reading the work of a man of genius, we are not contented with what we are reading; and it explains why it is that, with all our discontent, we still place Thackeray so high among the Victorian writers.

He wrote very well, very clearly and fluently, and at times, particularly in *Esmond,* with beautiful grace. He was always easy, and sometimes full of power. His eye for character was exceptionally sure. All the characters in *Esmond*, although they are drawn in low tones, are memorable; several of those in *Vanity Fair*, several in *Pendennis*, one or two in *The Newcomes* return to us as old friends when we re-read those books. *Barry Lyndon* is still unsurpassed in its own field. In the matter of character, these books, accordingly, although the character is simplified, have great excellence. Some of them are nearly a hundred years old, and we do not yet have to read them as antiques.

In the matter of theme, as I have suggested, they are less good. They sag. In the later books, especially, there are many pages where the pushing of a tired pen wearies the reader. But there are nearly always recoveries. Thackeray would be "in the mood" again; his fancy would become active; his shrewdness would kindle; melancholy would dawdle to a distance. For this reason, even the later books are full of pleasures. But how strange it is, they are the books of an old man—although Thackeray was only fifty-two when he died.

This leads me to remark that there is no notable difference in maturity between the early Thackeray and the later Thackeray. Although the "Shabby Genteel Story" is early, and its story poor, it has as much maturity as *The Newcomes*. So has *The Paris Sketch-book*, which is among Thackeray's earliest work. I think the truth is that Thackeray always had an old head on young shoulders. He was certainly an old man long before he died. The old head, observing the horrors of life at Charter House, stored many facts; as the shoulders too grew older, facts were collected. "It will serve me for a chapter."

It may be suggested: what a pity that Thackeray should have been forced to write so much, when time spent in planning might have given us modern books as good as *Esmond*! That is not quite the question that Trollope expected us to put. He would have given the answer, perhaps, that I now offer. Delicate, although he had a big frame and a big head, Thackeray wanted energy. He had been brought up in the belief that his income would be assured, however small. His young mind had not been prepared for the struggle which was to follow. But the lack of physical energy was constant. His mind suffered from lassitude. The task would be done; but no more. That it was done so well, and at times so brilliantly, is testimony to the native gifts. That it took on a peculiarly sedentary and reflective quality is an indication of a natural bent. Thackeray, like his own Major Pendennis, was a born clubman.

To my thinking, the novels of Thackeray, except when they rise to their highest levels, are the work of a clubman of genius. The author's interests were those of a clubman. He looked out of a window, and saw the world going by, full of odd characters. He looked around him in the library or the dining-room, and saw the majors, the bankers, the writers, the old men, and the young men. He heard stories of the past clubmen, of the great world of roses, of the lesser world of ordinary club members. He was always listening, always curious as to this man and that, this rule of conduct and that, this fortune and misfortune, that old way, old building, old book. His inclination was towards the past; the eighteenth-century writers were those upon whom he formed his style; the present was full of rivals and anxieties; the future was a darkness. If he could have had a sinecure, he might have kept journals as assiduously as Greville. As it was, he wrote novels about a world at one remove from the real world of yesterday. The best of them was about a world of the day before yesterday, when Steele and Addison and Swift could play parts agreeable or disagreeable at his whim. But he had then transcended the club; his emotion was aroused; he was engaged, at high pressure, in producing a romance which has ever since been used as a model.

" The humorous writer," says Thackeray, " professes to awaken and direct your love, your pity, your kindness—your scorn for untruth, pretension, imposture—your tenderness for the weak, the poor, the oppressed, the unhappy. To the best of his means and ability he comments on all the ordinary actions and passions of life almost. He takes upon himself to be the weekday preacher, so to speak. Accordingly, as he finds, and speaks, and feels the truth best, we regard him, esteem him—sometimes love him. And, as his business is to mark other people's lives and peculiarities, we moralize upon his life when he is gone —and yesterday's preacher becomes the text for to-day's sermon.''

ANTHONY TROLLOPE

1815-1882

BY
HUGH
WALPOLE

ANTHONY TROLLOPE

A MONG all the re-estimations of great Victorian figures in this volume, none surely can offer a stranger example of the irresponsibility of critical judgments than Trollope.

In 1883, the year that followed his death, it seemed that he was gone, and gone for ever. Now, in 1932, when the reputations of the Victorian novelists are in a very sad way indeed, Trollope, who was possibly of all the more prominent writers the least expected by his contemporaries to survive, has a firmer position with serious critics than any of them save Dickens and, possibly, Emily Brontë.

To men who, like myself, are now nearing fifty, this resurrection is all the more odd, because during the years when we first began to sit up and take notice, the years from 1895 to 1905, Trollope had vanished quite completely. Consult the columns of H. D. Traill's *Literature,* or the early and most excellent *Academy,* and you will find that when Trollope is mentioned at all it is with an air of patronizing pity. Even then he is the author of the Barchester novels only, and the Apologia takes the form of "Poor old Trollope. Hack writer by the clock! There was some good work hidden in that great mass of fiction, but we enlightened critics of to-day have alas! no time to search for it!"

Yet to-day we have writers as different as Miss Rebecca West, Mr. Forster, and Mrs. Woolf, lovers of the extreme examples of modernist literature, praising Trollope with an almost reverential fervour!

The personality and gifts that harmed him in 1883, that had drowned him by 1900, are precisely the personality and gifts that have made him popular again to-day. And behind the story lies a moral.

It is generally taken for granted that it was the publication of his extremely honest *Autobiography* that ruined him with his contemporaries. In that judgment there is, I think, only a half-truth. Trollope published, in all, fifty-one works of fiction. His books appeared, with very little break in time, from 1847 to 1882. For thirty-five years the readers of Great Britain were offered Trollope, and always very Trollopian Trollope. By that I mean that, whatever he wrote about Ireland, Barsetshire, or the House of Commons, he was too honest and simple a novelist to pretend to be other than he was. When a novelist publishes books steadily, year by year, over a very long period, both the critics and the general reader take him, after a while, for granted. They know thoroughly his gifts, his tricks, the subjects that suit him, the subjects that don't suit him. " Ah, here is Mr. Smith again," they say, " with his annual novel. Even though he is writing this time about pirates rather than curates, we know that his pirates will turn out to be curates in the end." The critics have long ago said their say, and prefer to exercise their wits upon someone new and original. This is natural history, and no author, although in the secrecy of his chamber he may be hurt by it, can possibly complain of it.

Time passes, and if the author has in him anything authentic, revenges will be brought in, and it will be discovered that no one will ever again write as that author did. He may have been no genius, but he had something unique to offer. This is especially true, I believe, of any novelist who creates reasonable human beings and has a credible story to tell. We are but little interested in the contemporary fashions and ideas of 1850, but the ladies of Cranford, the clergymen of Barchester, Charles Reade's adventures in the company of young Gerard, are still real to us. If a novelist wishes for some kind of immortality (and all immortalities are regrettably limited !), let his business be with the common simplicities of human nature, and his ghost will have a chance of gratifying his harmless vanity !

First of all, however, it is worthy of notice that Trollope himself had none of these immortal longings. His *Autobiography* is the most modest document ever given to us by any author ; and it is, what is more, a modesty above

suspicion. There is no pose in it, no theatrical disclaimer,
no jealousy of his contemporaries. He was sure that he
had no genius; if he boasted of anything, it was that he
was an honest workman who wrote because he enjoyed it,
because he had to support a family, because it was his
profession. Let other authors allow themselves their eccen-
tricities; he himself had none, and if, at the conclusion of
a novel, there were still ten minutes of his allotted time to
go, he would begin a new one! Henry James said of him:
" His great, his inestimable merit was a complete appreciation of the ' usual,' " and he carried this appreciation into
all his affairs without shame and without any pretence of
disgracing the name of artist.

It was because, in his *Autobiography,* he made no claim
to the name of artist that his contemporaries were so greatly
shocked. In 1883 it was beginning to be demanded that
the novel should be a conscious art, and this demand has
increased, until in our own day it has assumed, I think,
unwholesome proportions. It is all the more curious, then,
that the English novelist who, above all others, wished to
remark that he was no artist should, by the prophets of the
higher criticism, be now so generously acclaimed. It is this
that makes his position to-day so interesting and unusual;
it is this apparent paradox that is especially worth examination.

About Trollope the man there can be no possible difference of opinion. His simple and colossal outlines are there
for anyone to see. Here I may be allowed perhaps to
quote from my own analysis in my " English Men of
Letters " volume:

> " The standard presentation of him has become so
> definite as to be symbolic—almost Titanic in size—vast
> of shoulder and thigh, astride a horse as Titanic as
> himself, or bursting into the Garrick Club, bellowing
> forth some greeting, slapping a friend on the back,
> involved quickly in some discussion, tempestuous in
> agreement or argument, hailing friends with a roar and
> enemies with a frown, hospitable, generous, enthusi-
> astic, limited, bellicose, affectionate; and then behind
> this eager John Bull the second figure, rising at five-
> thirty of a morning (roused by a sleepy but ever-
> punctual groom), hurrying to his study, setting his
> watch before him, then gravely, without a moment's
> pause, slipping through the gates of his creation into

the well-known country, meeting without surprise or hesitation Lady Glencora or Sowerby or Mr. Slope, striding down the High Street of Barchester, or urging his nag down the lanes around Allington, not so much as a creative artist as a recording citizen.

" And then, behind this figure again, the third, the timid, shy, shrinking self-doubter of the early school-days longing for affection, but trained to show no feeling, dreading always what the next day will bring, dirty, dishevelled, and above all self-humiliated."

To this let me add something from the *Autobiography*:

" I think I became popular among those with whom I associated. I have long been aware of a certain weakness in my own character, which I may call a craving for love. I have ever had a wish to be liked by those around me—a wish that, during the first half of my life, was never gratified. In my schooldays no small part of my misery came from the envy with which I regarded the popularity of popular boys. They seemed to me to live in a social paradise, while the desolation of my pandemonium was complete. And afterwards, when I was in London as a young man, I had few friends.

" Among the clerks in the Post Office I held my own fairly well for the first two or three years; but even then, I regarded myself as something of a pariah. My Irish life had been much better: I had had my wife and children, and had been sustained by a feeling of general respect. But even in Ireland, I had in truth lived but little in society. Our means had been sufficient for our wants, but insufficient for entertaining others. It was not till we had settled ourselves at Waltham that I really began to live much with others. The Garrick Club was the first assemblage of men at which I felt myself to be popular."

And then, to this add the comment on his admiration of and affection for Millais, who illustrated several of his novels:

" To see him has always been a pleasure. His voice has been a sweet sound in my ears. Behind his back I have never heard him praised without joining the eulogist; I have never heard a word spoken against him without opposing the censurer. These words, should he ever see them, will come to him from the grave, and will tell him of my regard—as one living man never tells another.''

How significant is that last sentence ! In any portrait of Trollope to-day that very ugly word '' Inferiority complex,'' beloved by our modern psychologists, would have been used, but indeed the portrait is complete—the bulky blundering man (no glasses, however strong, seemed to correct his bad sight) with blustering voice, loud in argument, positive, often, it seemed, prejudiced—and, within this, shy, longing for affection, self-doubting.

No one of us ever recovers from the years of childhood : what they make us we, for ever after, are. Trollope was to be, and to remain, the abused, mocked, misunderstood schoolboy. But he was also the strong, courageous, unflinching man of letters. He allowed no one to perceive his timidity nor guess at his longing for affection. We may assume that much of that unflagging, unresting passion of work was a determination to risk none of the perils of the idle, unguarded moment.

His life was busy and successful. After the recognition of *Barchester Towers,* he never again wanted for money ; he had all the things that his physical self enjoyed—a house in the country with a garden, plenty of hunting, a perfect family life, clubs in London where he could see his friends, honour, and renown. He declares, in his *Autobiography,* that he had had a happy life, and yet we may wonder, as we may wonder about any man who has allowed us to see into his heart, whether all this was not a courageous enjoyment of the second-best. He wrote well, but he would wish to have written better ; he loved his family and his friends, but was to the last, perhaps, a lonely man. Nothing, we may suggest, was as real to him in later life as the terror and dismay of those early schooldays. This is possibly a sentimental emphasis, and it is only advanced because it is this very loneliness and unsatisfied longing that give so much of his work its especial quality. He lived, however, in a period when this kind of analysis was not encouraged ; a man, and especially a man with the physical attributes of Trollope, was expected to be a man. Never were the two sexes so resolutely separated in the psychological sense as in those Victorian years in England.

Moreover, Trollope himself approved of this simplicity of psychology. In his novels his men are men and his women

women with such a definite certainty that, when they meet, it is as though continent speaks to continent across a waste of waters; one reason, perhaps, why they are restfully refreshing to our modern generation. Trollope knew a great deal more about life than he was permitted to tell, and this with his own absolute approval. Not only did he refuse to bring a blush to any young maiden's cheek, but he would not bring a blush to his own either. It is astonishing that he was able to reveal so much of the life of his time with such honesty when the revelation of half of it was forbidden him. But that he knew as much of it as the frankest young novelist of to-day we cannot doubt.

What, then, did he set out to do? He set out deliberately to do nothing except make a little money from telling stories, and it is perfectly possible to see his career from first to last as a money-plotting concern, about which he was all the franker, because so many people were not. He could not endure that there should be any humbug about his pretences. "I am a writer, and I am paid for my work. I get all that I can. I enjoy telling you how much I did get. Every author wants money, and it is arrant humbug when he says that he doesn't."

As this honest declaration of Trollope's was the principal reason of his unpopularity in his own time, and is a principal reason of his popularity now, it is worth examination. Trollope's novels to-day do not meet the requirements of modern taste in the direction either of æsthetics or psychology, but they do meet it in the direction of reality. We tolerate humbug to-day with more impatience than any other of the vices, and Pecksniff is our great Aunt Sally. Trollope's honesty covers for us a multitude of his sins, his languor and his sentimentalities: we can forgive the Widow Bold and Lily Dale and the interminable thinness of *Is he Popenjoy?* or *Ralph the Heir,* because he never told a lie about anything. Did it matter to him as artist that he got as much as he could as often as he could? It did not matter, I think, unless he wrote with deliberate boldness to please a large public. But Trollope *was* a case of a novelist who wrote for money, and wrote sometimes less well than he might otherwise have done for that reason. His temptation, and the temptation, I am afraid, to which he too often yielded, was the Serial. The Serial scarcely exists to-day, and when it does exist, it is "a very little one," but in Trollope's time, if you were serialized in

Good Words or *Belgravia* or the *Cornhill,* you ran on
simply for evermore, and if you were published in shilling
monthly numbers you ran on longer than that! Weary
and impatient critics complain of the new passion for length
in the modern novel. Why, if Mr. Priestley and myself
and Miss Clemence Dane were to combine, and be together
as long as we knew how, we would not approach the inter-
minability of Dumas, Eugene Sue, Reynolds, Lever, and
the other serial writers of the 'forties and 'fifties!

It is important to add that the long novel to-day is
deliberately long. Trollope, however, thinned his novels
out to suit the magazine or monthly instalment—almost
all the defects of his talents come from yielding to this
temptation. On the other hand, he had two very admirable defences against this accusation. He did not,
in the first place, think he was yielding to temptation
because, with his eyes wide open and his hand on his heart,
he could declare that he preferred making money (or rather
supporting his family as it should be supported) to calling
himself an artist. He was not an artist: he did not think
that the novel *was* an art. It was an amusement.

And, secondly, however thin his novel might become, he
found himself, day by day, living in that creative world,
so "well in," as they say in *Alice,* that he could not step
outside to see whether the novel *were* unduly thinning.
This is undoubtedly one of the dangers for the writer of the
long novel, and one of the delights (if he is enjoying himself at all) of the reader. The writer of the long novel
moves month after month in a world of his own creating.
There is no reason why he should ever stop. He is simply
a citizen of his world, and it is his own fault if he is not
happy there. This is what Trollope was—happy in his own
world, too happy to be a suffering, conscious artist. He
contributes his happiness, his well-being, to his readers,
and it is often forgotten to-day, I think, what pleasure this
sense of the *author's* pleasure gives to the reader.

Trollope, then, has for us three great charms: he is real,
he is happy inside his creative world, and, we feel, rather
lonely and awkward outside it. We can therefore trust him
in what he tells us, be happy with him in his fables, and
feel warmly towards him in his daily life which, thanks
to his *Autobiography,* we know something about.

Of these three qualities it is his reality that is the most
important. In what sense is he real? Why, when he is so

x

obviously old-fashioned, do we of to-day still find him real? And is he *real* about everything? In answer to the first question, he is real within his own world. I can believe— and, indeed, we have contemporary witnesses to the fact —that many Deans and Archdeacons of his own day accused his *Barsetshire* of complete unreality. Trollope himself said that he knew little or nothing about cathedral towns, and had never lived in one. His reality, however, was not at all the modern realism of to-day. He had neither the technical knowledge of Mr. Kipling nor the psychological subtlety of Marcel Proust. He had not Mr. Joyce's catholicity of taste, nor the poetic imaging of Virginia Woolf. He trusted to the great truth that human nature is, basically, everywhere the same, that a hen-pecked husband, whether a bishop or a butcher, will feel very much as Bishop Proudie felt, and a poor muddled man accused of stealing will suffer as Mr. Crawley suffered. This is his great, his abiding, strength, that he was able to create men and women who were types as well as individuals, individuals as well as types.

I have said that he is real within his own world; that world is a limited one, but it happens that those very limitations are the ones that win our favour to-day. We want just now no nonsense, no heroics in our novels. We have been through the worst war, and are now experiencing the worst peace: the hero has to be very unheroic indeed to win our attention. That is just what Trollope's heroes are—most unheroic. Mr. Harding, Mr. Crawley, Johnny Eames, that delightful silent Briton in *The Belton Estate,* Phineas Phinn—all of these men are very ordinary, and Trollope insists on their ordinariness. It has been said that Trollope's world is unaware of poetry: there are certainly no mystics in it (unless you think Mr. Crawley absent-minded enough to be one), no other-worldliness, no shadows on the grass, no moons nor red red roses, neither Leprecauns nor Centaurs. Trollope quite frankly liked the daylight. When he attempted to terrify he was absurd, when he philosophized he was commonplace, when he was emotional about the heart he was sentimental.

But he had (and I do not know that the comparison has ever been made before) quite a piece of Balzac in his composition. Balzac would not have been ashamed to own the heroine of *The Eustace Diamonds*—Lizzie Eustace is one of the really great figures in the English novel—nor Planty

Pall nor Mrs. Proudie nor, especially, Mr. Crawley. Balzac
had a passion for painting solitary figures persecuted by
the world, and he was better with his persecutors than his
persecuted—his Valérie Marneffe rather than his Cousin
Pons ! Trollope, too, had the same hard, remorseless sense
of character, but he was cut off, as Balzac of course was
not, from so many things that he knew but could not say.
Then he wanted " a good time to be enjoyed by all." All
the good children in the English Victorian novel are re-
warded with matrimony. Trollope knew, as well as Balzac
did, that that was not the end of the question, but he writes
" Finis " across the page, winks at his other self, looks at
his watch, and begins the next novel. He was also like
Balzac in his creation of a World. He had a sense of
Space, one of the most important of the novelist's possessions : you feel the whole of the English counties spread
beneath your eye, and loosely, idly, in the comfortable air
of an English country day, the figures move, meet, seem
to have no destinies, and to be none the worse for that.
He did, what Balzac and Thackeray and Dumas have done
—reintroduced his characters from book to book. If you
are very solemn about the novel as an art, this is a disgrace-
ful thing to do, but if you are not very solemn it is often
delightful for both author and reader. Trollope did it
because his characters were so real to him that they never
died. This accounts partly for the sense you get, when
reading him, that you are moving, not only among people
whom you know, but among people who know *you* ! I am
quite conceited enough to believe that Mrs. Proudie knows
me very well and dislikes me very much. I am happy in
Mr. Harding's company (so long as his tearful daughter
is not present), but I am not at all sure whether *he* is happy
in mine !

This meeting with old friends in a novelist's books is,
I think, a very agreeable sensation. I am sure that it is
also a naïve and childish pleasure, but I believe that the
novel is the only literary form in which you can be naïve
if you wish—and certainly a great many people make
the most of the opportunity ! I don't see how you are to
escape that story-telling character of the novel. If you do
escape it, you are, it seems to me, writing something that
is not a novel at all. And surely that story-telling quality
is not to be despised ! You can see it at its easiest in
Trollope, and how charming, how restful it is ! He begins

539

Barchester Towers by saying that the only topic of the
moment is that the Bishop of Barchester is dead, and that
everyone is speculating about his successor. Well, how
simple and delightful that is! Here is a human situation
such as we can easily understand (a situation like the
Return of Ulysses, the elevation of Sancho Panza, the
introduction of the Wooden Horse into Troy, Christian's
adventures in Vanity Fair), and we are promised introductions to a number of people as stupid, vain, kindly, and
touching as are we ourselves. We come back, then, to
the two real reasons for Trollope's survival, his honesty
and his common humanity. He created a world and put
real people into it; he was kindly to his reader and intimate
with his characters. He is the most restful of all English
novelists, because of his knowledge of human nature, his
hatred of pose, his English humours, and his unawareness
that the novel ought to be an art.

   He wrote novels because he enjoyed writing them, and
because he made money *by* writing them. He had the great
good fortune to create a world in which he could do what
he pleased. Every once and again he permits us to go
with him. We follow that lumbering, thick-bearded, half-
blind, vociferous, shy, affectionate, and practical friend
into a country where it is always afternoon and, quite
unashamedly, English. English, yes, and Victorian. To
see Trollope against this background is to see at once that
he was made by his period, but avoided its gravest dangers.
The reason that Thackeray's literary stock is down with us
to-day while Trollope's seems to be rising is, I think, that
he was honest when Thackeray was not, loved his period
without patronizing it, believed in his period without
arrogance. The great Victorian virtues of courage, integrity, common sense, idealism, and humour he had in
abundance. The Victorian defects of hypocrisy, sentimentality, complacency, he (narrowly, perhaps) escaped.
The Victorians were often great because they believed that
life was important, that it meant something, that it was a
real battle in which something was eternally to be lost or
gained. That may seem to us now absurd (is it absurd?),
but at least it gave those figures size and colour. Trollope
shared those beliefs and ideals, but he succeeded in combining with them a great personal modesty. I do not mean
that he did not think that he was worthy of his hire—he
was thoroughly Victorian in that—but he was able, as so

many of the greater Victorians were able, to sink his personal adventure in a larger, more general one. It is, perhaps, our inability to do this that is our chief weakness to-day. We are brave but incredulous, honest but cynical. Trollope was a man of his time when he said: "These are the things that I am, here is what I have done. I think it is a decent record. I am not ashamed of it. But it is important only for its contribution to something bigger than Anthony Trollope."

He avoided much of the Victorian sentimentality (although he sometimes yielded to it) because his own early history stiffened his reserve. Thackeray, whose early story was more tragic than Trollope's, abandoned himself to the worst of all the Victorian vices—public demonstration of private feelings. I think that Thackeray was a greater novelist than Trollope, but he is not easy to read to-day, because he makes us so often shy: "Oh, Thackeray, please don't!" we murmur, but Trollope, with his more even tone, his steady, gruff narration, his refusal to allow us to share his private life, has the best of the Victorian common sense—the common sense that Surtees and the early Hardy and Mrs. Gaskell and the early George Eliot all shared.

What kind of writer would Trollope have been had he lived and worked from, say 1895 to 1930? It is noticeable that in the books of his last period—*An Eye for an Eye, Kept in the Dark,* the unfinished *Landleaguers,* he was less and less of a Victorian—that is, he penetrated (even though very slightly and without success) fields that the Victorians distrusted. Without the Victorian assurance he would have been, perhaps, psychologically a more interesting novelist. But he would have lost his supreme quality—his record of the Victorian security and stability. His novels move in a land where it is always afternoon, where storms do not threaten, where no ground quivers beneath his foot. In giving us once and for all that atmosphere he is of supreme importance in the Victorian record. He was exactly suited in his talent to be the historian of a settled, immovable world. The character of his period denied him other and important gifts, his contemporaries became impatient with him because his picture seemed to them monotonous in its accuracy. But for us who, alas, know nothing of the peace of monotony, he is an historian, enviable, trustworthy, and most friendly.

EDWARD BURNETT TYLOR

1832–1917

BY
G. ELLIOT
SMITH, F.R.S.

x*

EDWARD BURNETT TYLOR

TYLOR was the father of English Anthropology, and so, because the most vital thing in the world is the understanding of human nature, he was one of the most significant figures of the Victorian Age. The correct interpretation of the thoughts, feelings, and social behaviour of other human beings is a matter of the utmost moment to everyone. In fact, it concerns mankind more closely and intimately than any other knowledge. Although at every moment of their lives all men are wrestling with this intensely practical problem, the attempts of scholars to interpret the process involved in the everyday social intercourse of human beings, and the development of men's beliefs, and the springs of their actions, have revealed unexpected difficulties and the strangest contradictions. Seventy years ago the growth of knowledge at last forced thinking men publicly to admit that the Pentateuch did not represent all it was essential to know on these matters. Hence they were free to seek for the solution elsewhere. The man to whom circumstances provided the opportunity for shaping opinion on this essential issue was Edward Burnett Tylor.

The sixties of the nineteenth century witnessed the dawn of a new era, the renunciation of some of the traditions that for many centuries had obscured men's vision of the truth concerning themselves.

In the year 1859 Charles Darwin's *Origins of Species* was published. Whatever verdict posterity will pass on the validity of the theories of evolution put forward in this book, it certainly effected a revolution in men's attitude, not merely to the meaning of the world of living beings,

545

but also to the interpretation of all natural phenomena and man's relationship to them. Men's eyes were being opened to a new vision of the universe and their place in it. The world was becoming more alert and open-minded for the discovery of truth.

In that year, however, a relatively trivial incident was charged with more immediately momentous results for Tylor and his career. A group of English geologists, including Falconer, Prestwich, and Lyell, paid a visit to Abbeville and St. Acheul in France to examine the evidence upon which a wildly speculative genius, Boucher de Perthes, was vainly trying to convince his fellow-countrymen of the remote antiquity of man. The English visitors were able to confirm the genuineness of the flint implements Boucher was finding, and to establish the fact that the men who made them lived many thousands of years ago, when lions, cave bears, and elephants were roaming in Europe. The expression of their views converted the world of learned men to overcome their distrust of Boucher, and to admit the conclusion that man was vastly older than had been supposed. It is difficult for us to-day to appreciate the full effects of these events of 1859, which shattered old superstitions and gave men new confidence in the use of reason.

Boucher de Perthes secured in Edouard Lartet a most influential ally among his own countrymen. In his account of the excavations of the Grotto of Aurignac in 1861, Lartet provided independent and more generally recognized corroboration of the remote antiquity of mankind. With the help of Henry Christy, an English collaborator, he then began the excavation of the famous site at Les Eyzies. The care they displayed in their researches, and the sobriety with which they recorded their results, converted many who were repelled by the unrestrained enthusiasm of Boucher de Perthes, which found expression in much that was frankly nonsensical. In 1863 the seal was set on a great revolution in thought by the publication of Lyell's *Geological Evidence of the Antiquity of Man,* which was all the more devastating in its effects, because until then Lyell had been the hero of those who were opposed to the new teaching.

It was a time when the new ferment of emancipation from old errors was leavening the thoughts and aspirations of mankind in the whole range of science and the humanities. Men were discovering a new world vastly more wonderful and awe-inspiring than anything they had conceived before.

This time of intellectual upheaval witnessed the publication of Edward Burnett Tylor's *Researches into the Early History of Mankind*—a calm and serious statement of fact and inference, entirely free from any trace of the emotional storms that were raging around him.

It is peculiarly appropriate that the man who was destined to take advantage of the new freedom to restore a certain measure of sober common-sense to the study of mankind was one who, in his upbringing, had been singularly free from the influence of the forces of tradition and the tyranny of conventional scholasticism. Tylor was not educated in either a public school or a university. A Quaker school, a brass-founder's workshop, and world-wide travels in association with a scholar apt to guide his path to true learning, provided the educational discipline which gave him vision without prejudice.

To a man of such upbringing the appeal to reason was tempered by a reaction to the violent religious animosities of the times in which he was living and writing. While unimpeachable evidence and rational argument compelled him to accept the reality of the world-wide dispersal of civilization in early times, an emotional intuition also led him to compromise on the theological issue, and to assume, without adequate justification, " the prevalence of a belief," among primitive people, " in the continuance of the soul's existence after death."

The unwitting conflict which developed in Tylor's mind between the rational and emotional factors in his mental make-up was destined to have far-reaching reactions in the world, not only of ethnology, but also of the whole range of human interests, education, politics, and sociology.

It is just a century since Edward Burnett Tylor was born (on October 2nd, 1832) in Camberwell, twenty years after that suburb of London produced, in Robert Browning, another inspired student of human thought and aspirations. Tylor was the third son of a brass-founder. Until he was sixteen years of age, when he entered his father's foundry, he attended the Grove House School at Tottenham, belonging to the Society of Friends. Seven years later ill-health compelled him to give up his work. The year 1856 found him making a therapeutic pilgrimage in Cuba. One day, when travelling by bus in Havana, a lucky chance made him acquainted with Henry Christy, the ethnologist and archæologist, who soon afterwards, in collaboration with Lartet, played a prominent part in establishing the antiquity of man. They immediately struck up a friendship that was destined to shape Tylor's career and transform the study of mankind. It provided him with an interest which was congenial, and the opportunity in pursuing it for giving full scope to his distinctive abilities. Leaving Cuba, he accompanied Christy on his travels in Mexico. He returned to England in 1857, at a time when Christy's friends were all agog, not so much with the doctrine Charles Darwin was preparing to publish, as with the views put forward by Boucher de Perthes regarding early stone implements and the antiquity of man. The inspiring company of Christy and his friends, Darwin, Huxley, Lyell, Spencer, Lubbock, and others, who were shaping the nascent science of anthropology, was responsible for completing the process of Tylor's real education, which had been begun in Mexico. Thus he definitely adopted the career of a student of mankind, of which he was destined to become the pre-eminent leader.

In 1861 his first book was published under the title *Anahuac, or Mexico and the Mexicans*. It was not until 1865, however, when he published his *Researches into the Early History of Mankind,* that the emergence of a new force in humanistic studies was revealed. Much had been written on customs and beliefs before then; but Tylor's book marks the inauguration of a new epoch in such studies. The opening two paragraphs of the introduction to his *Researches into the Early History of Mankind* will make clear the spirit in which Tylor approached the subject of his investigation, and explain why he adopted an attitude destined to exert so profound an influence upon the new mode of approaching the study of mankind.

" In studying the phenomena of knowledge and art, religion and mythology, law and custom, and the rest of the complex whole which we call civilization, it is not enough to have in view the more advanced races, and to know their history so far as direct records have preserved it for us. The explanation of the state of things in which we live has often to be sought in the condition of rude and early tribes; and without a knowledge of this to guide us, we may miss the meaning even of familiar thoughts and practices. To take a trivial instance, the statement is true enough as it stands, that the women of modern Europe mutilate their ears to hang jewels in them, but the reason for their doing so is not to be fully found in the circumstances among which we are living now. The student who takes a wider view thinks of the rings and bones and feathers thrust through the cartilage of the nose; the weights that pull the slit ears in long nooses to the shoulder; the ivory studs let in at the corners of the mouth; the wooden plugs as big as tablespoons put through slits in the under-lip; the teeth of animals stuck point outwards through holes in the cheeks, all familiar things among the lower races up and down in the world. The modern ear-ring of the higher nations stands, not as a product of our own times, but as a relic of a ruder mental condition, one of the many cases in which the result of progress has not been positive in adding, but negative in taking away, something belonging to an earlier state of things."

The sanity of his outlook is revealed by his wise recognition of a fact that is often flagrantly ignored in recent controversy.

" It is indeed hardly too much to say that civilization, being a process of long and complex growth, can only be thoroughly understood when studied through its entire range; that the past is continually needed to explain the present, and the whole to explain the part."

When it is realized how just was Tylor's conception of the problems of anthropology and of the principles which should guide the investigator in solving them, why, it will be asked, did he depart from these principles?

Even in the introduction to his book, which on the whole is frankly an argument in favour of the reality of diffusion of early culture as the true explanation of the similarities revealed in distant areas, he refers to two factors, which eventually came to exert an increasingly great influence upon his attitude in the matter of the conflicting interpretations of human history. They determined the views, which afterwards took more concrete shape in his theory of " animism," and ultimately dominated his attitude towards the essential problem of ethnology, and in particular his opposition to the doctrine of diffusion.

" When similar arts, customs, or legends are found in several distant regions, among people not known to be of the same stock, how is this similarity to be accounted for? Sometimes it may be ascribed to the like working of men's minds under like conditions, and sometimes it is a proof of blood relationship or of intercourse, direct or indirect, between the races among whom it is found."

At this time, however, Tylor was a diffusionist. The interest of the last quotation lies in the evidence it affords that he was playing with the conflicting view. The next paragraph, however, contains the germ of Tylor's eventual repudiation of the diffusion of culture.

"The prevalence of a belief in the continuance of the soul's existence after death does not prove that all mankind have inherited such a belief from a common source. It may have been so, but the historical argument is made valueless by the fact that certain natural phenomena may have suggested to the mind of man, while in a certain stage of development, the idea of a future state, and this not once only, but again and again in different regions and at different times. These phenomena may prove nothing of the kind to us, but that is not the question. The reasoning of the savage is not to be judged by the rules which belong to a higher education ; and what the ethnologist requires in such a case, is not to know what the facts prove to his own mind, but what inference the very differently trained mind of the savage may draw from them.

"The belief that man has a soul capable of existing apart from the body it belongs to, and continuing to live, for a time at least, after that body is dead and buried, fits perfectly in such a mind with the fact that the shadowy forms of men and women do appear to others, when the men and women themselves are at a distance, and after they are dead."

It is quite clear that this attitude involves the claim for the independent development of culture and the repudiation of the spread of civilization. Thus he says: "When we find dim notions of a future state current in the remotest regions of the world, we must not thence assume that they were all devised from a single geographical centre. The case is one in which any one plausible explanation from natural causes is sufficient to bar the argument from historical connection."

Six years later (in 1871) he developed the argument of

ancestors in the Old World many thousands of years and much tribulation to do—and to do these things when their own kinsmen, living in more congenial surroundings, such as California and New England, remained steeped in barbarism and uncultured nomadism! What we have to discover is how Tylor, an eminently sane and reasonable thinker, who was engaged in applying to human studies the new discipline of reason which the great emancipation of the sixties made possible, persuaded his disciples to take this topsy-turvy view of human nature, in defiance of all experience.

From the eighteenth century the attitude of scholars had shown wide fluctuations between the extreme view taken up by Robertson, that civilization naturally developed in various parts of the world quite independently of similar happenings elsewhere, and the idea of the essential unity of civilization, resulting from the widespread diffusion of ideas and practices, such as we know to have happened in the case of religions like Christianity, Islam, and Buddhism, and of inventions such as the steam-engine and electric lighting. In 1815 the pendulum swung to the other extreme, when Baron von Humboldt cited cogent reasons for the diffusion of culture in the similarity of the arbitrary features of the calendrical systems and their symbolism, the architecture, the religions, and the arts and crafts of the Pre-Columbian people of America and those of Eastern Asia. During the fifty years which intervened between Humboldt and Tylor's first serious contribution to this discussion, opinion had fluctuated backwards and forwards from one extreme to the other. Although views were in a fluid state, it is clear that in 1865 feeling was more sympathetic to the general idea of the diffusion of culture as the explanations of the similarities of ancient civilizations than to the hypothesis of independent development. Hence it is not surprising that, in the *Early History of Mankind,* Tylor adopted a frankly diffusionist point of view, and vigorously criticized writers such at Nilsson, who dared to claim that the invention of the bow and arrow was a simple procedure which different people might have invented independently. In spite of the fact that Tylor from the beginning believed in the reality of the spread of culture, which he illustrated by the study of folk-tales and arbitrary arts and crafts throughout the world, he declined to accept this point of view in explanation of primitive religion. Impressed as he was by the widespread belief that objects which we consider inanimate, things of stone and wood, were regarded by some relatively uncultured people as being definitely alive, and equipped with something analogous to what European people call the soul, Tylor advanced the theory which he called "animism." He claimed that people instinctively believe the universe to be alive, and regard all the objects in it—the mountains, the trees, the rivers, objects of wood and stone—as animate beings possessing souls which make the whole world kin. From such a beginning, Tylor went on to claim that all human beings believe in the existence of a soul which survived after death. It is now widely recognized that there is no justification for such views. The stricter discipline of investigation, which Tylor's own work was responsible for stimulating, led his disciples to inquire into the evidence of popular beliefs and superstitions, and one of the first results of this critical examination was to demonstrate the baselessness of the claims upon which his theory of animism had developed. Even when such animistic hypotheses were being demolished, however, the inferences which Tylor had based upon their acceptance did not seem to be weakened, but gained a greater measure of influence. It is a familiar phenomenon that error and superstition flourish best when unhampered by reference to inconvenient evidence ! For, so Tylor argued, if all human beings instinctively adopt a belief in animism, why should they not also develop similar methods of thinking and doing in respect of other things? In other words, the adoption of the theory of animism was virtually an acceptance of the speculation of the independent development of culture, and as such was in direct antagonism to the diffusion of culture to which Tylor was already committed.

One of the most remarkable features of Tylor's life was the fact that, from 1865 to 1895, during the thirty years of his greatest activity, he simultaneously maintained a belief in these conflicting views. From time to time he called attention to what he regarded as undoubted cases of worldwide diffusion of culture from a single centre. In 1879 he traced the spread of games like backgammon from Egypt to America; in 1880 he described the diffusion of peculiar types of ornament and architectural symbolism from Babylonia to the ends of the earth; in 1894 he called attention to the identity of the arbitrary experiences of the soul recorded in Buddhist documents from Japan and in Aztec codices of Pre-Columbian Mexico. In every instance—and they are numerous during the years from 1865 to 1894 —he never hesitated to emphasize the inference that such cases demonstrated the reality of the world-wide diffusion of culture, and the essential unity of civilization's origin throughout the world.

Hence we have the strange phenomenon of a persuasive writer of transparent sincerity and exceptional authority maintaining, throughout thirty years of his life, the case for the diffusion of culture at the same time that he was the leading exponent of the diametrically opposite interpretation of human action, which is commonly called the independent development of culture. To the latter principle, with an amazing lack of cogency, he applied the wholly inappropriate label of " evolution," instead of the true biological analogy, the speculation known as " spontaneous generation." What is more, Tylor was responsible, however unwittingly, for inspiring his disciples to adopt this so-called evolutionary doctrine, and become, in many cases, the fanatical opponents of the theory of diffusion, at the very time when he was publishing arguments in favour of diffusion ! In the closing years of his active life he himself succumbed to the influence he had thus stirred up. The last article he wrote (" Anthropology," in the *Encyclopædia Britannica* of 1910) was an unrestrained outburst in opposition to the principle of diffusion, which is in pathetic contrast to everything he wrote before then.

How, it may be asked, could a man who was simultaneously maintaining two antagonistic doctrines become so influential a reformer as Tylor unquestionably was? The engaging charm of his impressive personality, the sobriety and lucidity of his exposition, and the frankness with which he stated and attempted to solve the great problems of human life and experience, provoked an honest discussion of these great subjects with a new seriousness and a new critical attitude. The very contradictions of his exposition acted as a provocation to scholars. As a result, widespread interest began to be taken in the problems of the simpler societies of the human family. A new zeal emerged for the collection of evidence and for the critical examination and interpretation of it.

The wave of enthusiasm excited by Tylor's writings in England rapidly spread to the Continent, to America, and,

555

in fact, to the whole world, and the acceptance of his ideas of animism overwhelmed the fashionable school of so-called "nature mythologists" of Max Müller and his disciples, and converted most of them into believers in animism. But the process of critical study and collection of evidence which was inaugurated by Tylor soon led to an extension of this process, one of the most surprising results of which was the overthrow of animism itself. As I have already mentioned, however, the strange thing is that the demolition of the speculation of animism, upon which has been built up the modern school of belief in the independent development of culture, did not destroy the latter doctrine. On the contrary, the destruction of all rational foundation for its existence seems to have given it a new lease of life, and a freedom from the necessity of justifying claims which are wholly unjustifiable.

It can be truly said of Tylor, however, that he provoked the serious study of the great problems of human life. If for a time his simultaneous acceptance of the two mutually contradictory views has caused provocation and confusion, out of the conflict there is now beginning to emerge a just and true appreciation of the continuity of cultural development, and of the part played by each civilized community in shaping and developing its share of the heritage which is common to the whole world.